THE **LEGEND** OF
LUTHER STRODE

IMAGE COMICS INC.

Robert Kirkman — Chief Operating Officer
Erik Larsen — Chief Financial Officer
Todd McFarlane — President
Marc Silvestri — Chief Executive Officer
Jim Valentino — Vice-President

Eric Stephenson — Publisher
Ron Richards — Director of Business Development
Jennifer de Guzman — PR & Marketing Director
Branwyn Bigglestone — Accounts Manager
Emily Miller — Accounting Assistant
Jamie Parreno — Marketing Assistant
Emilio Bautista — Sales Assistant
Susie Giroux — Administrative Assistant
Kevin Yuen — Digital Rights Coordinator
Tyler Shainline — Events Coordinator
David Brothers — Content Manager
Jonathan Chan — Production Manager
Drew Gill — Art Director
Jana Cook — Print Manger
Monica Garcia — Senior Production Artist
Vincent Kukua — Production Artist
Jenna Savage — Production Artist
www.imagecomics.com

THE LEGEND OF LUTHER STRODE
First printing.   August 2013.   ISBN: 978-1-60706-773-3

WRITTEN BY **JUSTIN JORDAN**

ART BY **TRADD MOORE**

COLORS BY **FELIPE SOBREIRO**

LETTERING BY **FONOGRAFIKS**

BOOK DESIGN BY **DREW GILL**

Where We Came From, Where We're Going.

The first volume of this series, *The Strange Talent of Luther Strode*, was about a reasonably normal kid, Luther, getting a book that unleashed superhuman powers in him. It did not go well for Luther. You don't have to have read that book to read this one, but it's probably helpful to understand where he and Petra are coming from.

Luther wanted what a lot of, maybe all, teenage boys want: he wanted to be buffed and awesome. He wanted to kick some ass and get the girl. He wanted to keep the people in his life safe.

And he got most of that. Almost all of it, in fact. But not the part that matters. In getting what he wished for, he lost everything he had: his home, his life, his best friend, and his mother.

He lost all the things that made him *him*. But he survived, despite his best attempt at suicide by cop. It was meant to be a tragedy where Luther's life was unwound by decisions that he couldn't help but make. This is the story of what comes after.

In classic tragedies, the hero usually dies, undone by his own fatal flaw. But I was interested in what you would do if you lost everything, by your own hand, and life went on. Luther's problems in the first series start from getting superpowers, but not having an Uncle Ben, his own Ma and Pa Kent or, hell, even Alfred, to help guide him.

Now he has even less. He's been reduced, in his own mind, to something less than human. All he sees, every time he looks at a person, is meat. Every glance tells him exactly how to kill them and how easy it would be.

That's the sort of thing that will fuck a kid up.

So this is what comes after tragedy. Luther wants to be punished or redeemed. There are certainly plenty of people who would love to help him out with the first one, but what he needs is someone, just one person, to believe that redemption is possible. Maybe that would be enough.

But maybe not.

- Justin

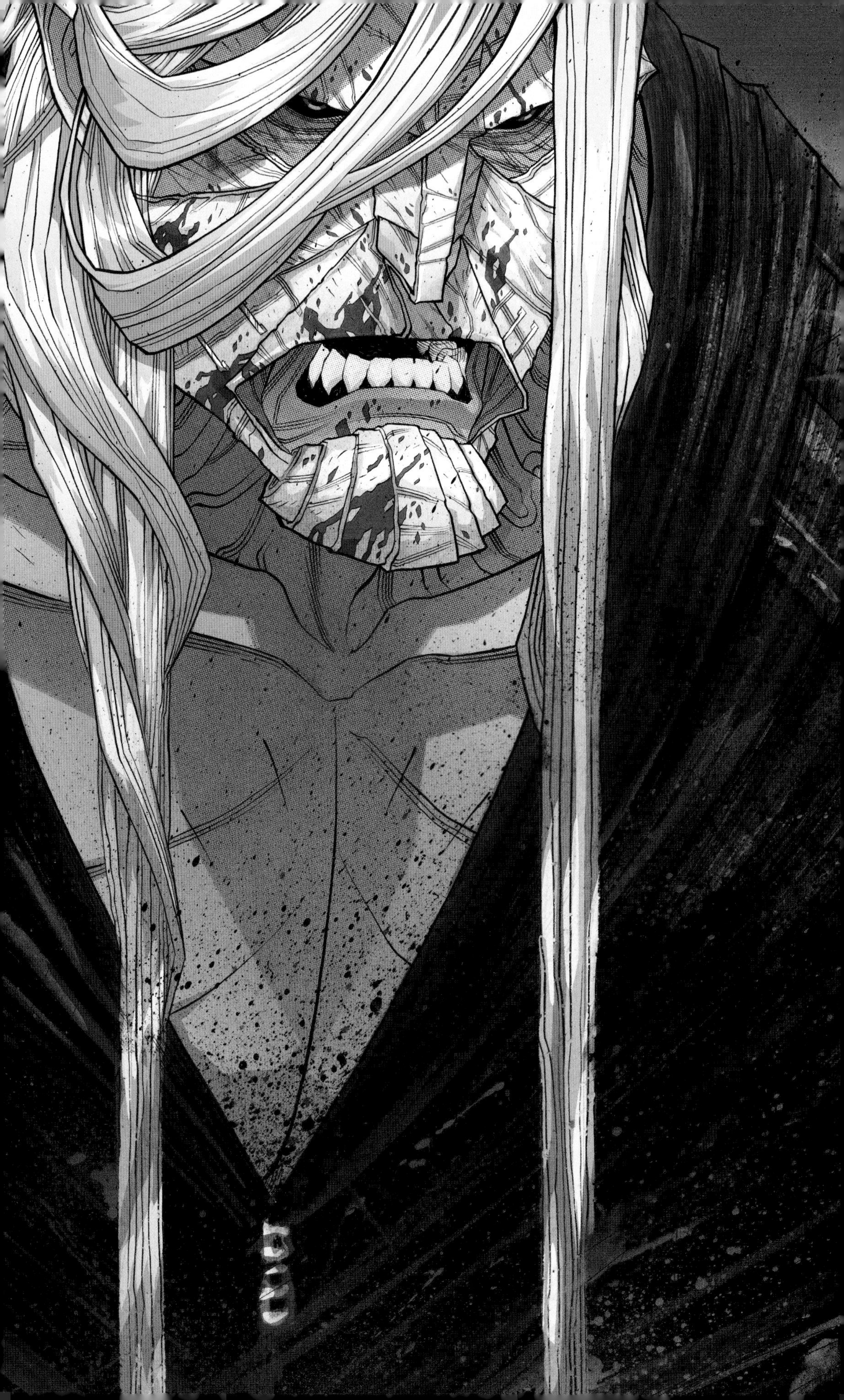

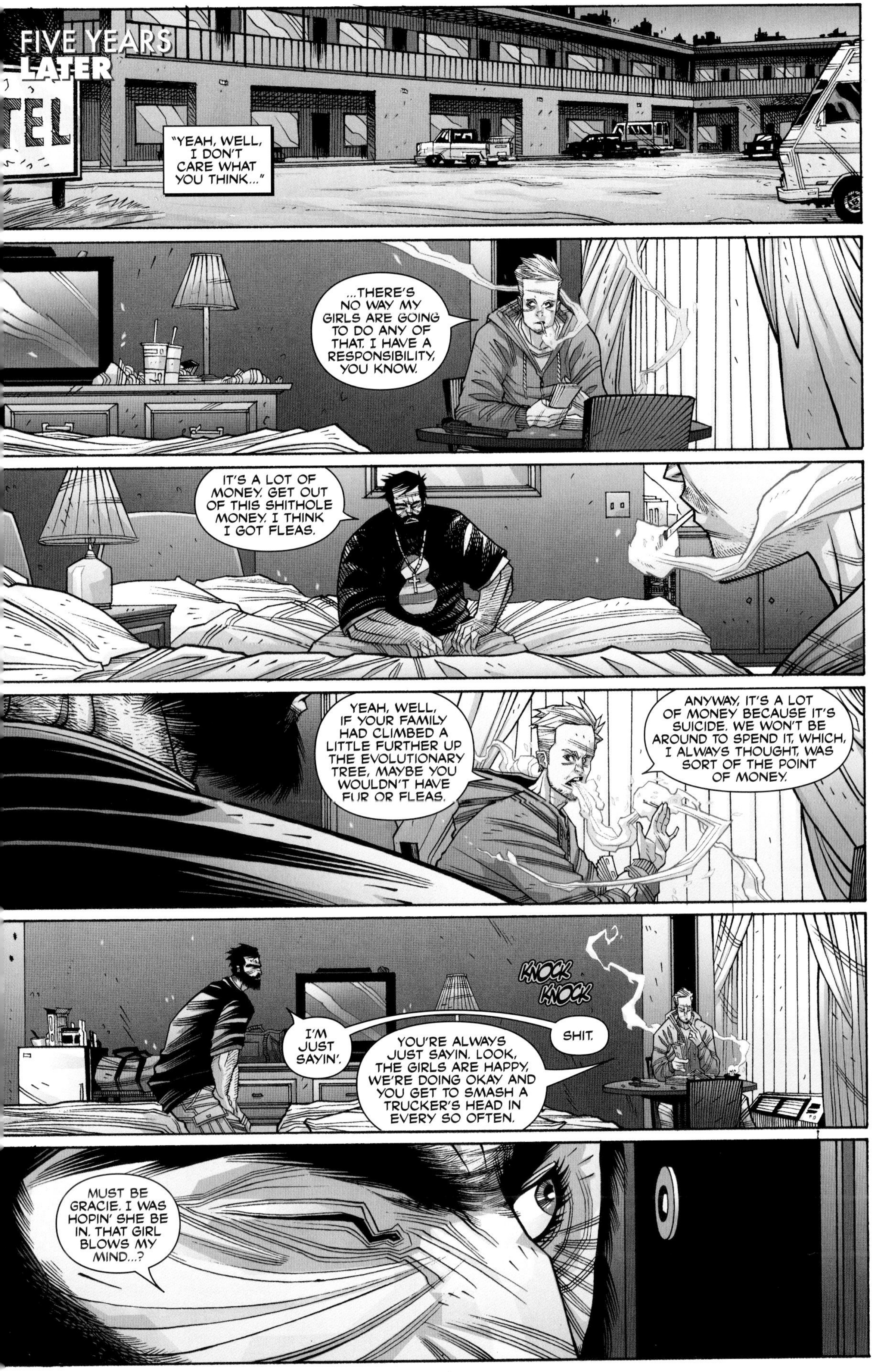
FIVE YEARS LATER
TEL
"YEAH, WELL, I DON'T CARE WHAT YOU THINK..."
...THERE'S NO WAY MY GIRLS ARE GOING TO DO ANY OF THAT. I HAVE A RESPONSIBILITY, YOU KNOW.
IT'S A LOT OF MONEY. GET OUT OF THIS SHITHOLE MONEY. I THINK I GOT FLEAS.
YEAH, WELL, IF YOUR FAMILY HAD CLIMBED A LITTLE FURTHER UP THE EVOLUTIONARY TREE, MAYBE YOU WOULDN'T HAVE FUR OR FLEAS.
ANYWAY, IT'S A LOT OF MONEY BECAUSE IT'S SUICIDE. WE WON'T BE AROUND TO SPEND IT, WHICH, I ALWAYS THOUGHT, WAS SORT OF THE POINT OF MONEY.
I'M JUST SAYIN'.
YOU'RE ALWAYS JUST SAYIN. LOOK, THE GIRLS ARE HAPPY, WE'RE DOING OKAY AND YOU GET TO SMASH A TRUCKER'S HEAD IN EVERY SO OFTEN.
KNOCK KNOCK
SHIT.
MUST BE GRACIE. I WAS HOPIN' SHE BE IN. THAT GIRL BLOWS MY MIND...?

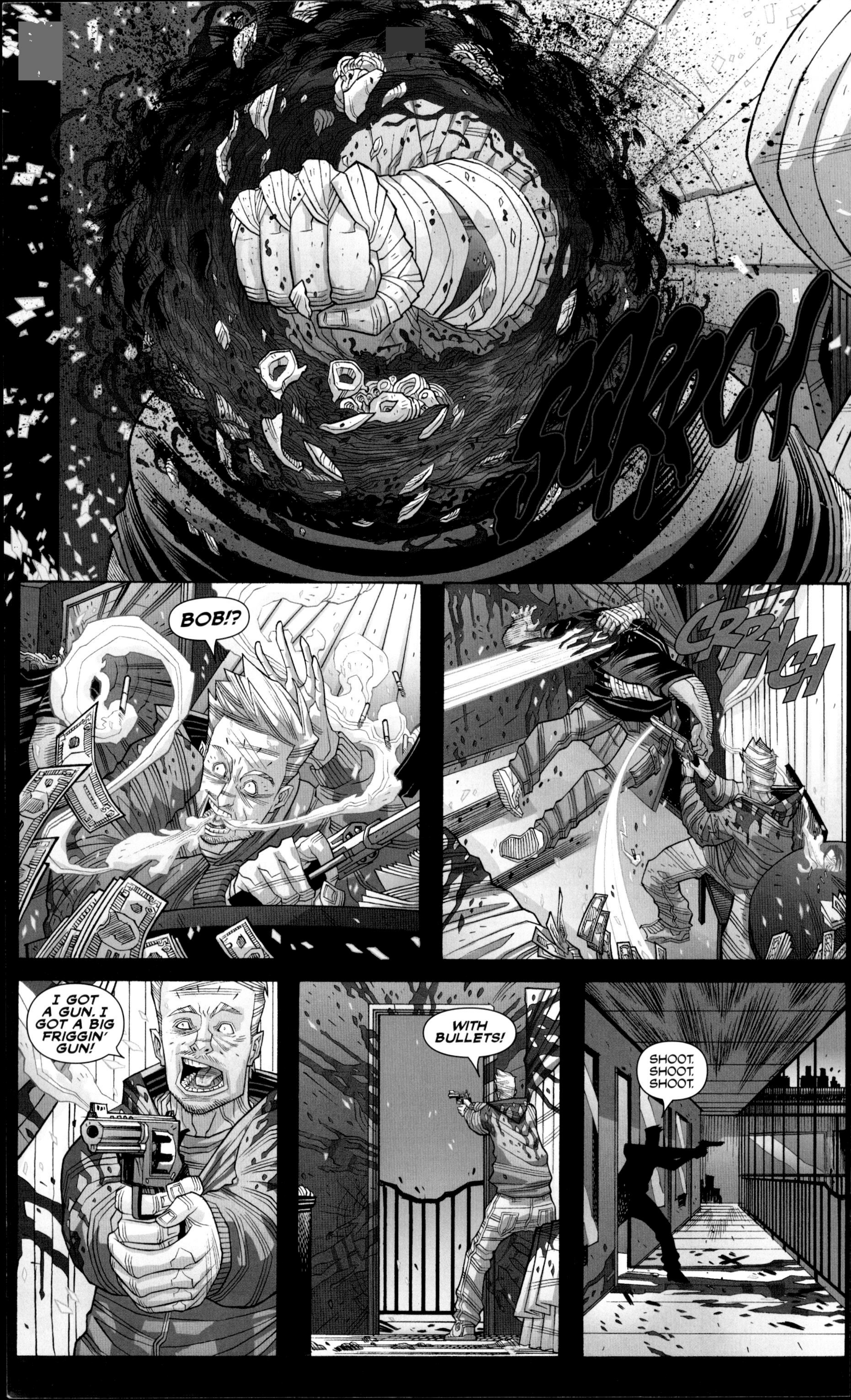
BOB!?
I GOT A GUN. I GOT A BIG FRIGGIN' GUN!
WITH BULLETS!
SHOOT. SHOOT. SHOOT.

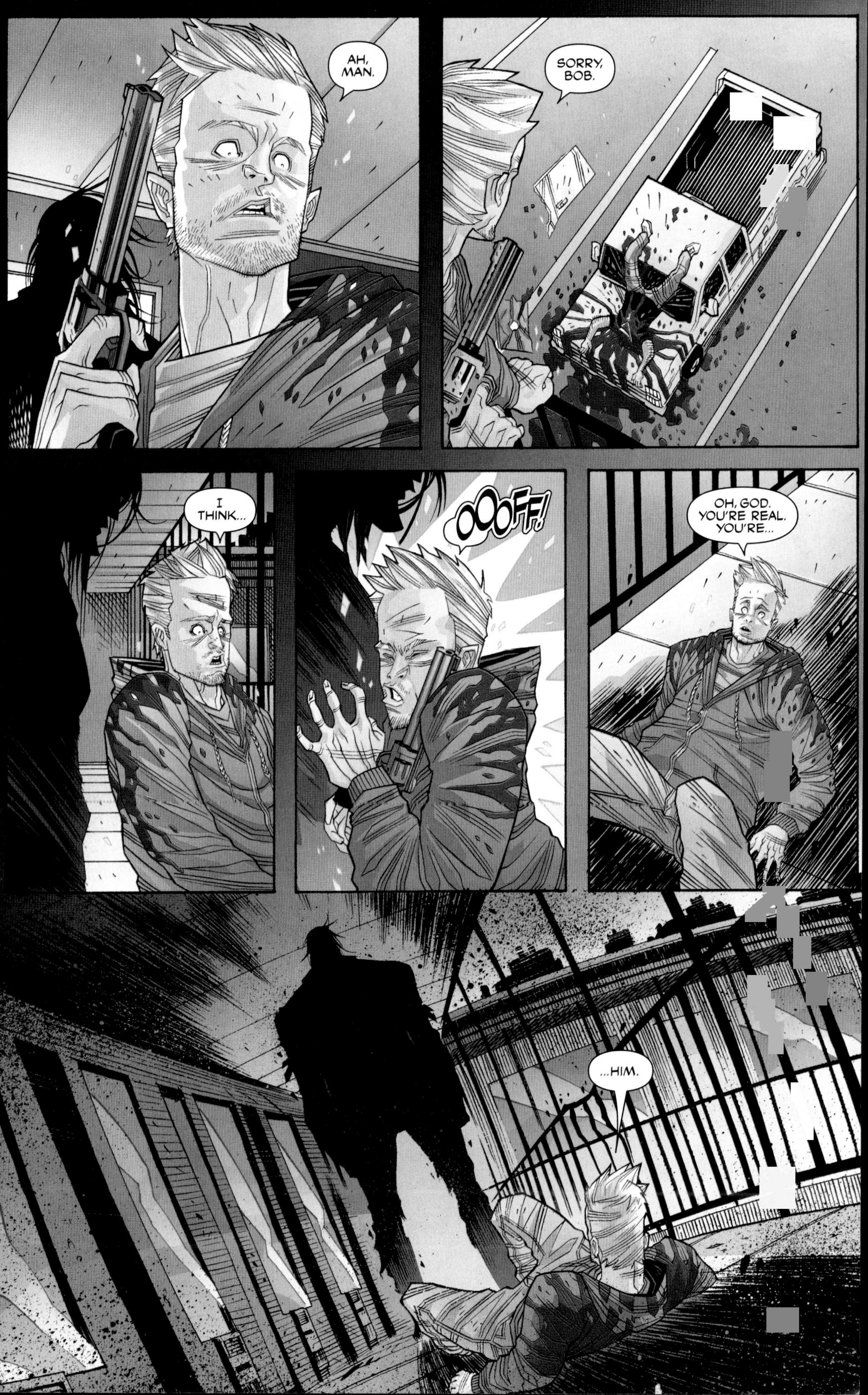
AH, MAN.
SORRY, BOB.
I THINK...
OOOFF!
OH, GOD. YOU'RE REAL. YOU'RE...
...HIM.

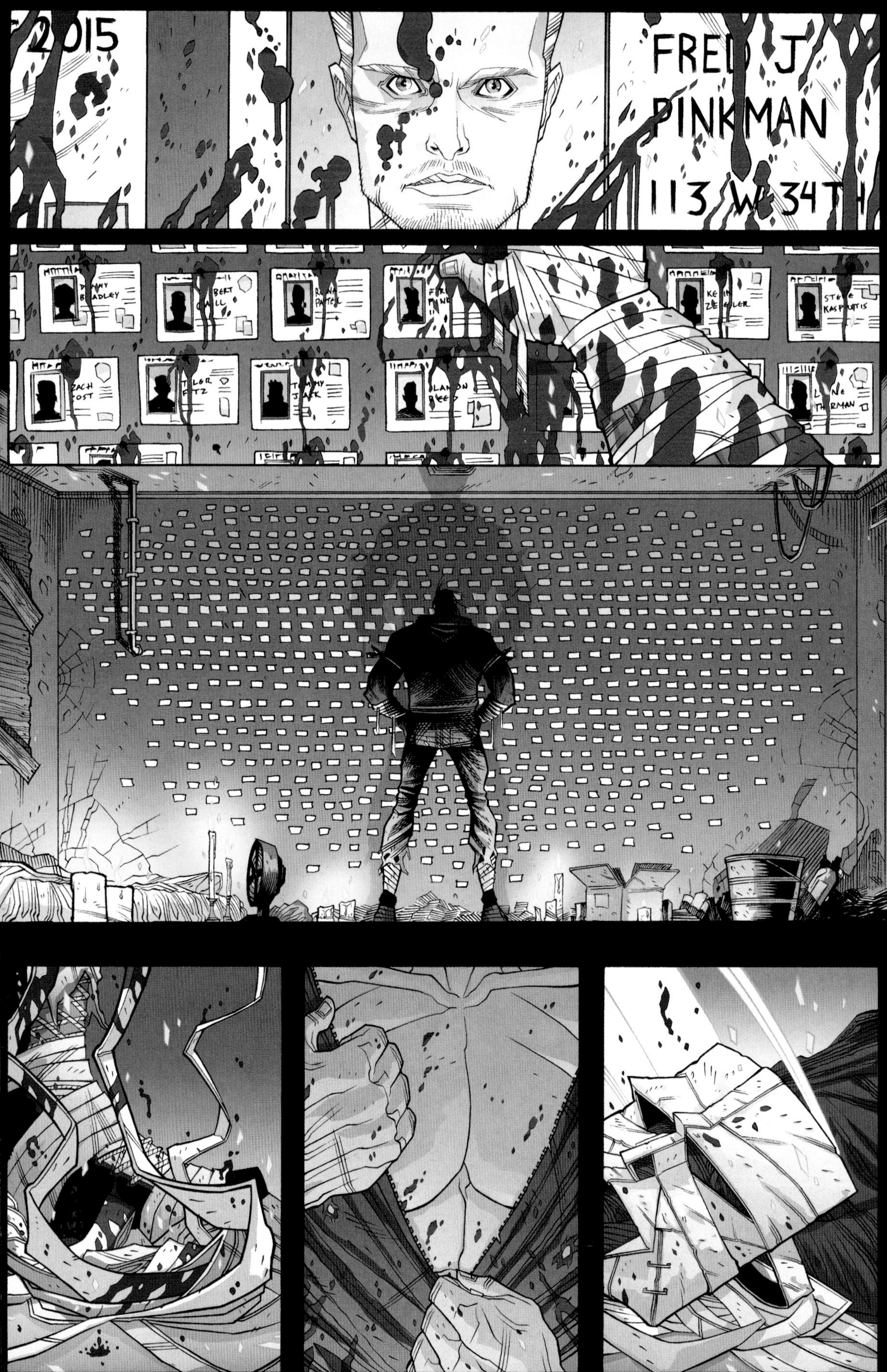
2015
FRED J
PINKMAN
113 W 34TH

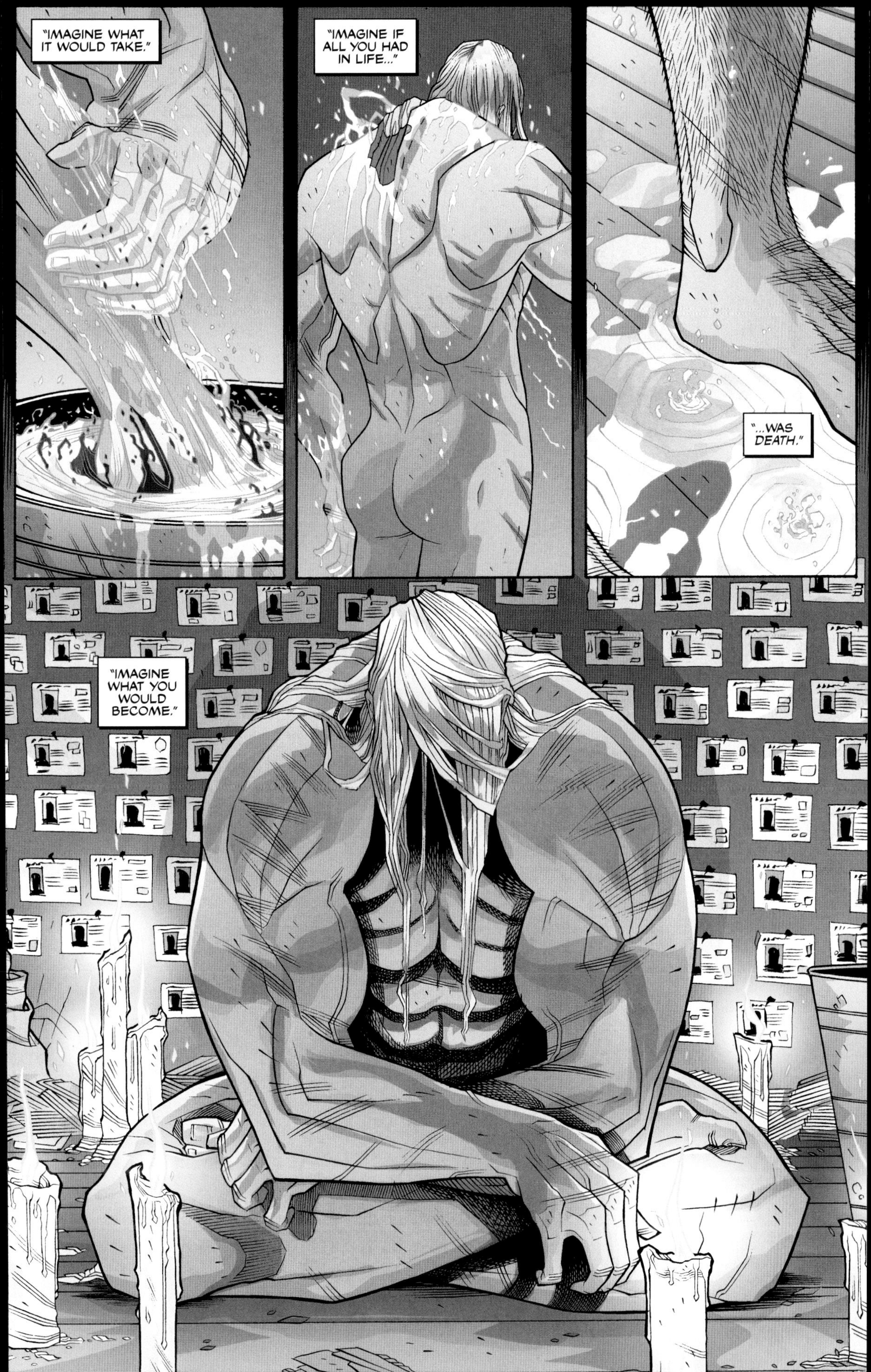
"IMAGINE WHAT IT WOULD TAKE."
"IMAGINE IF ALL YOU HAD IN LIFE..."
"...WAS DEATH."
"IMAGINE WHAT YOU WOULD BECOME."

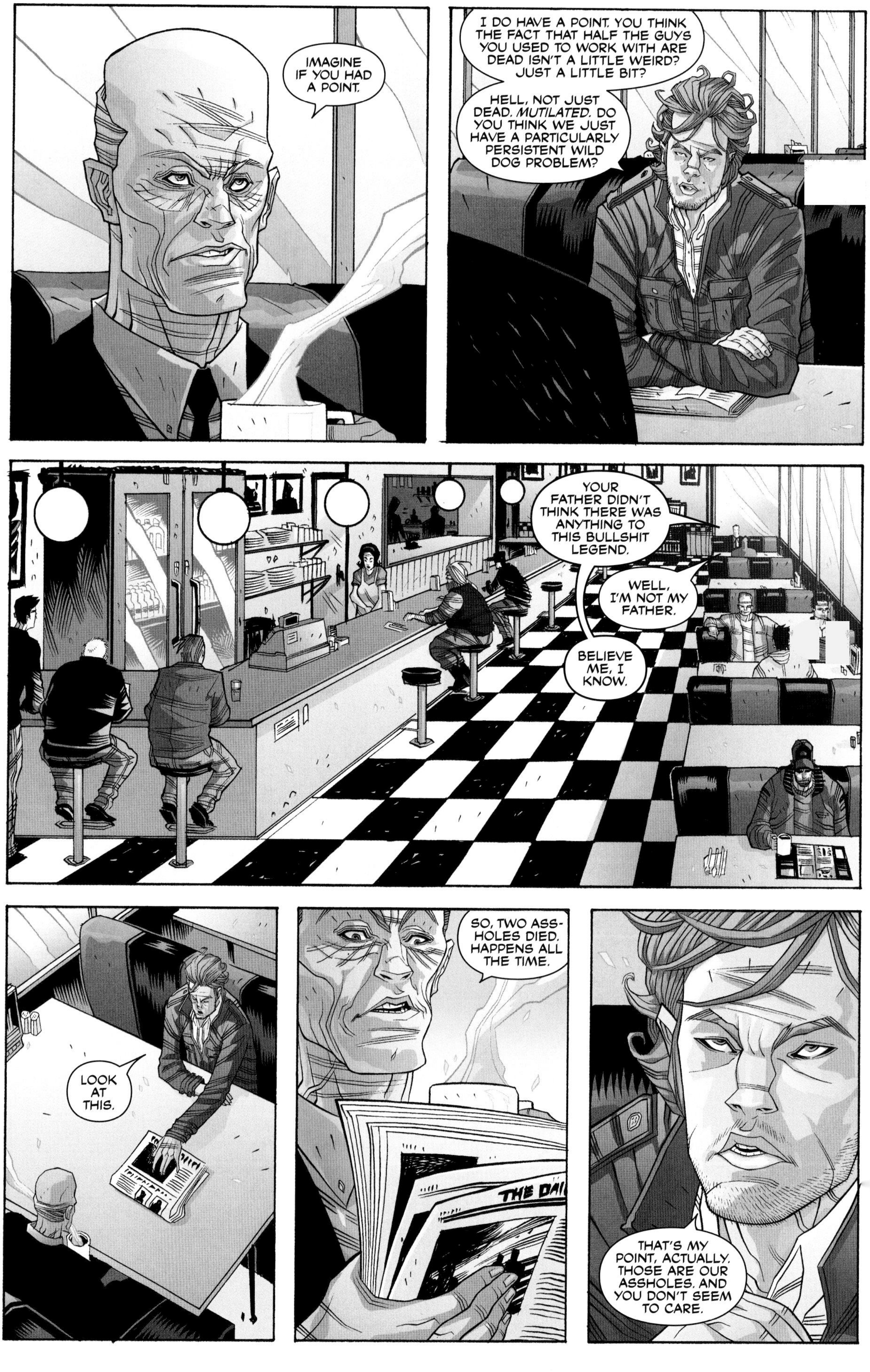
IMAGINE IF YOU HAD A POINT.
I DO HAVE A POINT. YOU THINK THE FACT THAT HALF THE GUYS YOU USED TO WORK WITH ARE DEAD ISN'T A LITTLE WEIRD? JUST A LITTLE BIT?
HELL, NOT JUST DEAD. *MUTILATED.* DO YOU THINK WE JUST HAVE A PARTICULARLY PERSISTENT WILD DOG PROBLEM?
YOUR FATHER DIDN'T THINK THERE WAS ANYTHING TO THIS BULLSHIT LEGEND.
WELL, I'M NOT MY FATHER.
BELIEVE ME, I KNOW.
LOOK AT THIS.
SO, TWO ASS-HOLES DIED. HAPPENS ALL THE TIME.
THE DAI
THAT'S MY POINT, ACTUALLY. THOSE ARE OUR ASSHOLES. AND YOU DON'T SEEM TO CARE.

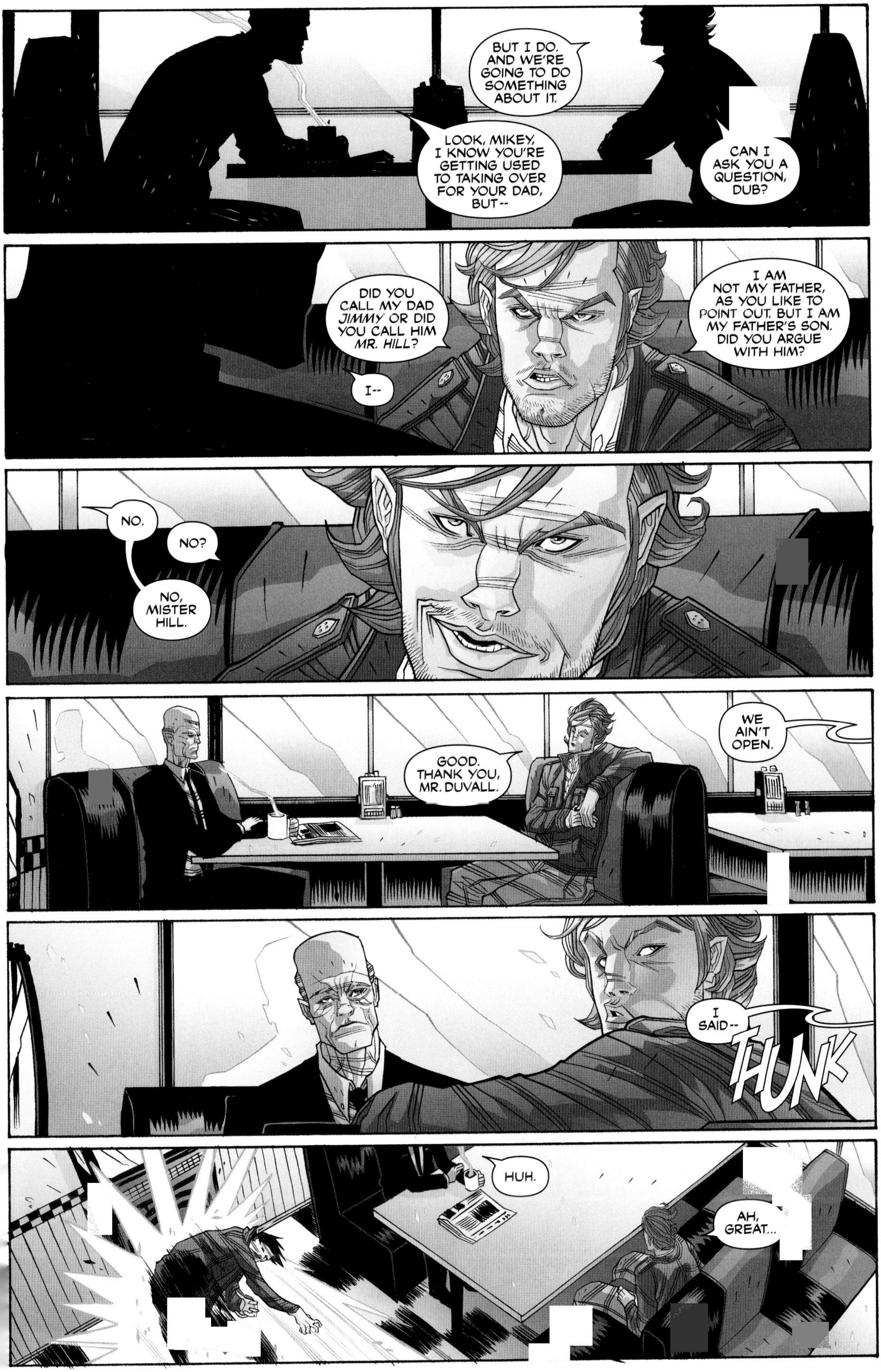
BUT I DO. AND WE'RE GOING TO DO SOMETHING ABOUT IT.
LOOK, MIKEY, I KNOW YOU'RE GETTING USED TO TAKING OVER FOR YOUR DAD, BUT--
CAN I ASK YOU A QUESTION, DUB?
DID YOU CALL MY DAD *JIMMY* OR DID YOU CALL HIM *MR. HILL*?
I--
I AM NOT MY FATHER, AS YOU LIKE TO POINT OUT. BUT I AM MY FATHER'S SON. DID YOU ARGUE WITH HIM?
NO.
NO?
NO, MISTER HILL.
GOOD. THANK YOU, MR. DUVALL.
WE AIN'T OPEN.
I SAID--
THUNK
HUH.
AH, GREAT...

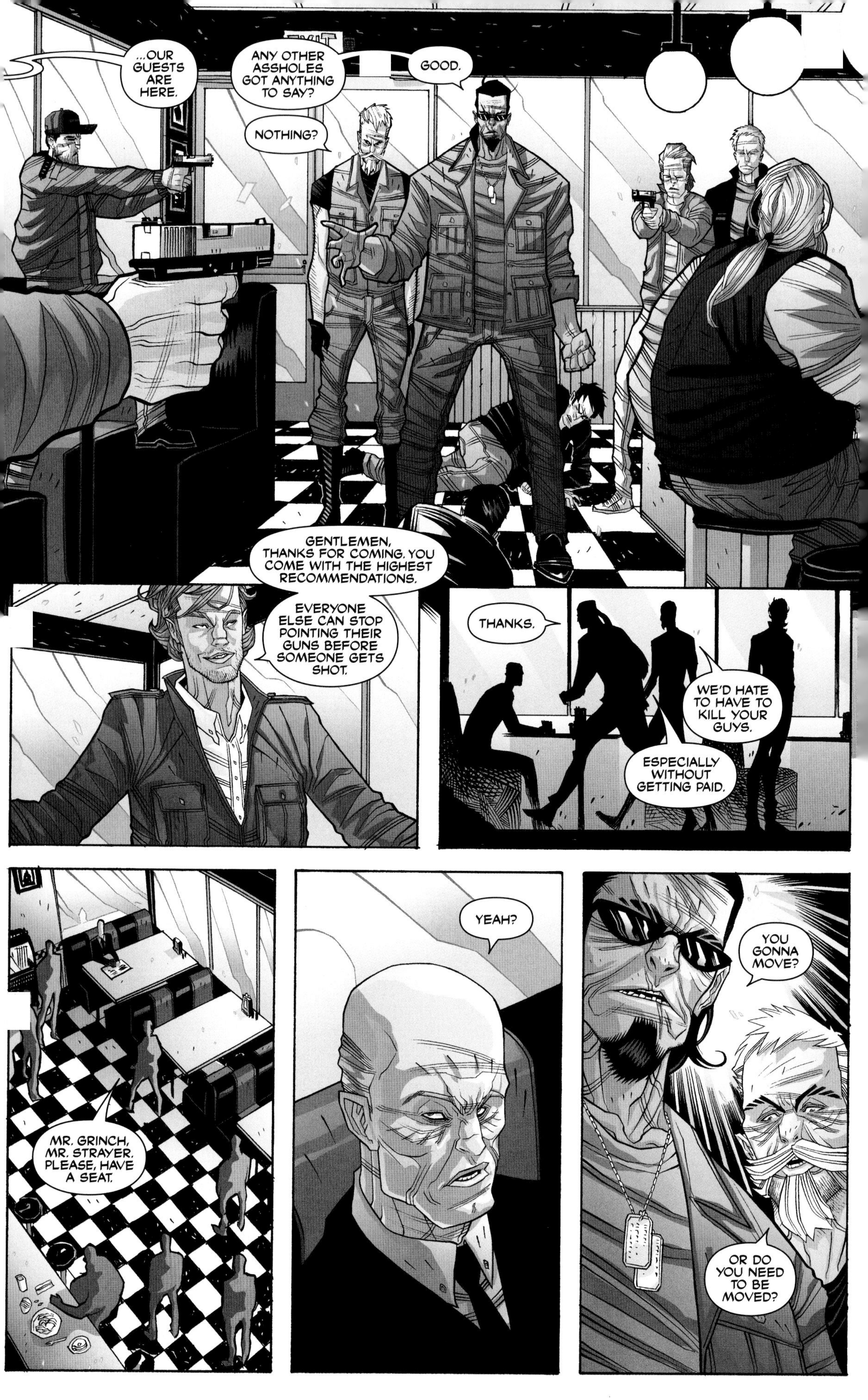
...OUR GUESTS ARE HERE.
ANY OTHER ASSHOLES GOT ANYTHING TO SAY?
GOOD.
NOTHING?
GENTLEMEN, THANKS FOR COMING. YOU COME WITH THE HIGHEST RECOMMENDATIONS.
EVERYONE ELSE CAN STOP POINTING THEIR GUNS BEFORE SOMEONE GETS SHOT.
THANKS.
WE'D HATE TO HAVE TO KILL YOUR GUYS.
ESPECIALLY WITHOUT GETTING PAID.
MR. GRINCH, MR. STRAYER. PLEASE, HAVE A SEAT.
YEAH?
YOU GONNA MOVE?
OR DO YOU NEED TO BE MOVED?

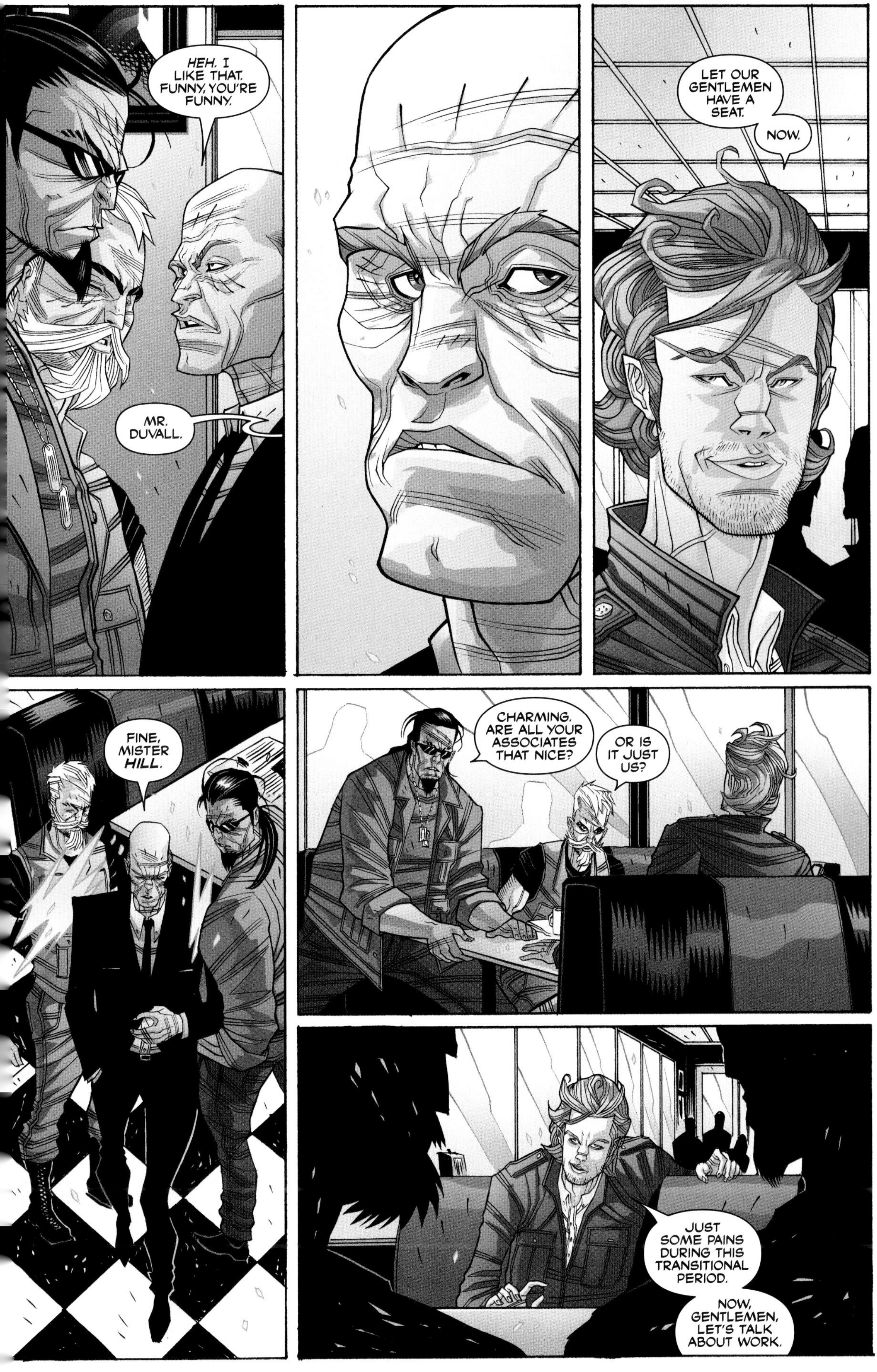
HEH. I LIKE THAT. FUNNY, YOU'RE FUNNY.
MR. DUVALL.
LET OUR GENTLEMEN HAVE A SEAT.
NOW.
FINE, MISTER HILL.
CHARMING. ARE ALL YOUR ASSOCIATES THAT NICE?
OR IS IT JUST US?
JUST SOME PAINS DURING THIS TRANSITIONAL PERIOD.
NOW, GENTLEMEN, LET'S TALK ABOUT WORK.

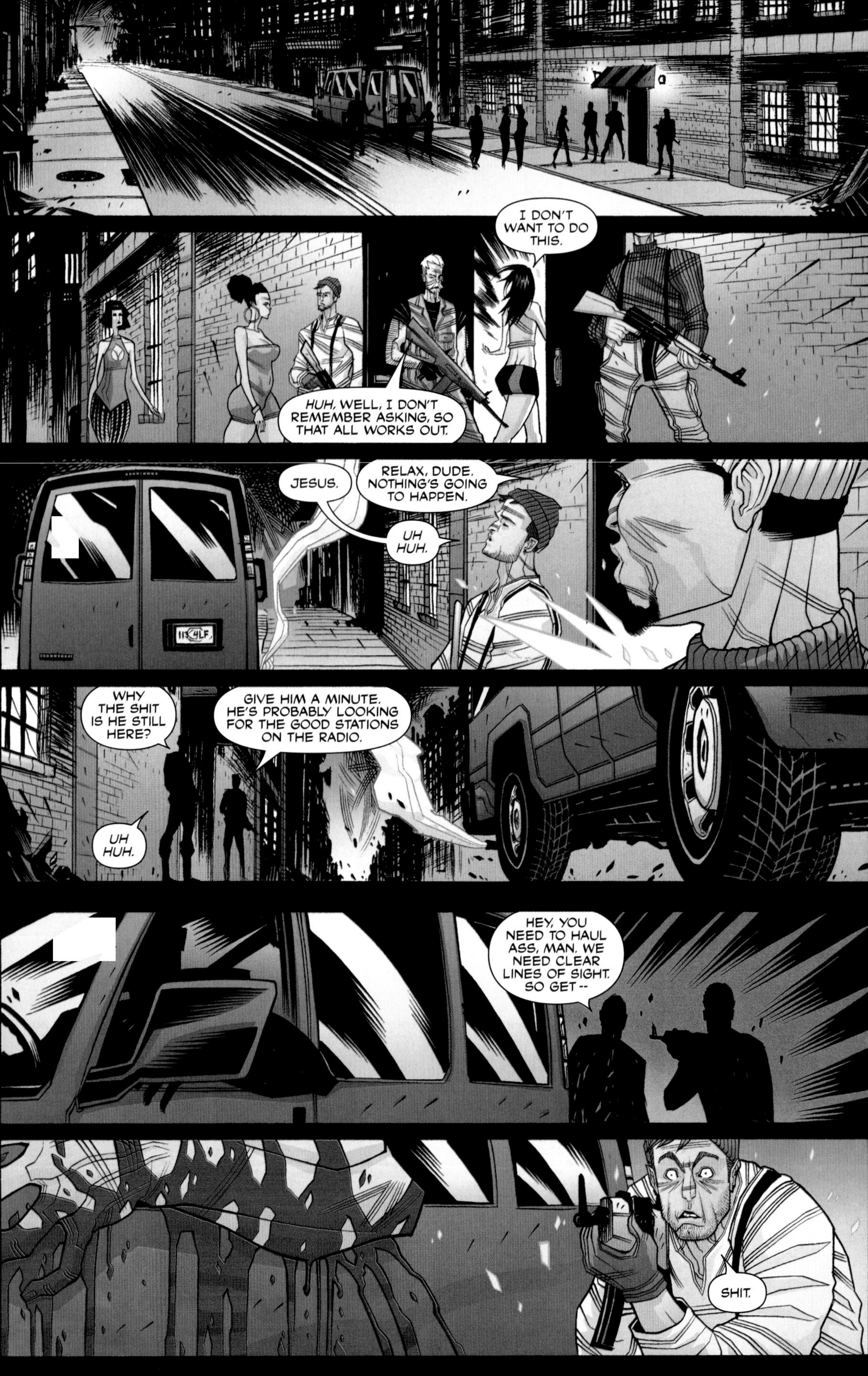
I DON'T WANT TO DO THIS.
HUH, WELL, I DON'T REMEMBER ASKING, SO THAT ALL WORKS OUT.
JESUS.
RELAX, DUDE. NOTHING'S GOING TO HAPPEN.
UH HUH.
WHY THE SHIT IS HE STILL HERE?
GIVE HIM A MINUTE. HE'S PROBABLY LOOKING FOR THE GOOD STATIONS ON THE RADIO.
UH HUH.
HEY, YOU NEED TO HAUL ASS, MAN. WE NEED CLEAR LINES OF SIGHT. SO GET --
SHIT.

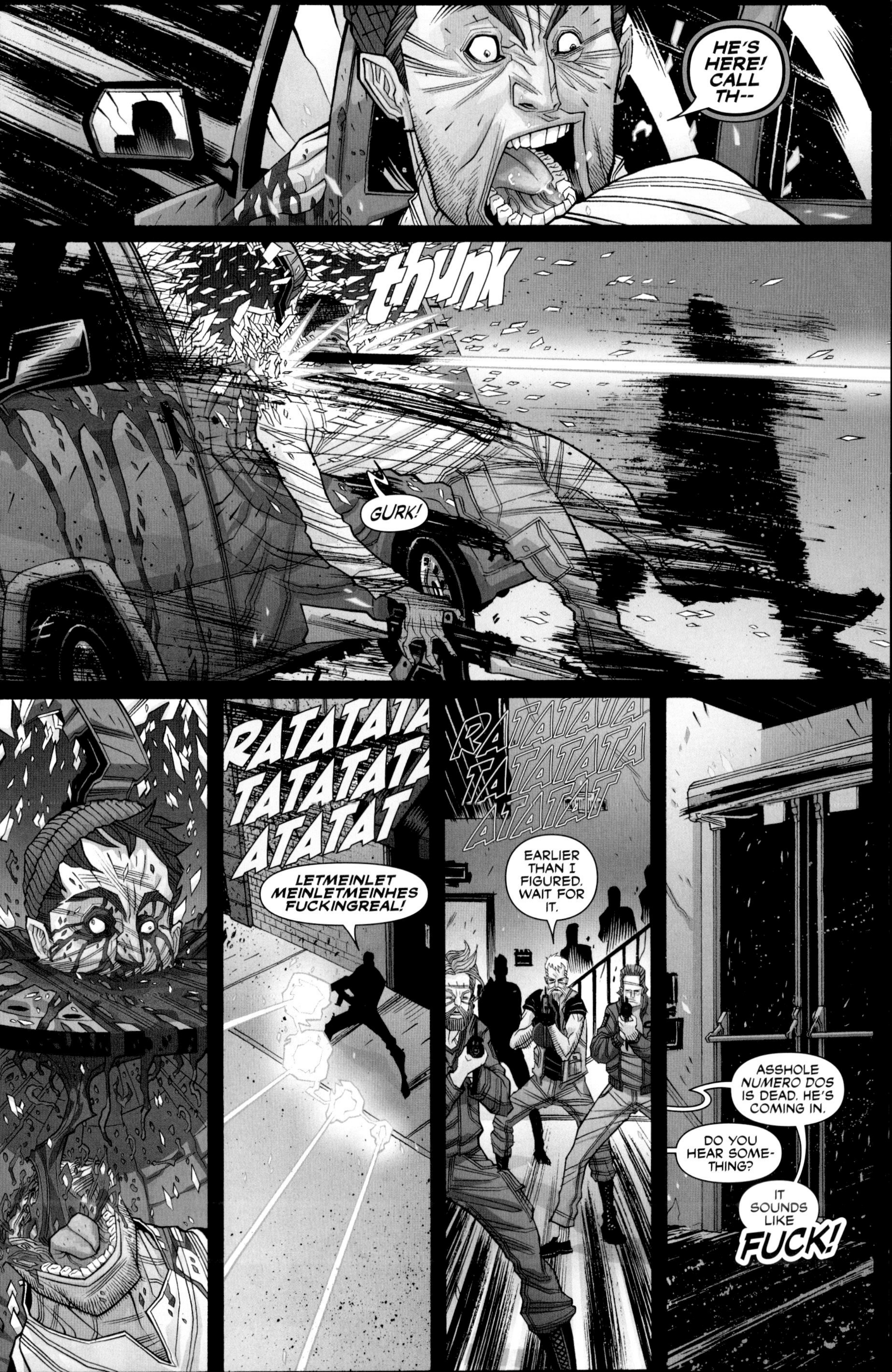
HE'S HERE! CALL TH--
thunk
GURK!
RATATATA TATATATA ATATAT
LETMEINLET MEINLETMEINHES FUCKINGREAL!
RATATATA TATATATA ATATAT
EARLIER THAN I FIGURED. WAIT FOR IT.
ASSHOLE NUMERO DOS IS DEAD. HE'S COMING IN.
DO YOU HEAR SOME-THING?
IT SOUNDS LIKE
FUCK!

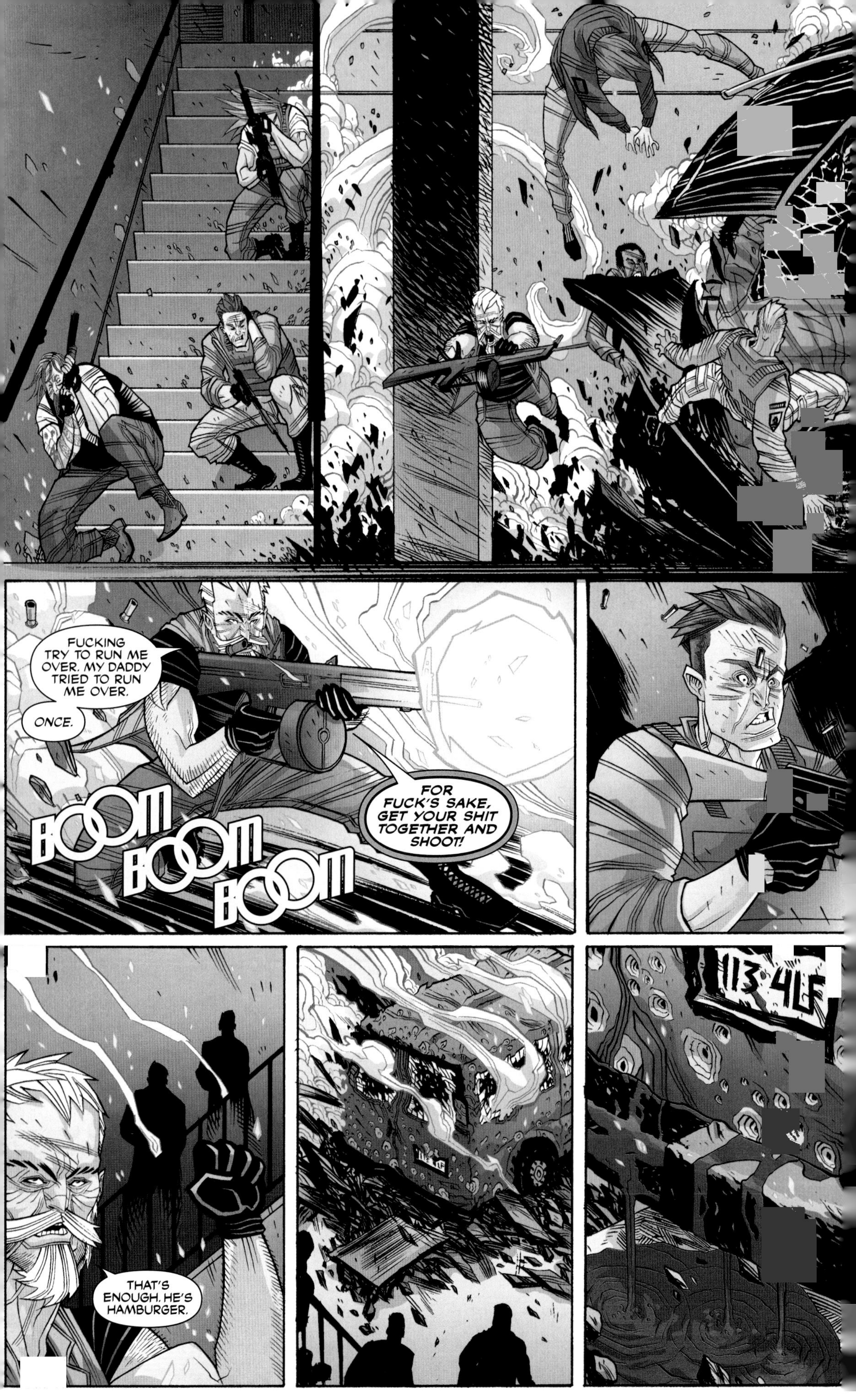
FUCKING TRY TO RUN ME OVER. MY DADDY TRIED TO RUN ME OVER.
ONCE.
BOOM BOOM BOOM
FOR FUCK'S SAKE, GET YOUR SHIT TOGETHER AND SHOOT!
THAT'S ENOUGH. HE'S HAMBURGER.
113 4LF

SMASH

RATATA TATATA ATAT

RATATA TATATA ATAT

RATATA TATATA TATATATA TATATATA

BOOM BOOM BOOM

BANG BANG BANG

BANG BANGBANG BANG

KEEP IT TOGETHER. AND FOR FUCK'S SAKE, DON'T SHOOT ME. THAT SHIT PISSES ME OFF.

DISTRACTION! HE'S COMING IN SOME OTHER WAY. GET YOUR ASSES TURNED AND YOUR EYES OPEN.

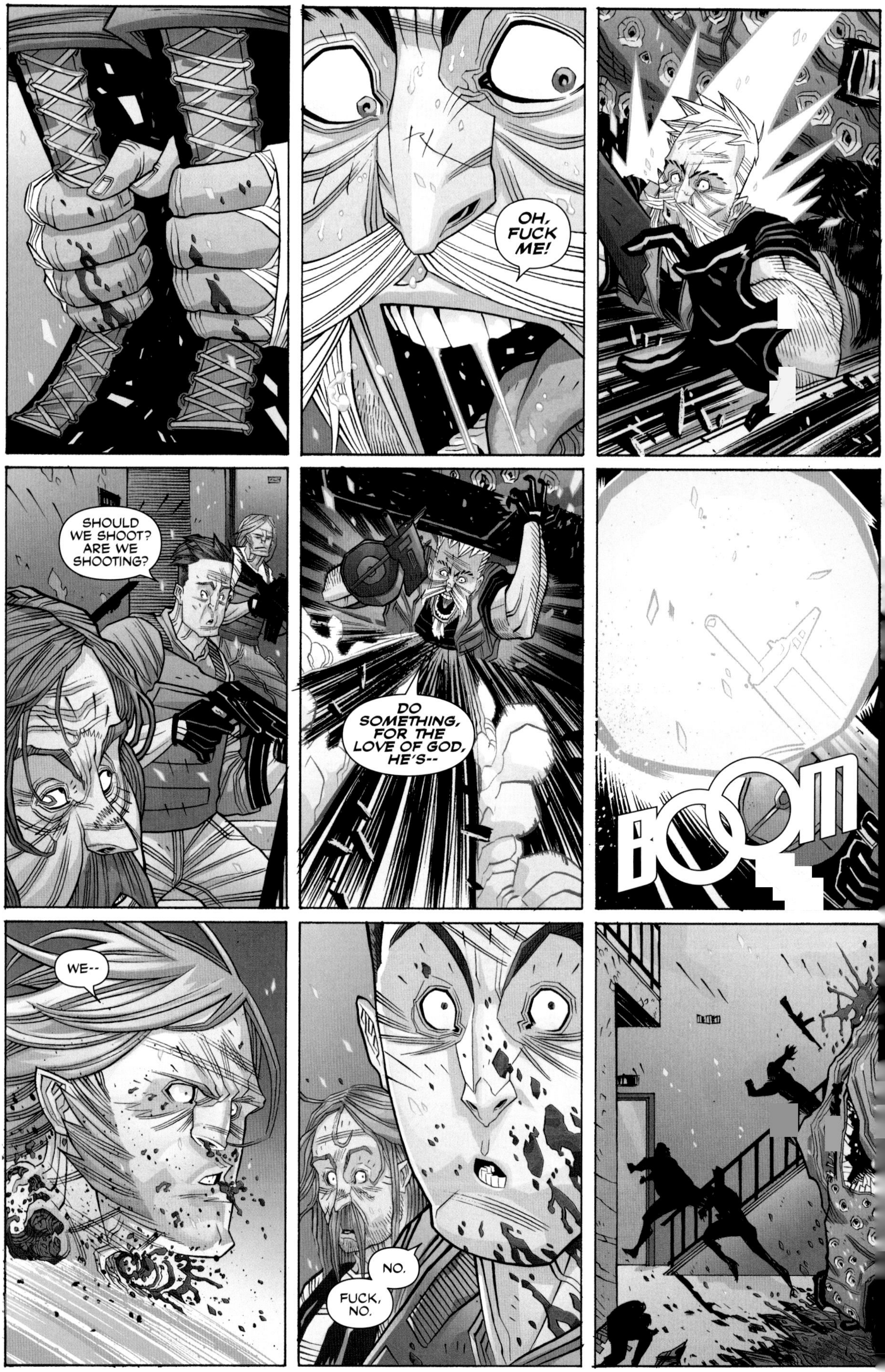
OH, FUCK ME!
SHOULD WE SHOOT? ARE WE SHOOTING?
DO SOMETHING, FOR THE LOVE OF GOD, HE'S--
BOOM
WE--
NO.
FUCK, NO.

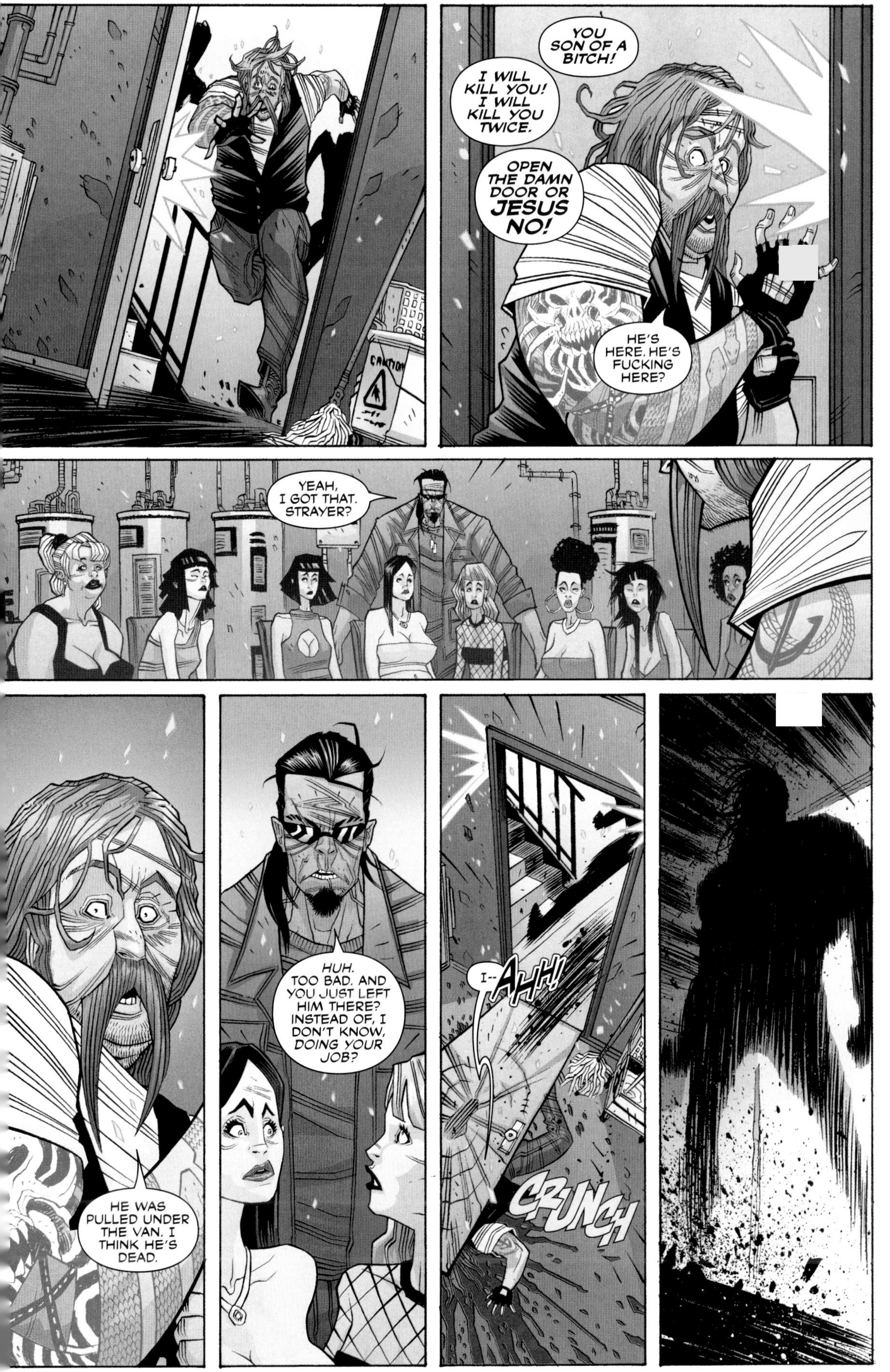
YOU SON OF A BITCH!
I WILL KILL YOU! I WILL KILL YOU TWICE.
OPEN THE DAMN DOOR OR JESUS NO!
HE'S HERE. HE'S FUCKING HERE?
YEAH, I GOT THAT. STRAYER?
HE WAS PULLED UNDER THE VAN. I THINK HE'S DEAD.
HUH. TOO BAD. AND YOU JUST LEFT HIM THERE? INSTEAD OF, I DON'T KNOW, DOING YOUR JOB?
I--AHH!
CRUNCH

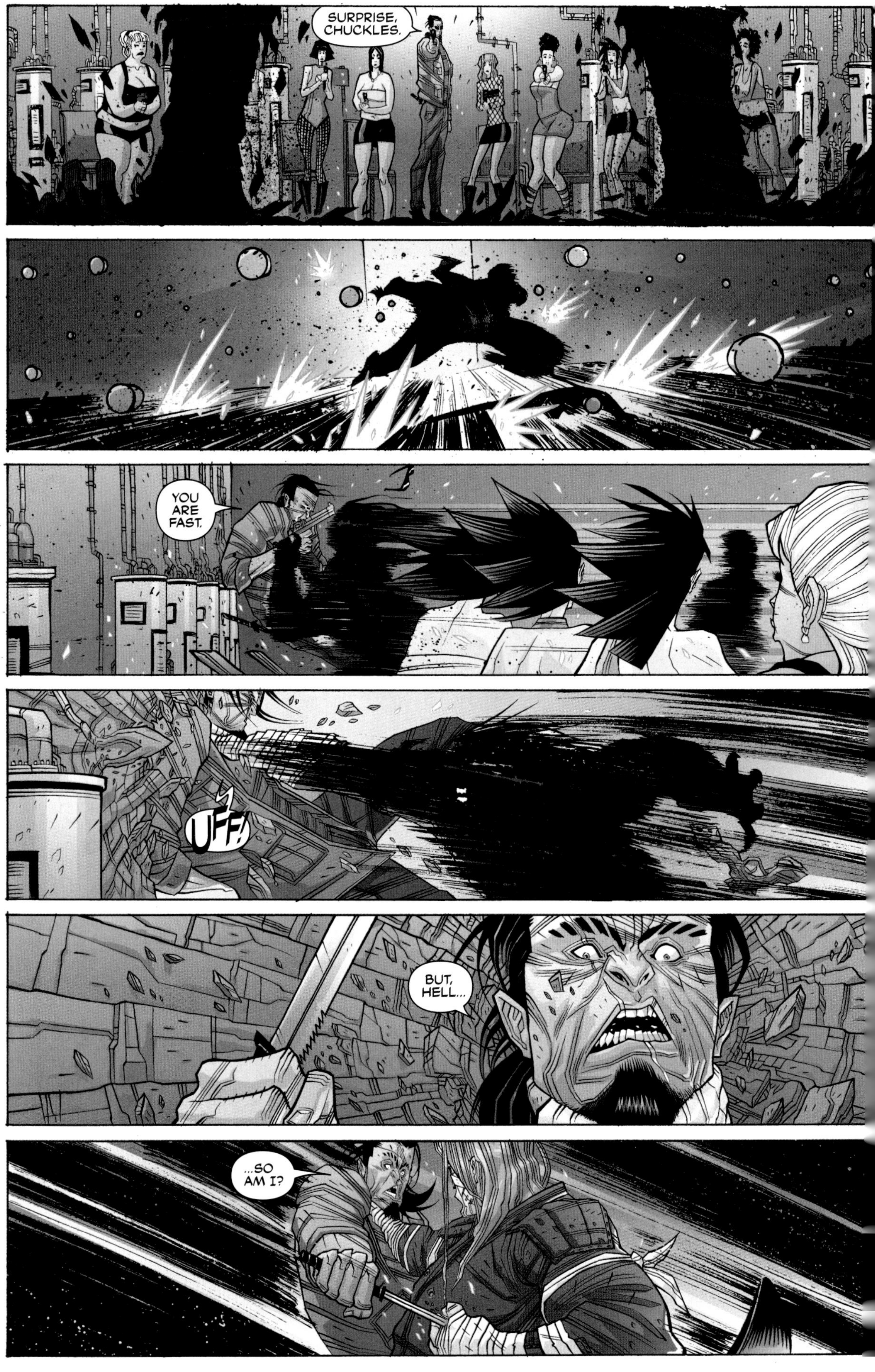
SURPRISE, CHUCKLES.
YOU ARE FAST.
UFF!
BUT, HELL...
...SO AM I?

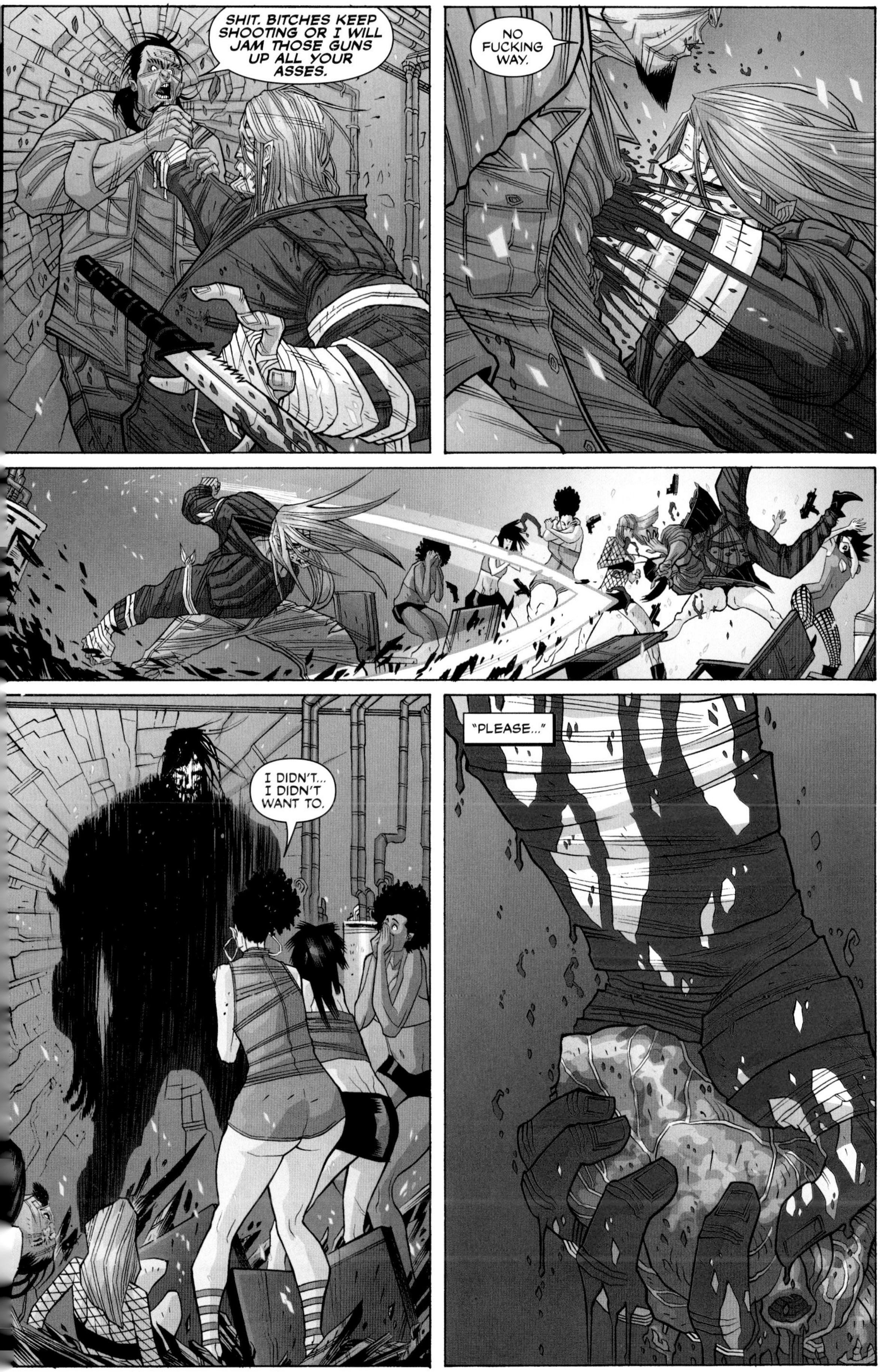
SHIT. BITCHES KEEP SHOOTING OR I WILL JAM THOSE GUNS UP ALL YOUR ASSES.
NO FUCKING WAY.
I DIDN'T... I DIDN'T WANT TO.
"PLEASE..."

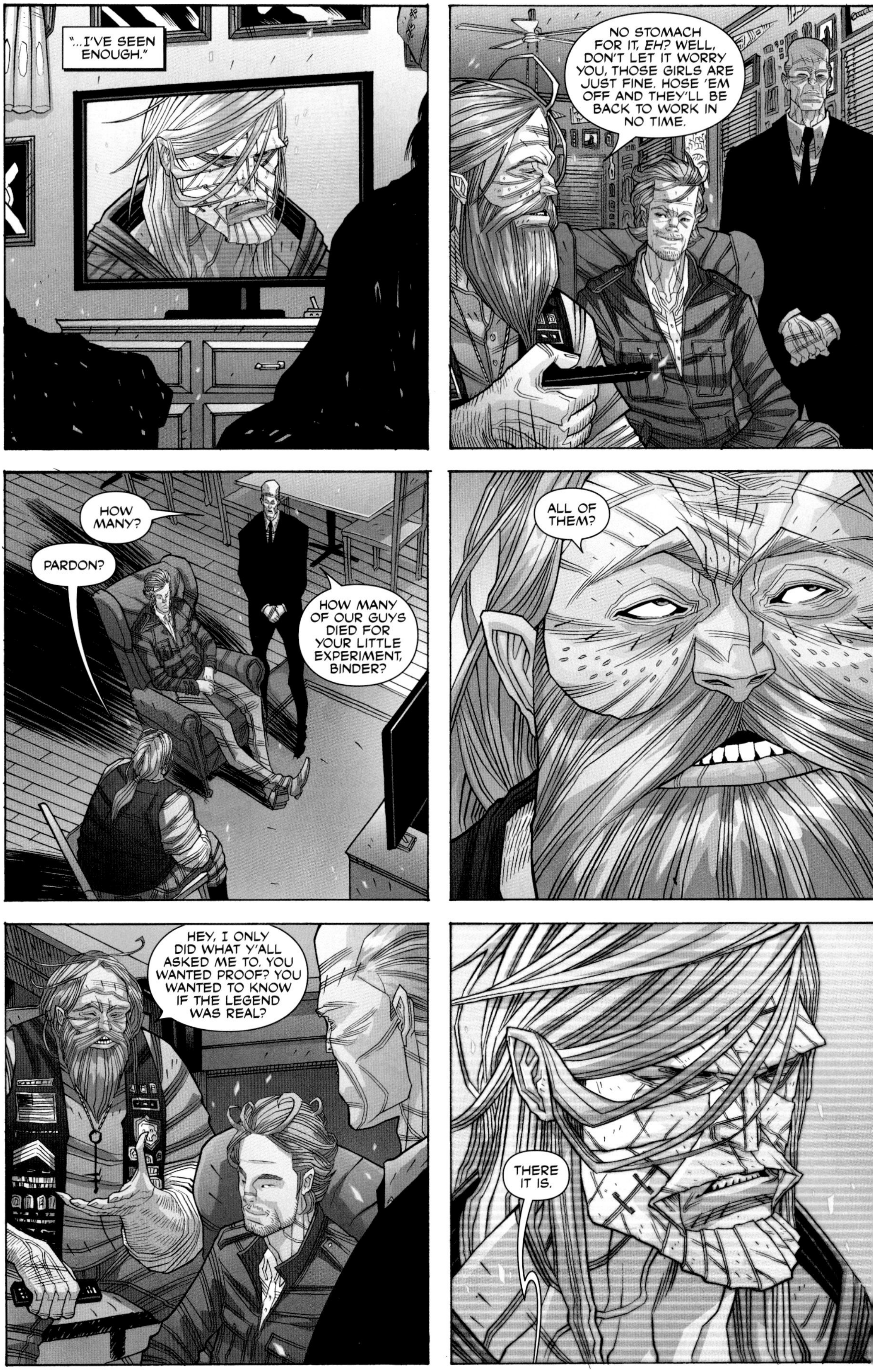
"...I'VE SEEN ENOUGH."
NO STOMACH FOR IT, EH? WELL, DON'T LET IT WORRY YOU, THOSE GIRLS ARE JUST FINE. HOSE 'EM OFF AND THEY'LL BE BACK TO WORK IN NO TIME.
HOW MANY?
PARDON?
HOW MANY OF OUR GUYS DIED FOR YOUR LITTLE EXPERIMENT, BINDER?
ALL OF THEM?
HEY, I ONLY DID WHAT Y'ALL ASKED ME TO. YOU WANTED PROOF? YOU WANTED TO KNOW IF THE LEGEND WAS REAL?
THERE IT IS.

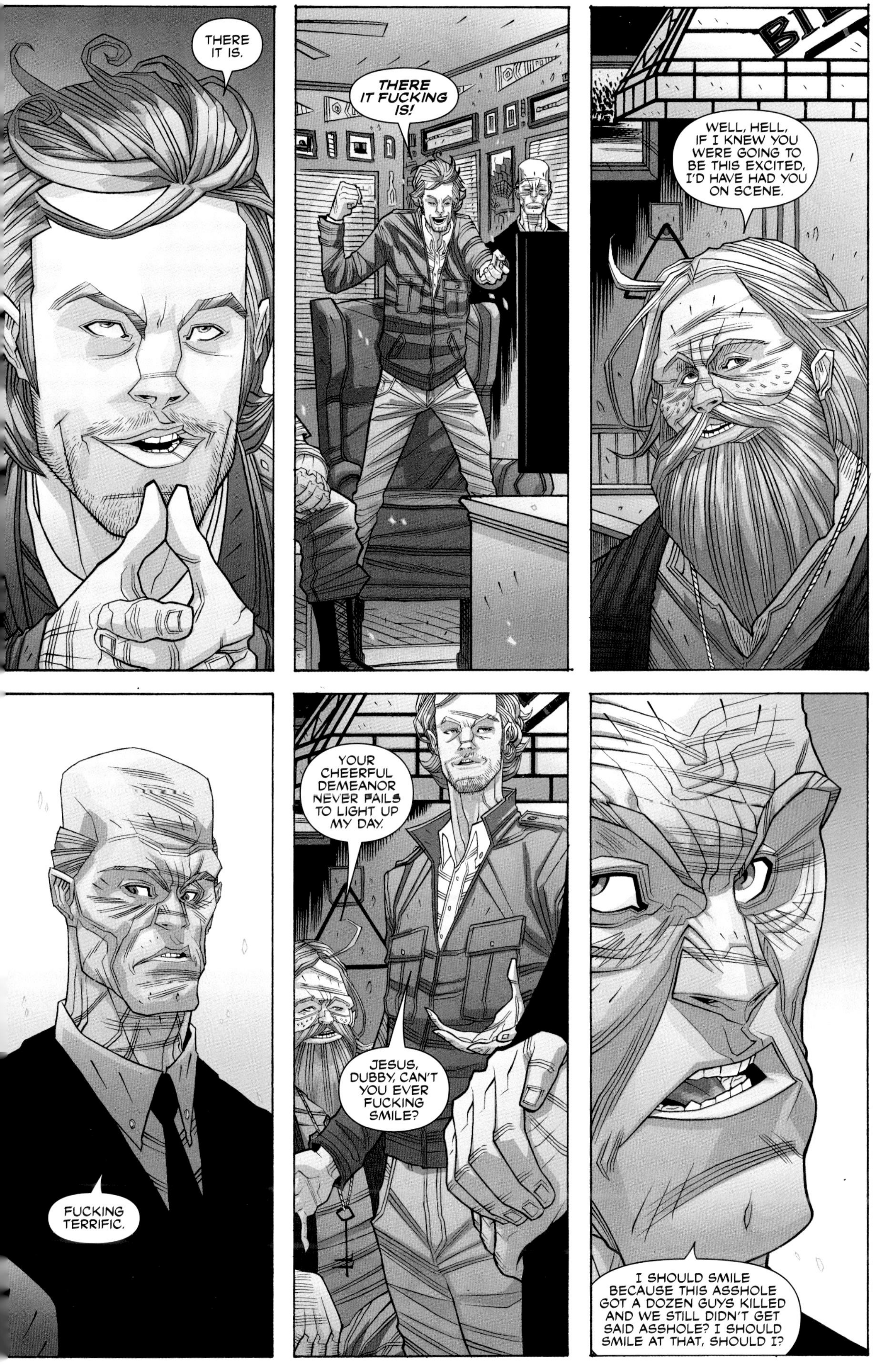
THERE IT IS.
THERE IT FUCKING IS!
WELL, HELL, IF I KNEW YOU WERE GOING TO BE THIS EXCITED, I'D HAVE HAD YOU ON SCENE.
FUCKING TERRIFIC.
YOUR CHEERFUL DEMEANOR NEVER FAILS TO LIGHT UP MY DAY.
JESUS, DUBBY, CAN'T YOU EVER FUCKING SMILE?
I SHOULD SMILE BECAUSE THIS ASSHOLE GOT A DOZEN GUYS KILLED AND WE STILL DIDN'T GET SAID ASSHOLE? I SHOULD SMILE AT THAT, SHOULD I?

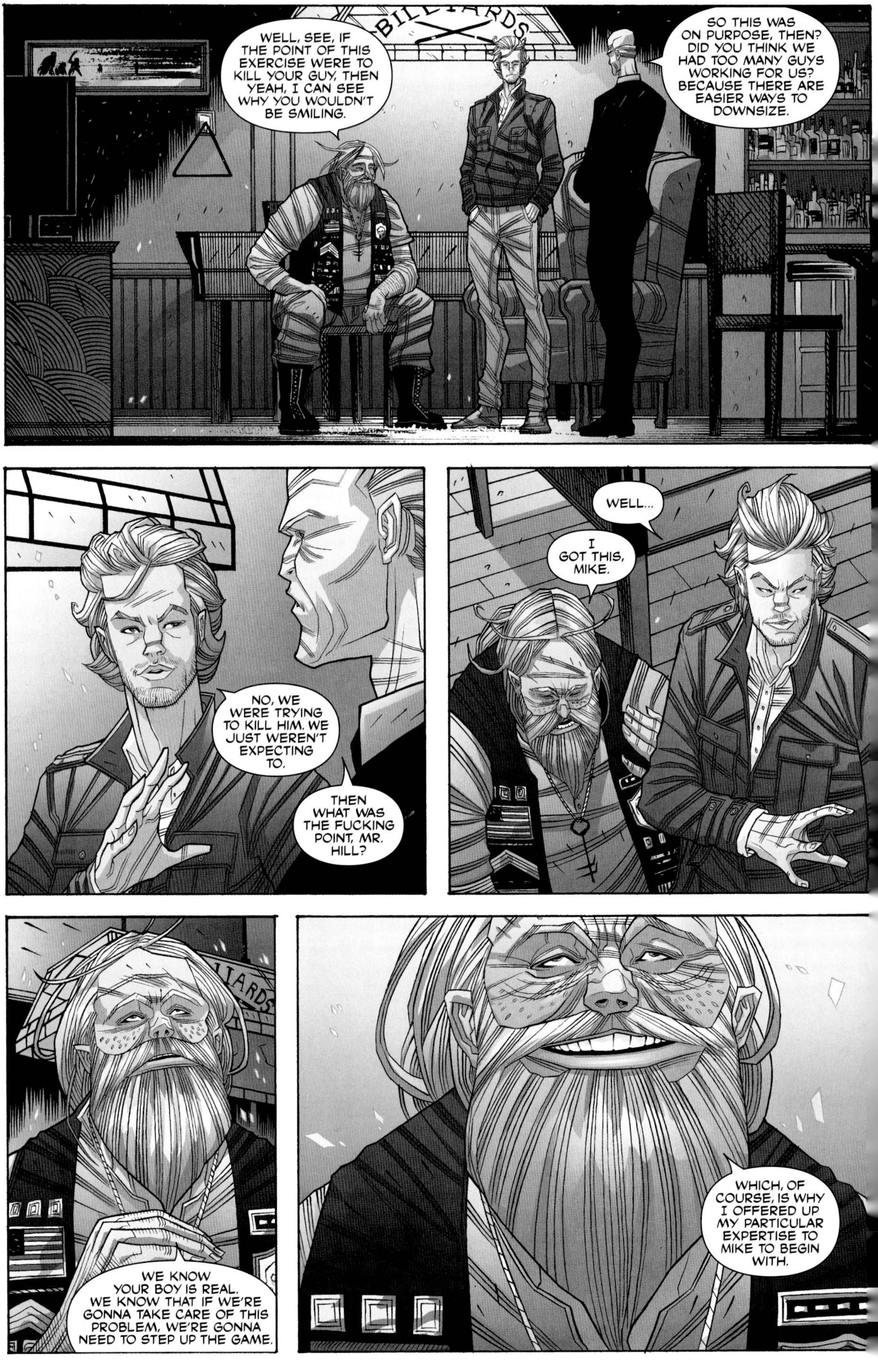
BILLIARDS
WELL, SEE, IF THE POINT OF THIS EXERCISE WERE TO KILL YOUR GUY, THEN YEAH, I CAN SEE WHY YOU WOULDN'T BE SMILING.
SO THIS WAS ON PURPOSE, THEN? DID YOU THINK WE HAD TOO MANY GUYS WORKING FOR US? BECAUSE THERE ARE EASIER WAYS TO DOWNSIZE.
NO, WE WERE TRYING TO KILL HIM. WE JUST WEREN'T EXPECTING TO.
THEN WHAT WAS THE FUCKING POINT, MR. HILL?
WELL...
I GOT THIS, MIKE.
WE KNOW YOUR BOY IS REAL. WE KNOW THAT IF WE'RE GONNA TAKE CARE OF THIS PROBLEM, WE'RE GONNA NEED TO STEP UP THE GAME.
WHICH, OF COURSE, IS WHY I OFFERED UP MY PARTICULAR EXPERTISE TO MIKE TO BEGIN WITH.

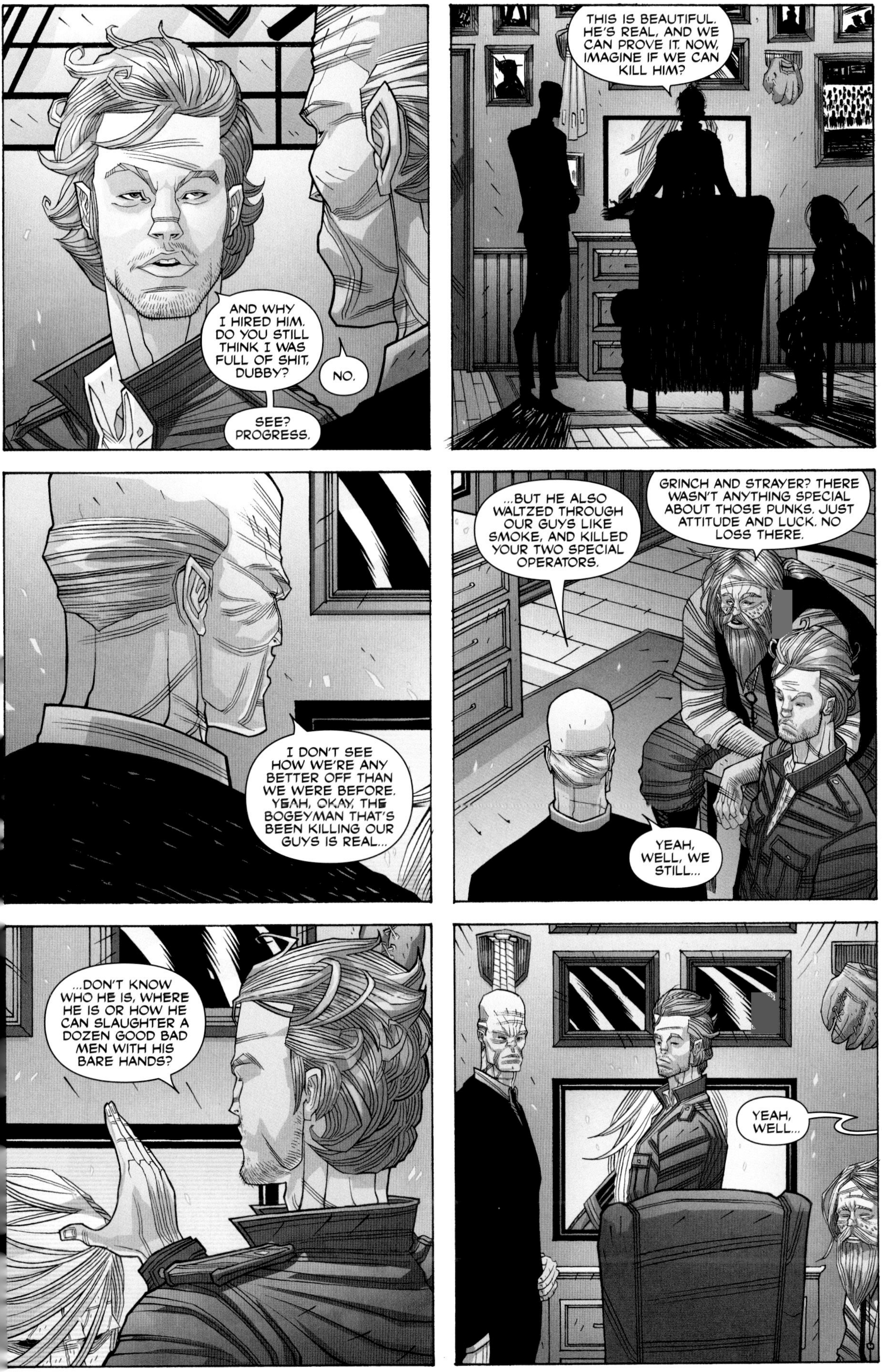
AND WHY I HIRED HIM. DO YOU STILL THINK I WAS FULL OF SHIT, DUBBY?
NO.
SEE? PROGRESS.
THIS IS BEAUTIFUL. HE'S REAL, AND WE CAN PROVE IT. NOW, IMAGINE IF WE CAN KILL HIM?
I DON'T SEE HOW WE'RE ANY BETTER OFF THAN WE WERE BEFORE. YEAH, OKAY, THE BOGEYMAN THAT'S BEEN KILLING OUR GUYS IS REAL...
...BUT HE ALSO WALTZED THROUGH OUR GUYS LIKE SMOKE, AND KILLED YOUR TWO SPECIAL OPERATORS.
GRINCH AND STRAYER? THERE WASN'T ANYTHING SPECIAL ABOUT THOSE PUNKS. JUST ATTITUDE AND LUCK. NO LOSS THERE.
YEAH, WELL, WE STILL...
...DON'T KNOW WHO HE IS, WHERE HE IS OR HOW HE CAN SLAUGHTER A DOZEN GOOD BAD MEN WITH HIS BARE HANDS?
YEAH, WELL...

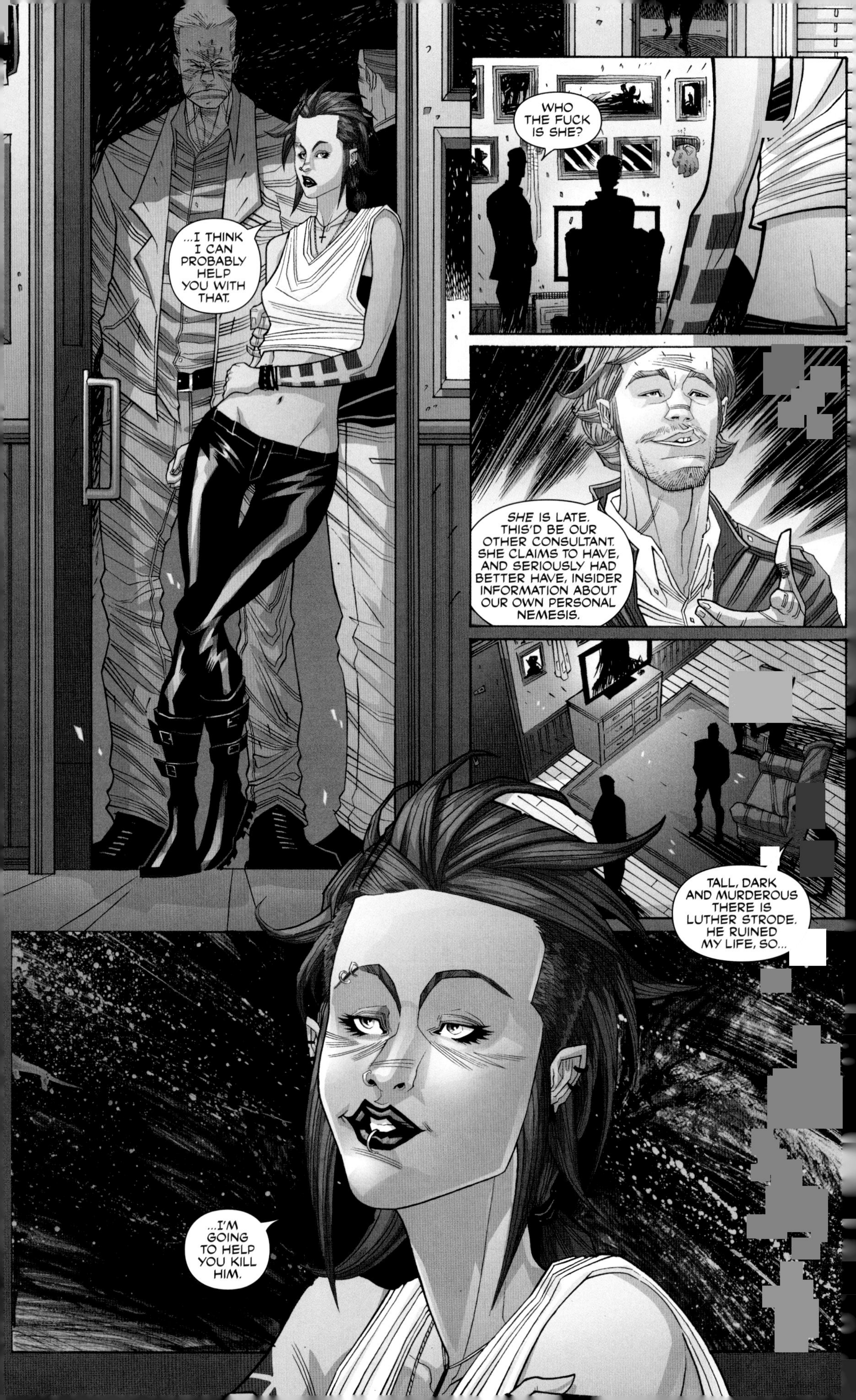
...I THINK I CAN PROBABLY HELP YOU WITH THAT.
WHO THE FUCK IS SHE?
SHE IS LATE. THIS'D BE OUR OTHER CONSULTANT. SHE CLAIMS TO HAVE, AND SERIOUSLY HAD BETTER HAVE, INSIDER INFORMATION ABOUT OUR OWN PERSONAL NEMESIS.
TALL, DARK AND MURDEROUS THERE IS LUTHER STRODE. HE RUINED MY LIFE, SO...
...I'M GOING TO HELP YOU KILL HIM.

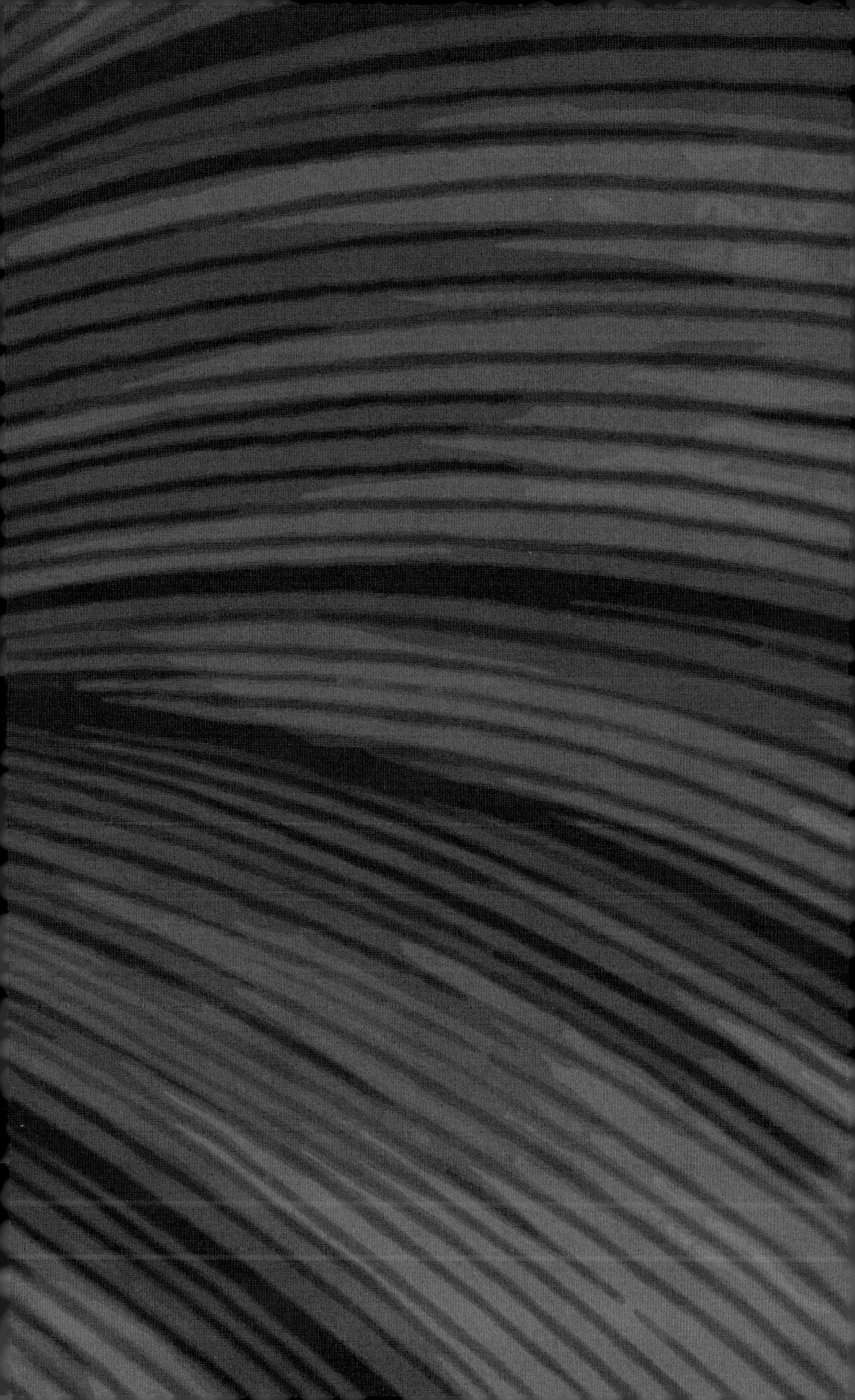

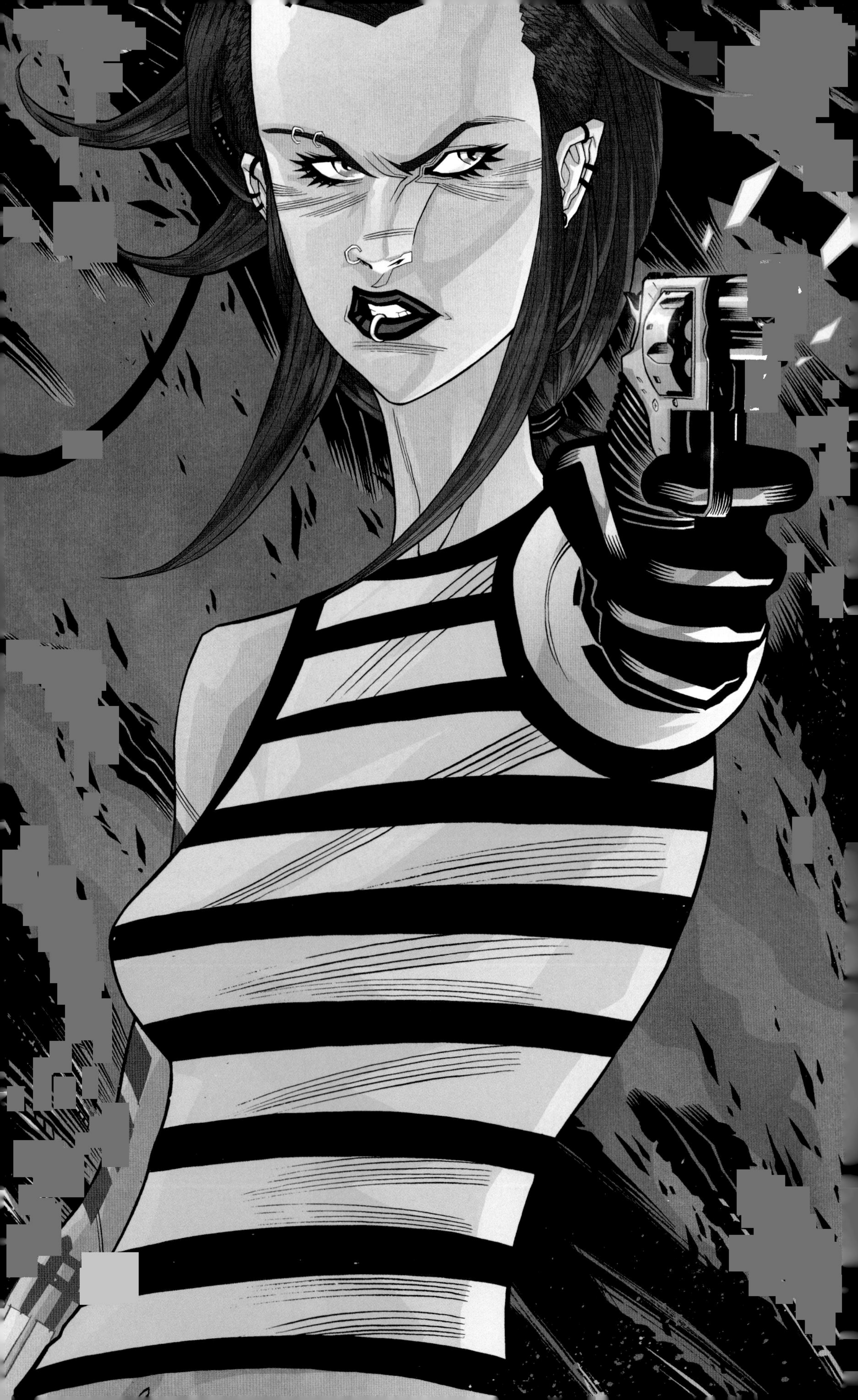

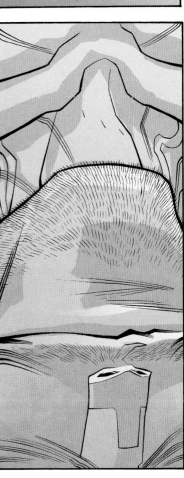

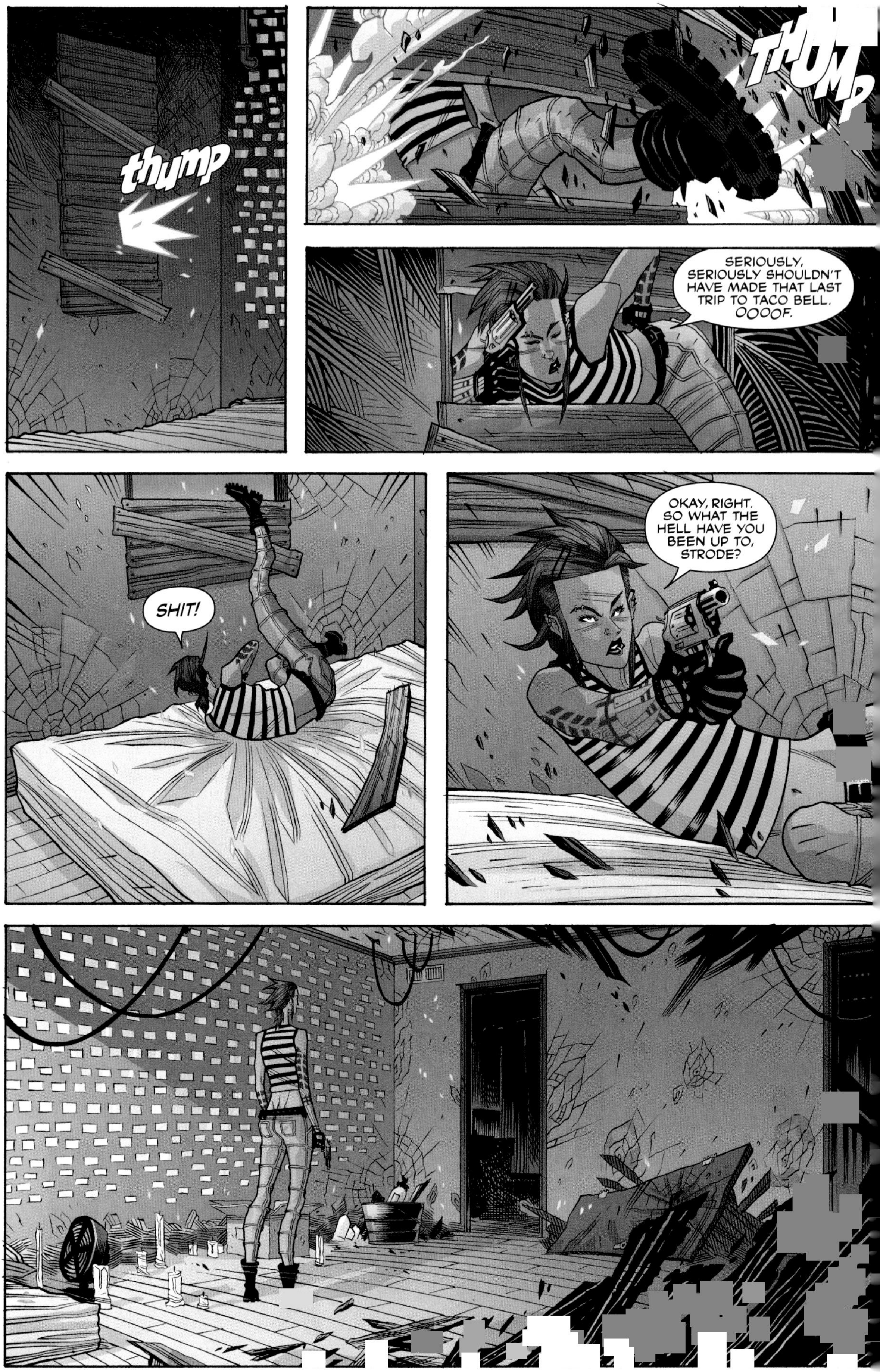
thump
THUMP
SERIOUSLY, SERIOUSLY SHOULDN'T HAVE MADE THAT LAST TRIP TO TACO BELL. OOOOF.
SHIT!
OKAY, RIGHT. SO WHAT THE HELL HAVE YOU BEEN UP TO, STRODE?

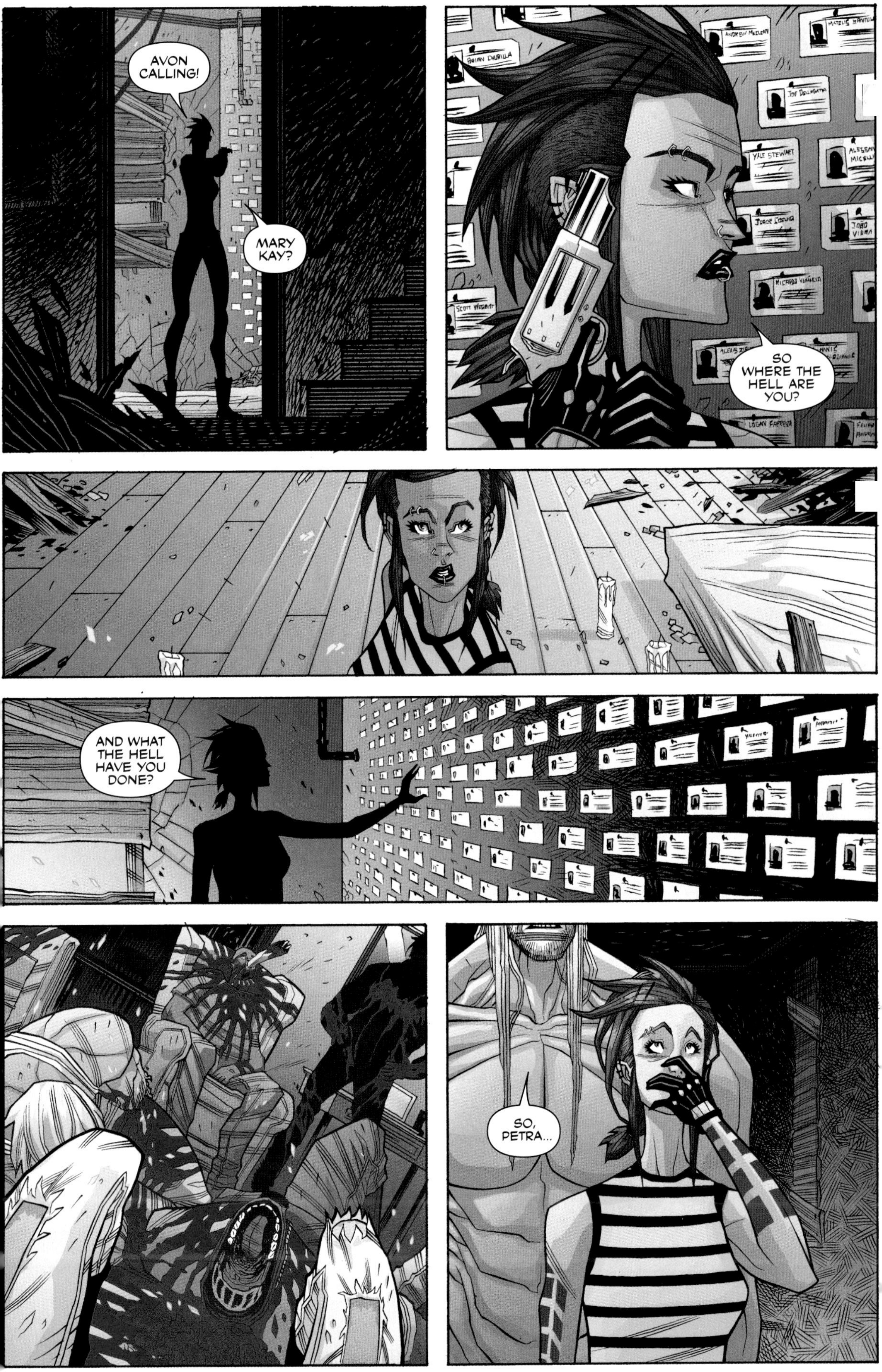
AVON CALLING!
MARY KAY?
SO WHERE THE HELL ARE YOU?
AND WHAT THE HELL HAVE YOU DONE?
SO, PETRA...

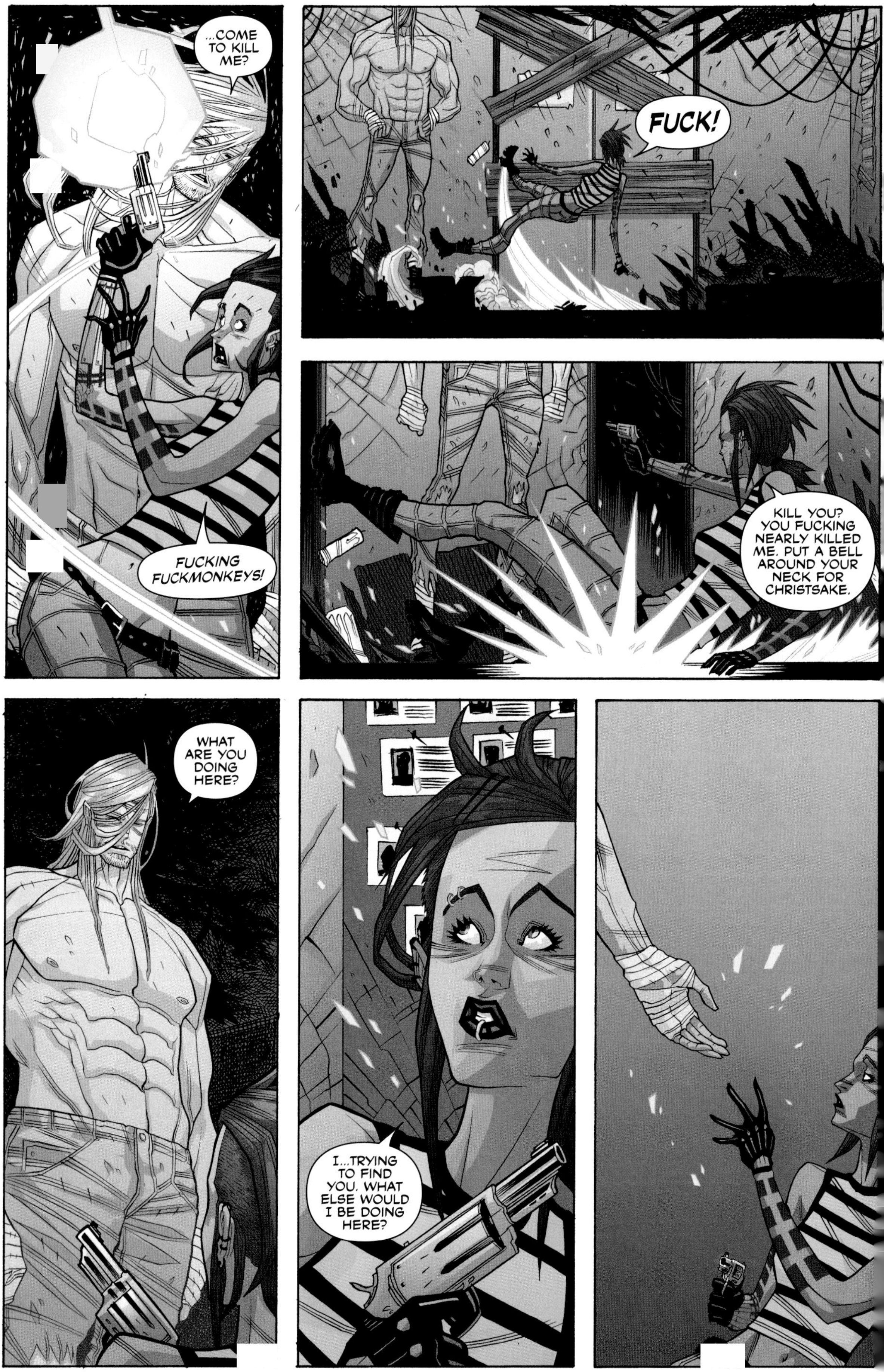
...COME TO KILL ME?
FUCKING FUCKMONKEYS!
FUCK!
KILL YOU? YOU FUCKING NEARLY KILLED ME. PUT A BELL AROUND YOUR NECK FOR CHRISTSAKE.
WHAT ARE YOU DOING HERE?
I...TRYING TO FIND YOU. WHAT ELSE WOULD I BE DOING HERE?

YOU'RE GOING TO TEAR MY ARM OFF, AREN'T YOU?

I WAS KIDDING. JESUS CHRIST, YOU STILL HAVEN'T GROWN A SENSE OF HUMOR TO GO WITH THOSE MUSCLES, HAVE YOU?

NO. YOU LOOK... DIFFERENT. YOU'VE CHANGED.

I'VE CHANGED? YOU'VE CHANGED.

NO, I HAVEN'T.

JESUS, STRODE. WHAT'S HAPPENED TO YOU?

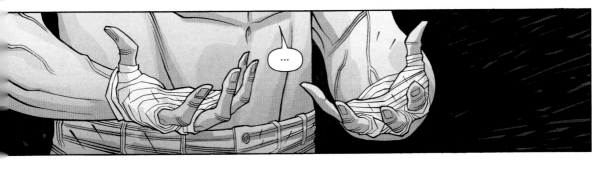

...

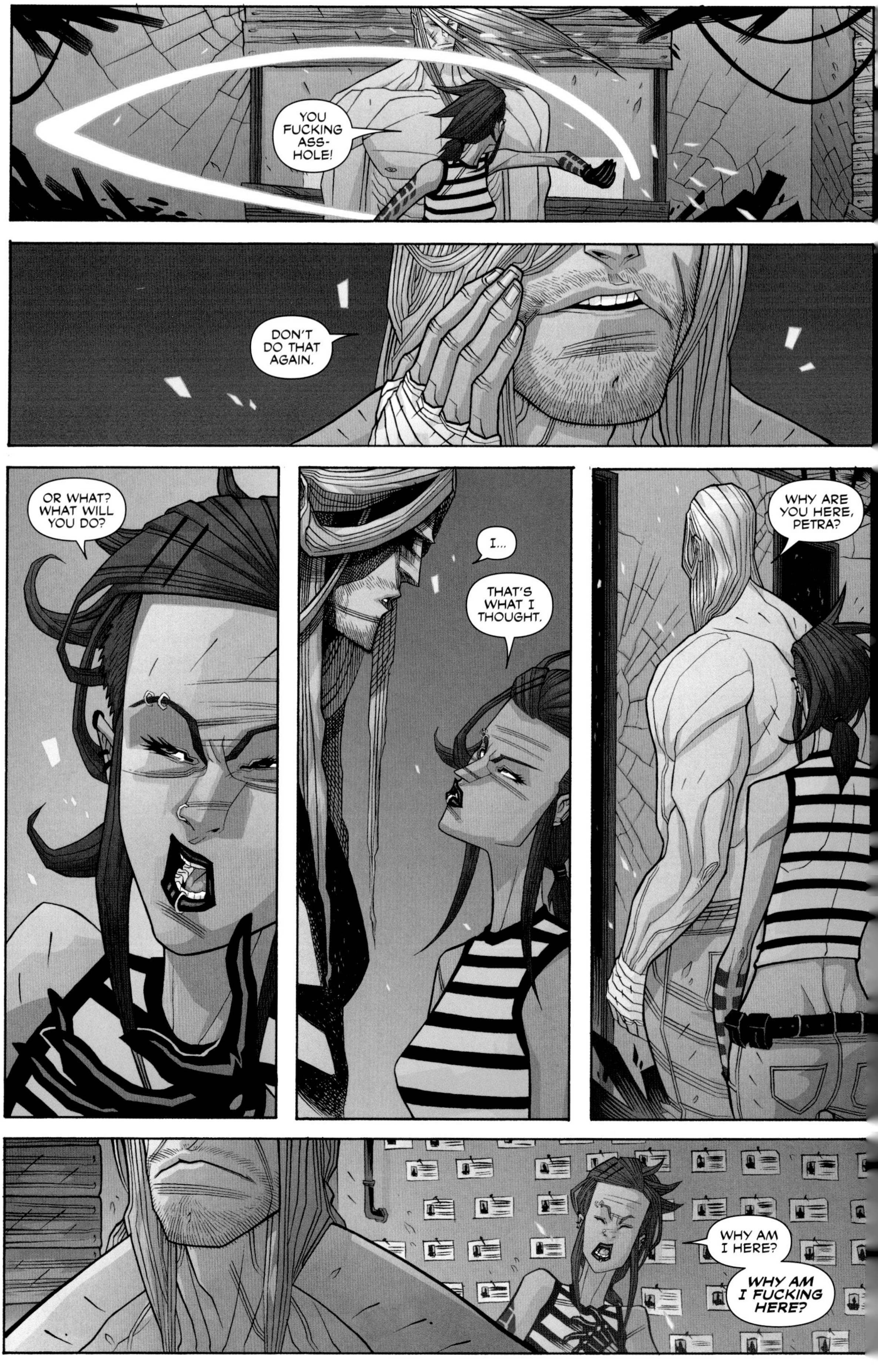
YOU FUCKING ASS-HOLE!
DON'T DO THAT AGAIN.
OR WHAT? WHAT WILL YOU DO?
I...
THAT'S WHAT I THOUGHT.
WHY ARE YOU HERE, PETRA?
WHY AM I HERE?
WHY AM I FUCKING HERE?

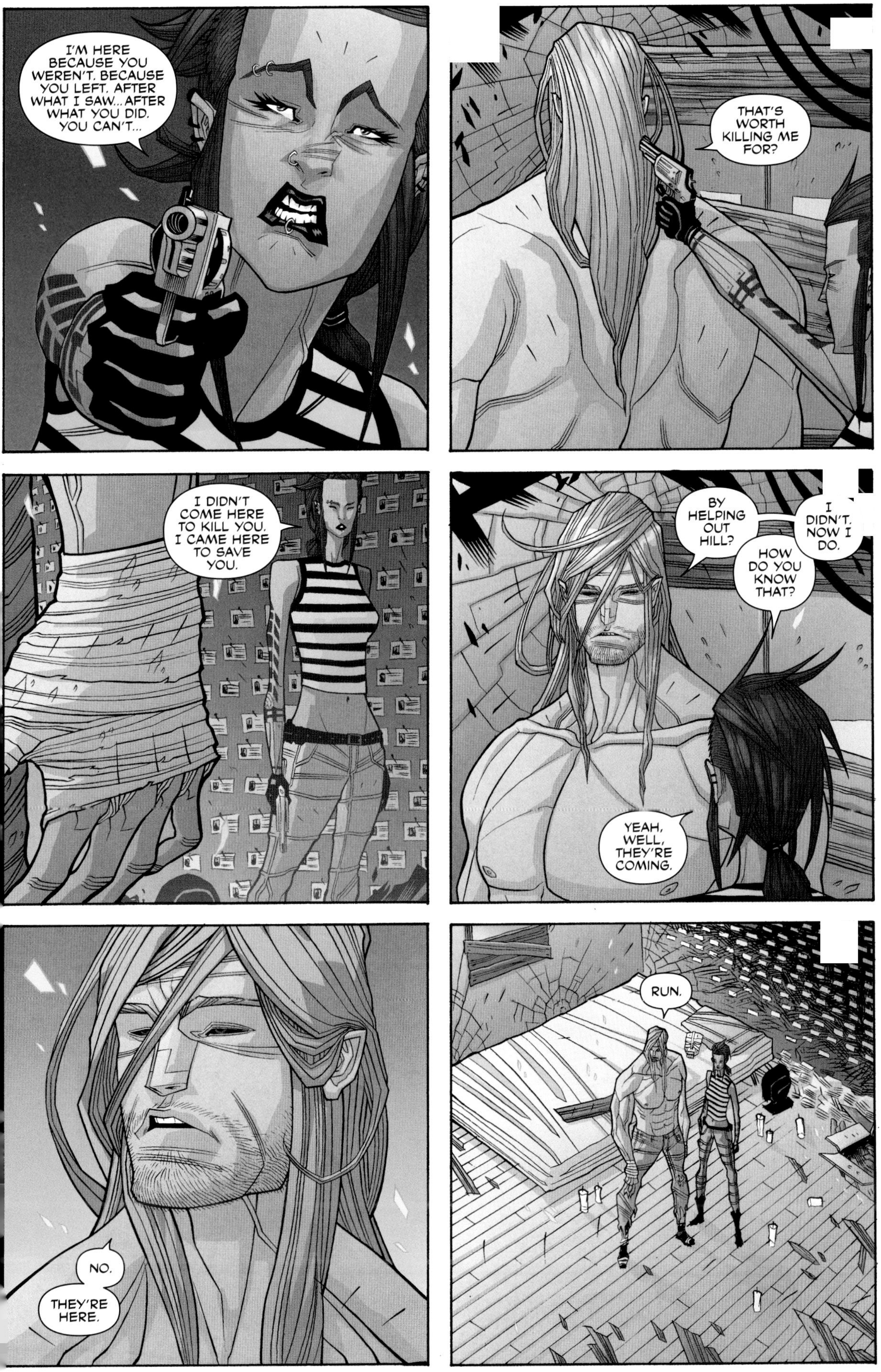
I'M HERE BECAUSE YOU WEREN'T. BECAUSE YOU LEFT. AFTER WHAT I SAW... AFTER WHAT YOU DID. YOU CAN'T...
THAT'S WORTH KILLING ME FOR?
I DIDN'T COME HERE TO KILL YOU. I CAME HERE TO SAVE YOU.
BY HELPING OUT HILL?
HOW DO YOU KNOW THAT?
I DIDN'T. NOW I DO.
YEAH, WELL, THEY'RE COMING.
NO.
THEY'RE HERE.
RUN.

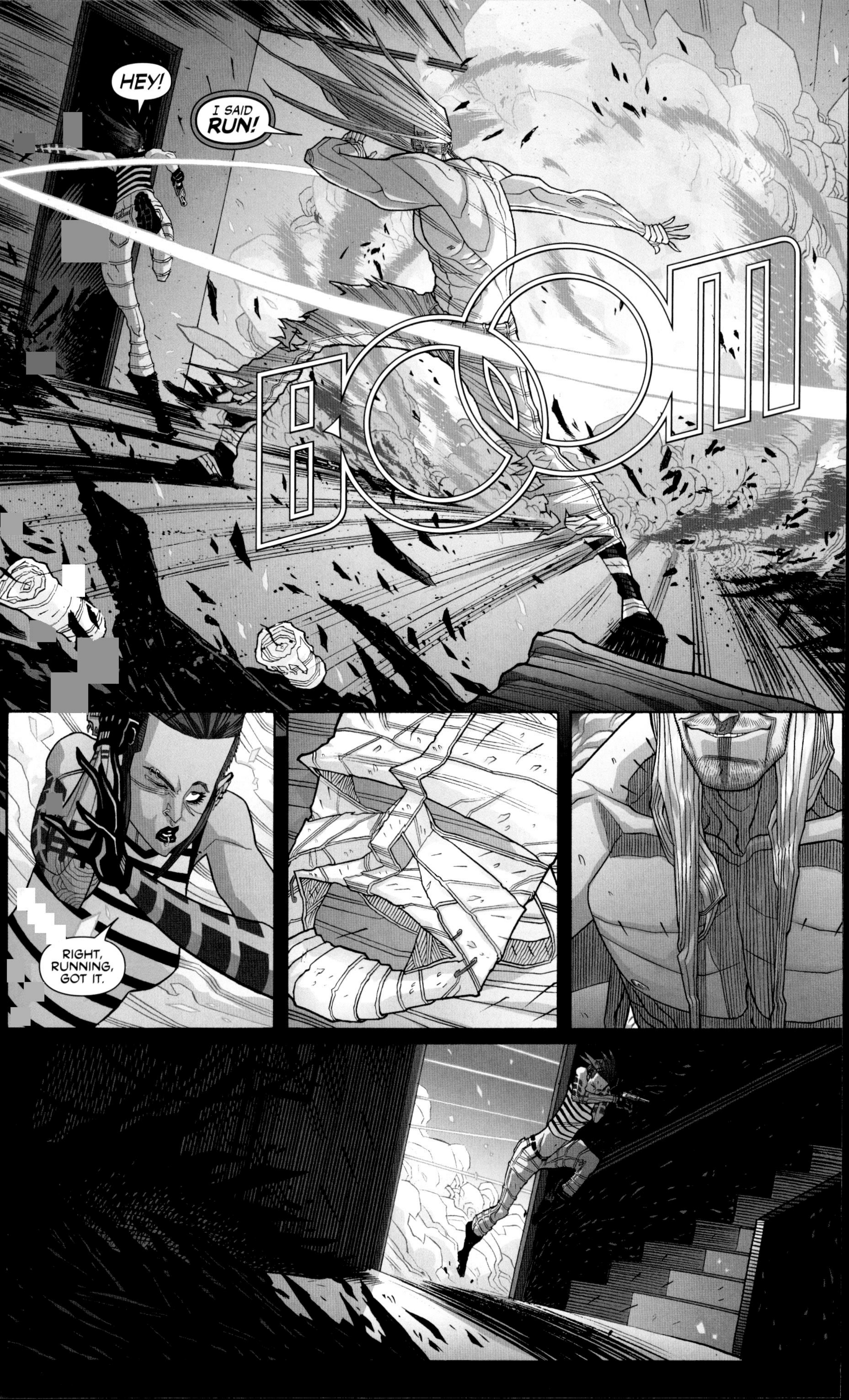
HEY!
I SAID RUN!
BOOM
RIGHT, RUNNING, GOT IT.

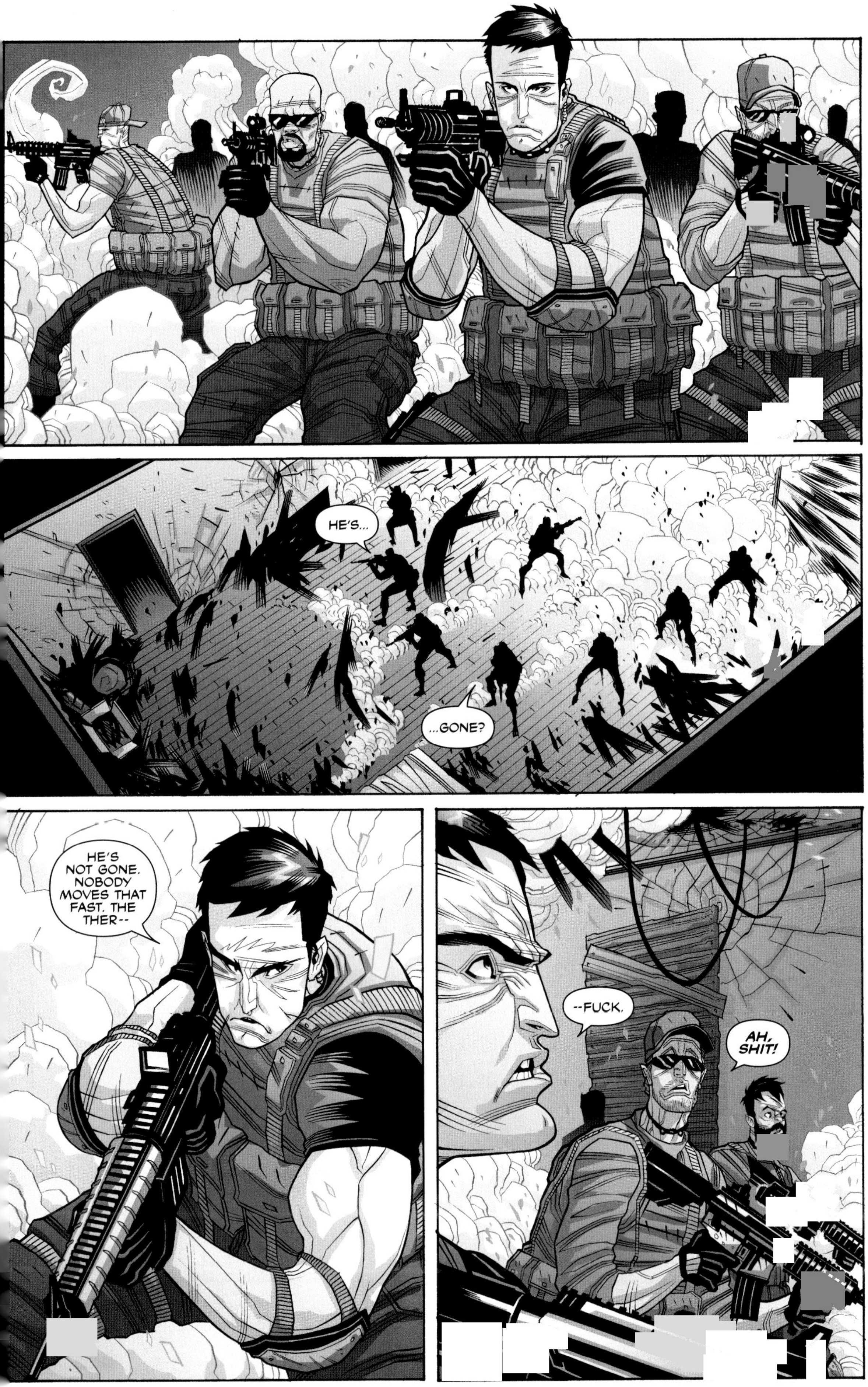
HE'S...
...GONE?
HE'S NOT GONE. NOBODY MOVES THAT FAST. THE THER--
--FUCK.
AH, SHIT!

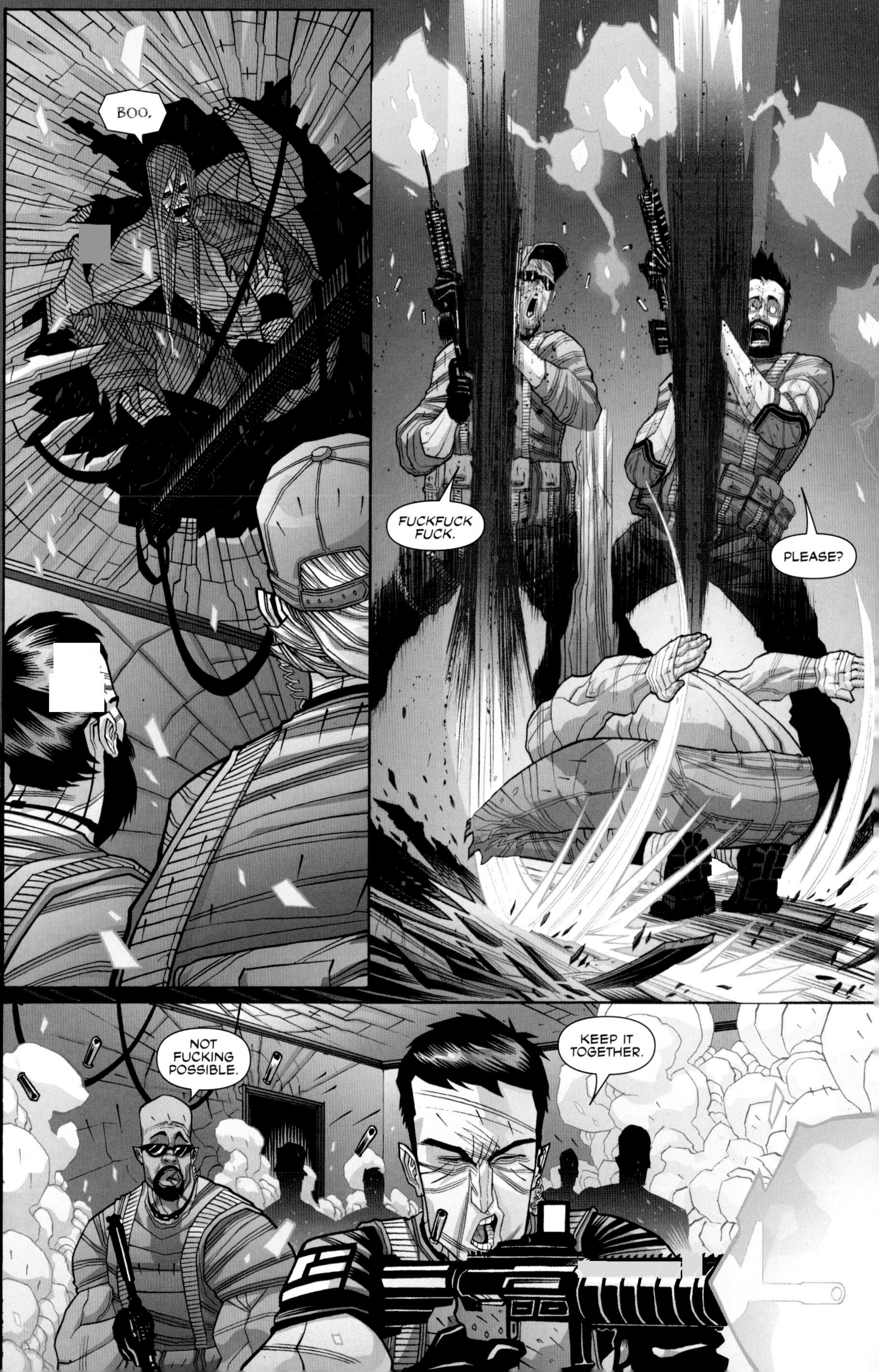
BOO.
FUCKFUCK FUCK.
PLEASE?
NOT FUCKING POSSIBLE.
KEEP IT TOGETHER.

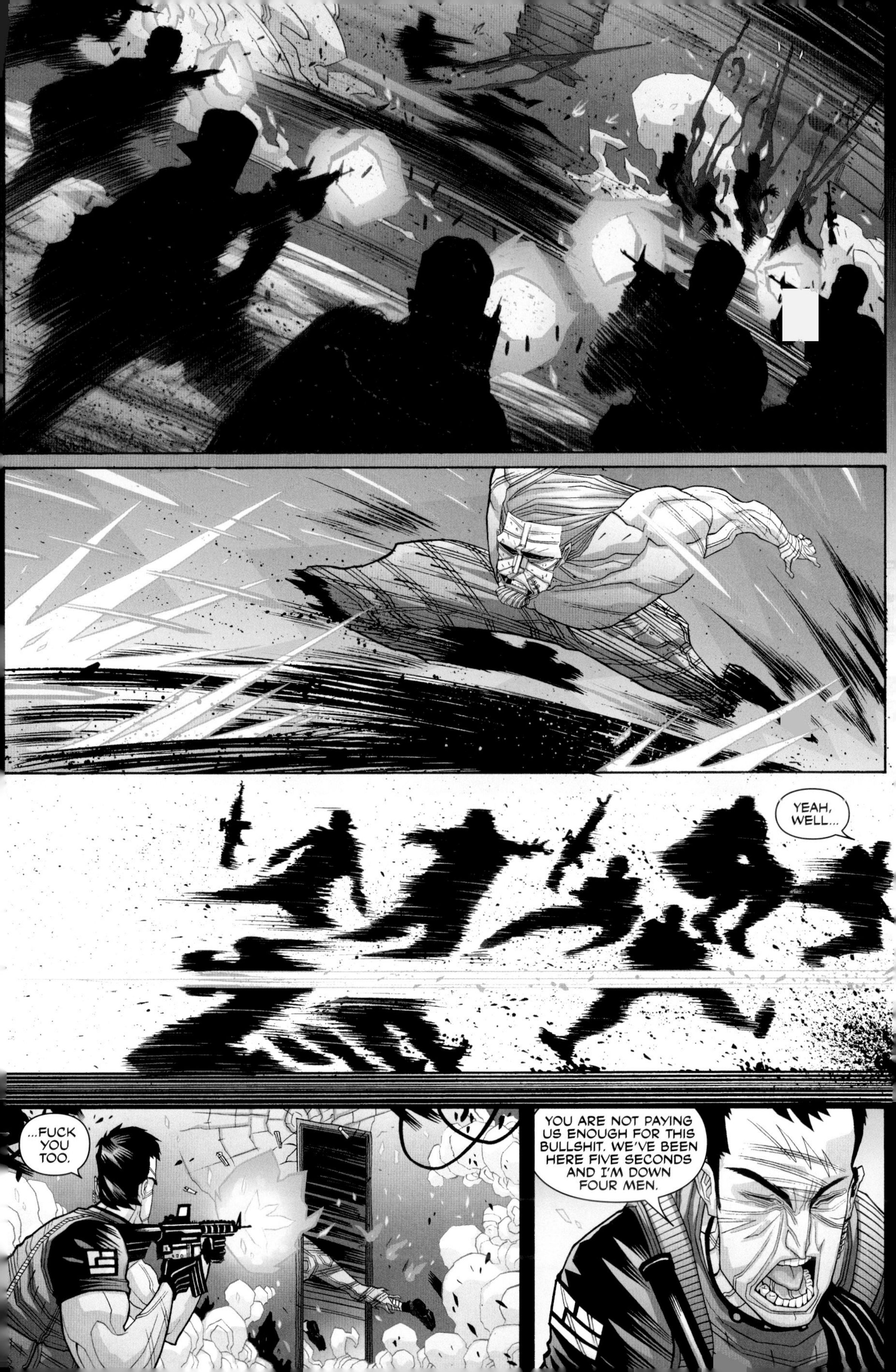
YEAH, WELL...
...FUCK YOU TOO.
YOU ARE NOT PAYING US ENOUGH FOR THIS BULLSHIT. WE'VE BEEN HERE FIVE SECONDS AND I'M DOWN FOUR MEN.

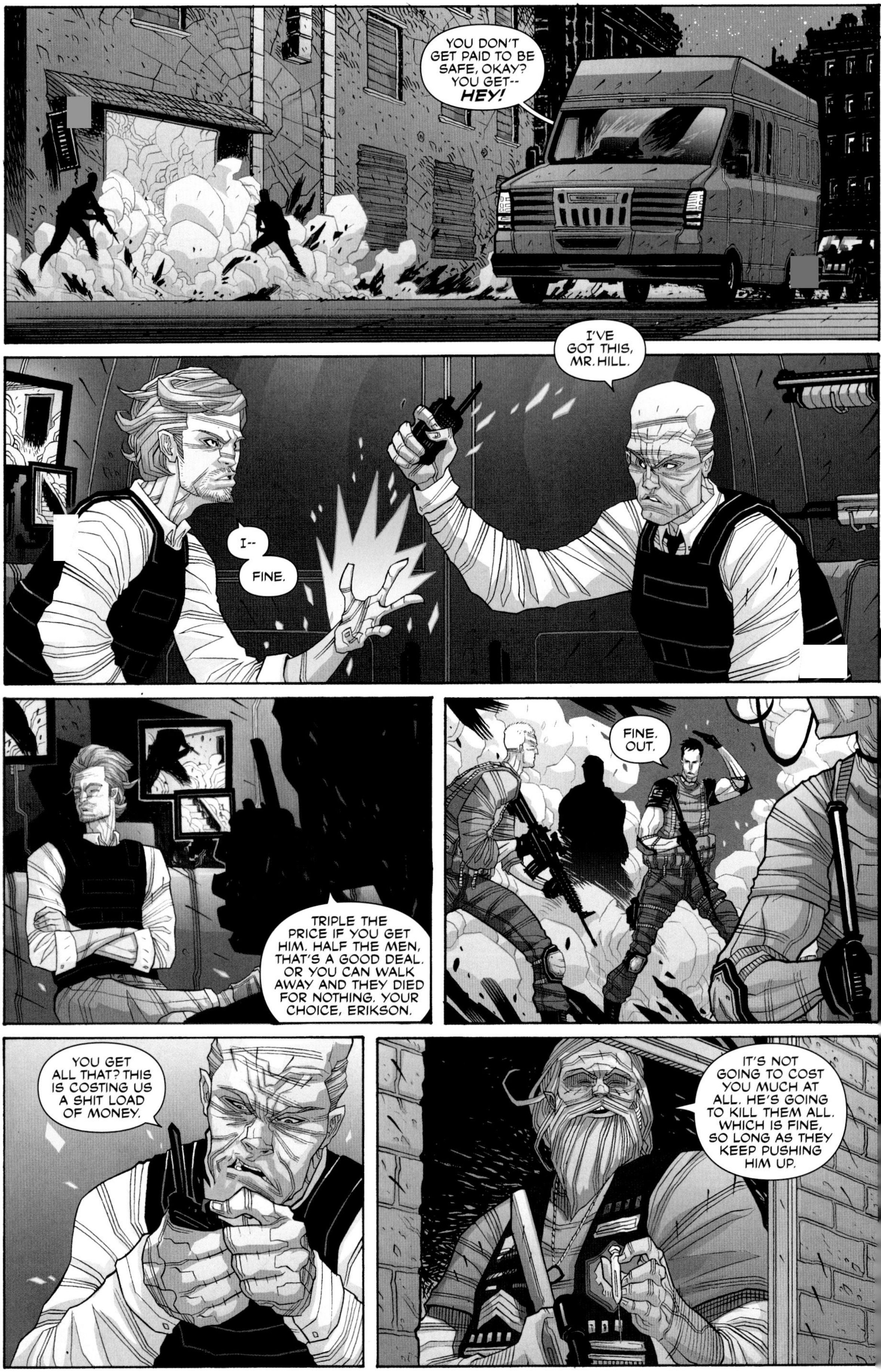

YOU DON'T GET PAID TO BE SAFE, OKAY? YOU GET-- HEY!
I'VE GOT THIS, MR. HILL.
I--
FINE.
TRIPLE THE PRICE IF YOU GET HIM. HALF THE MEN, THAT'S A GOOD DEAL. OR YOU CAN WALK AWAY AND THEY DIED FOR NOTHING. YOUR CHOICE, ERIKSON.
FINE. OUT.
YOU GET ALL THAT? THIS IS COSTING US A SHIT LOAD OF MONEY.
IT'S NOT GOING TO COST YOU MUCH AT ALL. HE'S GOING TO KILL THEM ALL. WHICH IS FINE, SO LONG AS THEY KEEP PUSHING HIM UP.

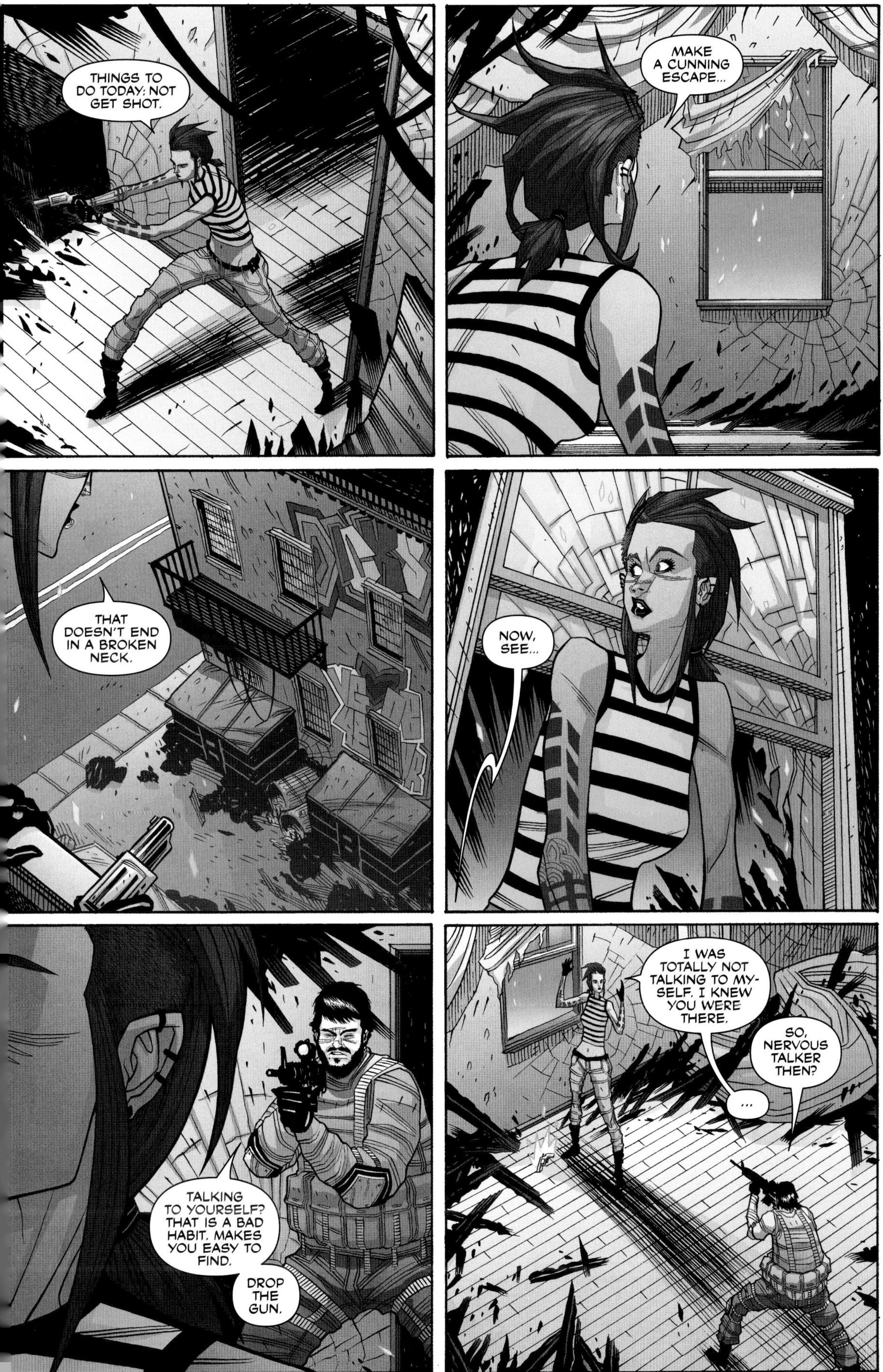
THINGS TO DO TODAY: NOT GET SHOT.
MAKE A CUNNING ESCAPE...
THAT DOESN'T END IN A BROKEN NECK.
NOW, SEE...
TALKING TO YOURSELF? THAT IS A BAD HABIT. MAKES YOU EASY TO FIND.
DROP THE GUN.
I WAS TOTALLY NOT TALKING TO MY-SELF. I KNEW YOU WERE THERE.
...
SO, NERVOUS TALKER THEN?

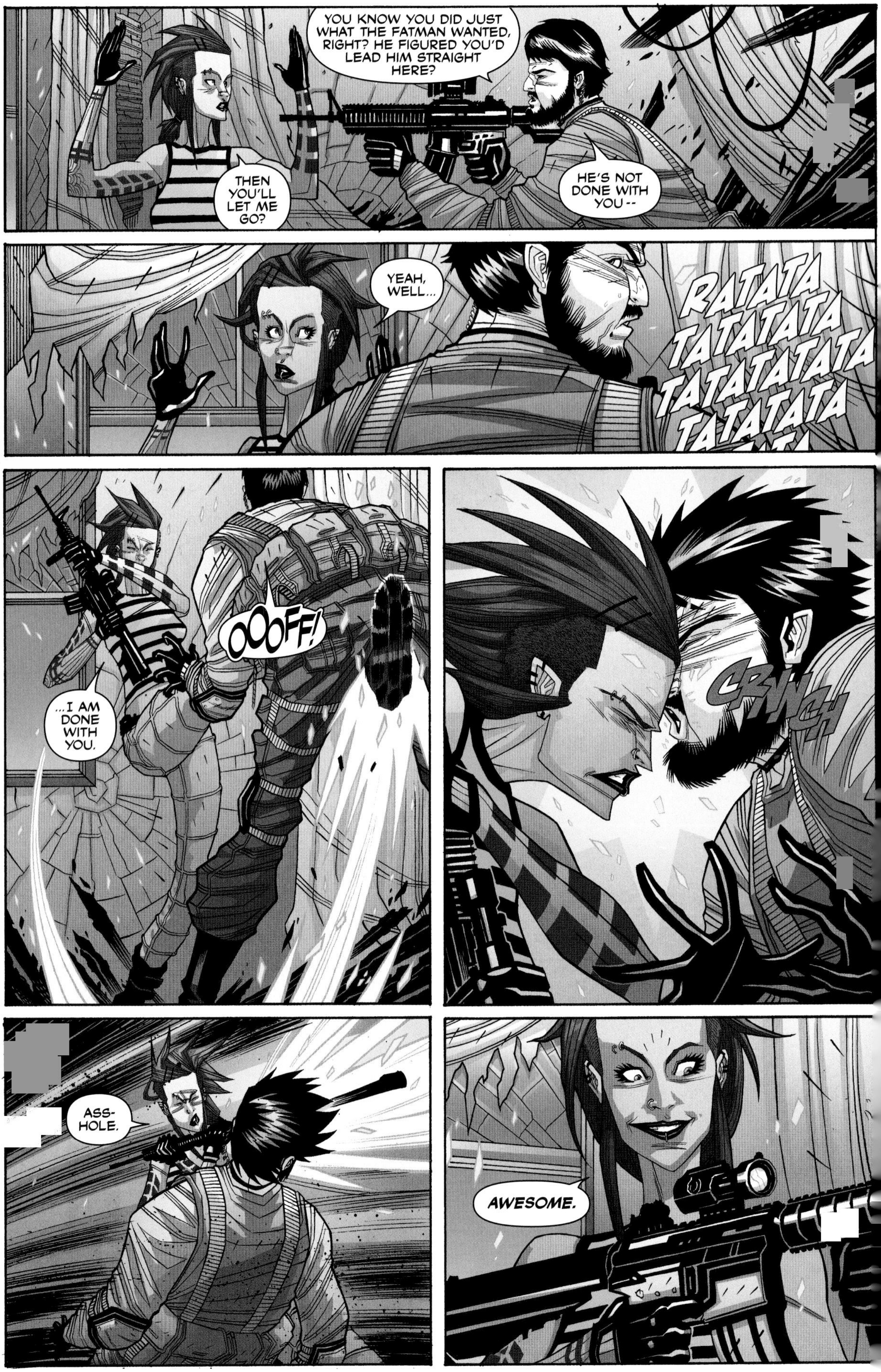
YOU KNOW YOU DID JUST WHAT THE FATMAN WANTED, RIGHT? HE FIGURED YOU'D LEAD HIM STRAIGHT HERE?
THEN YOU'LL LET ME GO?
HE'S NOT DONE WITH YOU --
YEAH, WELL...
RATATA TATATATA TATATATATA TATATATA
OOOFF!
...I AM DONE WITH YOU.
CRUNCH
ASS-HOLE.
AWESOME.

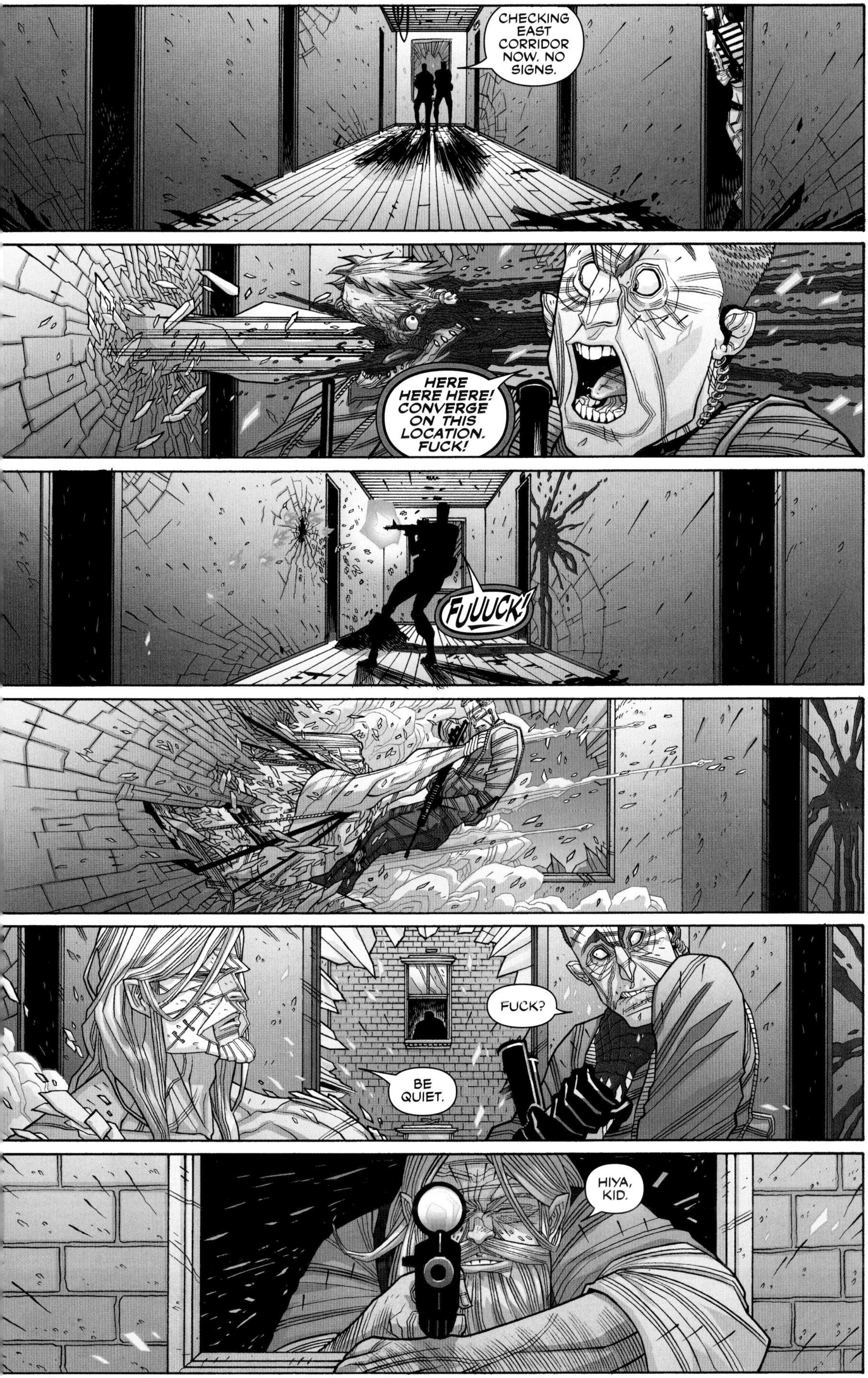
CHECKING EAST CORRIDOR NOW. NO SIGNS.
HERE HERE HERE! CONVERGE ON THIS LOCATION. FUCK!
FUUUCK!
FUCK?
BE QUIET.
HIYA, KID.

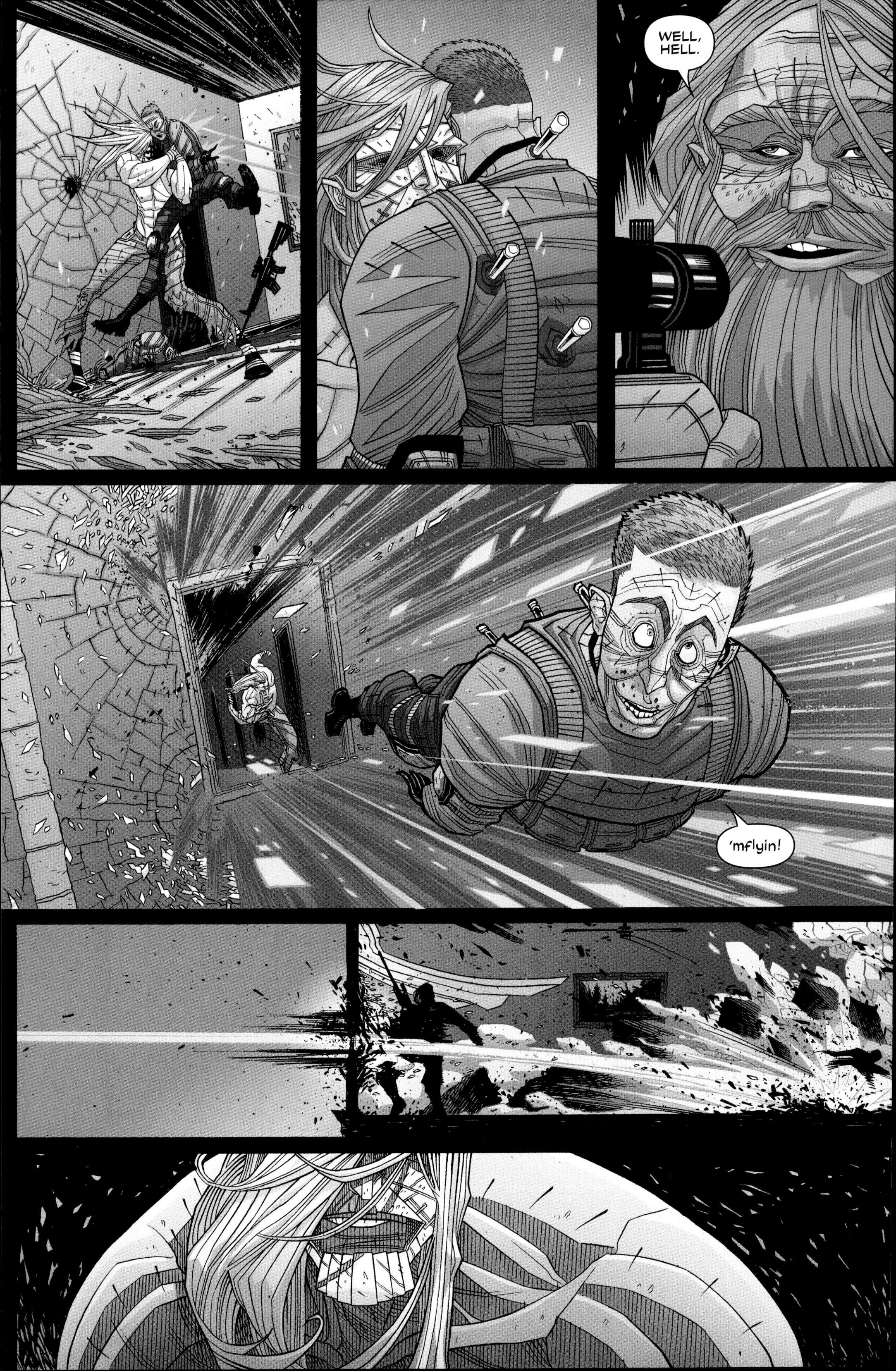
WELL, HELL.
'mflyin!

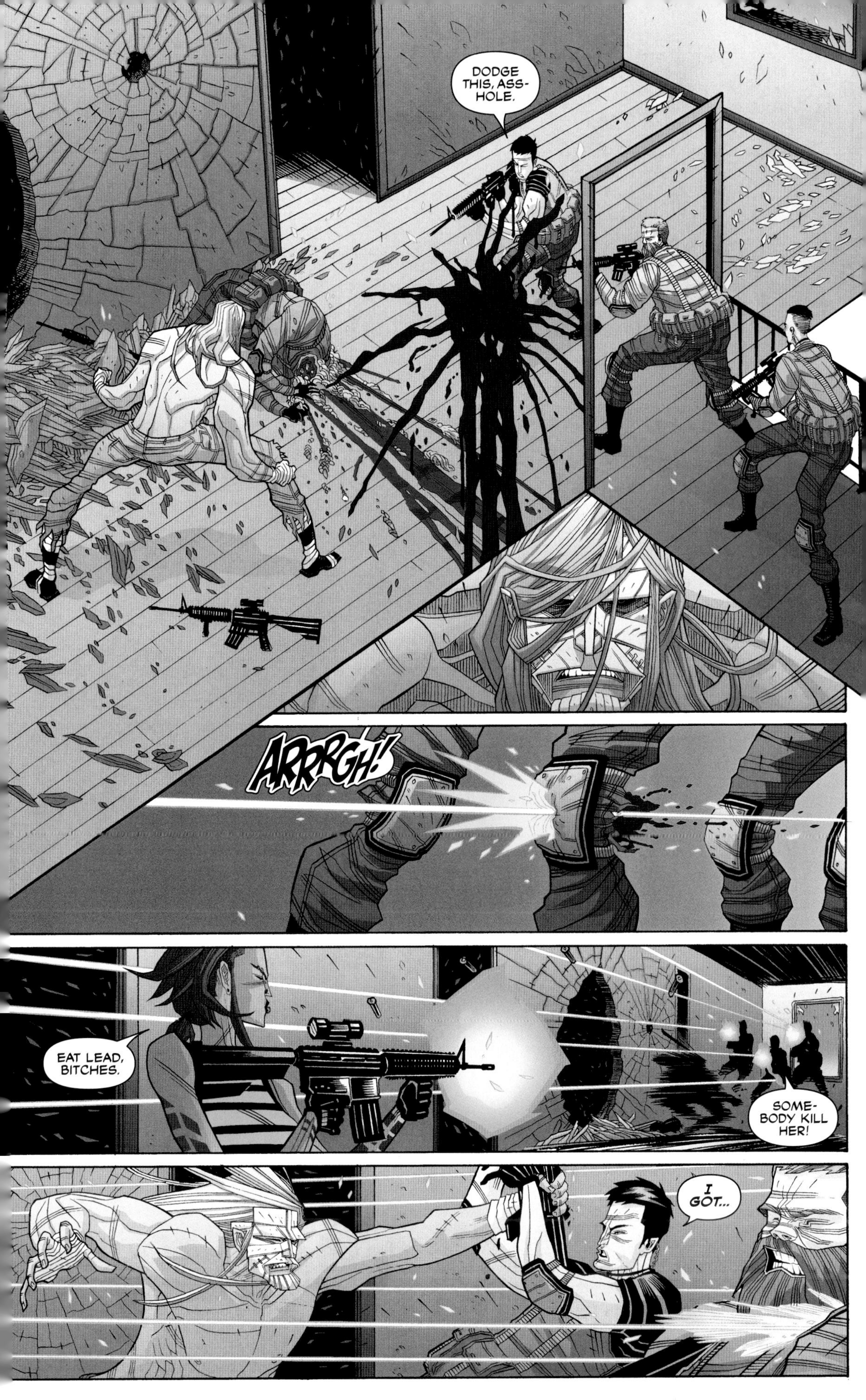
DODGE THIS, ASS-HOLE.
ARRRGH!
EAT LEAD, BITCHES.
SOME-BODY KILL HER!
I GOT...

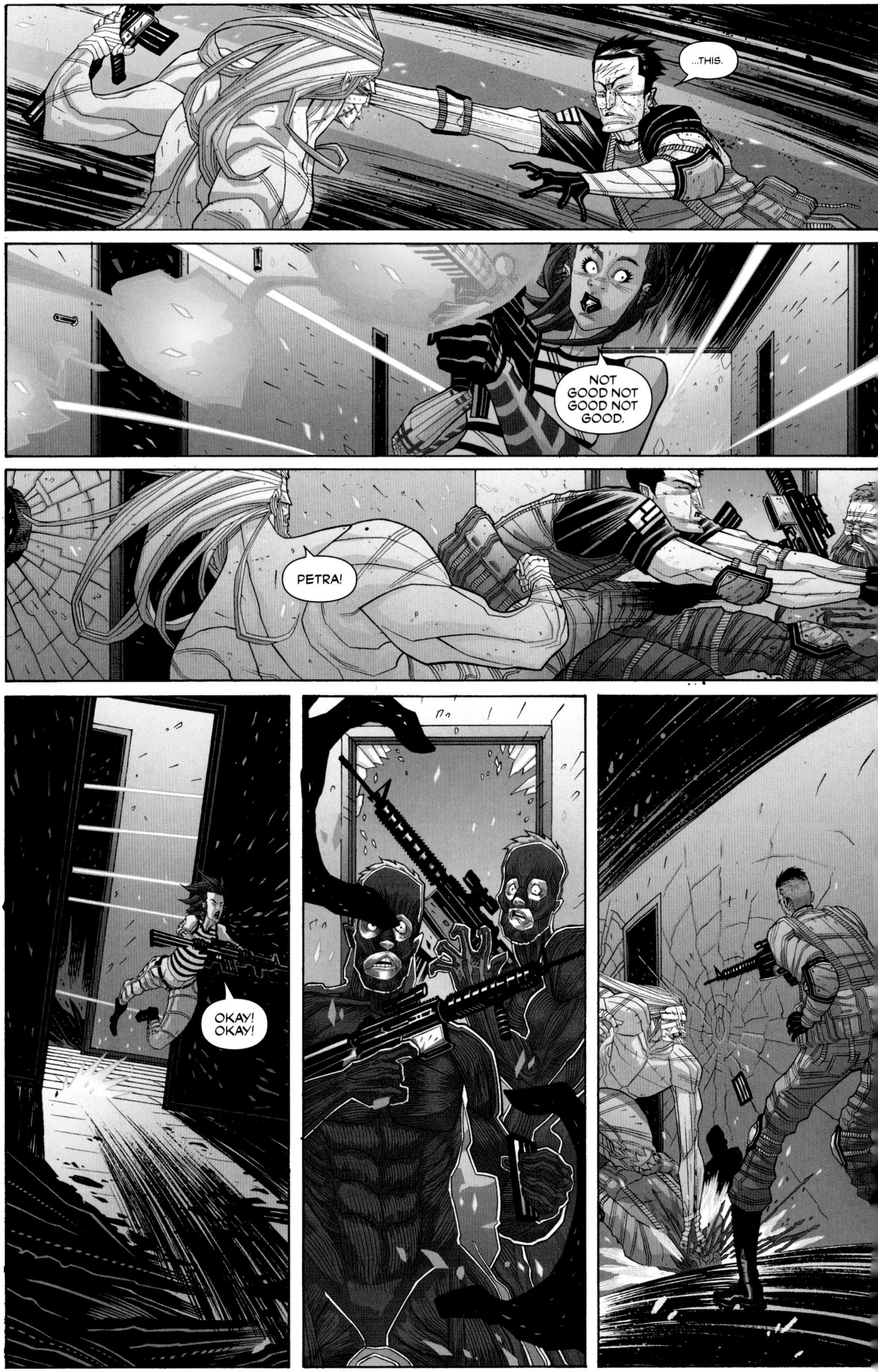
...THIS.
NOT GOOD NOT GOOD NOT GOOD.
PETRA!
OKAY! OKAY!

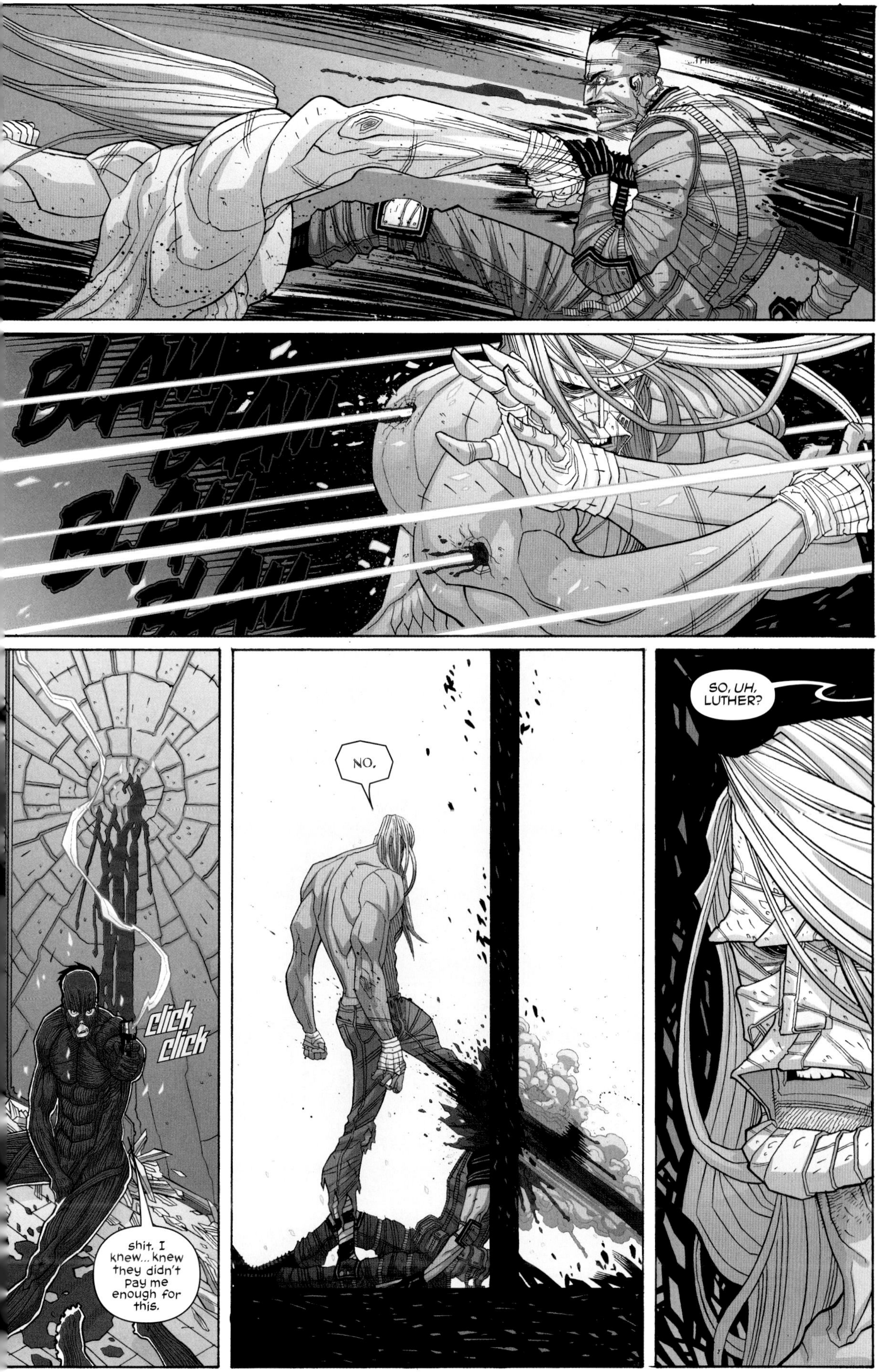
...THIS
BLAM BLAM
BLAM BLAM
click click
shit. I knew... knew they didn't pay me enough for this.
NO.
SO, UH, LUTHER?

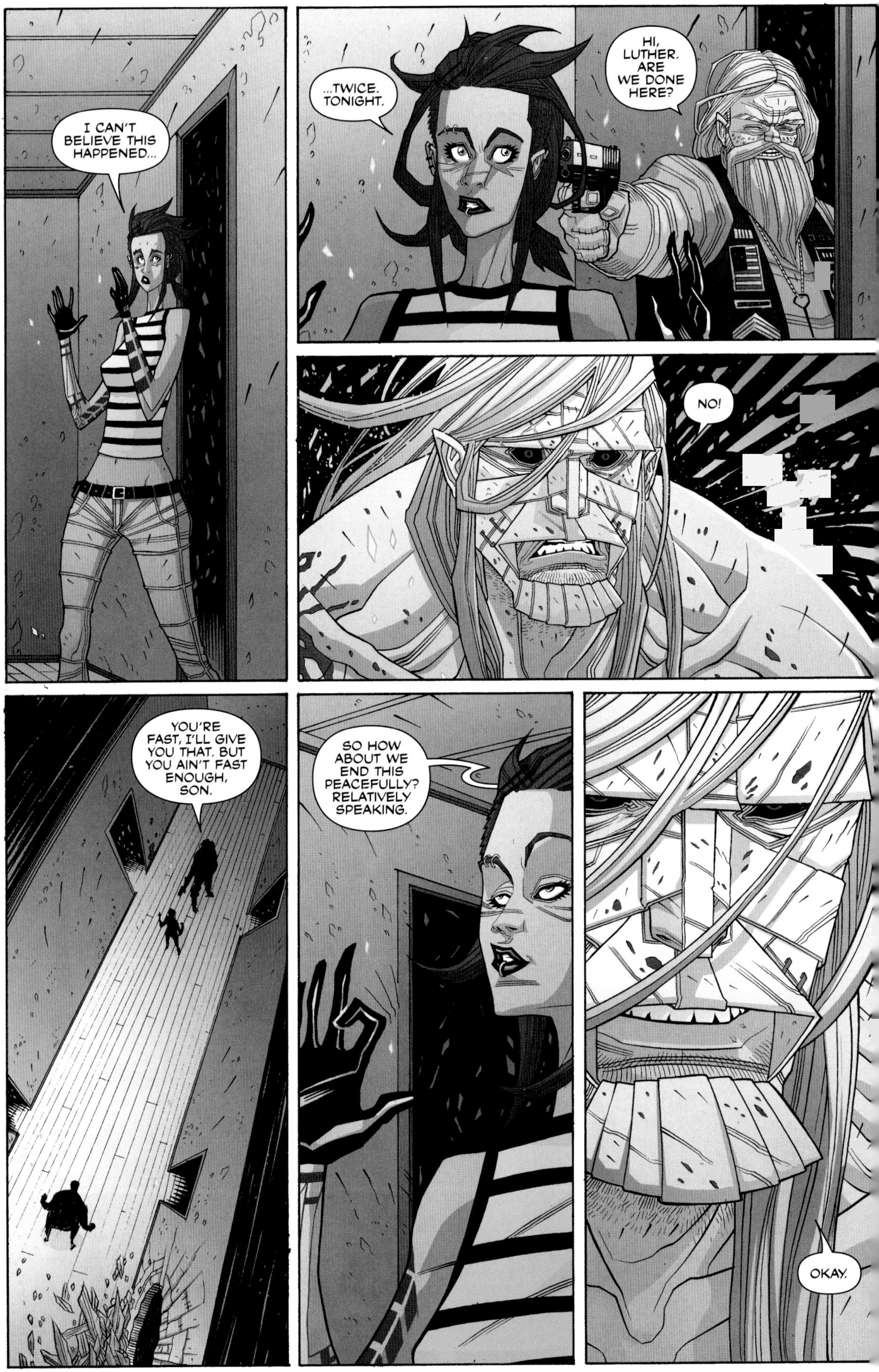
I CAN'T BELIEVE THIS HAPPENED...
...TWICE. TONIGHT.
HI, LUTHER. ARE WE DONE HERE?
NO!
YOU'RE FAST, I'LL GIVE YOU THAT. BUT YOU AIN'T FAST ENOUGH, SON.
SO HOW ABOUT WE END THIS PEACEFULLY? RELATIVELY SPEAKING.
OKAY.

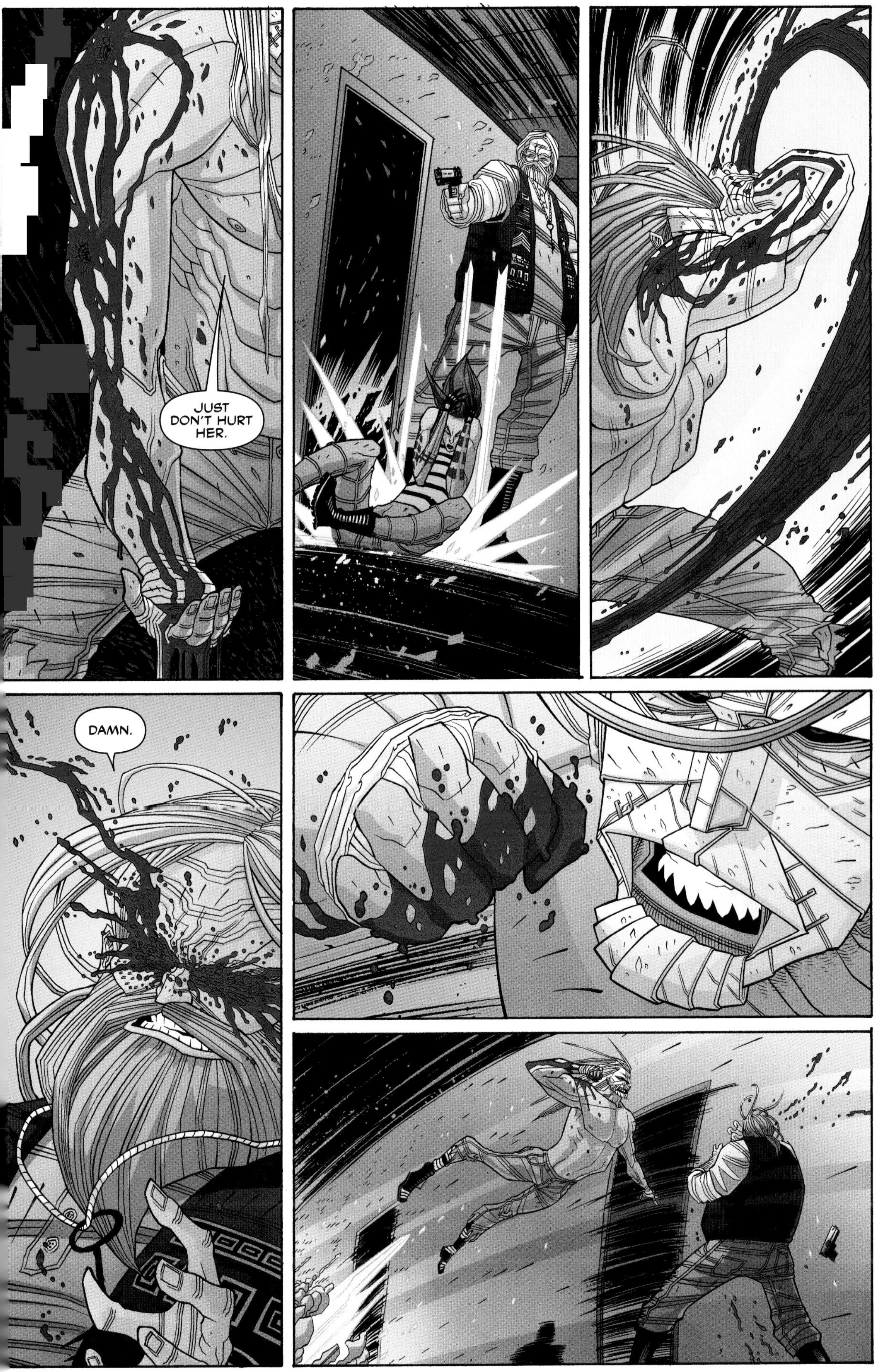
JUST DON'T HURT HER.
DAMN.

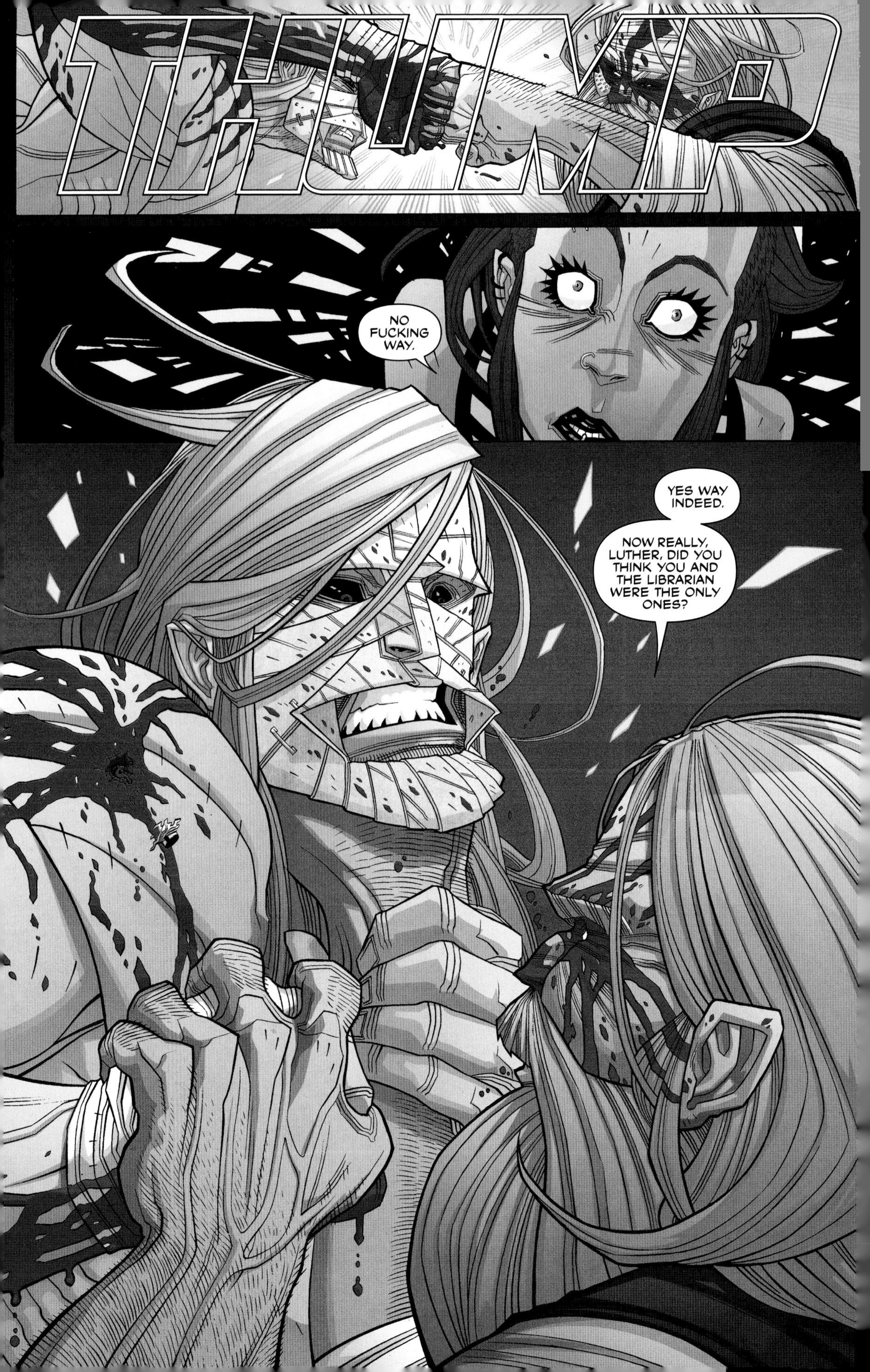
THUMP
NO FUCKING WAY.
YES WAY INDEED.
NOW REALLY, LUTHER, DID YOU THINK YOU AND THE LIBRARIAN WERE THE ONLY ONES?

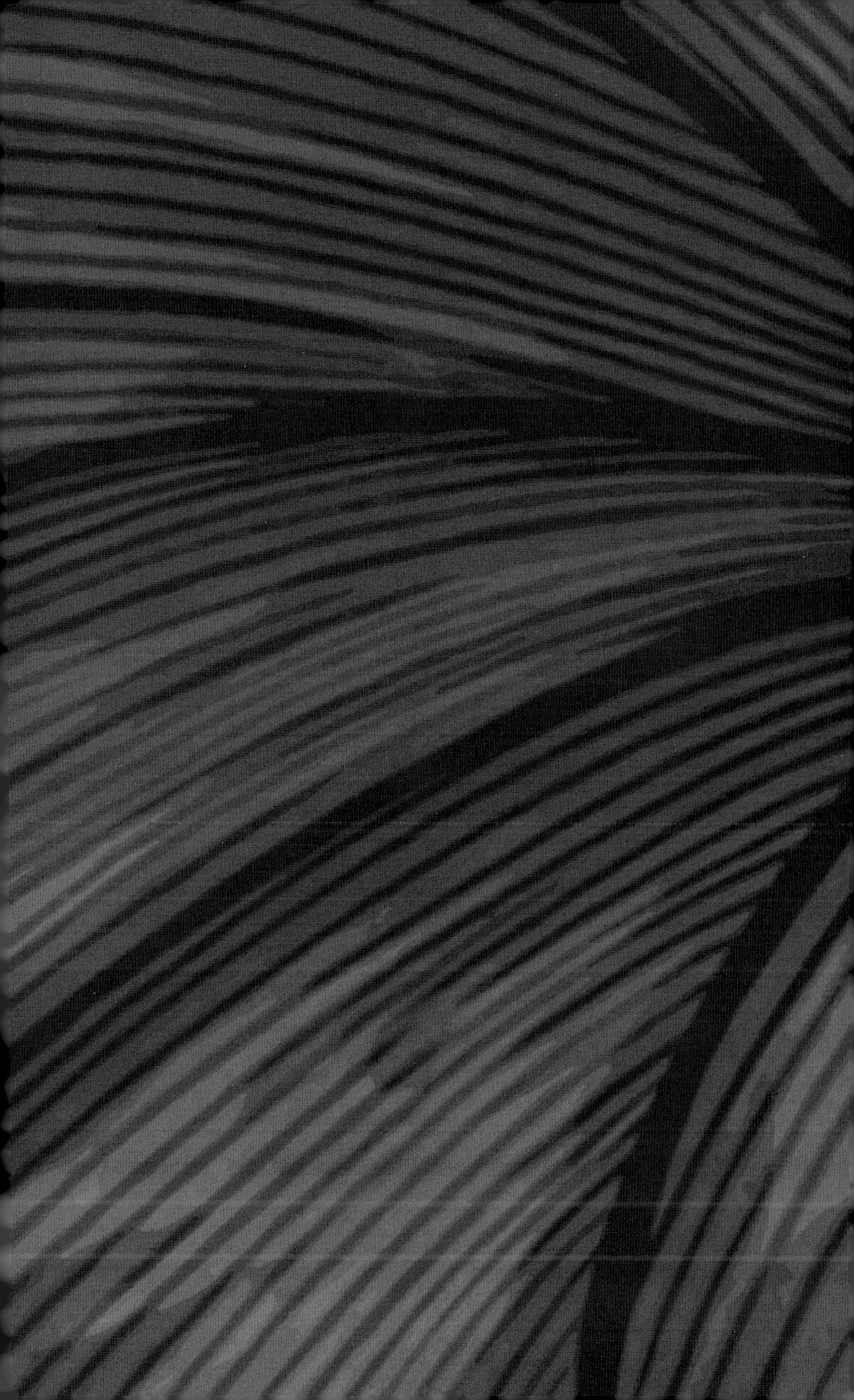

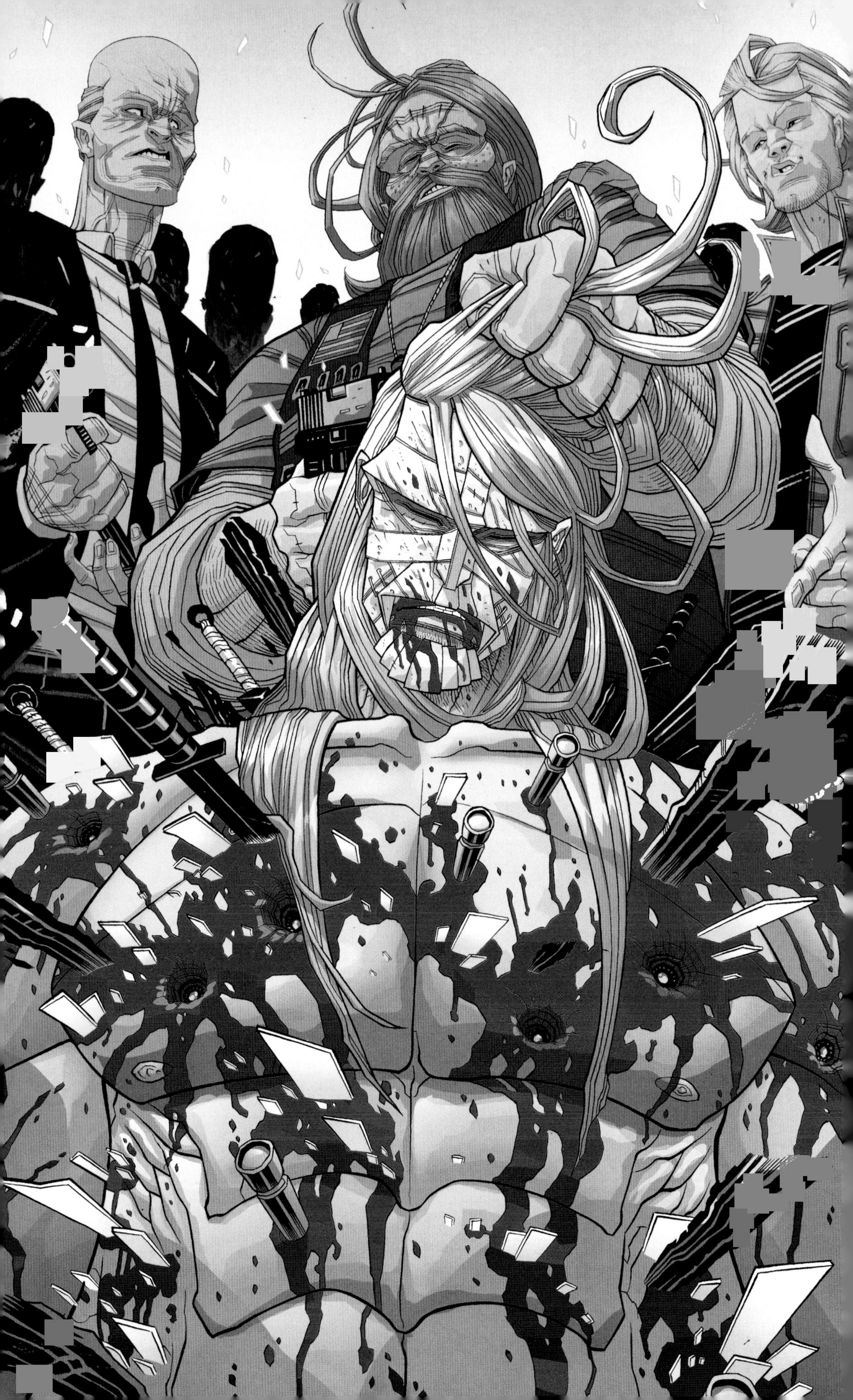

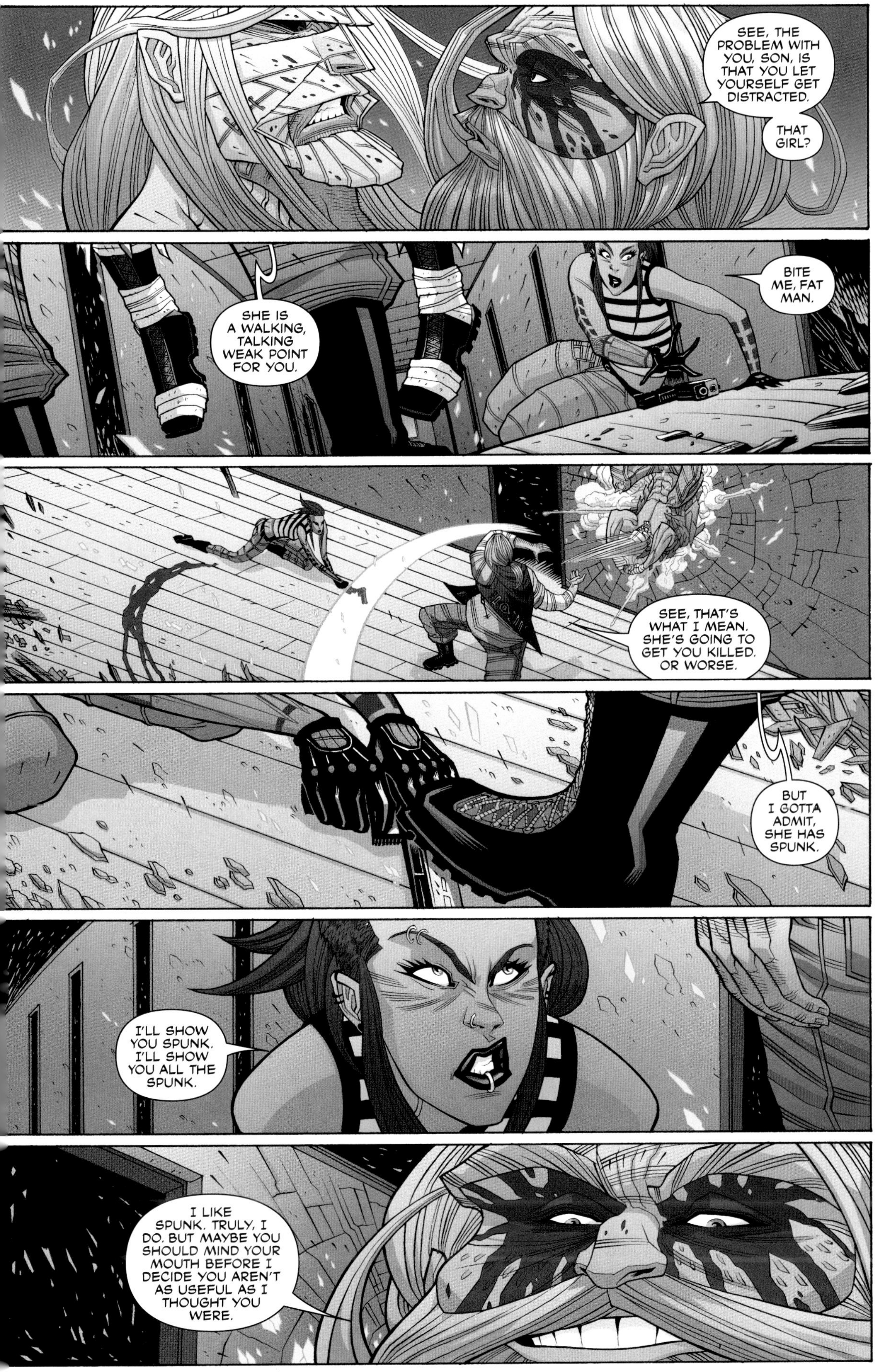
SEE, THE PROBLEM WITH YOU, SON, IS THAT YOU LET YOURSELF GET DISTRACTED.
THAT GIRL?
SHE IS A WALKING, TALKING WEAK POINT FOR YOU.
BITE ME, FAT MAN.
SEE, THAT'S WHAT I MEAN. SHE'S GOING TO GET YOU KILLED. OR WORSE.
BUT I GOTTA ADMIT, SHE HAS SPUNK.
I'LL SHOW YOU SPUNK. I'LL SHOW YOU ALL THE SPUNK.
I LIKE SPUNK. TRULY, I DO. BUT MAYBE YOU SHOULD MIND YOUR MOUTH BEFORE I DECIDE YOU AREN'T AS USEFUL AS I THOUGHT YOU WERE.

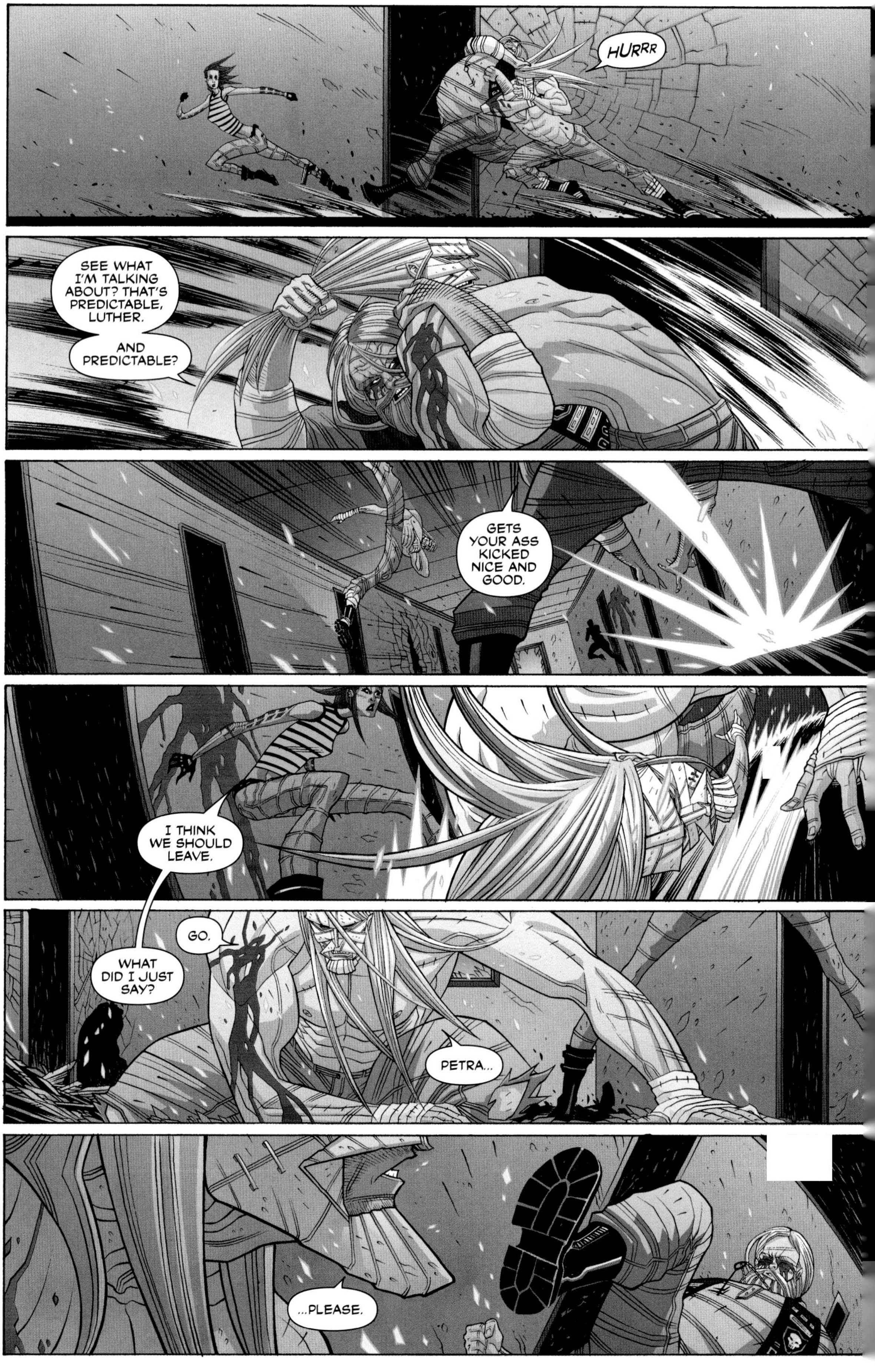
HURRR
SEE WHAT I'M TALKING ABOUT? THAT'S PREDICTABLE, LUTHER.
AND PREDICTABLE?
GETS YOUR ASS KICKED NICE AND GOOD.
I THINK WE SHOULD LEAVE.
GO.
WHAT DID I JUST SAY?
PETRA...
...PLEASE.

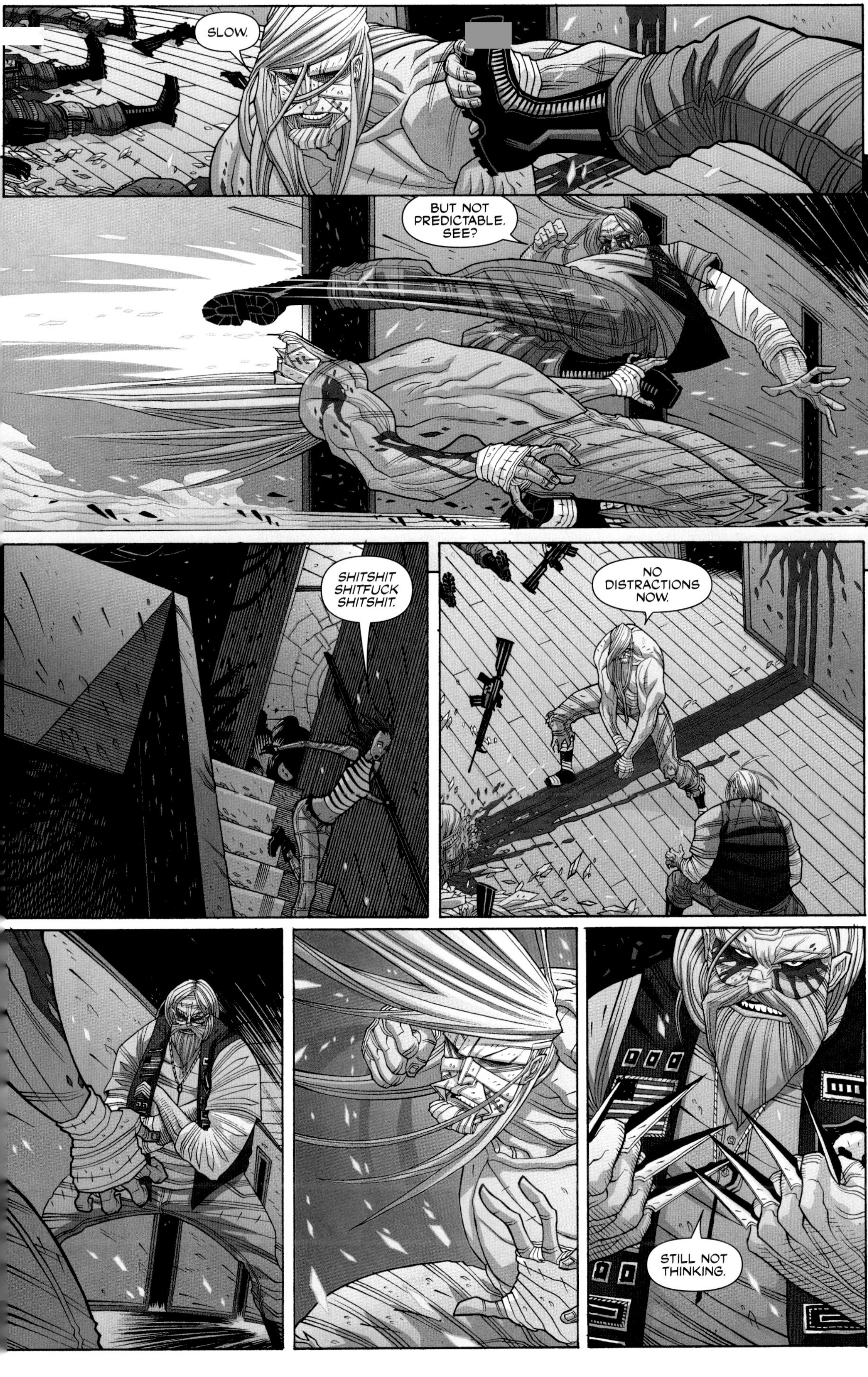
SLOW.
BUT NOT PREDICTABLE. SEE?
SHITSHIT SHITFUCK SHITSHIT.
NO DISTRACTIONS NOW.
STILL NOT THINKING.

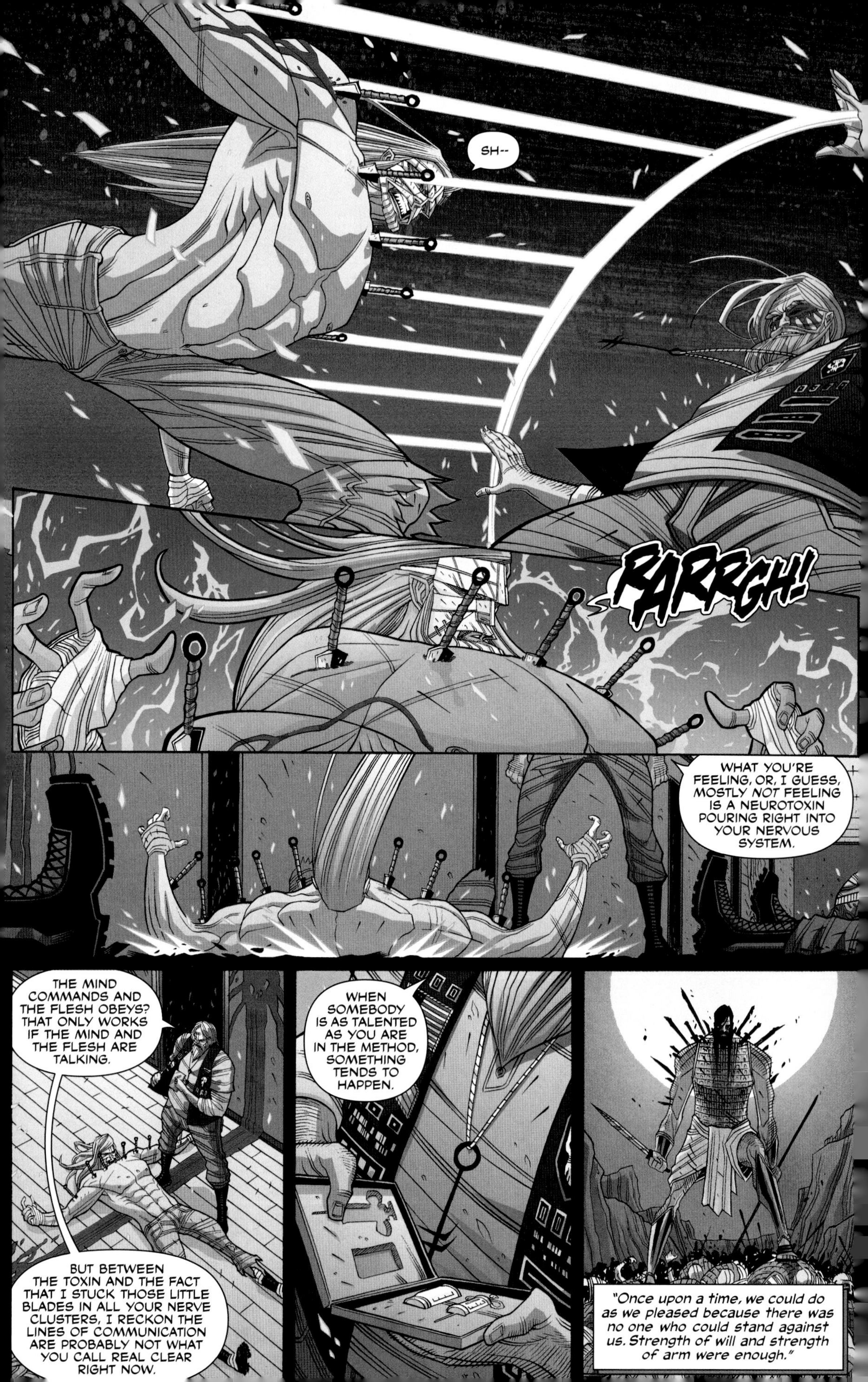

SH--
RARRGH!
WHAT YOU'RE FEELING, OR, I GUESS, MOSTLY NOT FEELING IS A NEUROTOXIN POURING RIGHT INTO YOUR NERVOUS SYSTEM.
THE MIND COMMANDS AND THE FLESH OBEYS? THAT ONLY WORKS IF THE MIND AND THE FLESH ARE TALKING.
BUT BETWEEN THE TOXIN AND THE FACT THAT I STUCK THOSE LITTLE BLADES IN ALL YOUR NERVE CLUSTERS, I RECKON THE LINES OF COMMUNICATION ARE PROBABLY NOT WHAT YOU CALL REAL CLEAR RIGHT NOW.
WHEN SOMEBODY IS AS TALENTED AS YOU ARE IN THE METHOD, SOMETHING TENDS TO HAPPEN.
"Once upon a time, we could do as we pleased because there was no one who could stand against us. Strength of will and strength of arm were enough."

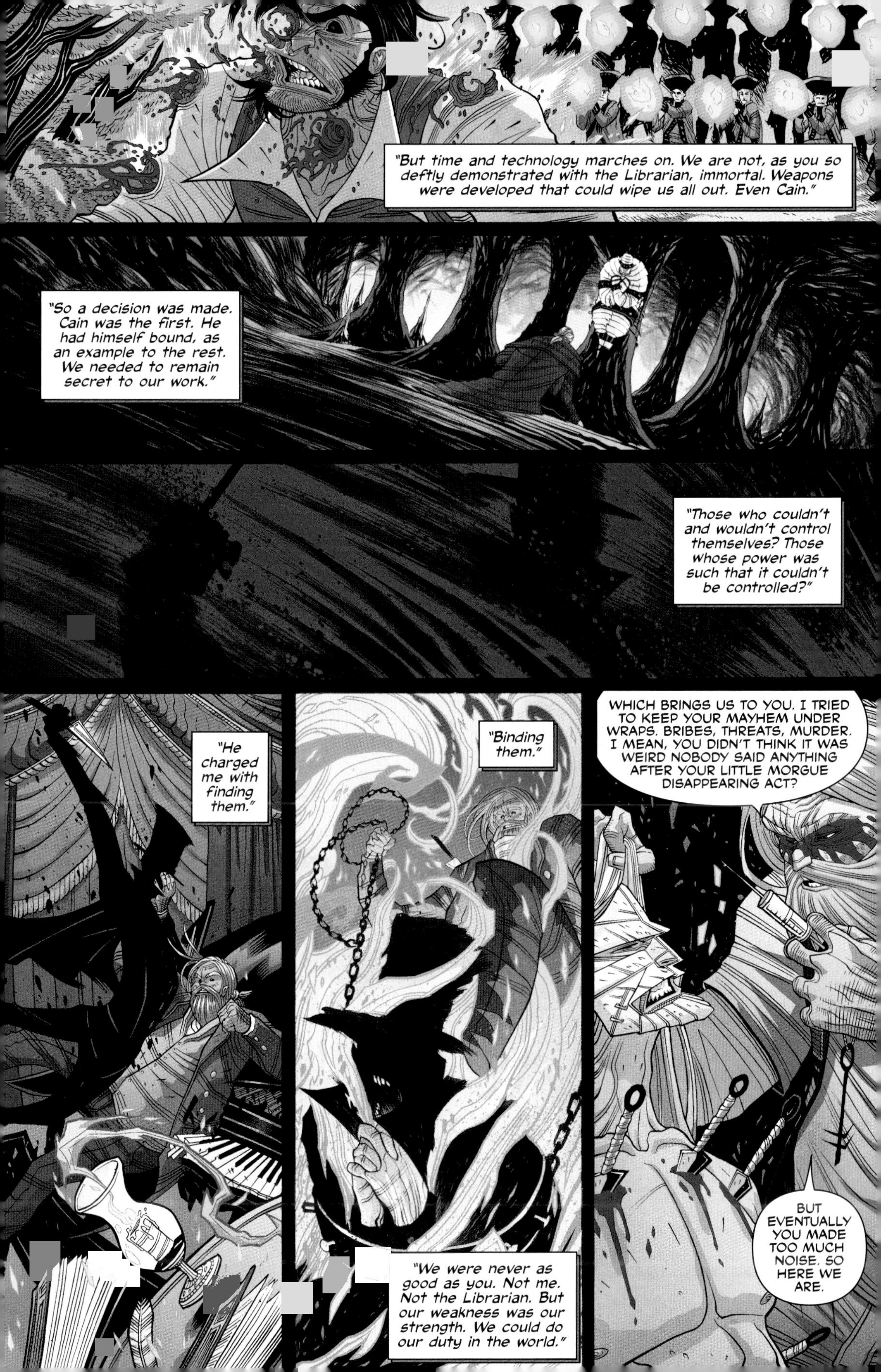
"But time and technology marches on. We are not, as you so deftly demonstrated with the Librarian, immortal. Weapons were developed that could wipe us all out. Even Cain."
"So a decision was made. Cain was the first. He had himself bound, as an example to the rest. We needed to remain secret to our work."
"Those who couldn't and wouldn't control themselves? Those whose power was such that it couldn't be controlled?"
"He charged me with finding them."
"Binding them."
"We were never as good as you. Not me. Not the Librarian. But our weakness was our strength. We could do our duty in the world."
WHICH BRINGS US TO YOU. I TRIED TO KEEP YOUR MAYHEM UNDER WRAPS. BRIBES, THREATS, MURDER. I MEAN, YOU DIDN'T THINK IT WAS WEIRD NOBODY SAID ANYTHING AFTER YOUR LITTLE MORGUE DISAPPEARING ACT?
BUT EVENTUALLY YOU MADE TOO MUCH NOISE. SO HERE WE ARE.

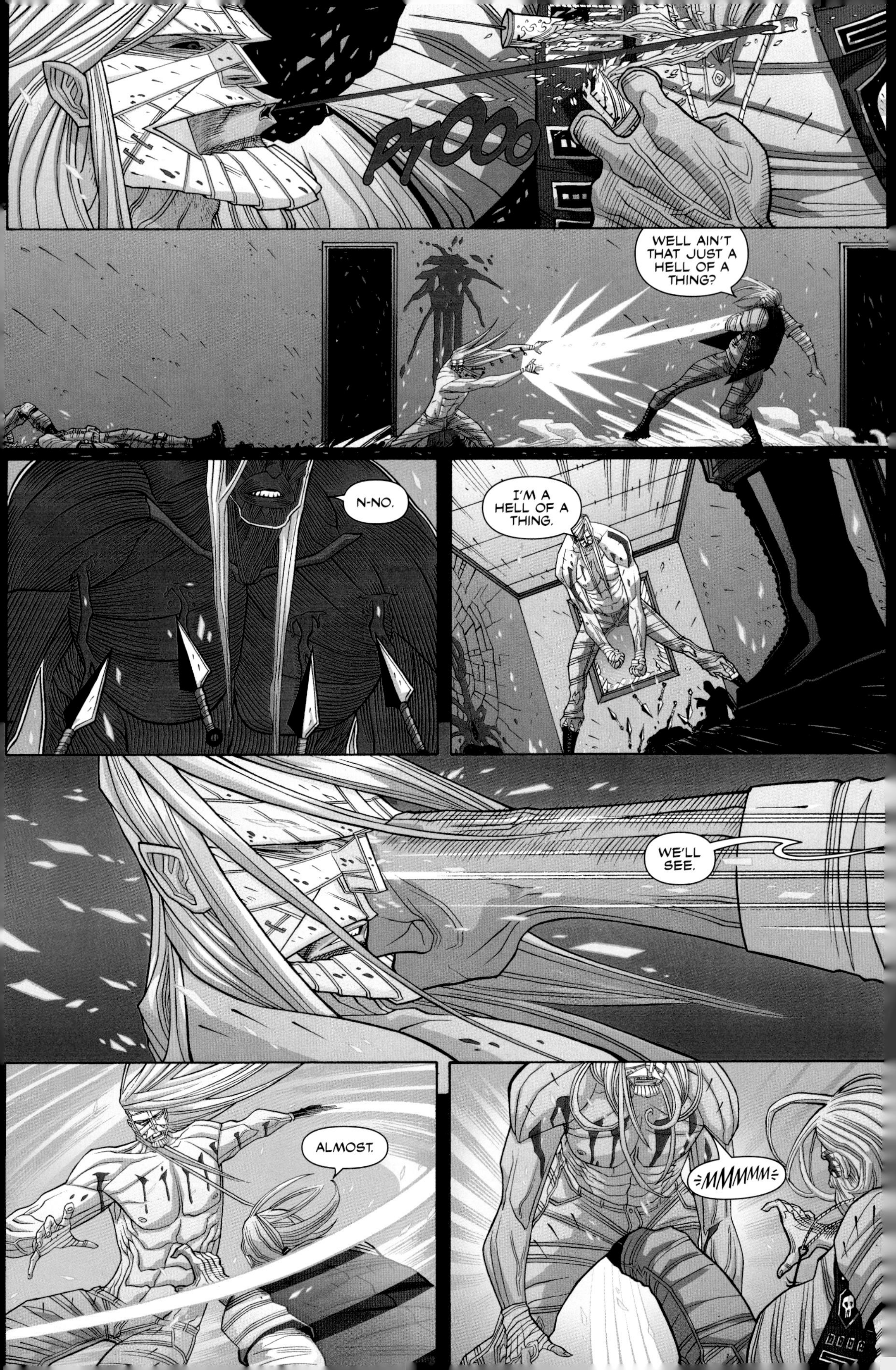
PTOOO
WELL AIN'T THAT JUST A HELL OF A THING?
N-NO.
I'M A HELL OF A THING.
WE'LL SEE.
ALMOST.
MMMMM

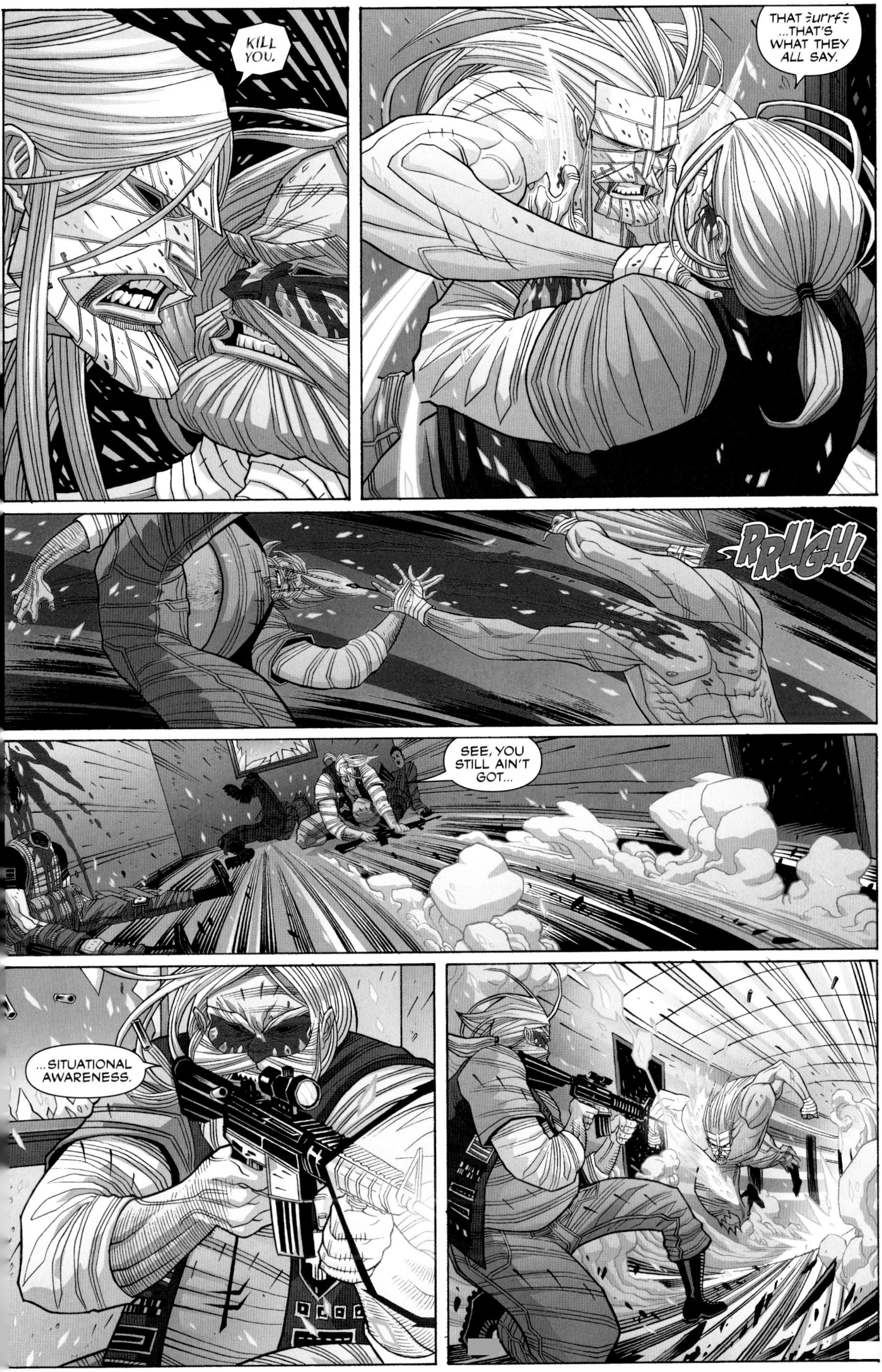
KILL YOU.
THAT urrf ...THAT'S WHAT THEY ALL SAY.
RRUGH!
SEE, YOU STILL AIN'T GOT...
...SITUATIONAL AWARENESS.

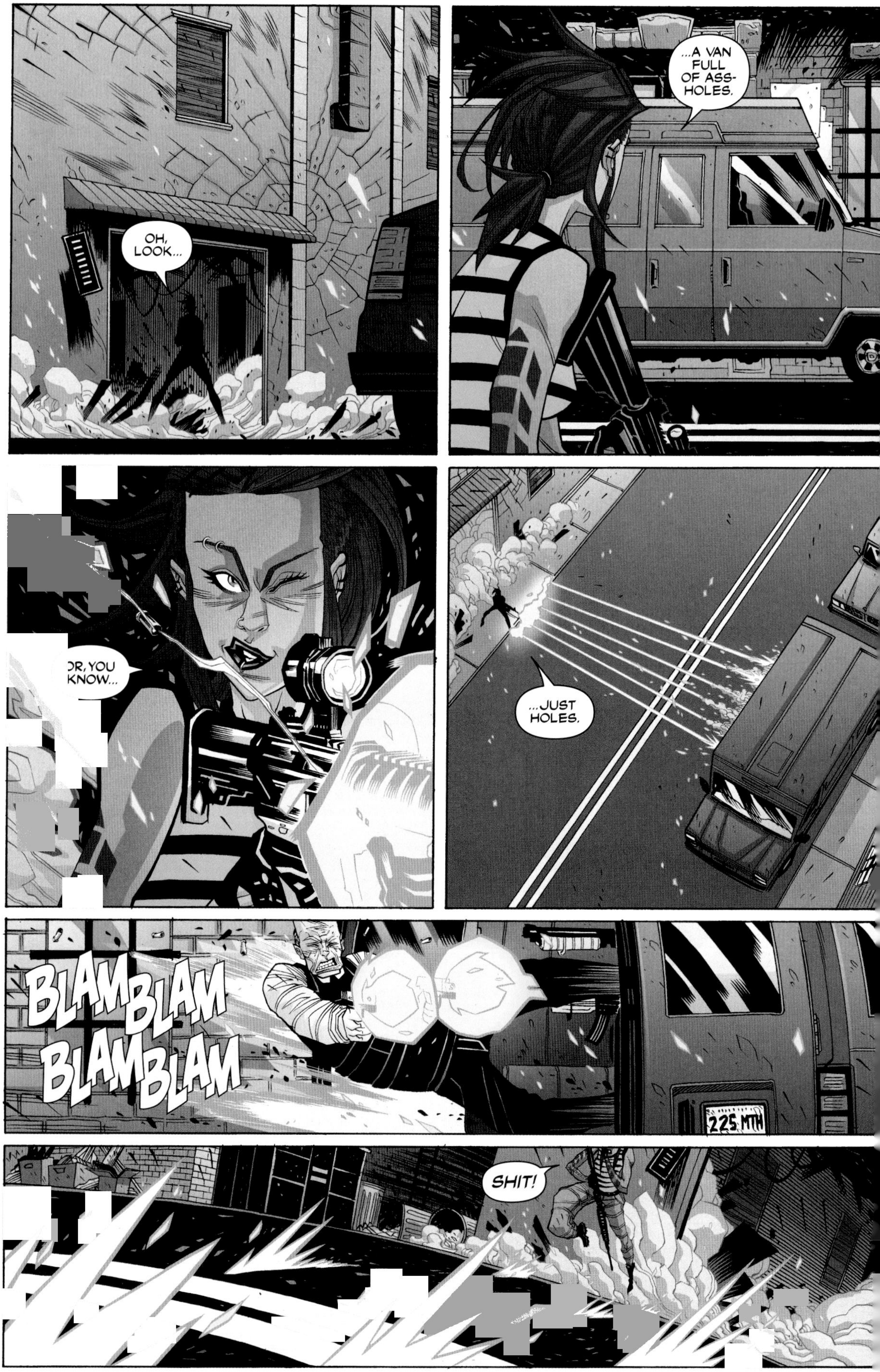
OH, LOOK...
...A VAN FULL OF ASS-HOLES.
OR, YOU KNOW...
...JUST HOLES.
BLAMBLAM BLAMBLAM
225 MTH
SHIT!

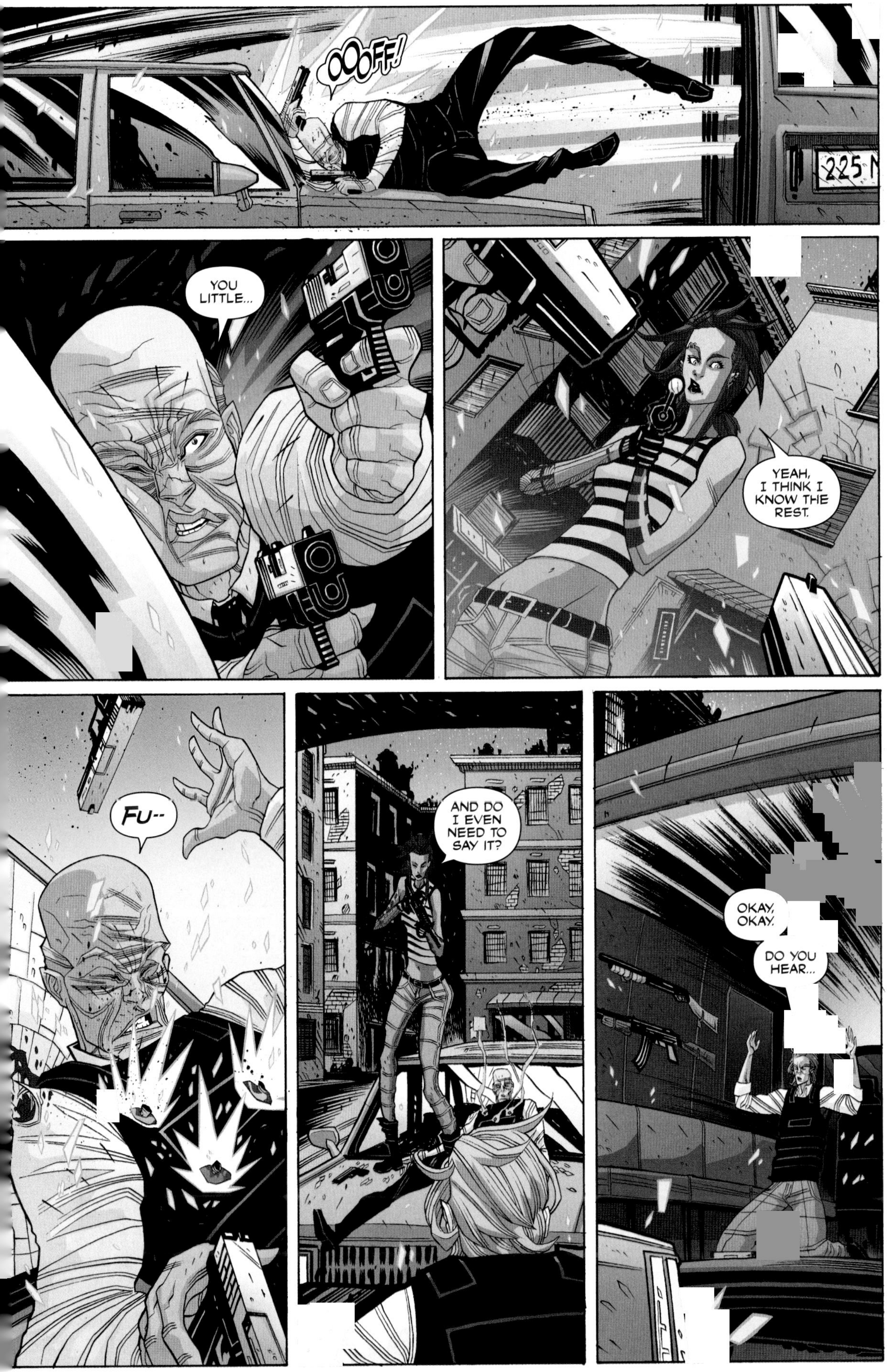
OOOFF!
225 N
YOU LITTLE...
YEAH, I THINK I KNOW THE REST.
FU--
AND DO I EVEN NEED TO SAY IT?
OKAY, OKAY.
DO YOU HEAR...

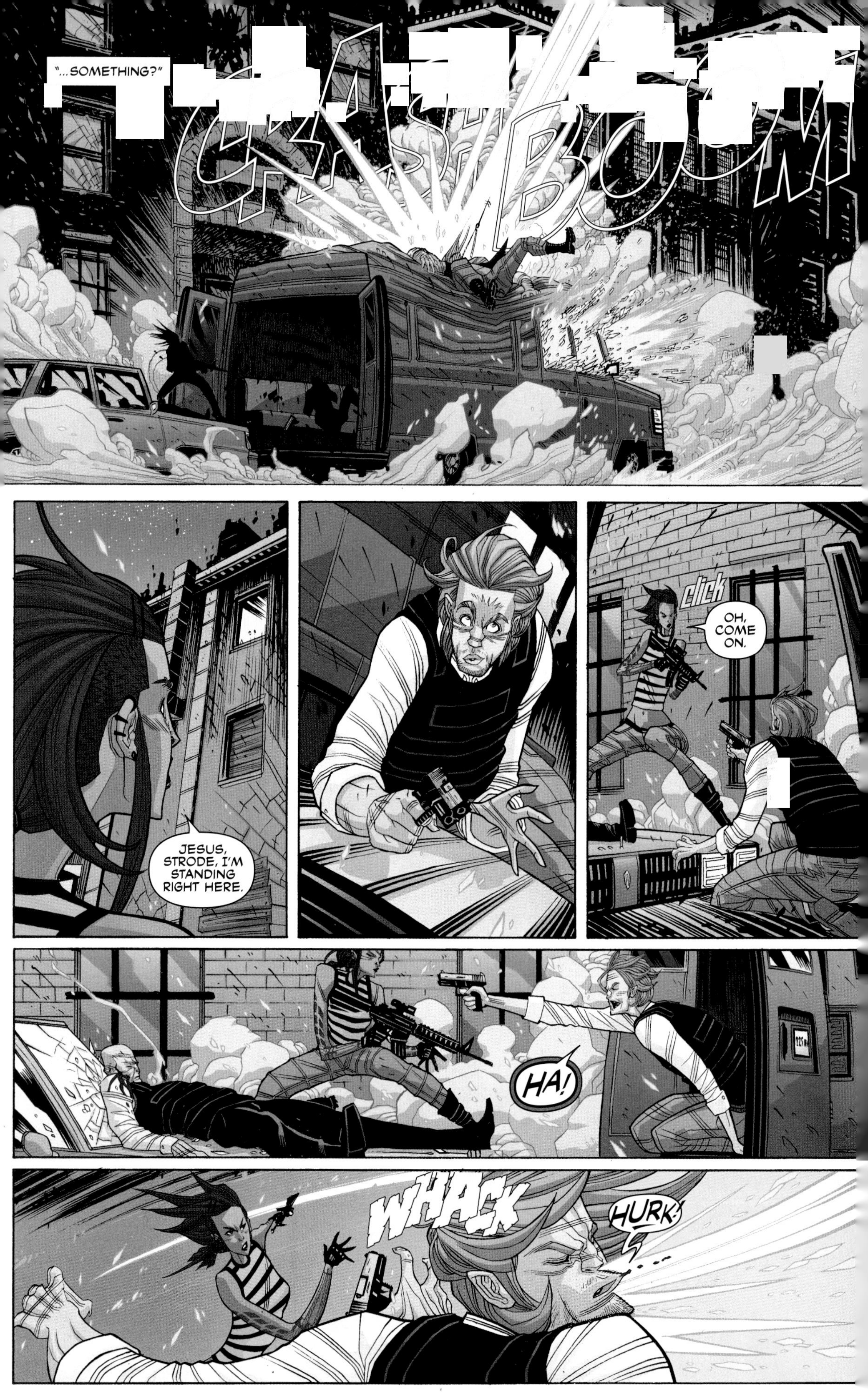
"...SOMETHING?"
JESUS, STRODE, I'M STANDING RIGHT HERE.
click
OH, COME ON.
HA!
WHACK
HURK!

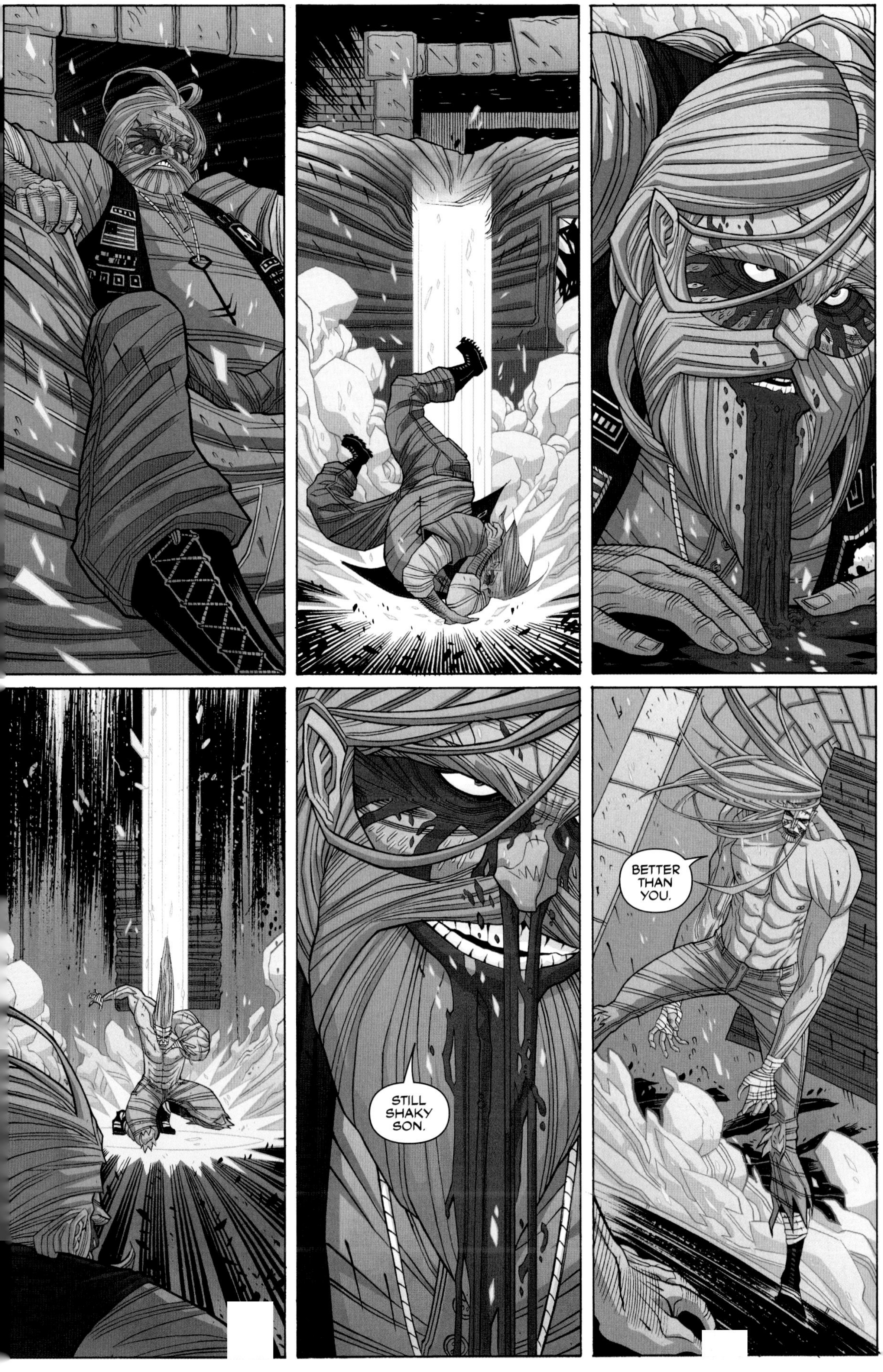
STILL SHAKY SON.
BETTER THAN YOU.

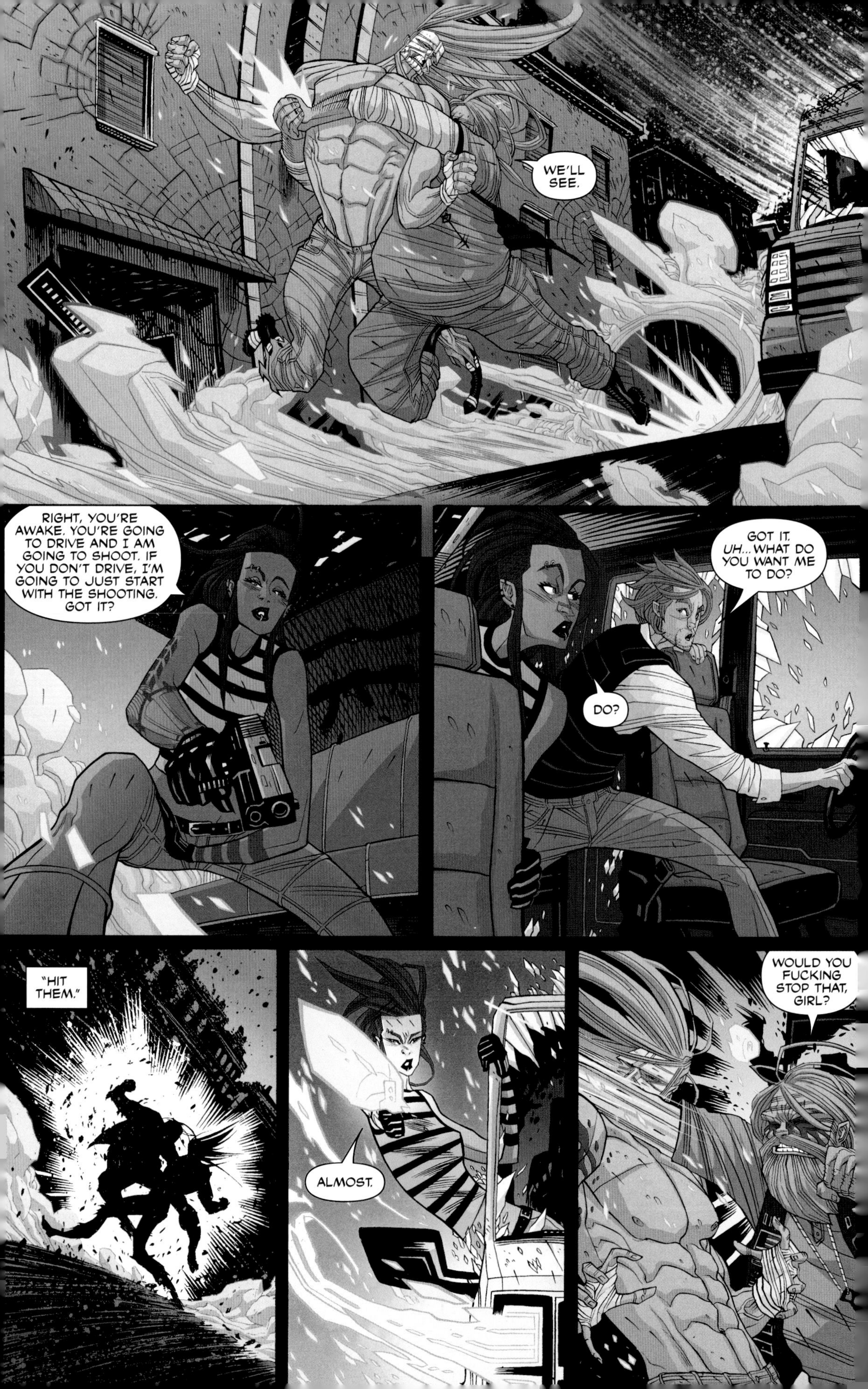
WE'LL SEE.
RIGHT, YOU'RE AWAKE. YOU'RE GOING TO DRIVE AND I AM GOING TO SHOOT. IF YOU DON'T DRIVE, I'M GOING TO JUST START WITH THE SHOOTING. GOT IT?
GOT IT. *UH*... WHAT DO YOU WANT ME TO DO?
DO?
"HIT THEM."
ALMOST.
WOULD YOU FUCKING STOP THAT, GIRL?

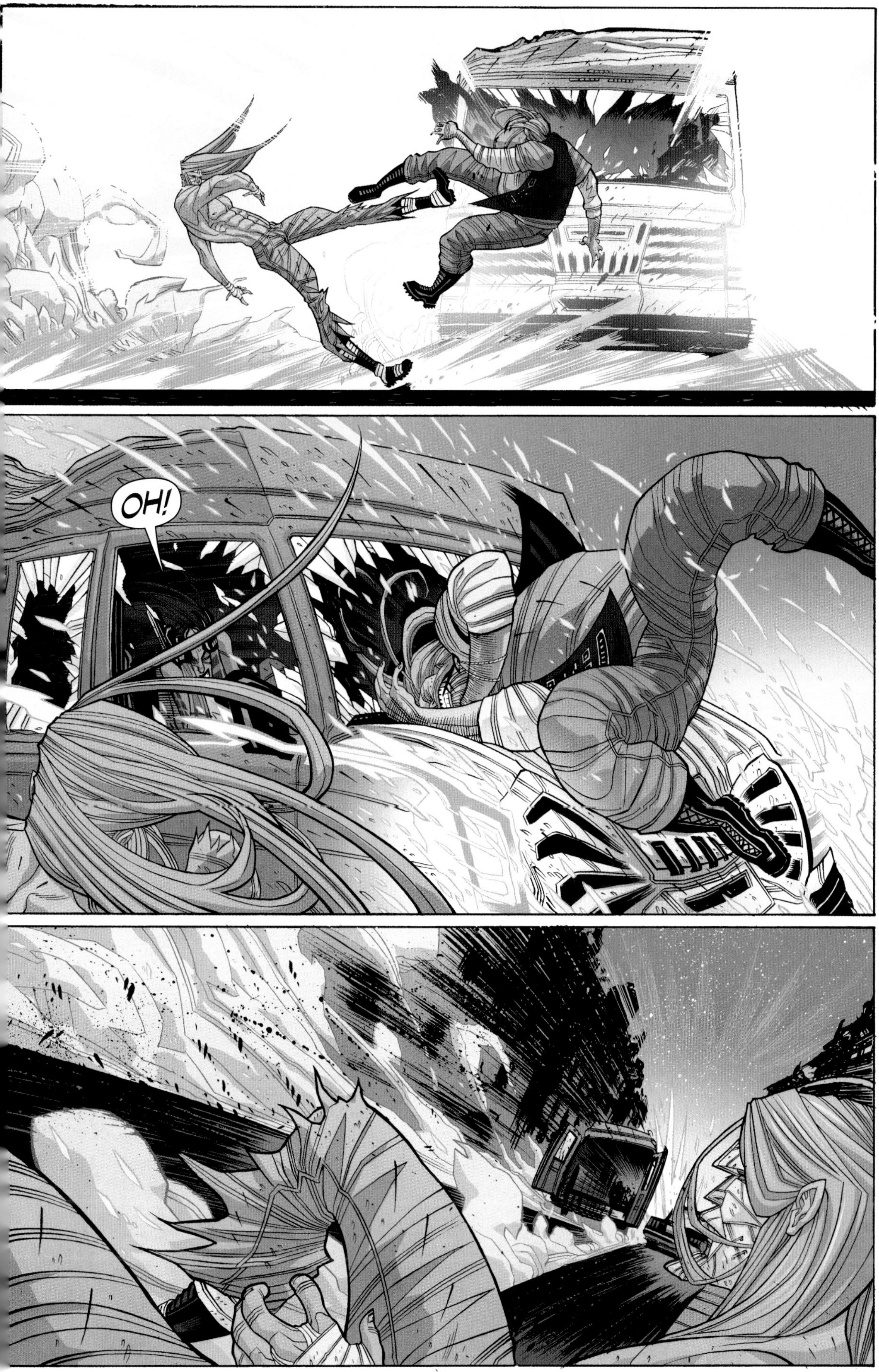
OH!

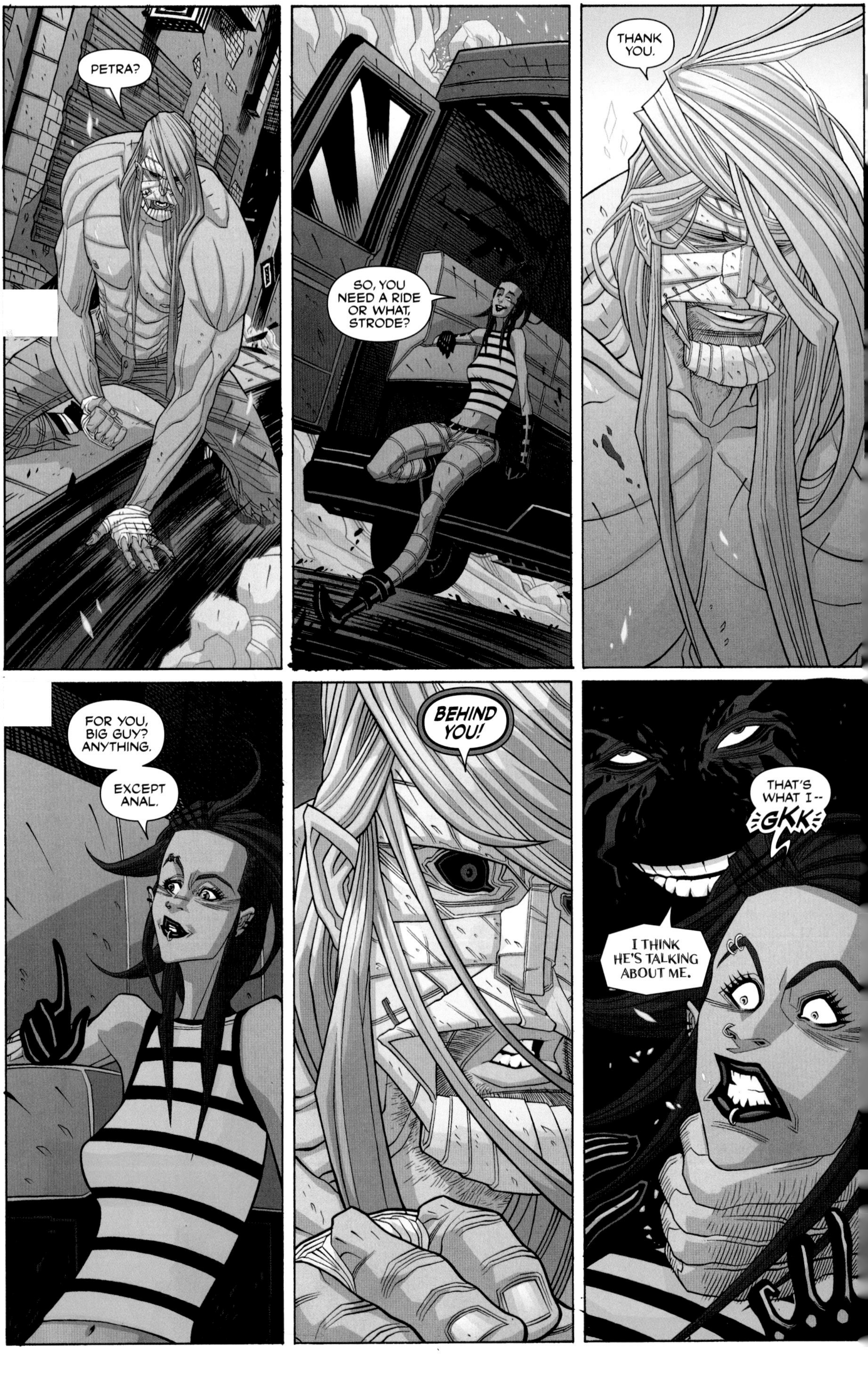
PETRA?
SO, YOU NEED A RIDE OR WHAT, STRODE?
THANK YOU.
FOR YOU, BIG GUY? ANYTHING.
EXCEPT ANAL.
BEHIND YOU!
THAT'S WHAT I --
GKK
I THINK HE'S TALKING ABOUT ME.

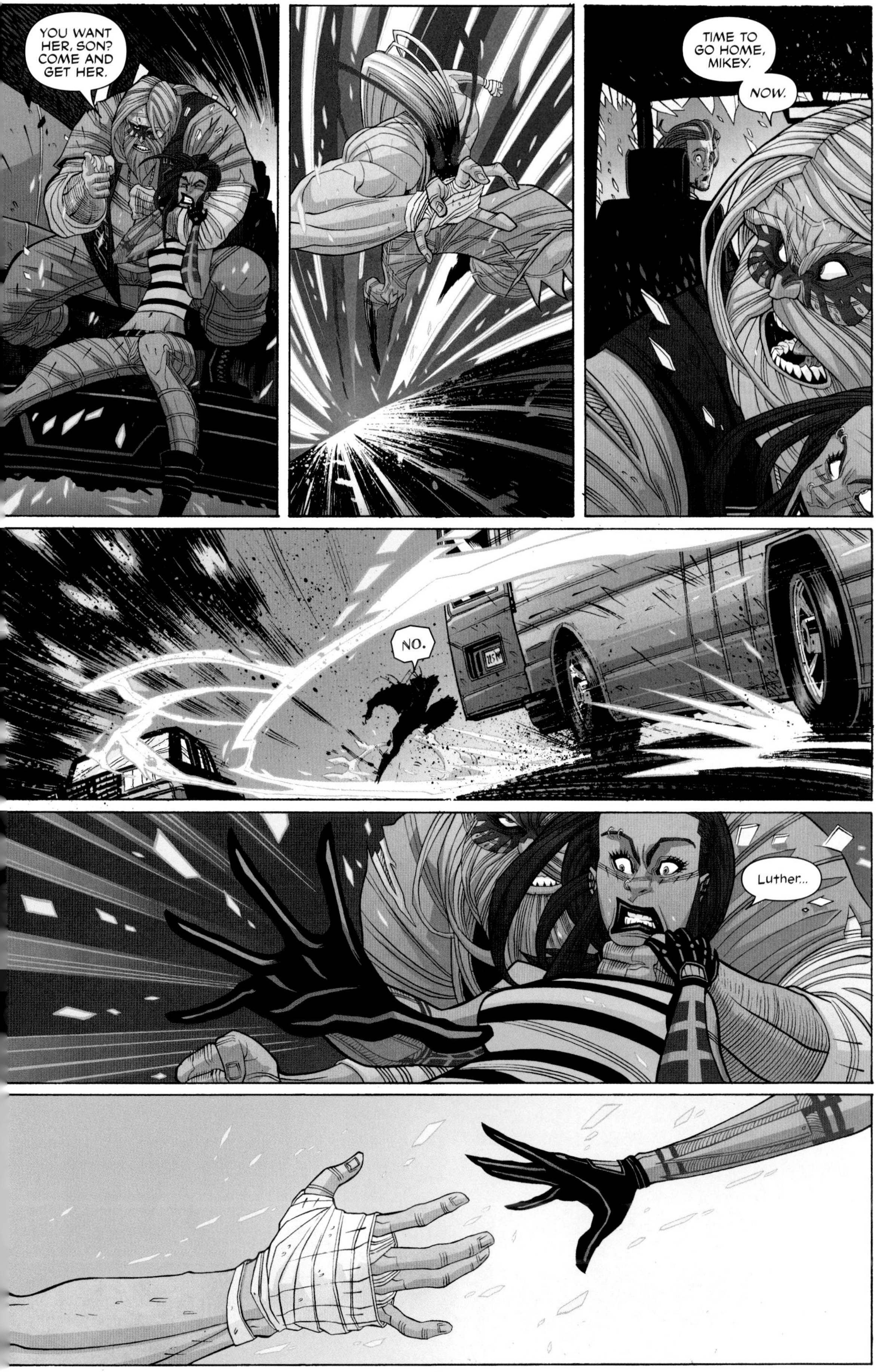
YOU WANT HER, SON? COME AND GET HER.
TIME TO GO HOME, MIKEY.
NOW.
NO.
Luther...

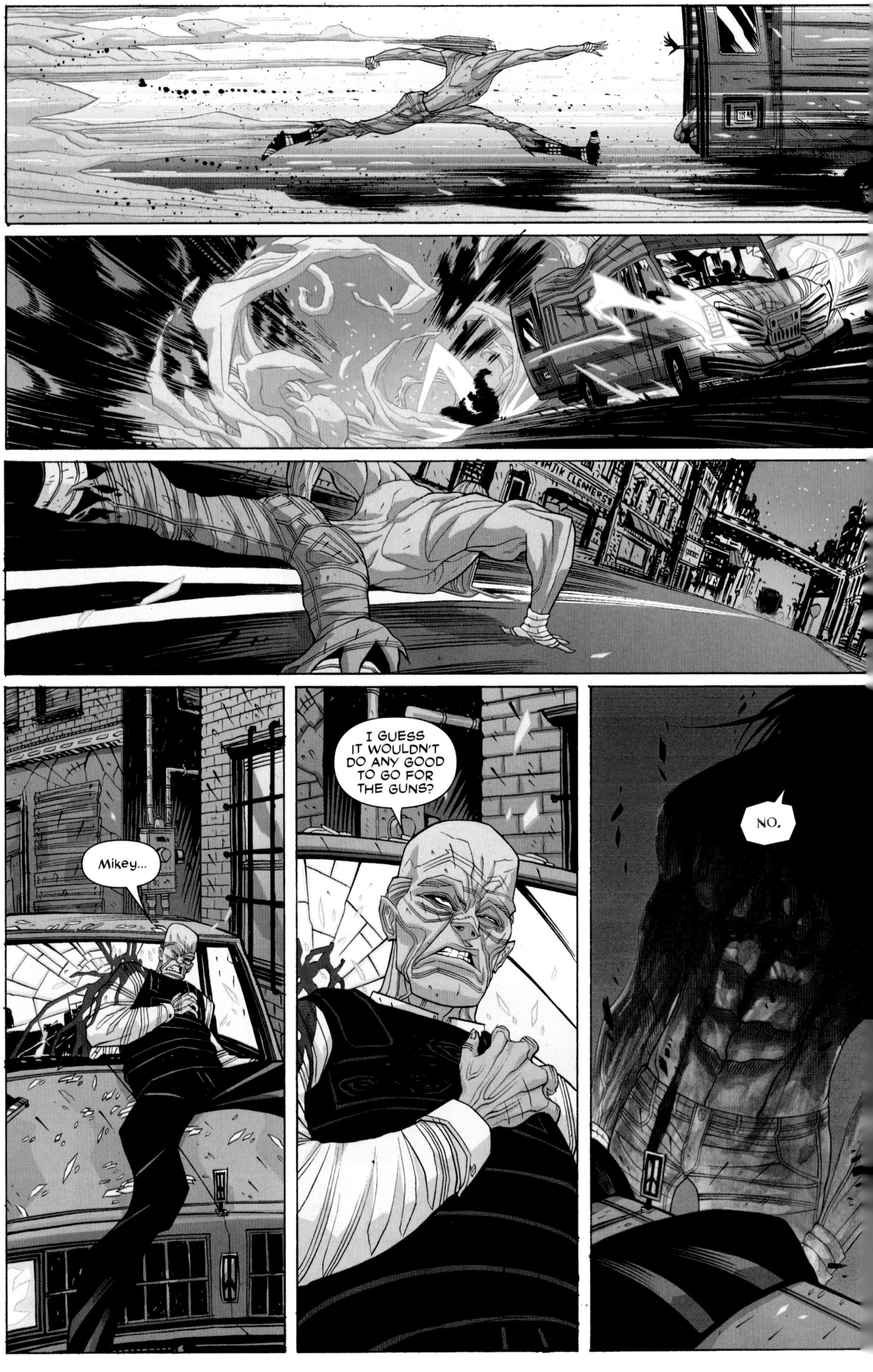
Mikey...
I GUESS IT WOULDN'T DO ANY GOOD TO GO FOR THE GUNS?
NO.

WHERE?

FUCK YOU. GET IT OVER WITH.

YOU DON'T UNDERSTAND WHAT YOU'RE DEALING WITH.

THEN TAKE ME TO HIM.

NOT WITH ME. NOT WITH HIM. YOU KNOW THAT HE USED YOU, RIGHT? THAT YOU, YOUR MEN AND ALL OF THAT WERE JUST TO SOFTEN ME UP.

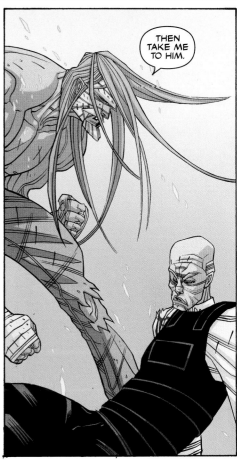

YEAH, I FIGURED THAT ONE OUT.

GOOD. I CAN KILL YOU, IF THAT'S WHAT YOU WANT. BUT HE'S GOING TO KILL YOU ALL. SO TELL ME... IS THERE ANYTHING YOU CARE ABOUT?

YES.

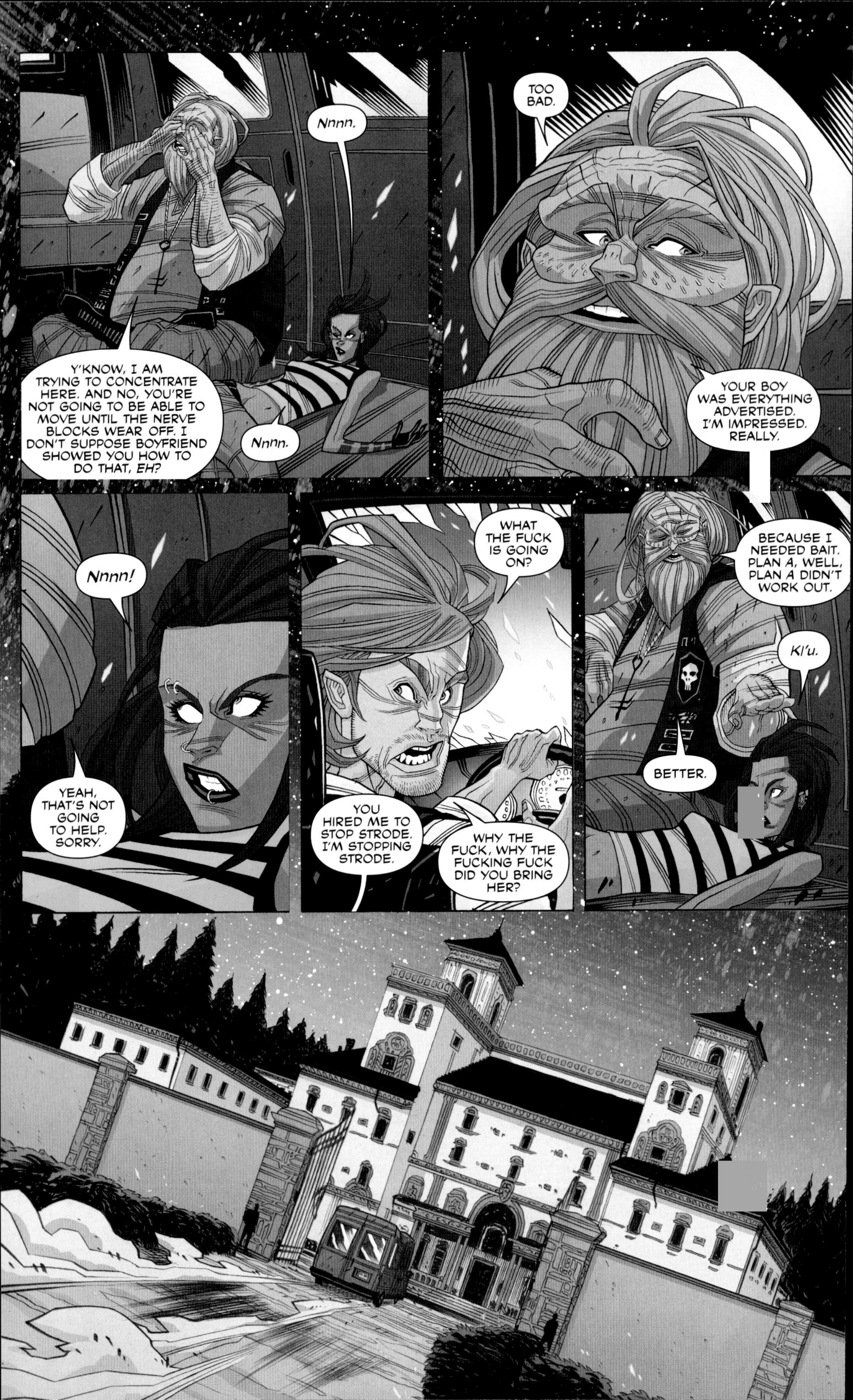
Nnnn.
Y'KNOW, I AM TRYING TO CONCENTRATE HERE. AND NO, YOU'RE NOT GOING TO BE ABLE TO MOVE UNTIL THE NERVE BLOCKS WEAR OFF. I DON'T SUPPOSE BOYFRIEND SHOWED YOU HOW TO DO THAT, EH?
Nnnn.
TOO BAD.
YOUR BOY WAS EVERYTHING ADVERTISED. I'M IMPRESSED. REALLY.
Nnnn!
YEAH, THAT'S NOT GOING TO HELP. SORRY.
WHAT THE FUCK IS GOING ON?
YOU HIRED ME TO STOP STRODE. I'M STOPPING STRODE.
WHY THE FUCK, WHY THE FUCKING FUCK DID YOU BRING HER?
BECAUSE I NEEDED BAIT. PLAN A, WELL, PLAN A DIDN'T WORK OUT.
Kl'u.
BETTER.

SO WE'RE FUCKED. GOOD TO KNOW.

WE'RE NOT. I DON'T HAVE JUST THE ONE PLAN. IN FACT, SHE'S GOING TO COME IN HANDY. BECAUSE WHERE SHE GOES, STRODE FOLLOWS.

AND THAT'S *GOOD*? HE JUST KILLED A DOZEN GUYS WITH HIS BARE HANDS.

HE'S A TALENTED GUY.

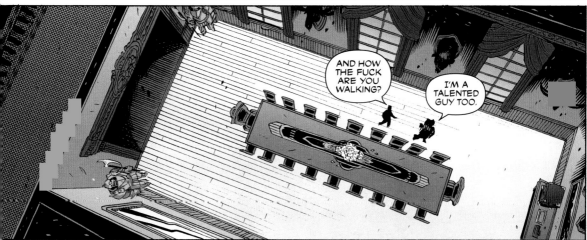

AND HOW THE FUCK ARE YOU WALKING?

I'M A TALENTED GUY TOO.

FFK!

SORRY ABOUT THAT.

I DON'T--

UNDERSTAND? YEAH, I HEARD YOU. I WAS HOPING TO STOP STRODE AT HIS... *LAIR*, I GUESS? BUT IT DIDN'T WORK, SO...

PLAN B.

PLAN B?

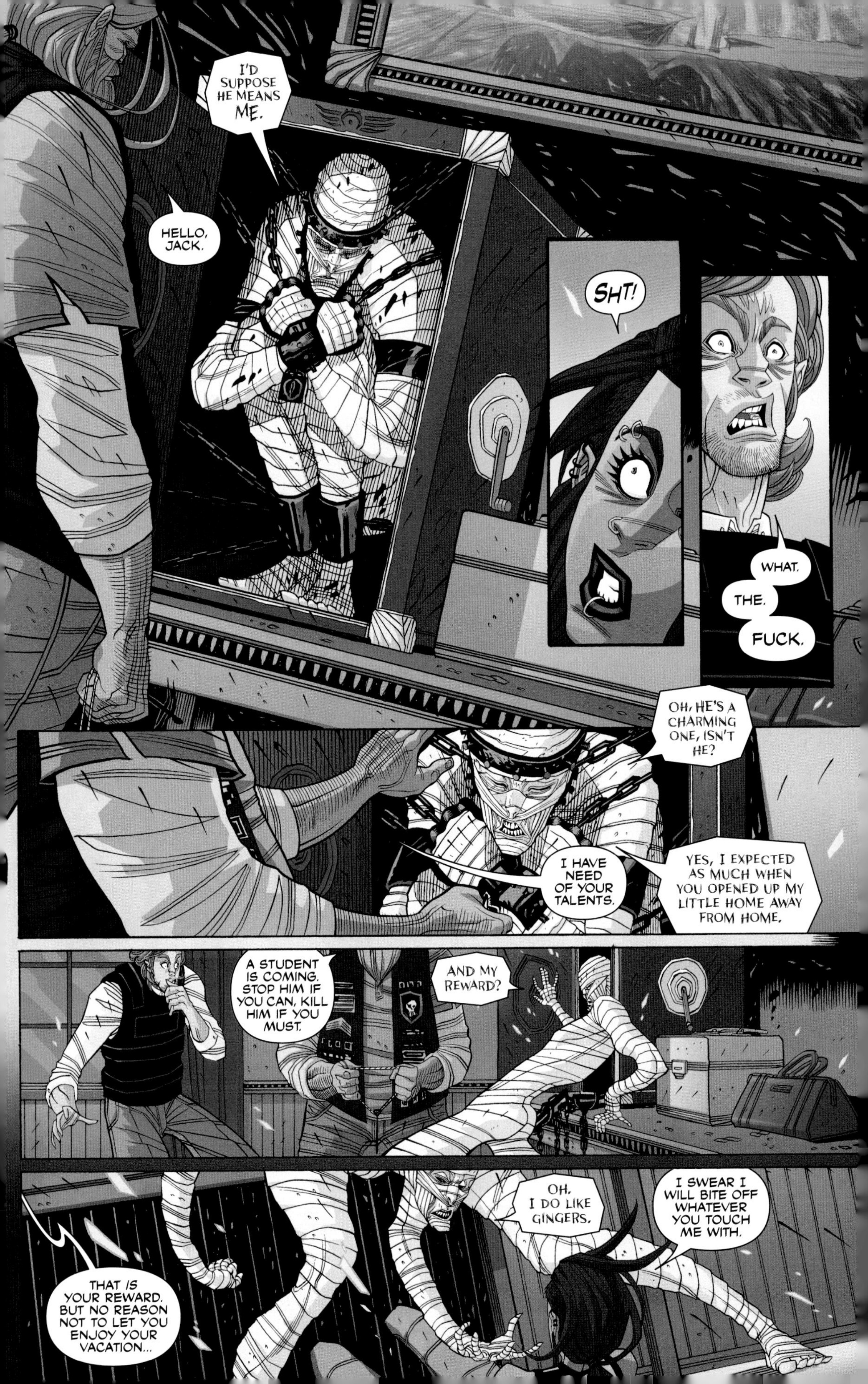
I'D SUPPOSE HE MEANS ME.
HELLO, JACK.
SHT!
WHAT.
THE.
FUCK.
OH, HE'S A CHARMING ONE, ISN'T HE?
I HAVE NEED OF YOUR TALENTS.
YES, I EXPECTED AS MUCH WHEN YOU OPENED UP MY LITTLE HOME AWAY FROM HOME.
A STUDENT IS COMING. STOP HIM IF YOU CAN, KILL HIM IF YOU MUST.
AND MY REWARD?
OH, I DO LIKE GINGERS.
I SWEAR I WILL BITE OFF WHATEVER YOU TOUCH ME WITH.
THAT IS YOUR REWARD. BUT NO REASON NOT TO LET YOU ENJOY YOUR VACATION...

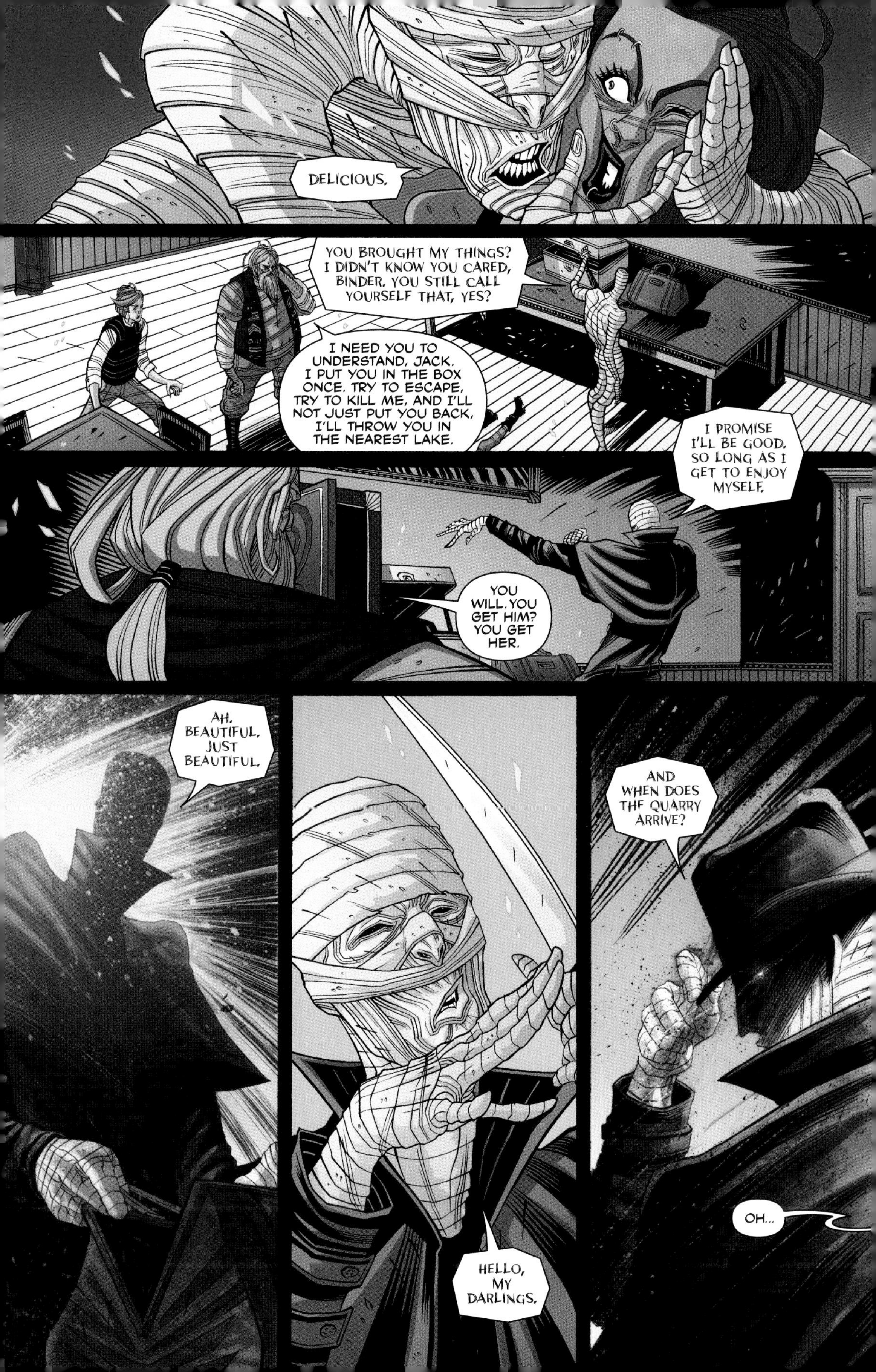
DELICIOUS.
YOU BROUGHT MY THINGS? I DIDN'T KNOW YOU CARED, BINDER. YOU STILL CALL YOURSELF THAT, YES?
I NEED YOU TO UNDERSTAND, JACK. I PUT YOU IN THE BOX ONCE. TRY TO ESCAPE, TRY TO KILL ME, AND I'LL NOT JUST PUT YOU BACK, I'LL THROW YOU IN THE NEAREST LAKE.
I PROMISE I'LL BE GOOD, SO LONG AS I GET TO ENJOY MYSELF.
YOU WILL. YOU GET HIM? YOU GET HER.
AH, BEAUTIFUL, JUST BEAUTIFUL.
HELLO, MY DARLINGS.
AND WHEN DOES THE QUARRY ARRIVE?
OH...

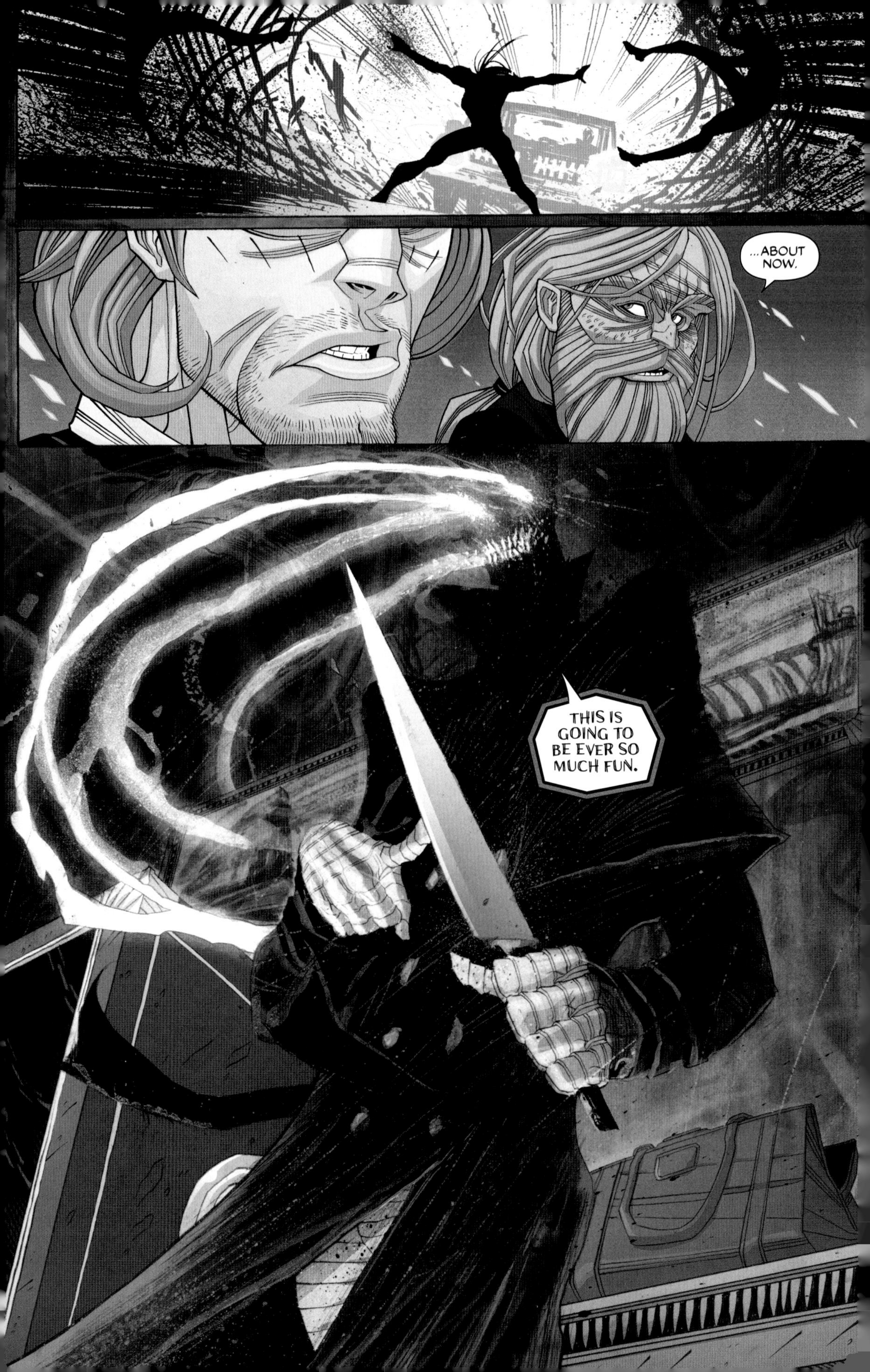
...ABOUT NOW.
THIS IS GOING TO BE EVER SO MUCH FUN.

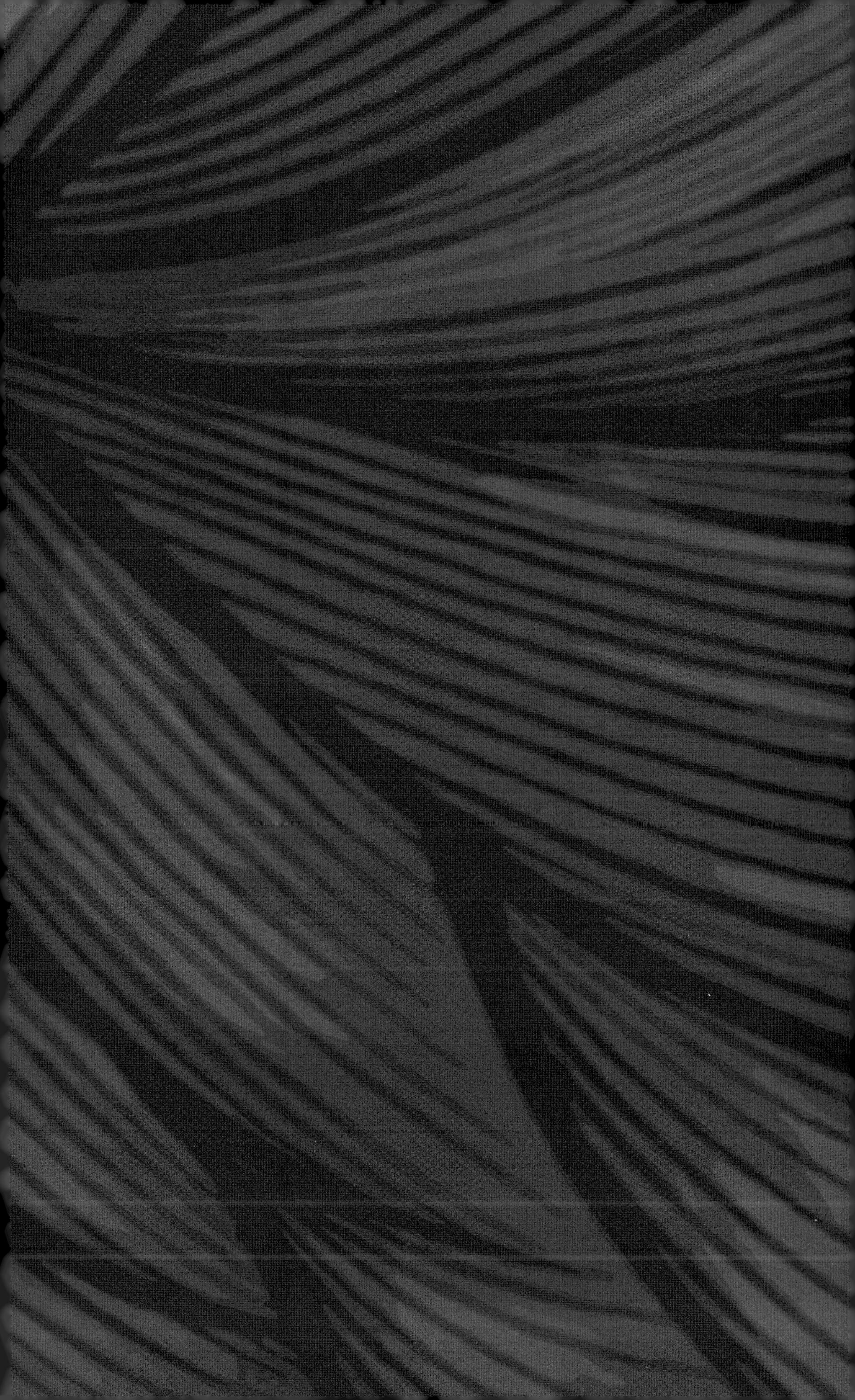

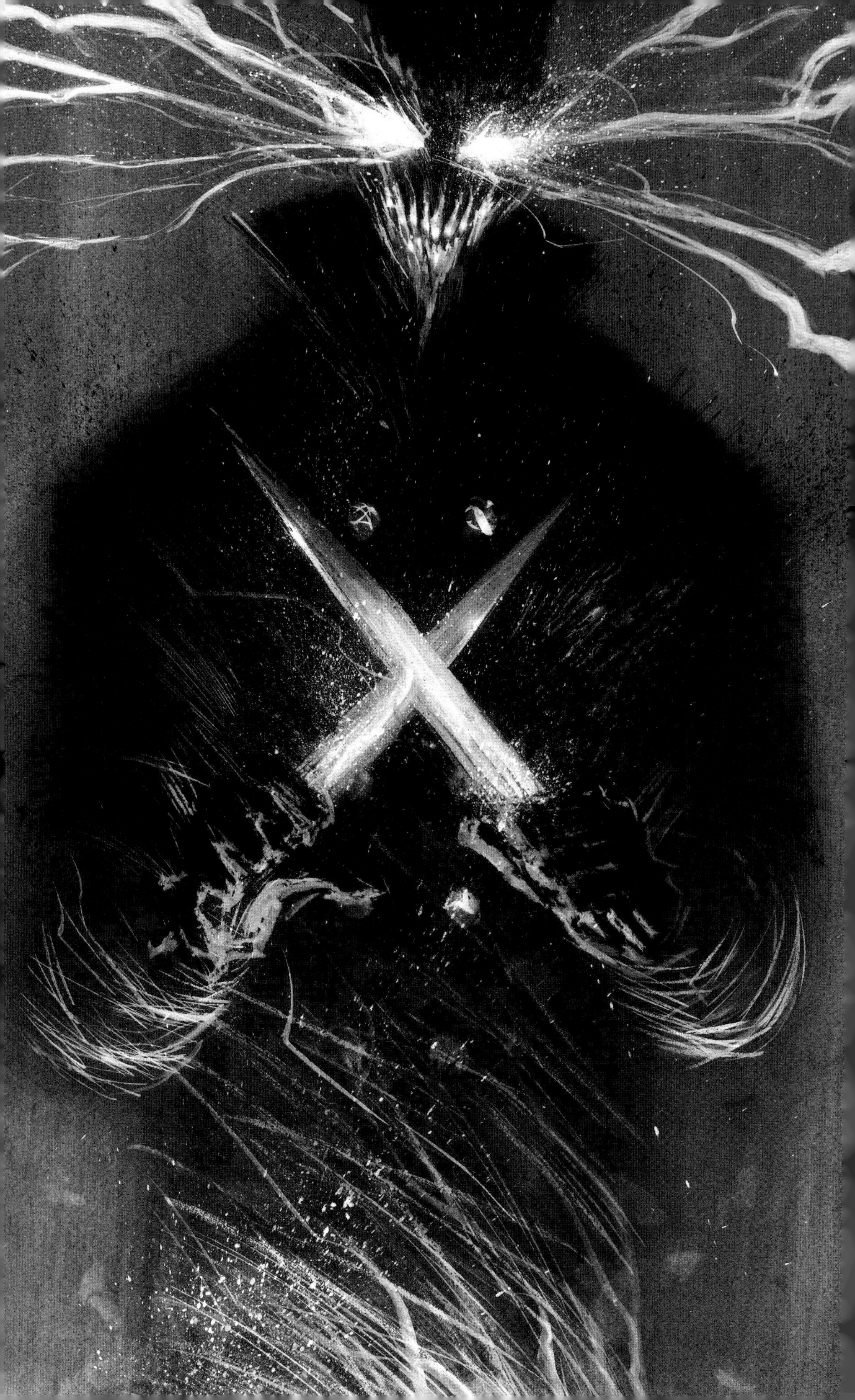

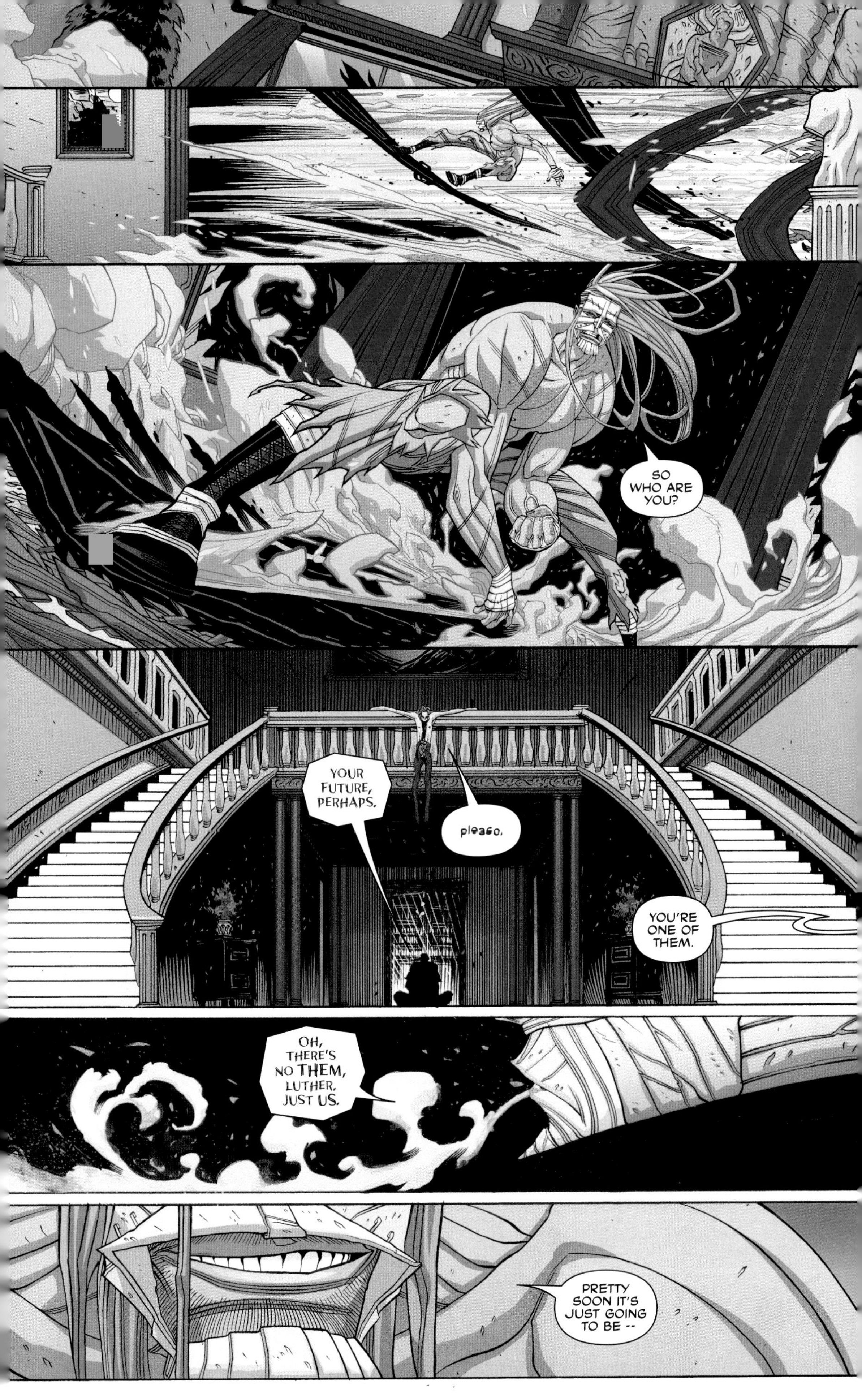
SO WHO ARE YOU?
YOUR FUTURE, PERHAPS.
please.
YOU'RE ONE OF THEM.
OH, THERE'S NO THEM, LUTHER. JUST US.
PRETTY SOON IT'S JUST GOING TO BE --

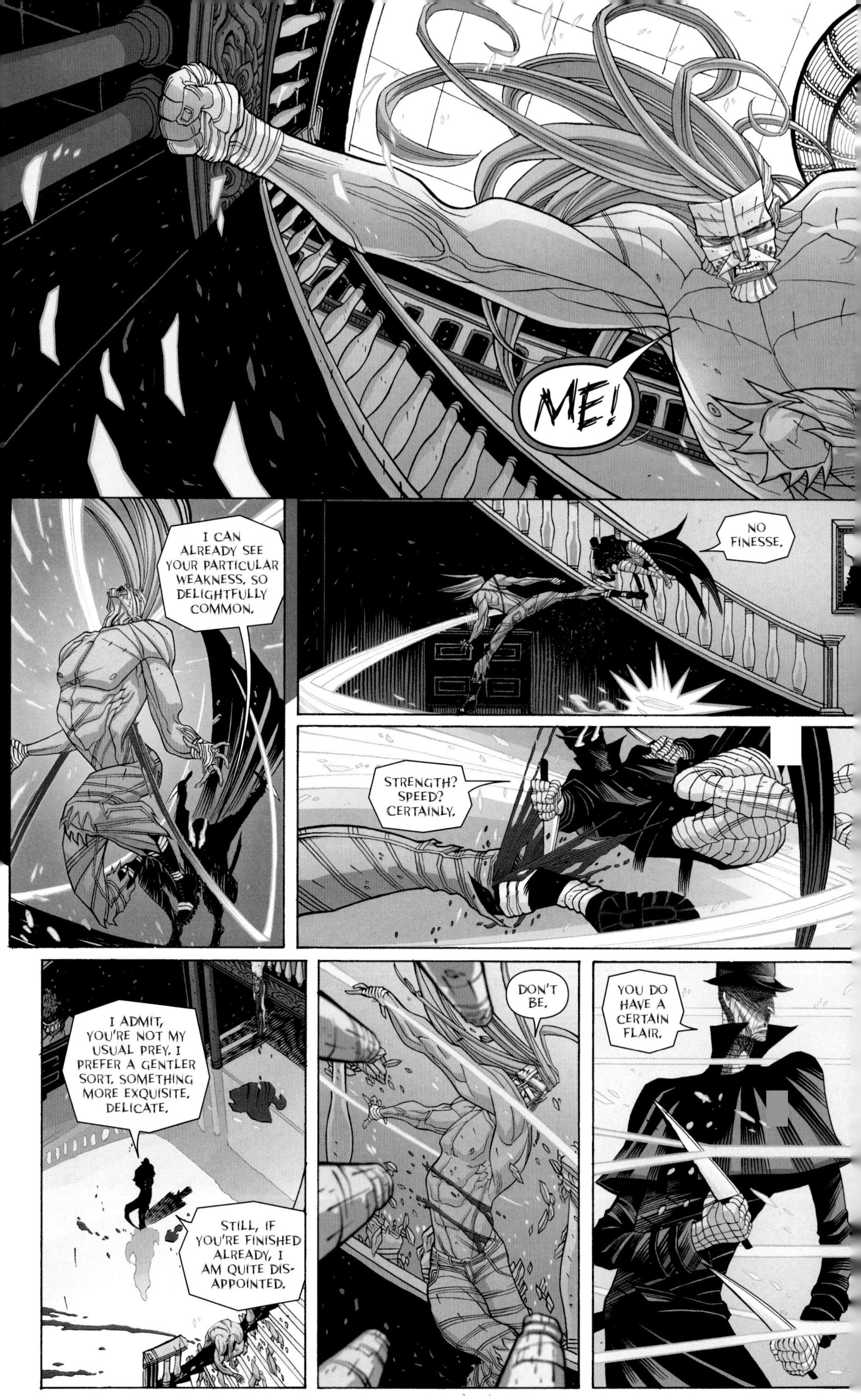
ME!
I CAN ALREADY SEE YOUR PARTICULAR WEAKNESS, SO DELIGHTFULLY COMMON.
NO FINESSE.
STRENGTH? SPEED? CERTAINLY.
I ADMIT, YOU'RE NOT MY USUAL PREY. I PREFER A GENTLER SORT. SOMETHING MORE EXQUISITE, DELICATE.
STILL, IF YOU'RE FINISHED ALREADY, I AM QUITE DIS-APPOINTED.
DON'T BE.
YOU DO HAVE A CERTAIN FLAIR.

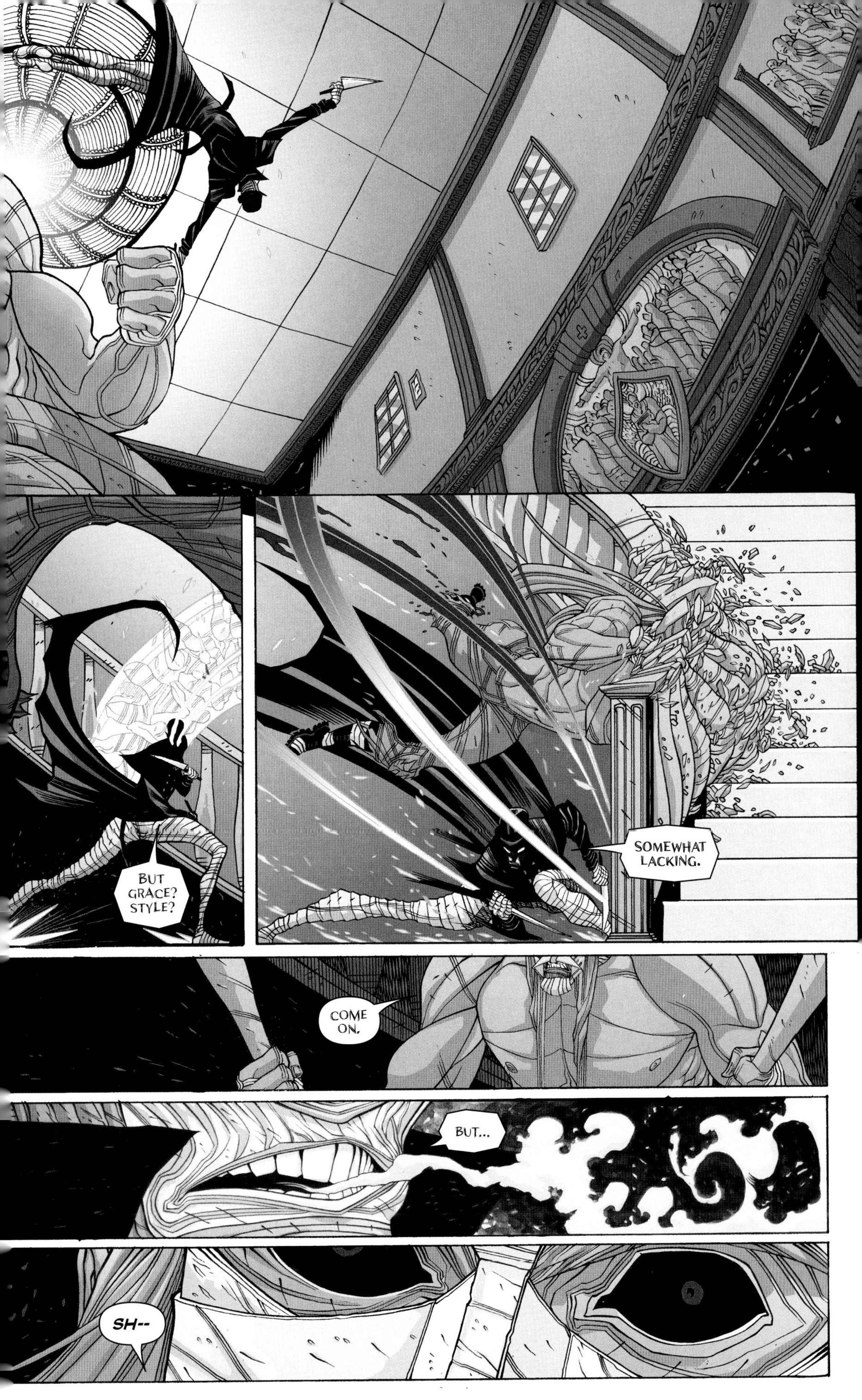
BUT GRACE? STYLE?
SOMEWHAT LACKING.
COME ON.
BUT...
SH--

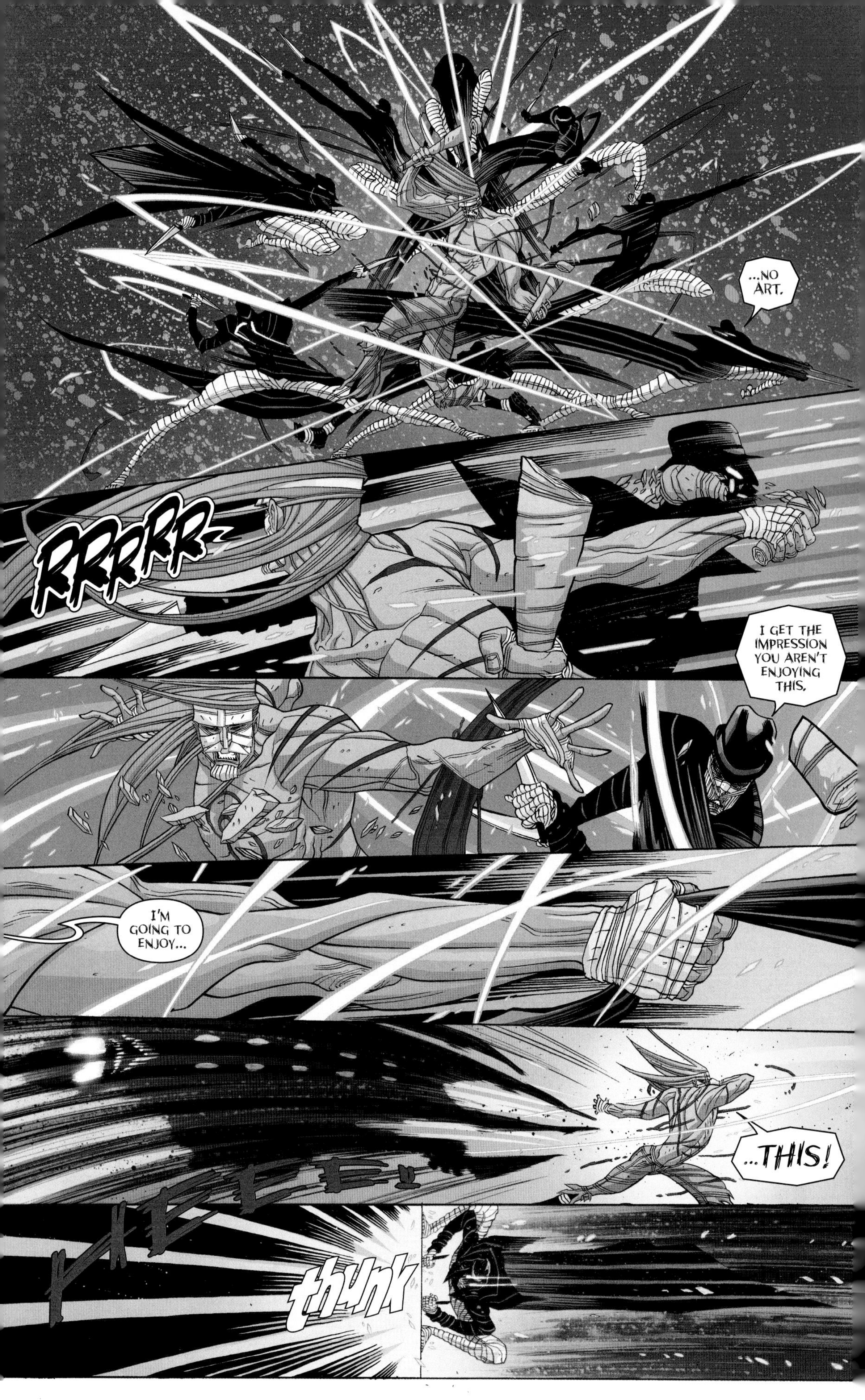
...NO ART.
RRRRR
I GET THE IMPRESSION YOU AREN'T ENJOYING THIS.
I'M GOING TO ENJOY...
...THIS!
thunk

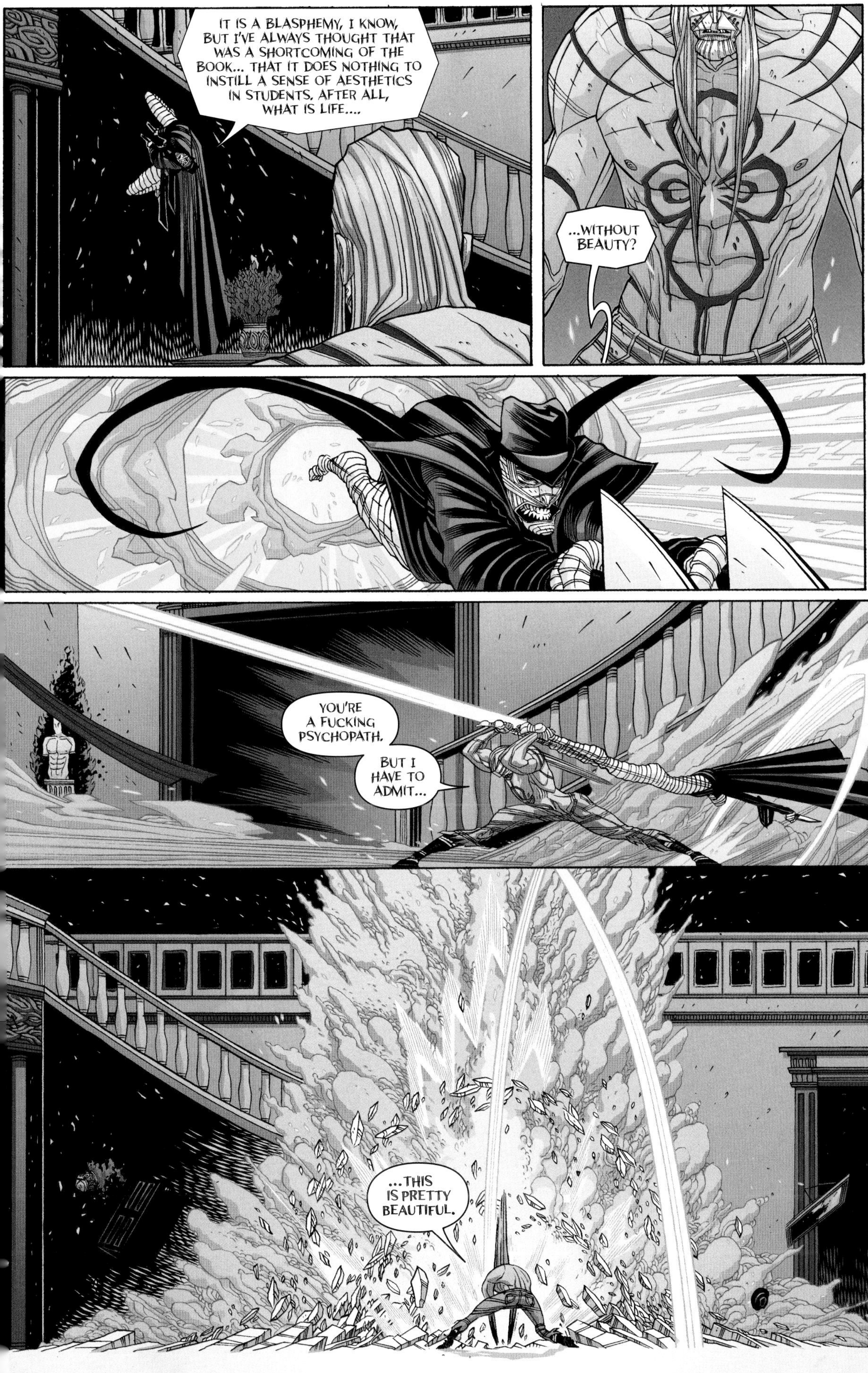
IT IS A BLASPHEMY, I KNOW, BUT I'VE ALWAYS THOUGHT THAT WAS A SHORTCOMING OF THE BOOK... THAT IT DOES NOTHING TO INSTILL A SENSE OF AESTHETICS IN STUDENTS. AFTER ALL, WHAT IS LIFE....
...WITHOUT BEAUTY?
YOU'RE A FUCKING PSYCHOPATH.
BUT I HAVE TO ADMIT...
...THIS IS PRETTY BEAUTIFUL.

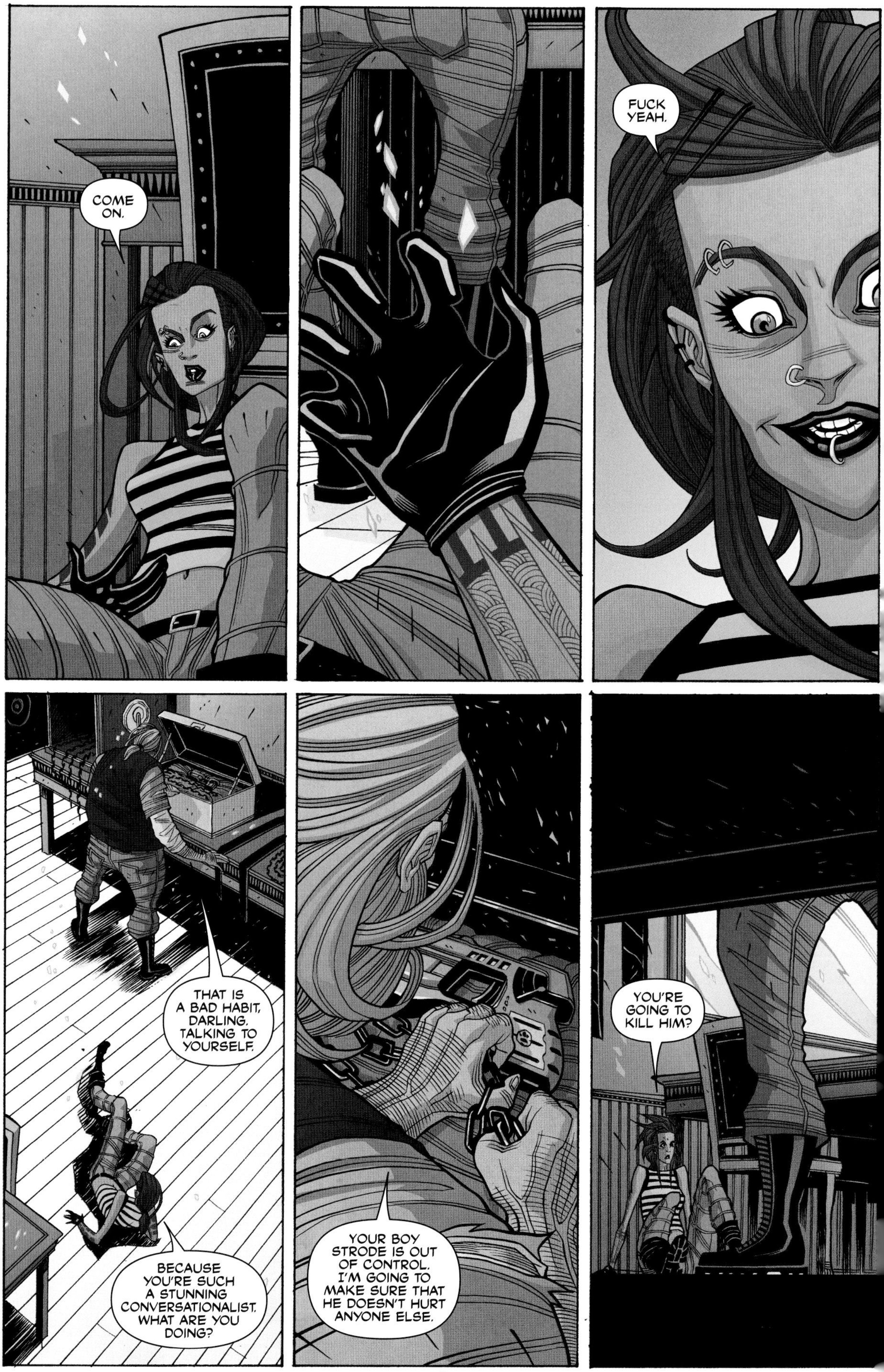
COME ON.
FUCK YEAH.
THAT IS A BAD HABIT, DARLING, TALKING TO YOURSELF.
BECAUSE YOU'RE SUCH A STUNNING CONVERSATIONALIST. WHAT ARE YOU DOING?
YOUR BOY STRODE IS OUT OF CONTROL. I'M GOING TO MAKE SURE THAT HE DOESN'T HURT ANYONE ELSE.
YOU'RE GOING TO KILL HIM?

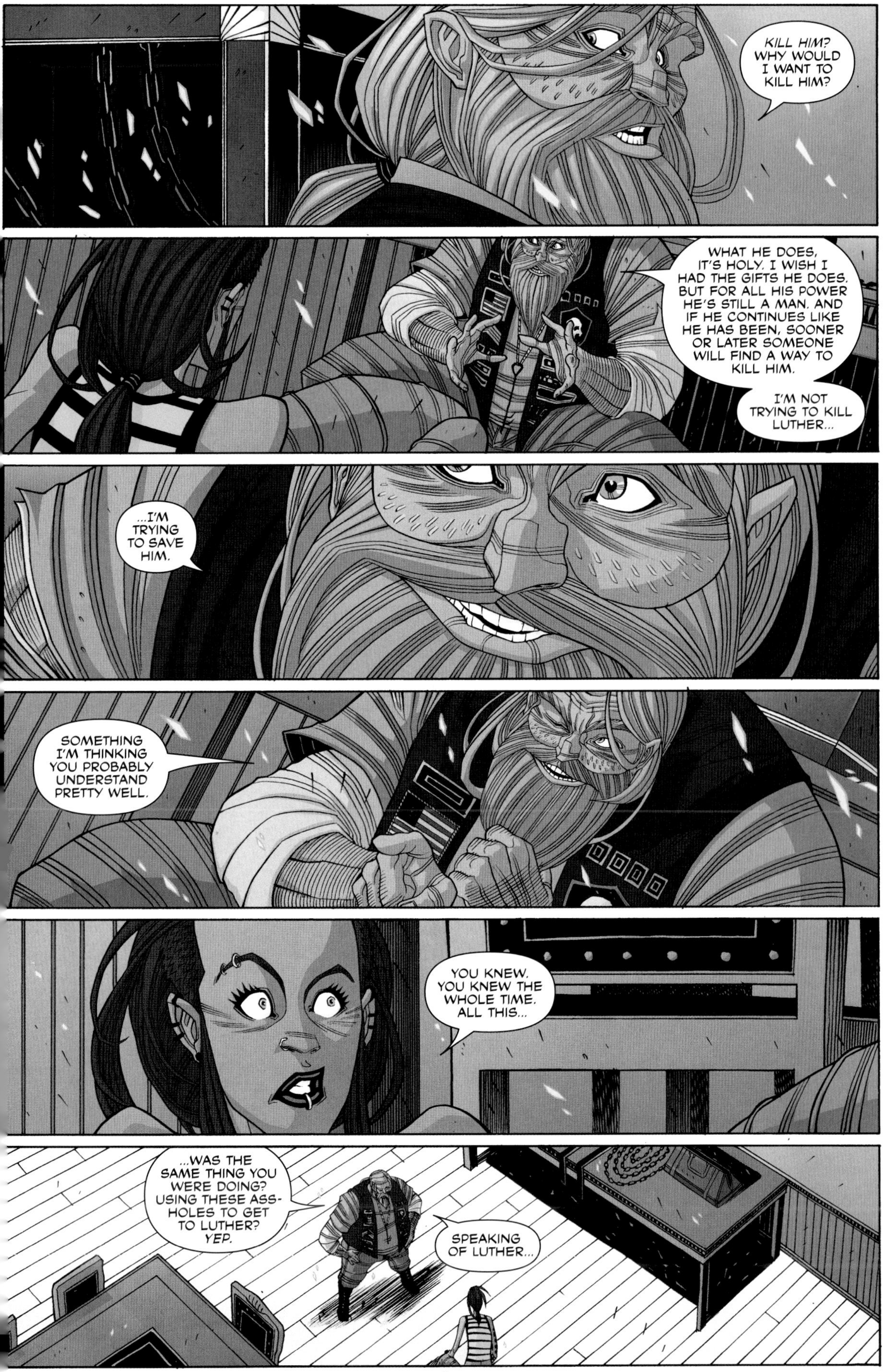
KILL HIM? WHY WOULD I WANT TO KILL HIM?
WHAT HE DOES, IT'S HOLY. I WISH I HAD THE GIFTS HE DOES. BUT FOR ALL HIS POWER HE'S STILL A MAN. AND IF HE CONTINUES LIKE HE HAS BEEN, SOONER OR LATER SOMEONE WILL FIND A WAY TO KILL HIM.
I'M NOT TRYING TO KILL LUTHER...
...I'M TRYING TO SAVE HIM.
SOMETHING I'M THINKING YOU PROBABLY UNDERSTAND PRETTY WELL.
YOU KNEW. YOU KNEW THE WHOLE TIME. ALL THIS...
...WAS THE SAME THING YOU WERE DOING? USING THESE ASS-HOLES TO GET TO LUTHER? *YEP.*
SPEAKING OF LUTHER...

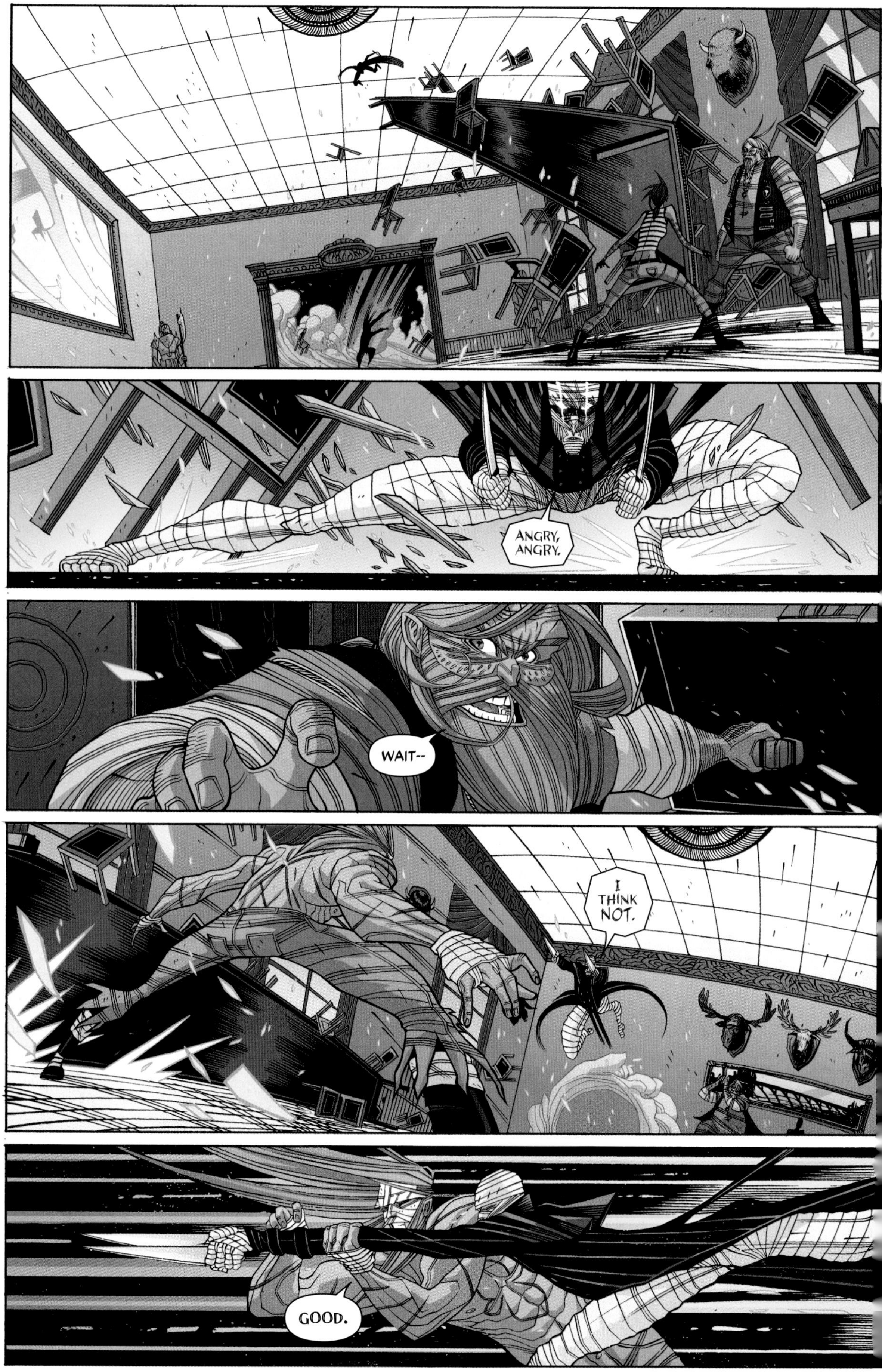
ANGRY, ANGRY.
WAIT--
I THINK NOT.
GOOD.

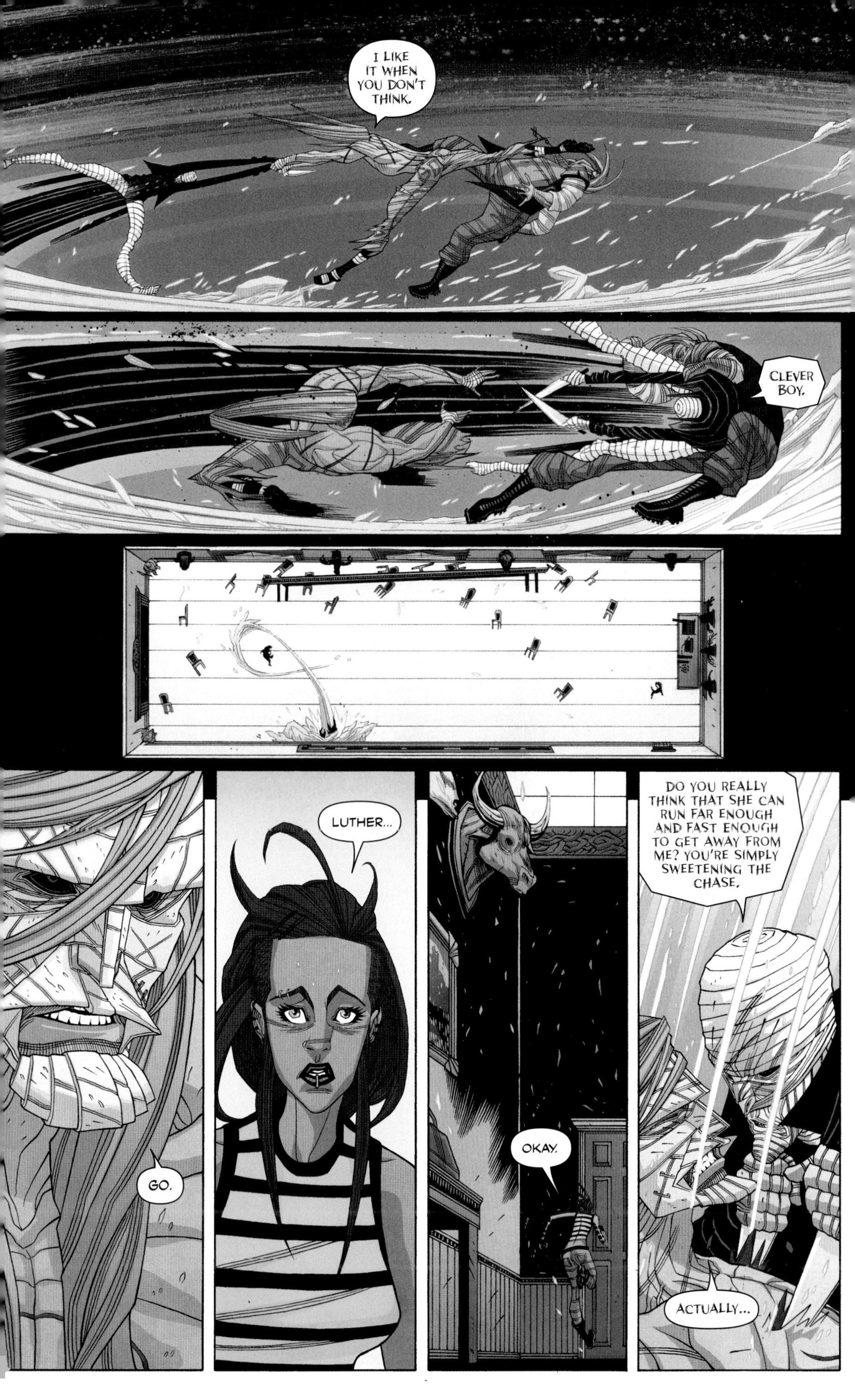
I LIKE IT WHEN YOU DON'T THINK.
CLEVER BOY.
GO.
LUTHER...
OKAY.
DO YOU REALLY THINK THAT SHE CAN RUN FAR ENOUGH AND FAST ENOUGH TO GET AWAY FROM ME? YOU'RE SIMPLY SWEETENING THE CHASE.
ACTUALLY...

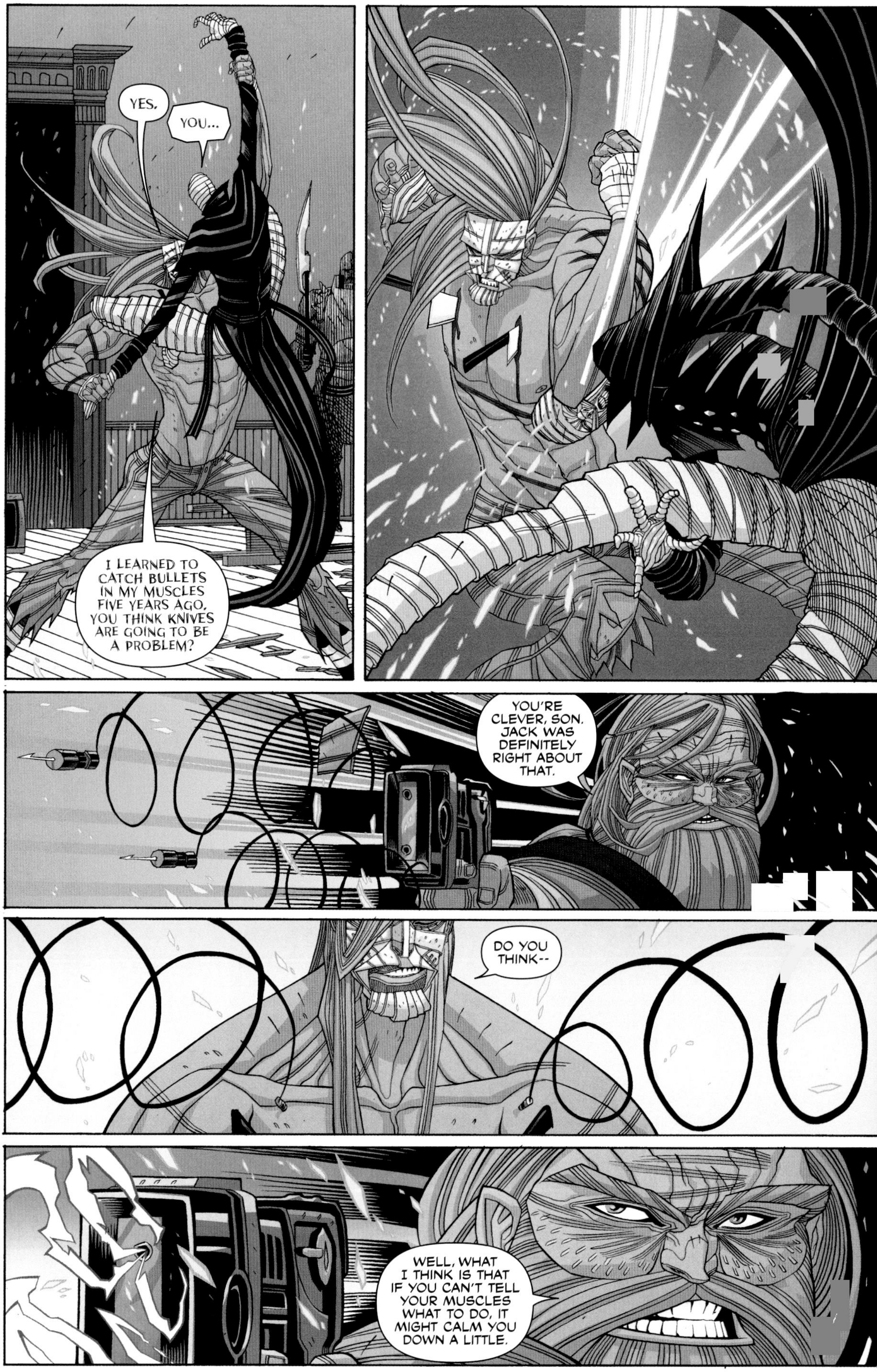
YES,
YOU...
I LEARNED TO CATCH BULLETS IN MY MUSCLES FIVE YEARS AGO, YOU THINK KNIVES ARE GOING TO BE A PROBLEM?
YOU'RE CLEVER, SON. JACK WAS DEFINITELY RIGHT ABOUT THAT.
DO YOU THINK--
WELL, WHAT I THINK IS THAT IF YOU CAN'T TELL YOUR MUSCLES WHAT TO DO, IT MIGHT CALM YOU DOWN A LITTLE.

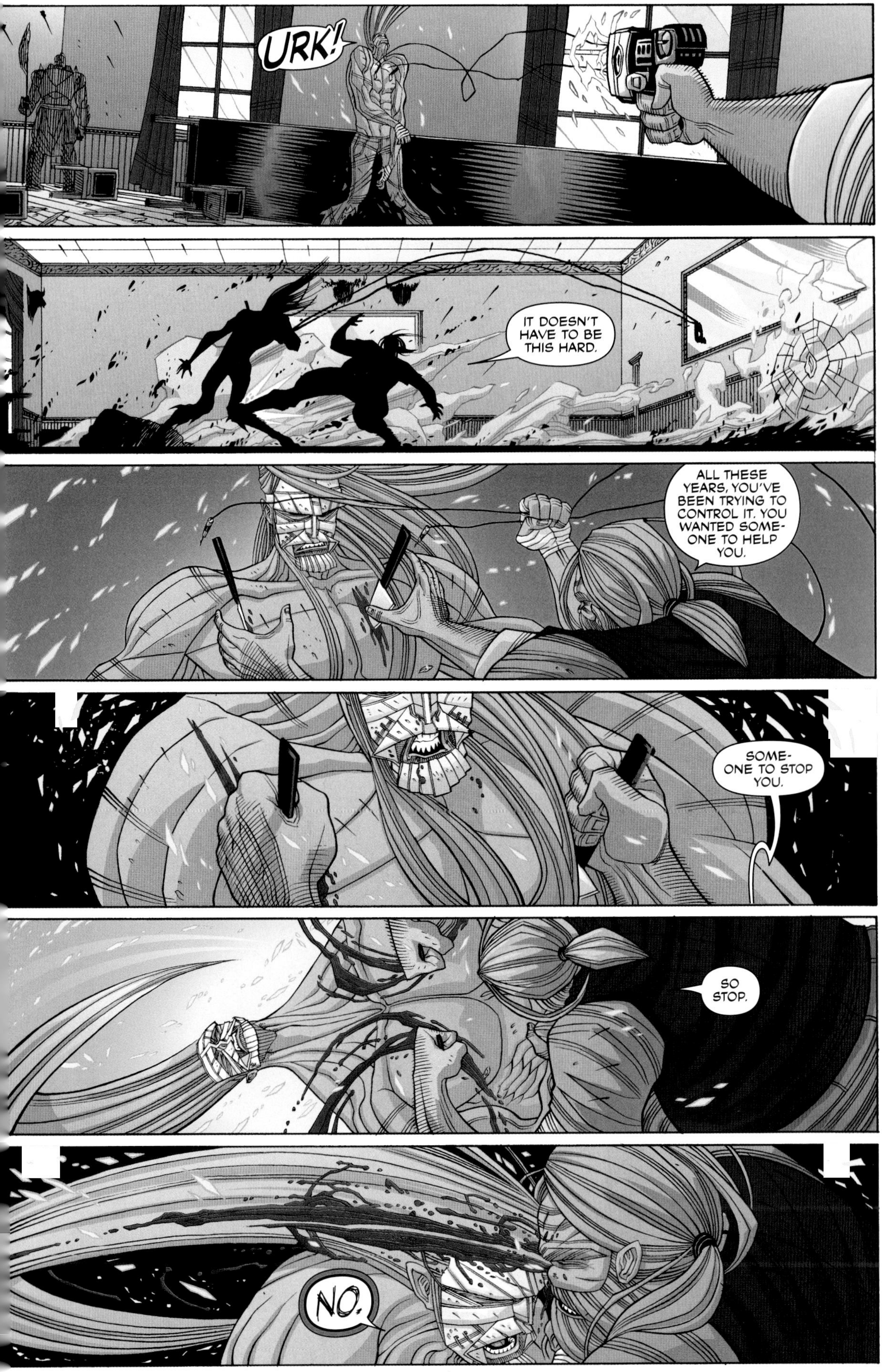
URK!
IT DOESN'T HAVE TO BE THIS HARD.
ALL THESE YEARS, YOU'VE BEEN TRYING TO CONTROL IT. YOU WANTED SOME-ONE TO HELP YOU.
SOME-ONE TO STOP YOU.
SO STOP.
NO.

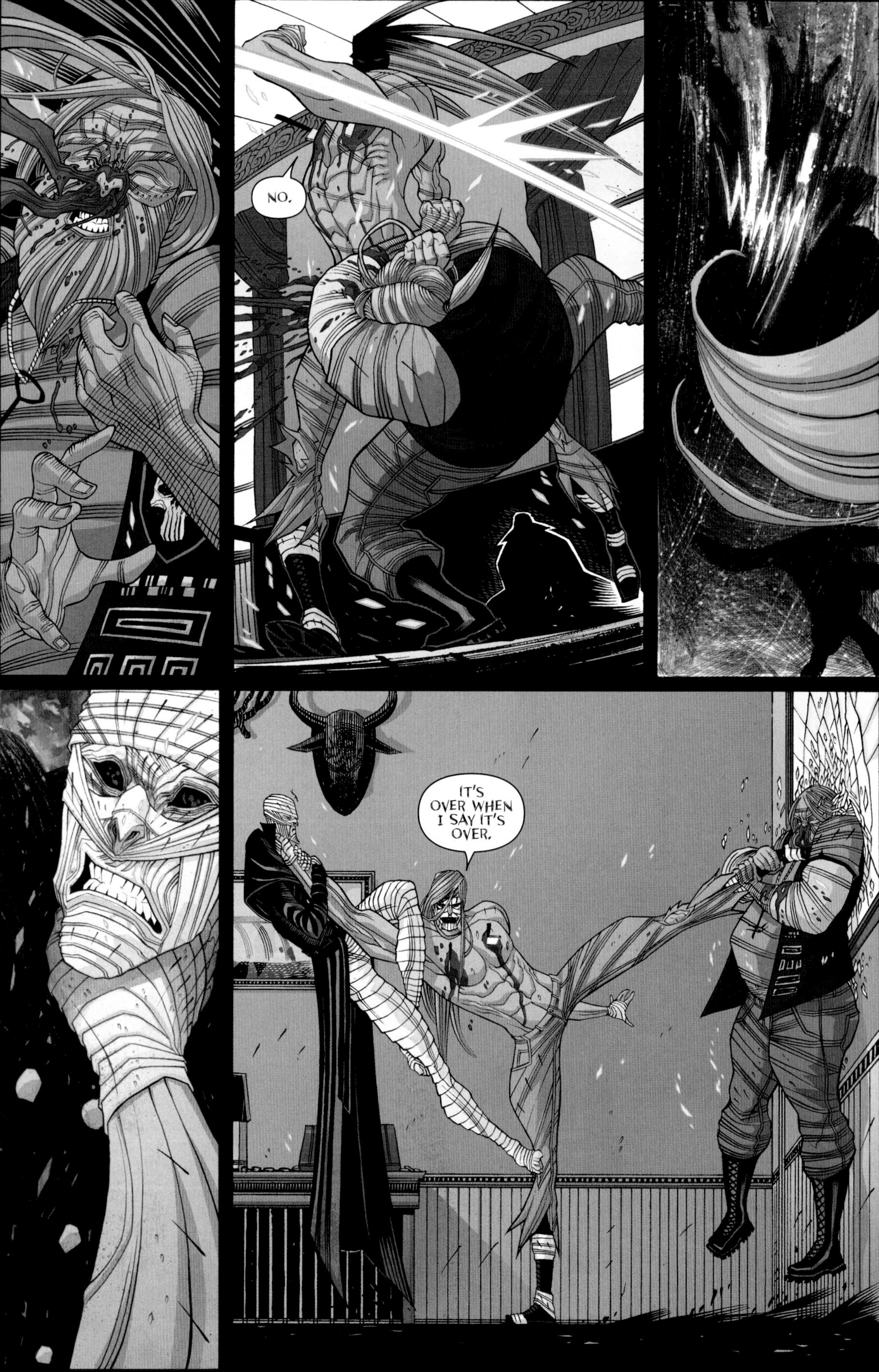
NO.
IT'S OVER WHEN I SAY IT'S OVER.

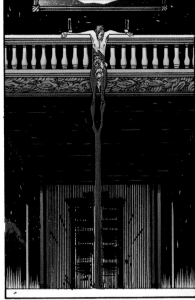

OH
SHIT.

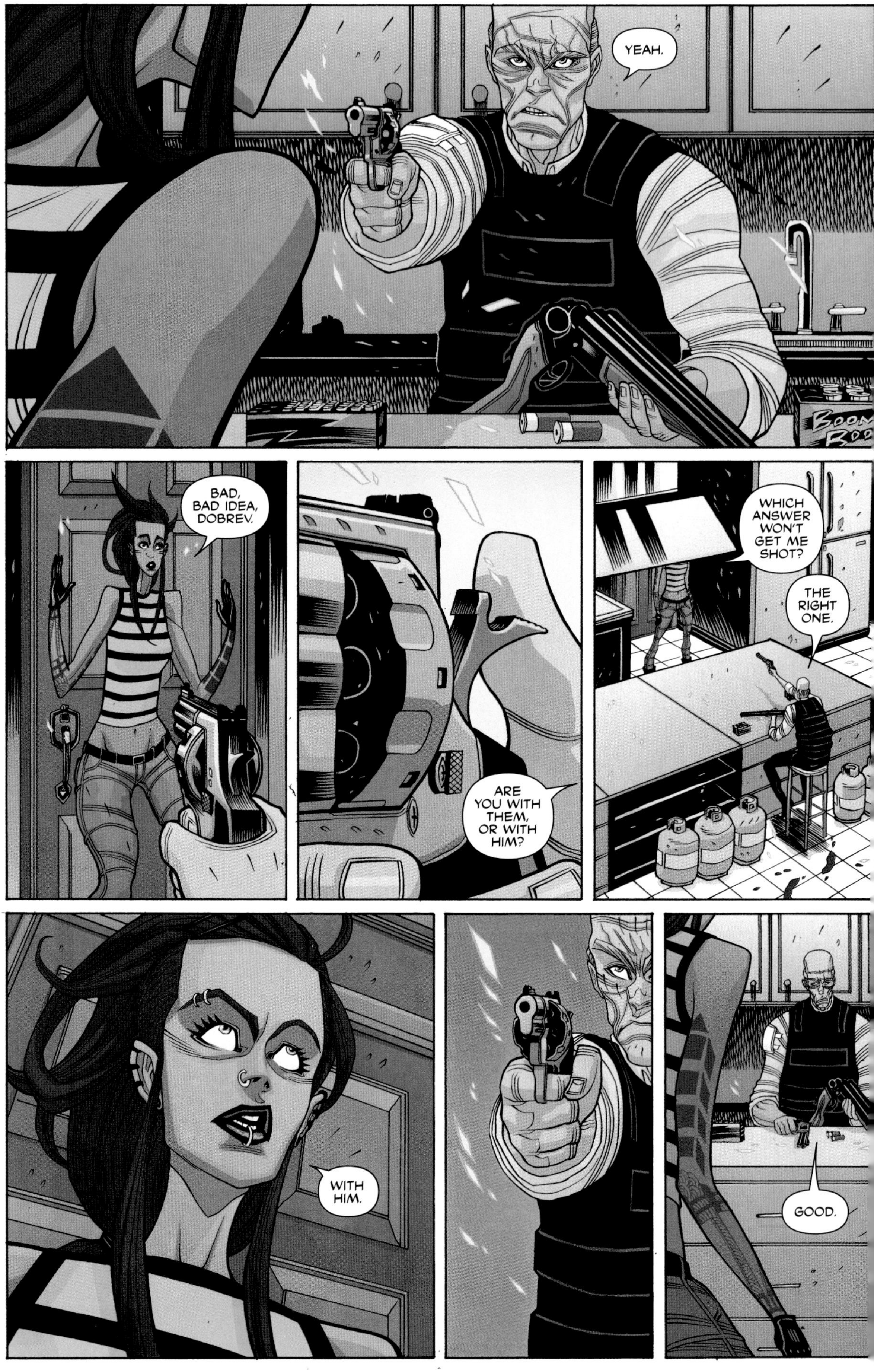
YEAH.
BAD, BAD IDEA, DOBREV.
ARE YOU WITH THEM, OR WITH HIM?
WHICH ANSWER WON'T GET ME SHOT?
THE RIGHT ONE.
WITH HIM.
GOOD.

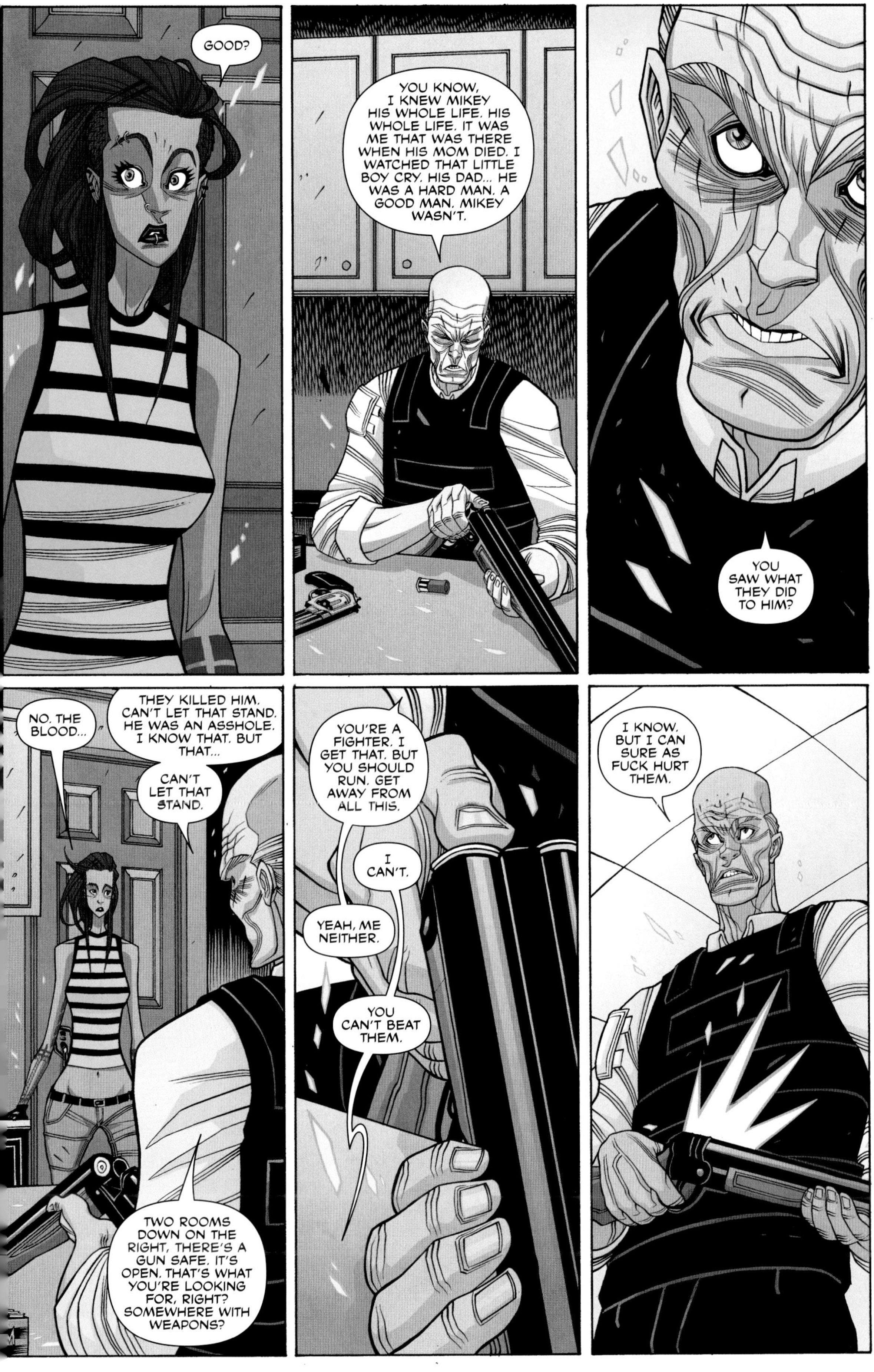
GOOD?
YOU KNOW, I KNEW MIKEY HIS WHOLE LIFE. HIS WHOLE LIFE. IT WAS ME THAT WAS THERE WHEN HIS MOM DIED. I WATCHED THAT LITTLE BOY CRY. HIS DAD... HE WAS A HARD MAN. A GOOD MAN. MIKEY WASN'T.
YOU SAW WHAT THEY DID TO HIM?
NO. THE BLOOD...
THEY KILLED HIM. CAN'T LET THAT STAND. HE WAS AN ASSHOLE. I KNOW THAT. BUT THAT...
CAN'T LET THAT STAND.
TWO ROOMS DOWN ON THE RIGHT, THERE'S A GUN SAFE. IT'S OPEN. THAT'S WHAT YOU'RE LOOKING FOR, RIGHT? SOMEWHERE WITH WEAPONS?
YOU'RE A FIGHTER. I GET THAT. BUT YOU SHOULD RUN. GET AWAY FROM ALL THIS.
I CAN'T.
YEAH, ME NEITHER.
YOU CAN'T BEAT THEM.
I KNOW. BUT I CAN SURE AS FUCK HURT THEM.

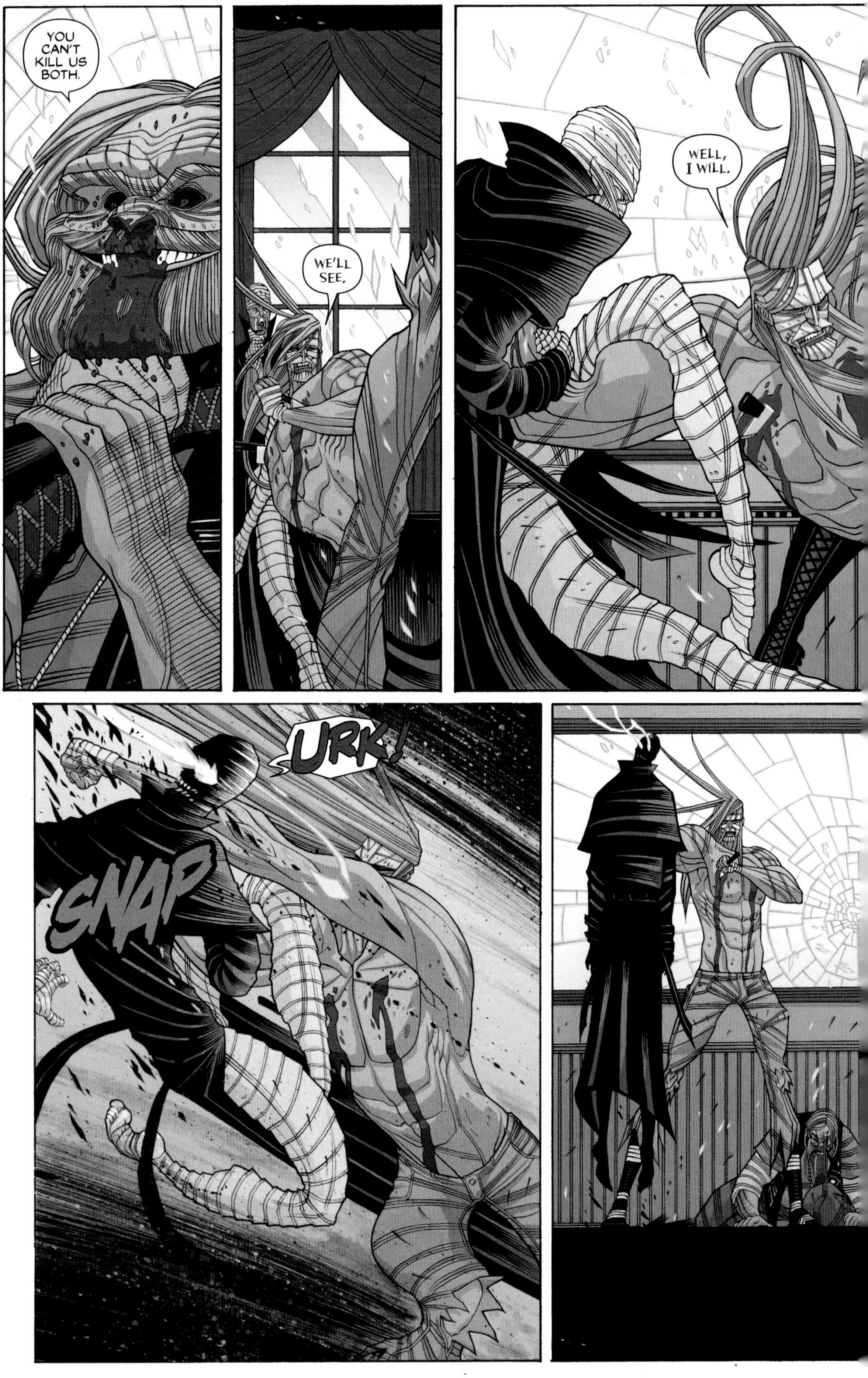
YOU CAN'T KILL US BOTH.
WE'LL SEE.
WELL, I WILL.
URK!
SNAP

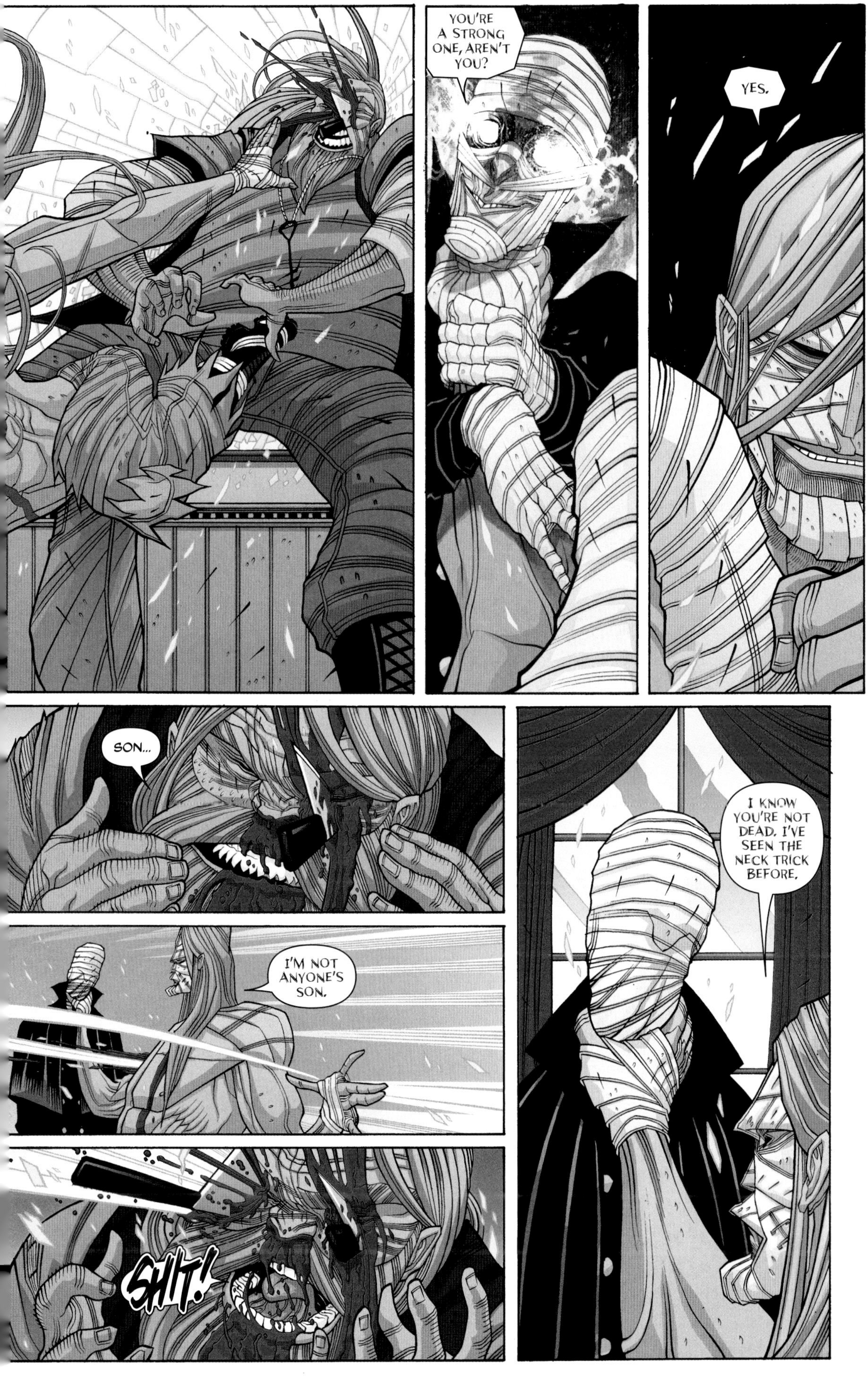
YOU'RE A STRONG ONE, AREN'T YOU?
YES.
SON...
I'M NOT ANYONE'S SON.
SHLIT!
I KNOW YOU'RE NOT DEAD. I'VE SEEN THE NECK TRICK BEFORE.

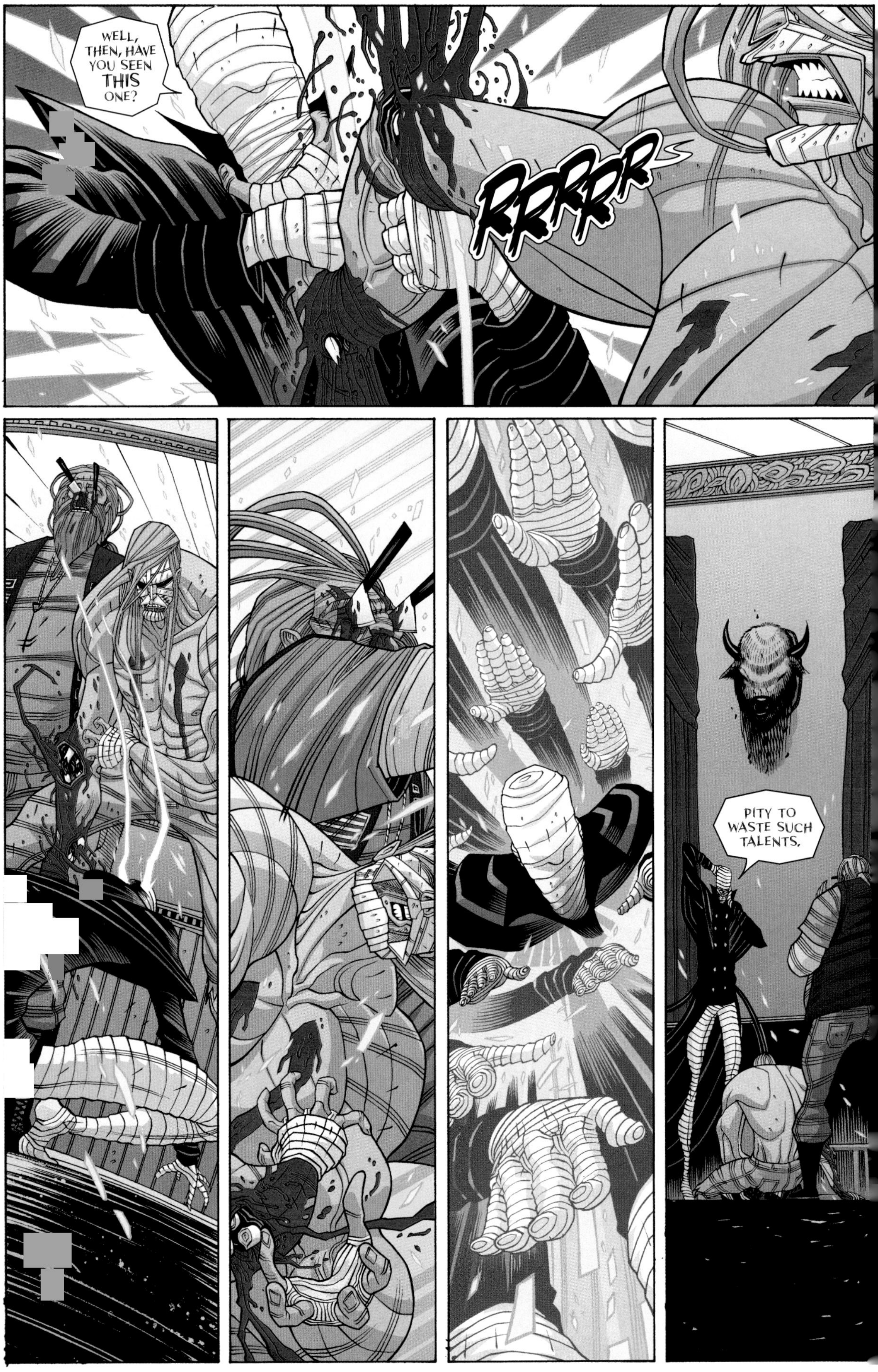
WELL, THEN, HAVE YOU SEEN THIS ONE?
RRRRR
PITY TO WASTE SUCH TALENTS.

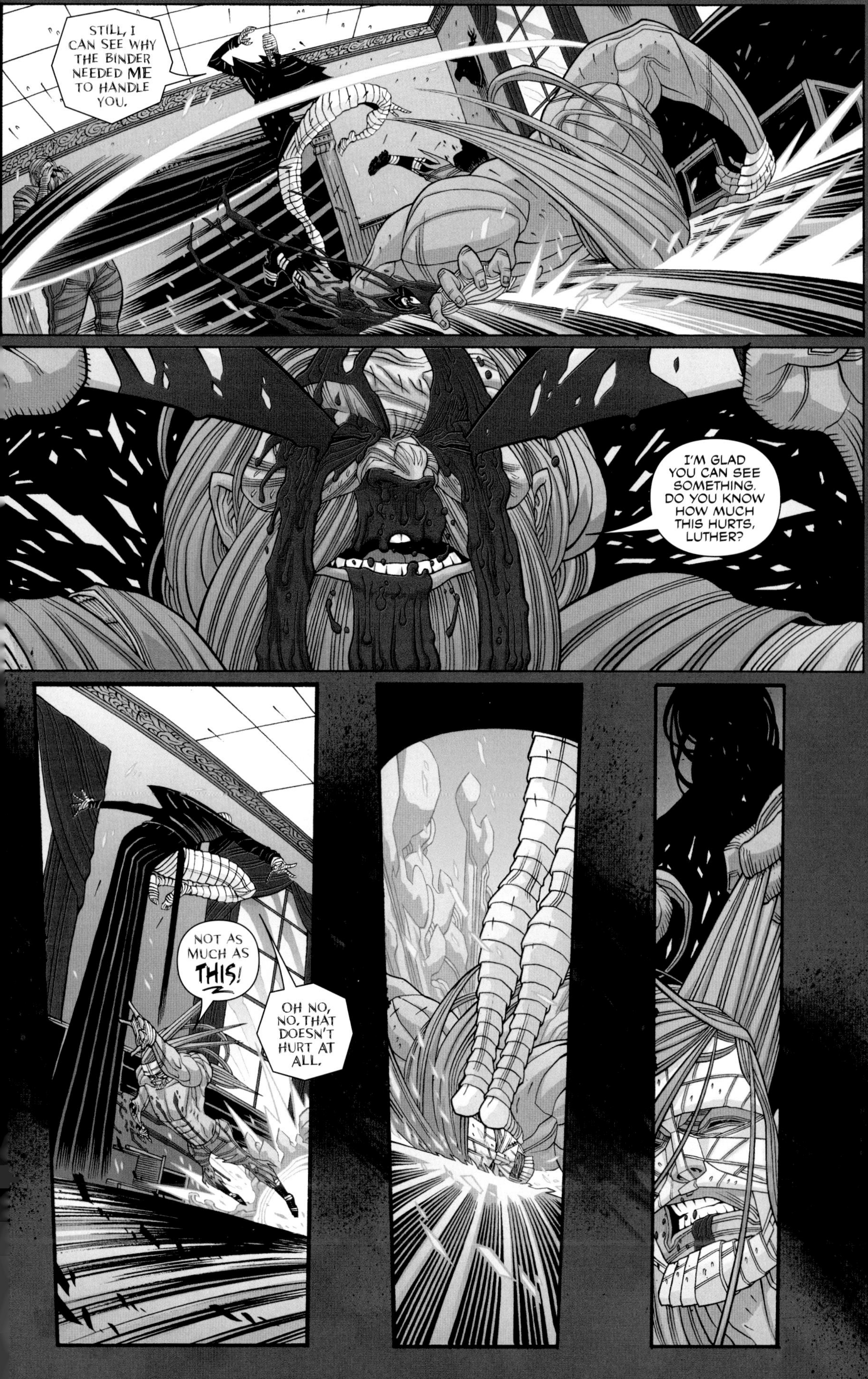
STILL, I CAN SEE WHY THE BINDER NEEDED ME TO HANDLE YOU.
I'M GLAD YOU CAN SEE SOMETHING. DO YOU KNOW HOW MUCH THIS HURTS, LUTHER?
NOT AS MUCH AS THIS!
OH NO, NO, THAT DOESN'T HURT AT ALL.

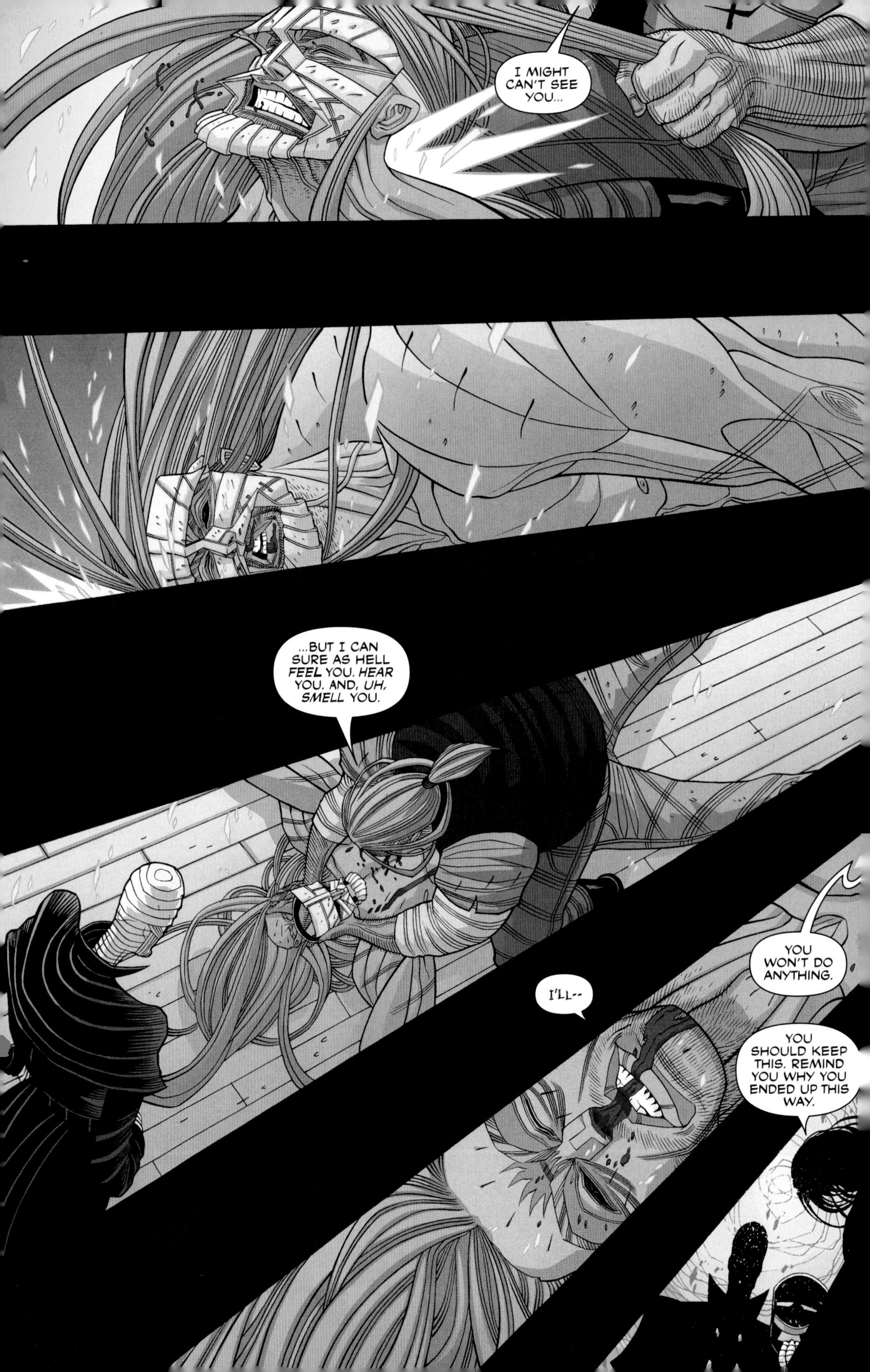
I MIGHT CAN'T SEE YOU...
...BUT I CAN SURE AS HELL FEEL YOU. HEAR YOU. AND, UH, SMELL YOU.
I'LL--
YOU WON'T DO ANYTHING.
YOU SHOULD KEEP THIS. REMIND YOU WHY YOU ENDED UP THIS WAY.

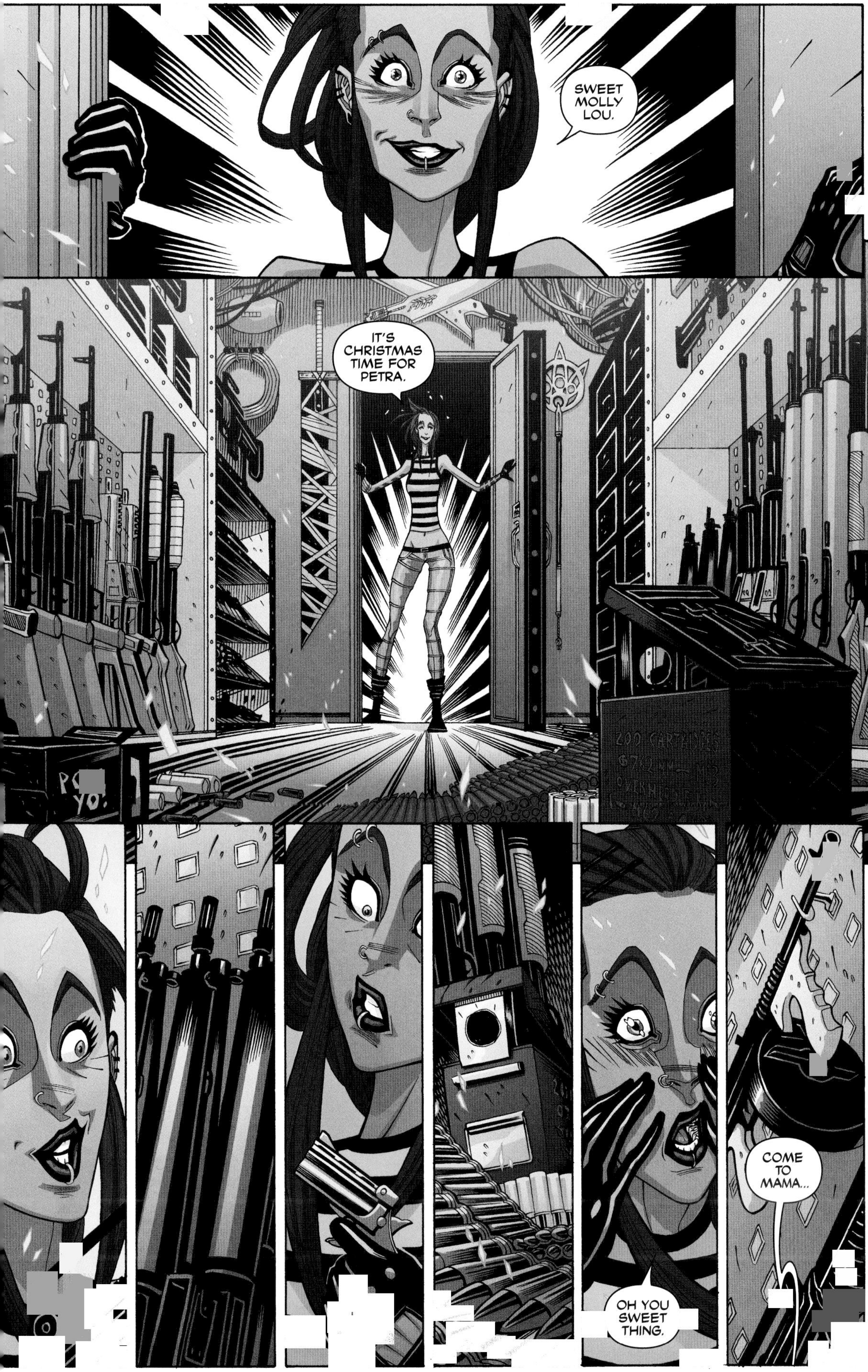
SWEET MOLLY LOU.
IT'S CHRISTMAS TIME FOR PETRA.
OH YOU SWEET THING.
COME TO MAMA...

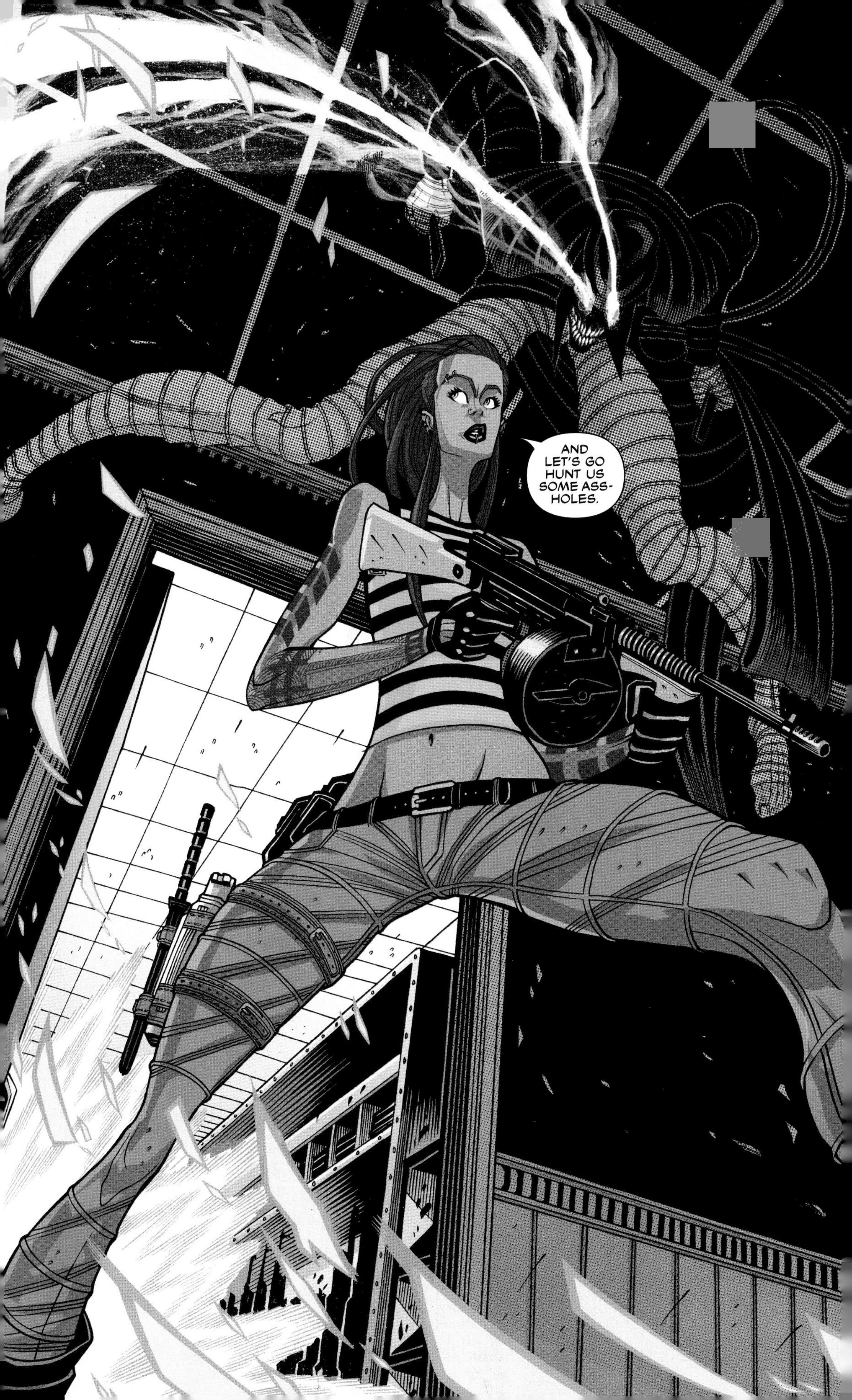
AND LET'S GO HUNT US SOME ASS-HOLES.

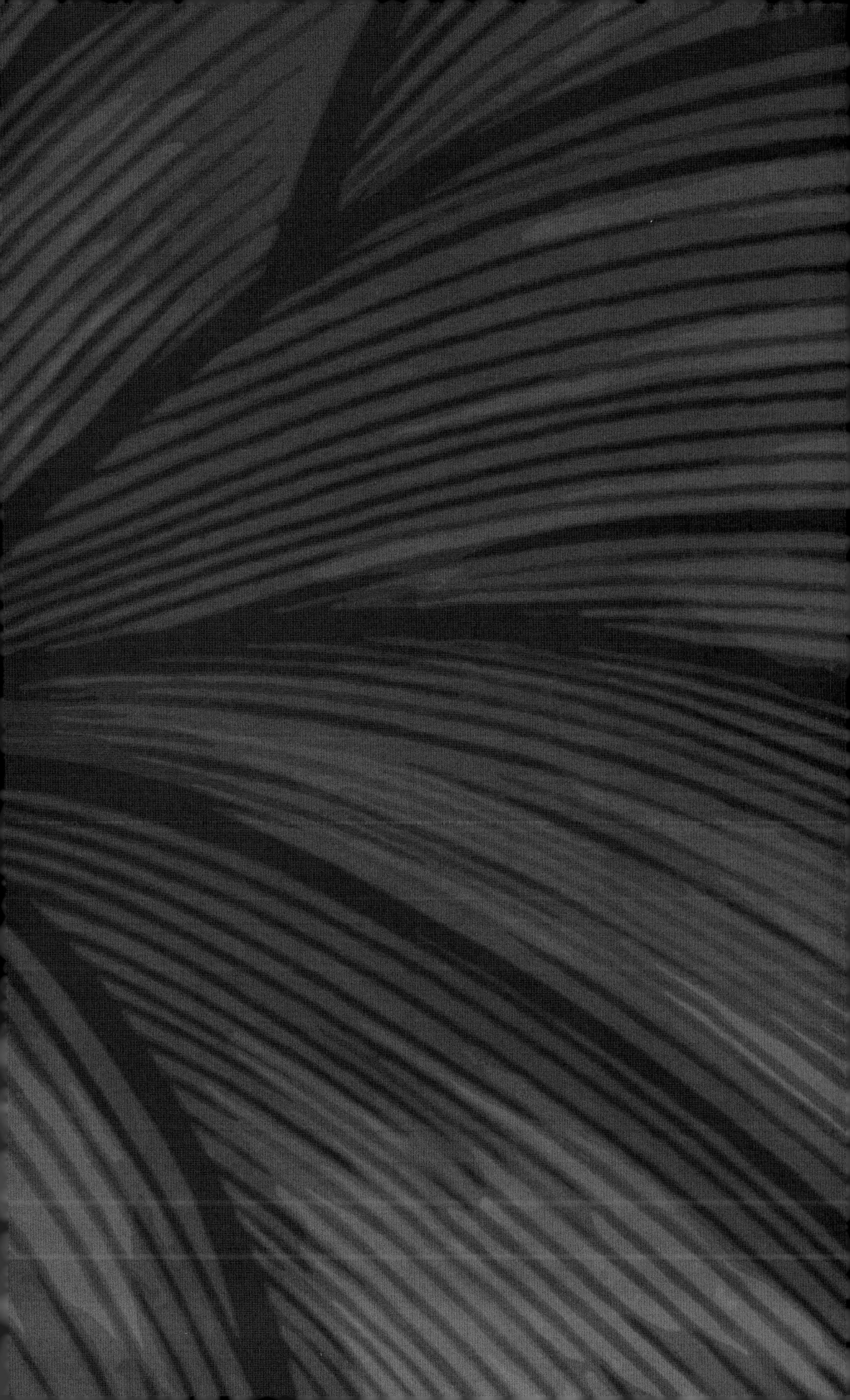

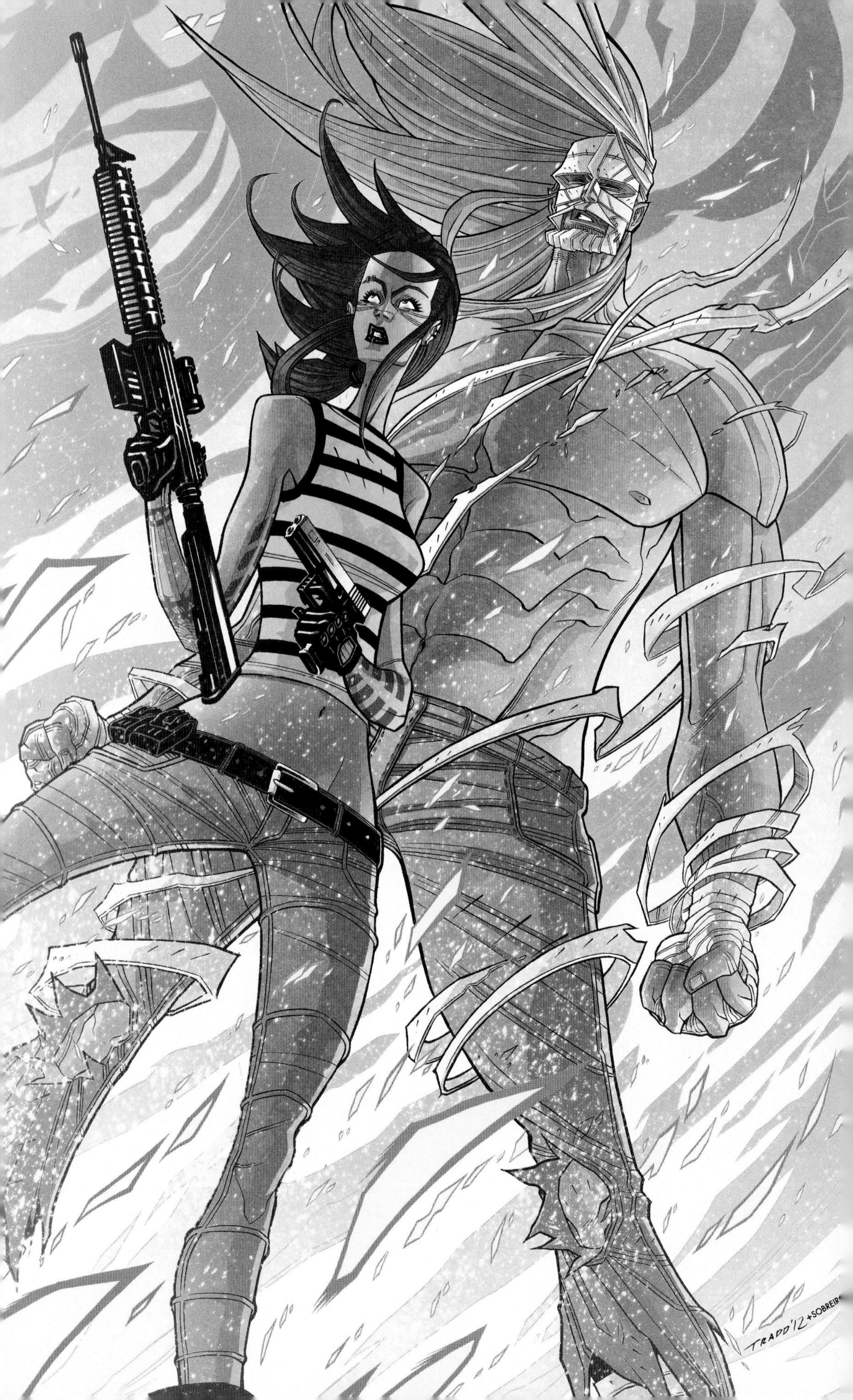
TRADD'12

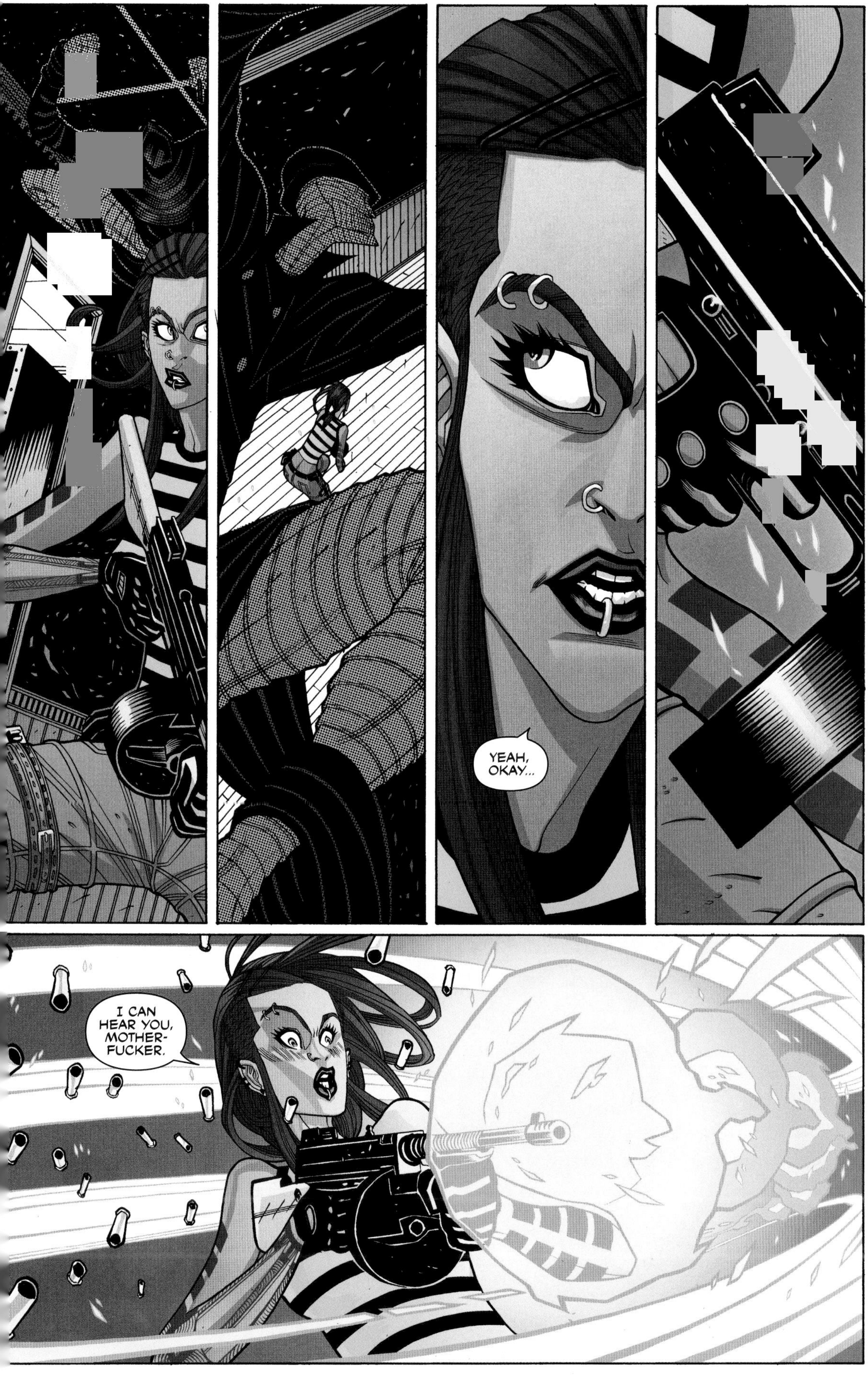
YEAH, OKAY...
I CAN HEAR YOU, MOTHER-FUCKER.

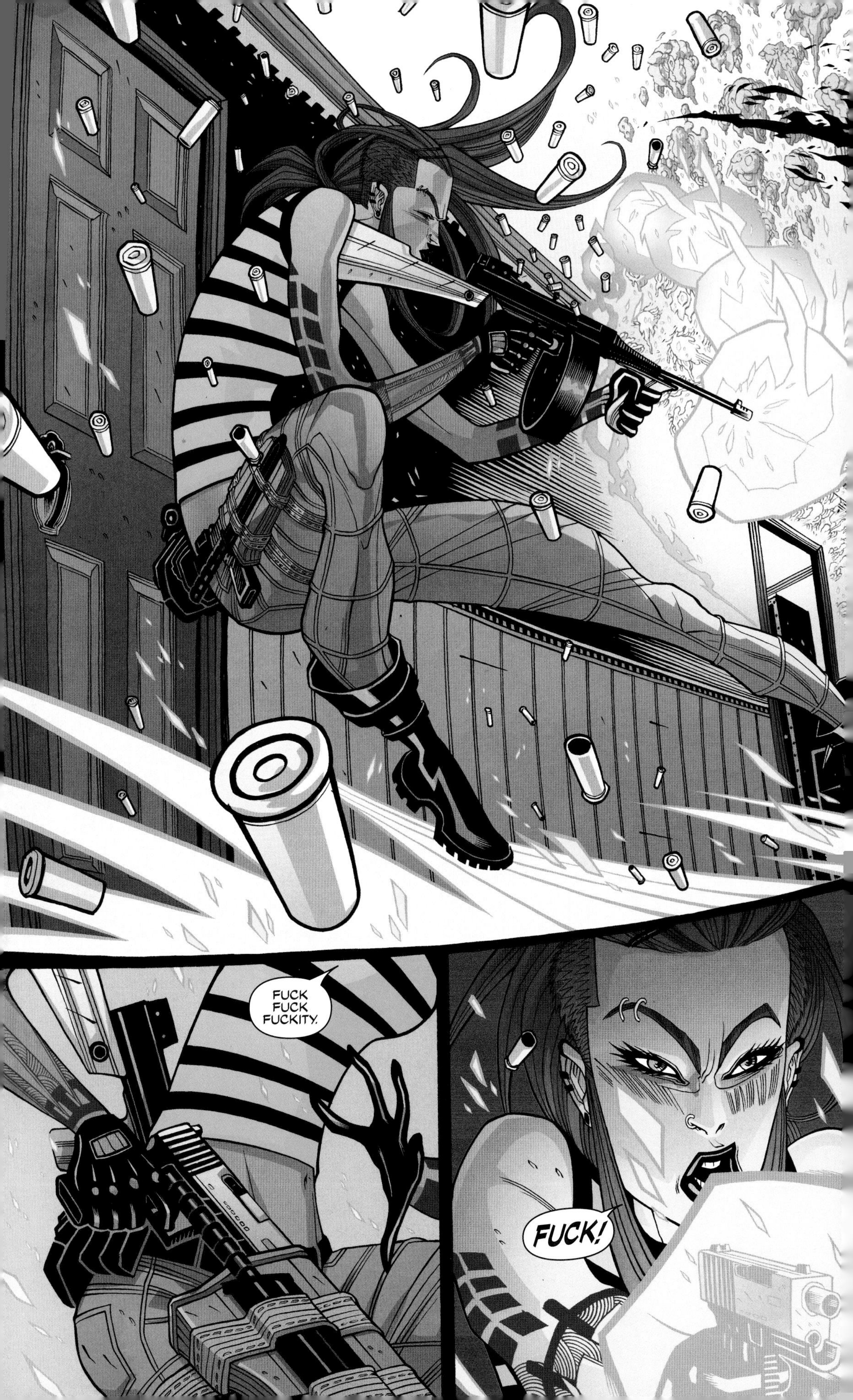
FUCK
FUCK
FUCKITY.
FUCK!

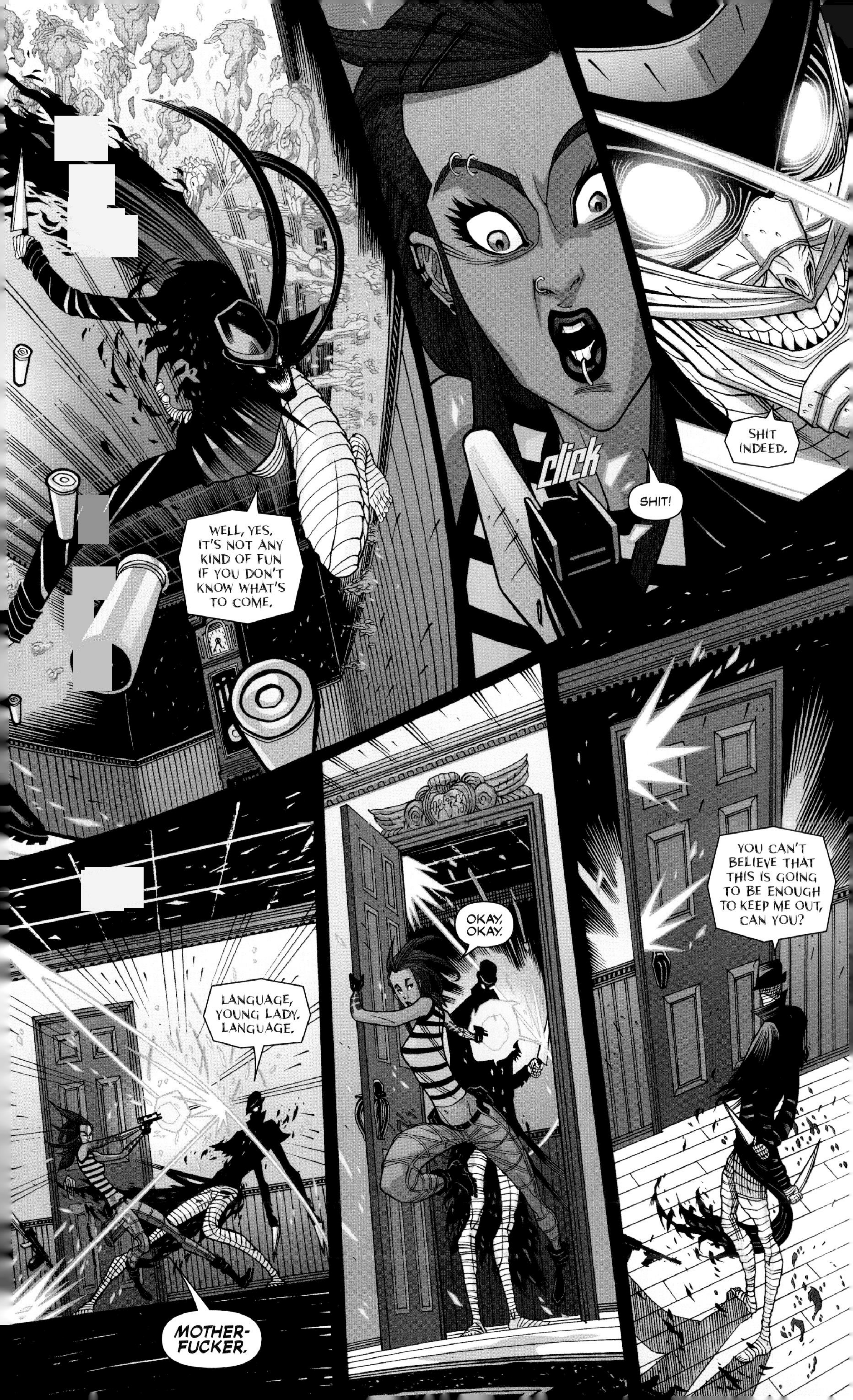
WELL, YES. IT'S NOT ANY KIND OF FUN IF YOU DON'T KNOW WHAT'S TO COME.
click
SHIT!
SHIT INDEED.
MOTHER-FUCKER.
LANGUAGE, YOUNG LADY. LANGUAGE.
OKAY, OKAY.
YOU CAN'T BELIEVE THAT THIS IS GOING TO BE ENOUGH TO KEEP ME OUT, CAN YOU?

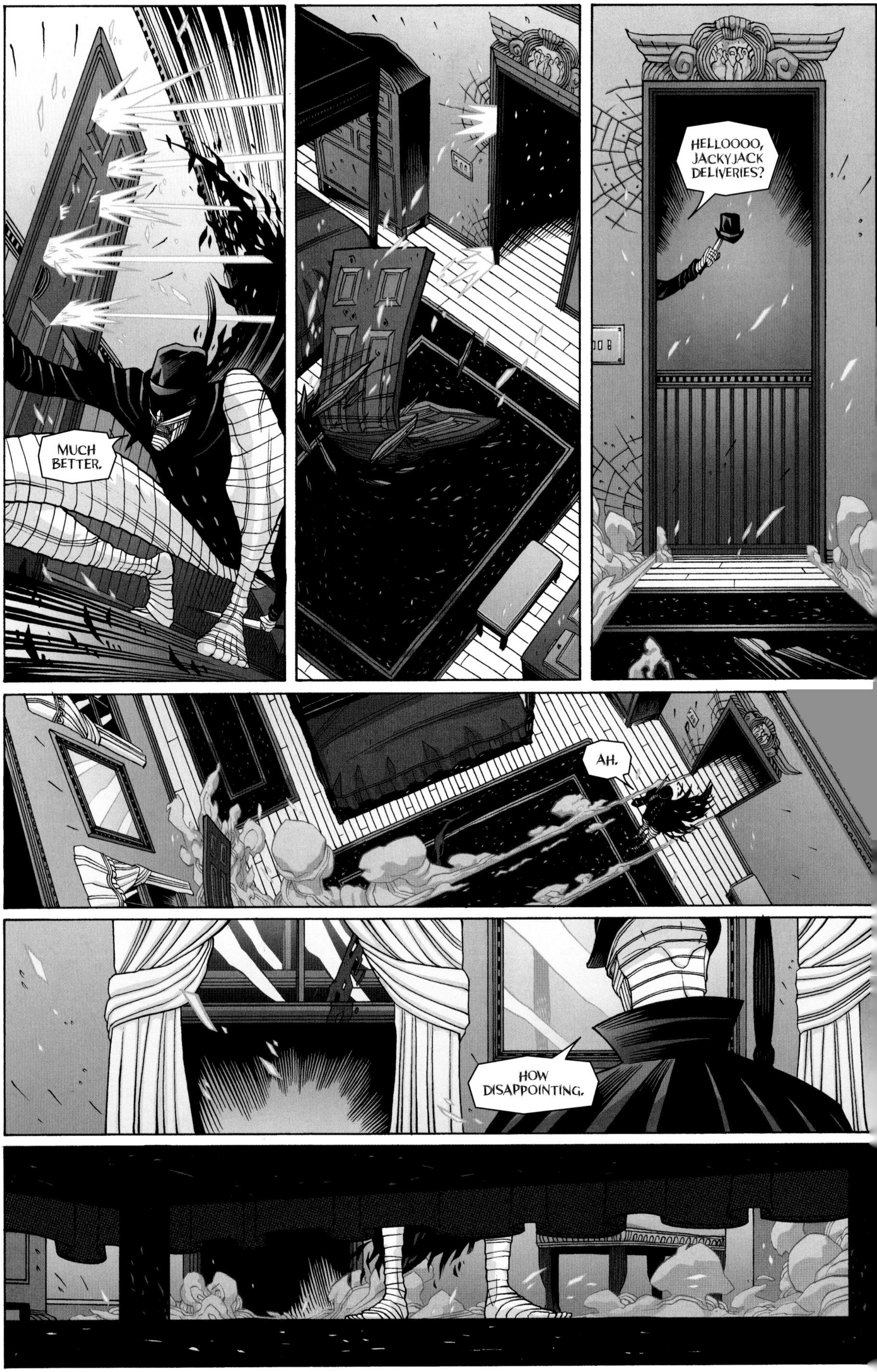
MUCH BETTER.
HELLOOOO, JACKYJACK DELIVERIES?
AH.
HOW DISAPPOINTING.

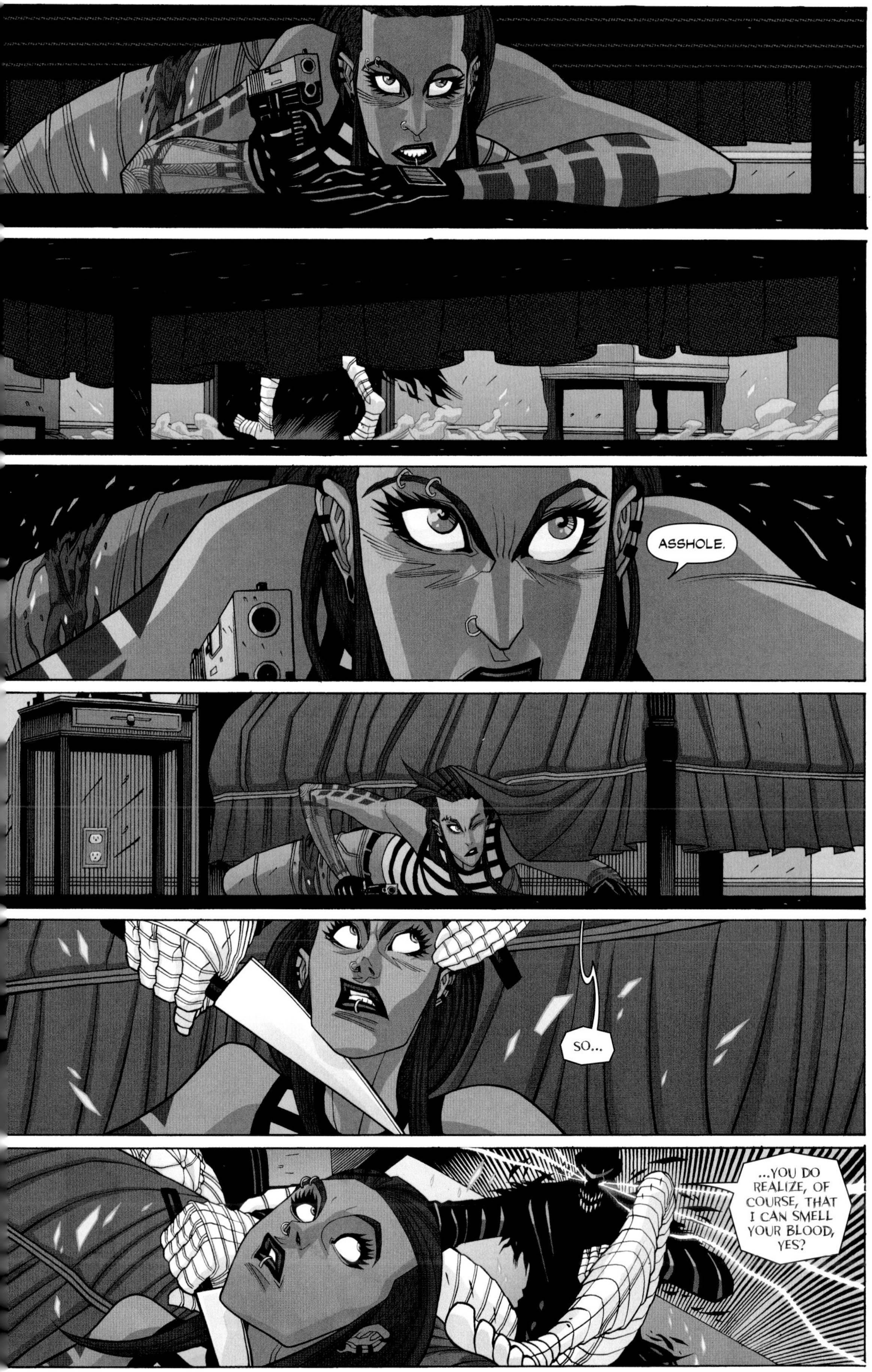
ASSHOLE.
SO...
...YOU DO REALIZE, OF COURSE, THAT I CAN SMELL YOUR BLOOD, YES?

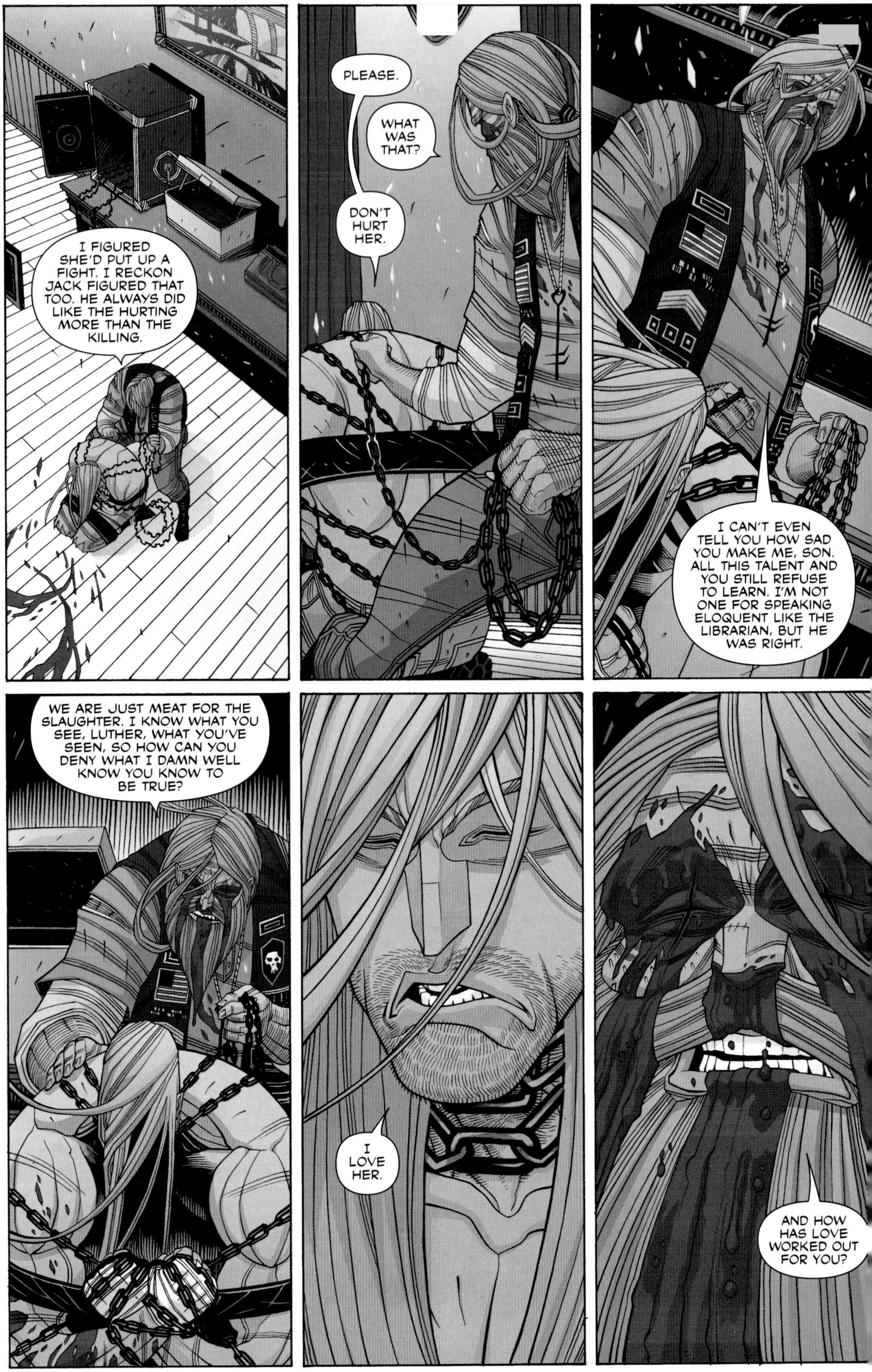
I FIGURED SHE'D PUT UP A FIGHT. I RECKON JACK FIGURED THAT TOO. HE ALWAYS DID LIKE THE HURTING MORE THAN THE KILLING.
PLEASE.
WHAT WAS THAT?
DON'T HURT HER.
I CAN'T EVEN TELL YOU HOW SAD YOU MAKE ME, SON. ALL THIS TALENT AND YOU STILL REFUSE TO LEARN. I'M NOT ONE FOR SPEAKING ELOQUENT LIKE THE LIBRARIAN, BUT HE WAS RIGHT.
WE ARE JUST MEAT FOR THE SLAUGHTER. I KNOW WHAT YOU SEE, LUTHER, WHAT YOU'VE SEEN, SO HOW CAN YOU DENY WHAT I DAMN WELL KNOW YOU KNOW TO BE TRUE?
I LOVE HER.
AND HOW HAS LOVE WORKED OUT FOR YOU?

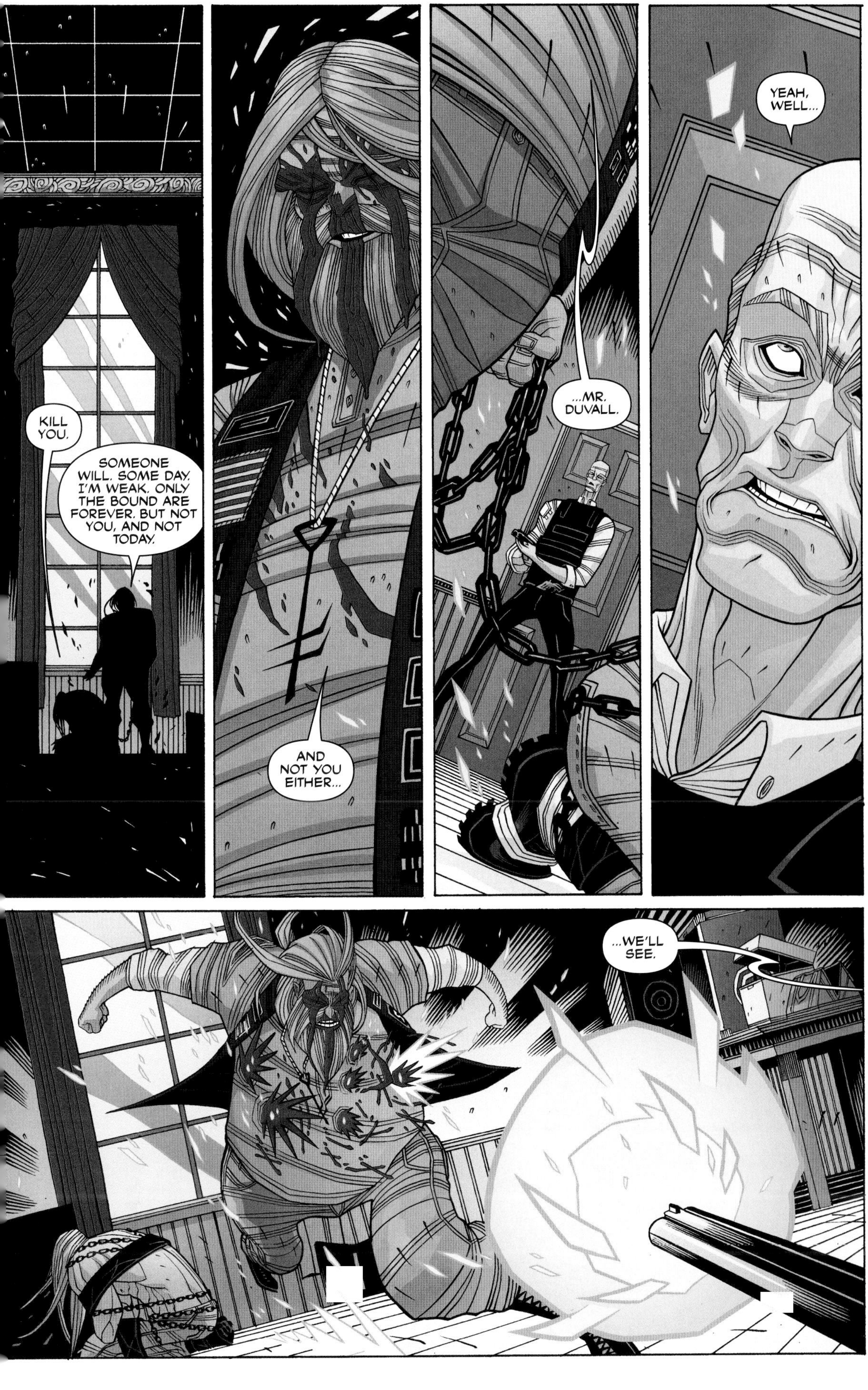
KILL YOU.
SOMEONE WILL. SOME DAY. I'M WEAK. ONLY THE BOUND ARE FOREVER. BUT NOT YOU, AND NOT TODAY.
AND NOT YOU EITHER...
...MR. DUVALL.
YEAH, WELL...
...WE'LL SEE.

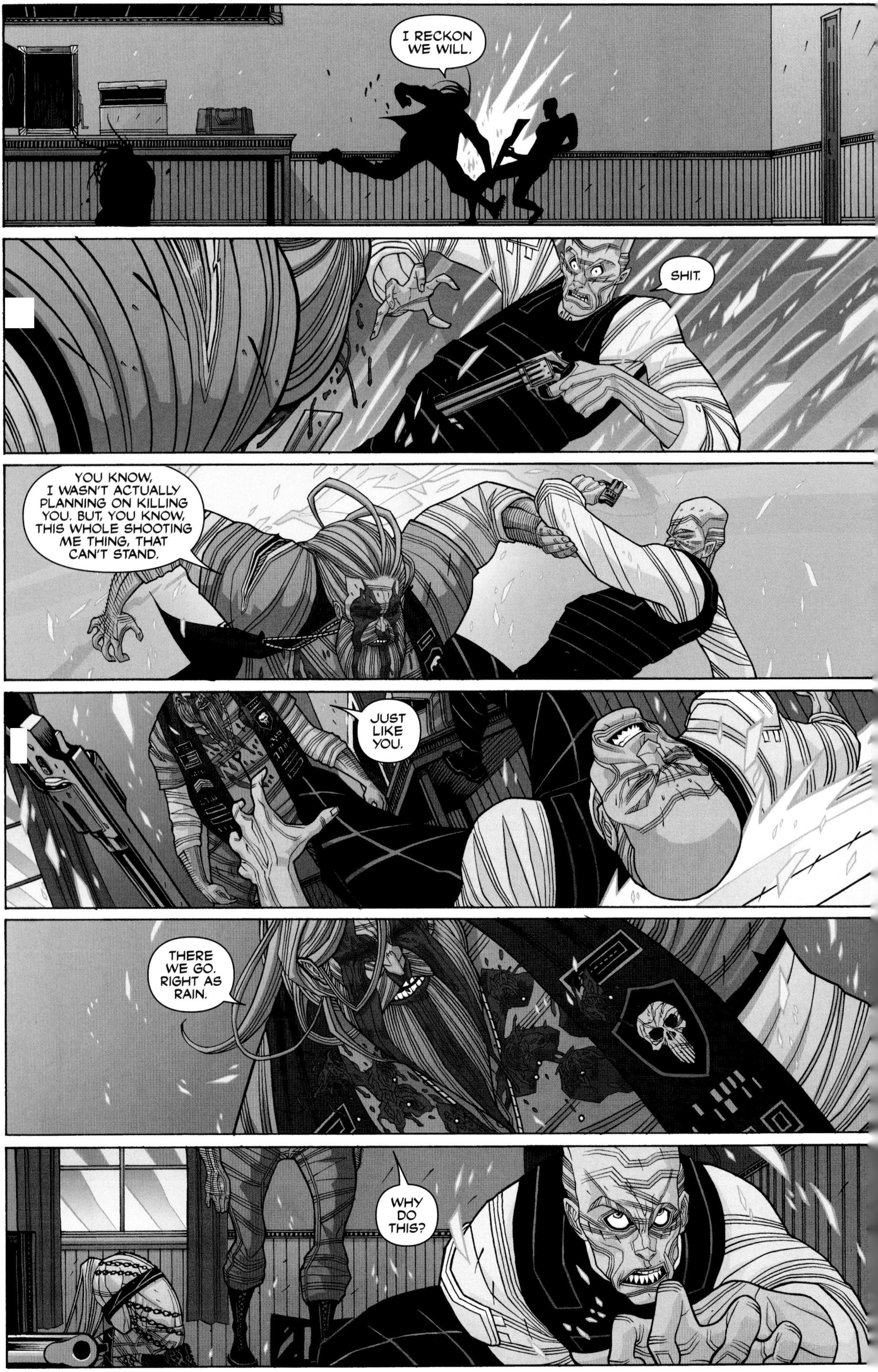
I RECKON WE WILL.
SHIT.
YOU KNOW, I WASN'T ACTUALLY PLANNING ON KILLING YOU. BUT, YOU KNOW, THIS WHOLE SHOOTING ME THING, THAT CAN'T STAND.
JUST LIKE YOU.
THERE WE GO. RIGHT AS RAIN.
WHY DO THIS?

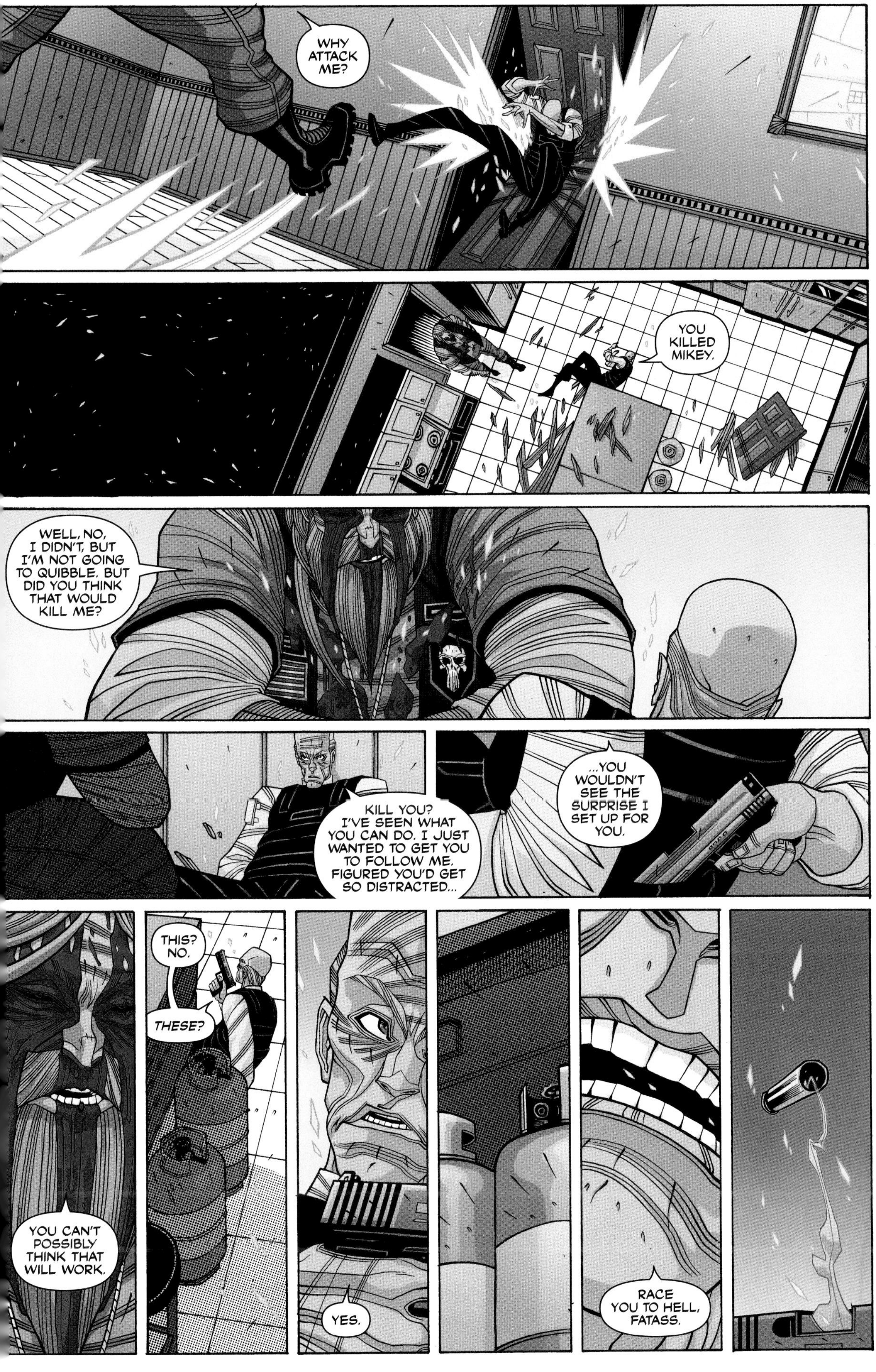
WHY ATTACK ME?
YOU KILLED MIKEY.
WELL, NO, I DIDN'T, BUT I'M NOT GOING TO QUIBBLE. BUT DID YOU THINK THAT WOULD KILL ME?
KILL YOU? I'VE SEEN WHAT YOU CAN DO. I JUST WANTED TO GET YOU TO FOLLOW ME. FIGURED YOU'D GET SO DISTRACTED...
...YOU WOULDN'T SEE THE SURPRISE I SET UP FOR YOU.
YOU CAN'T POSSIBLY THINK THAT WILL WORK.
THIS? NO.
THESE?
YES.
RACE YOU TO HELL, FATASS.

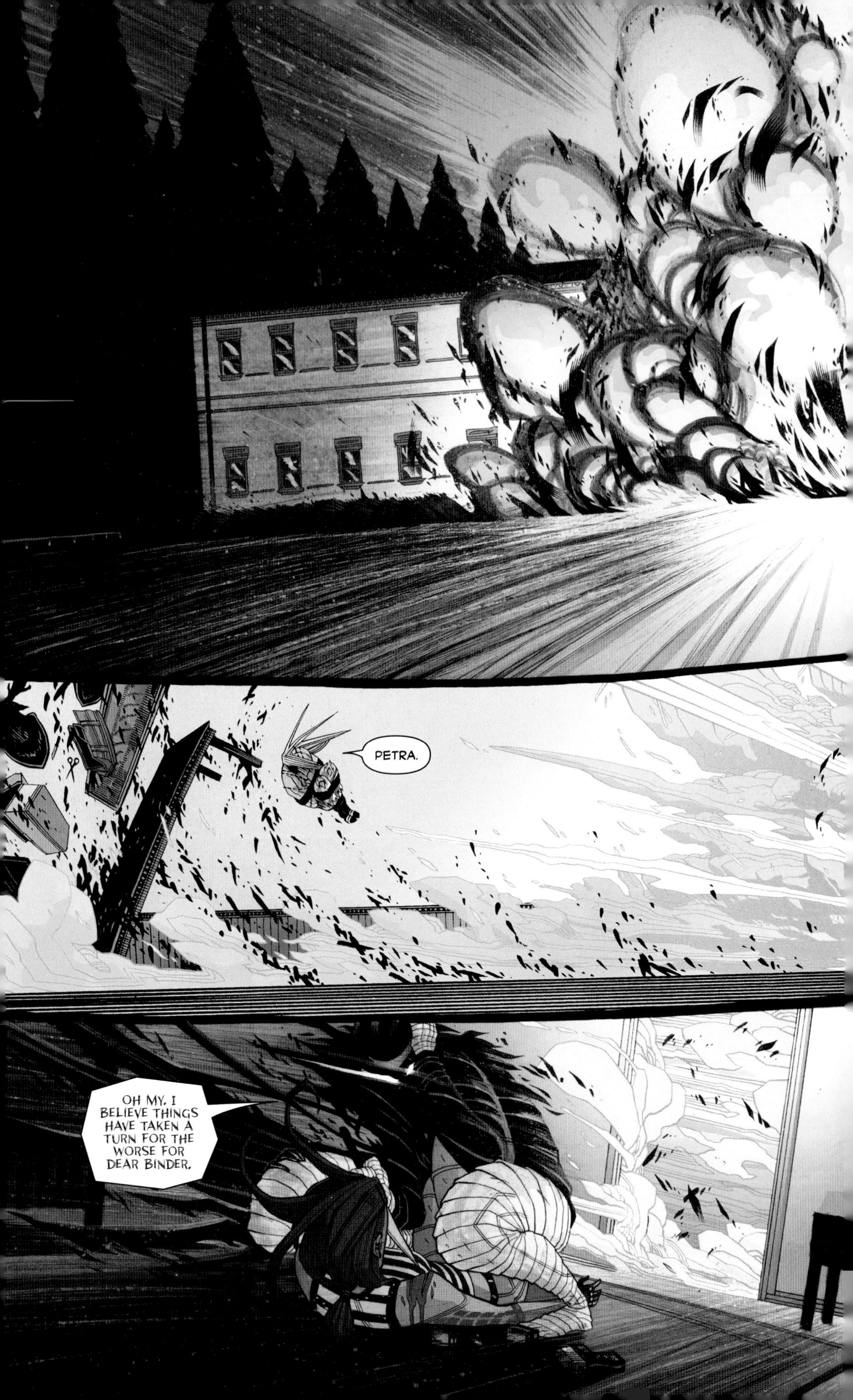
PETRA.
OH MY. I BELIEVE THINGS HAVE TAKEN A TURN FOR THE WORSE FOR DEAR BINDER.

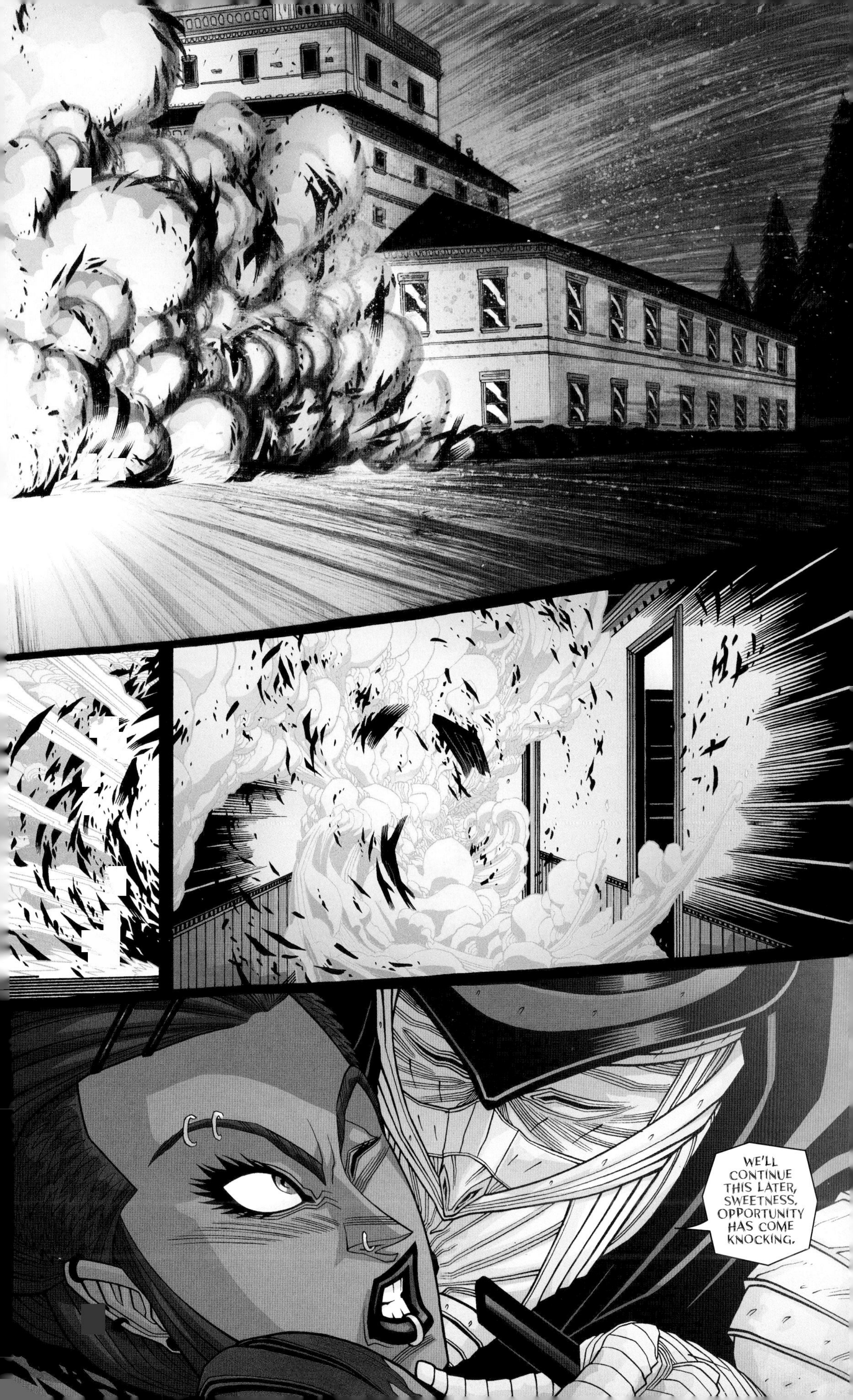
WE'LL CONTINUE THIS LATER, SWEETNESS. OPPORTUNITY HAS COME KNOCKING.

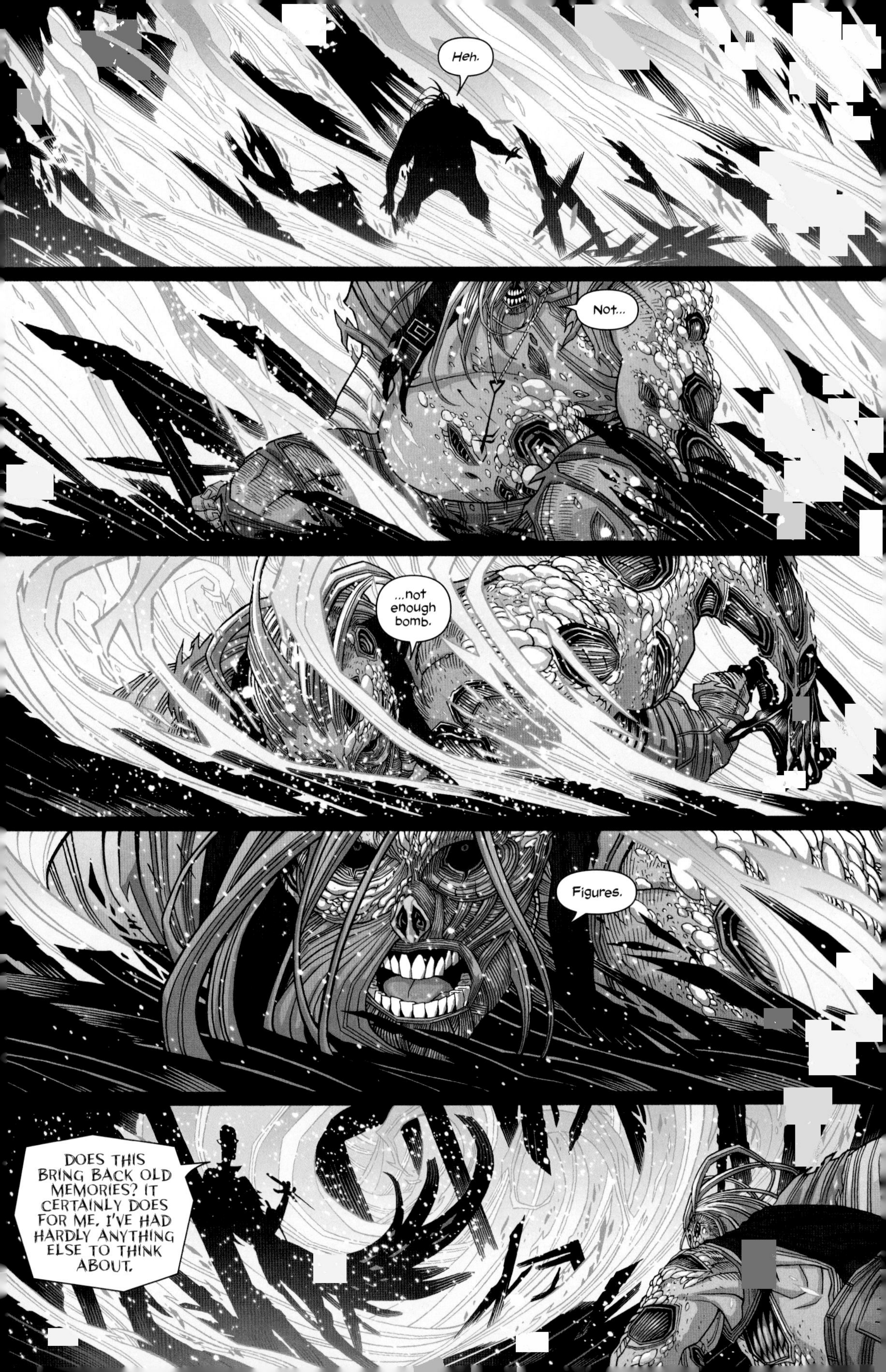
Heh.
Not...
...not enough bomb.
Figures.
DOES THIS BRING BACK OLD MEMORIES? IT CERTAINLY DOES FOR ME, I'VE HAD HARDLY ANYTHING ELSE TO THINK ABOUT.

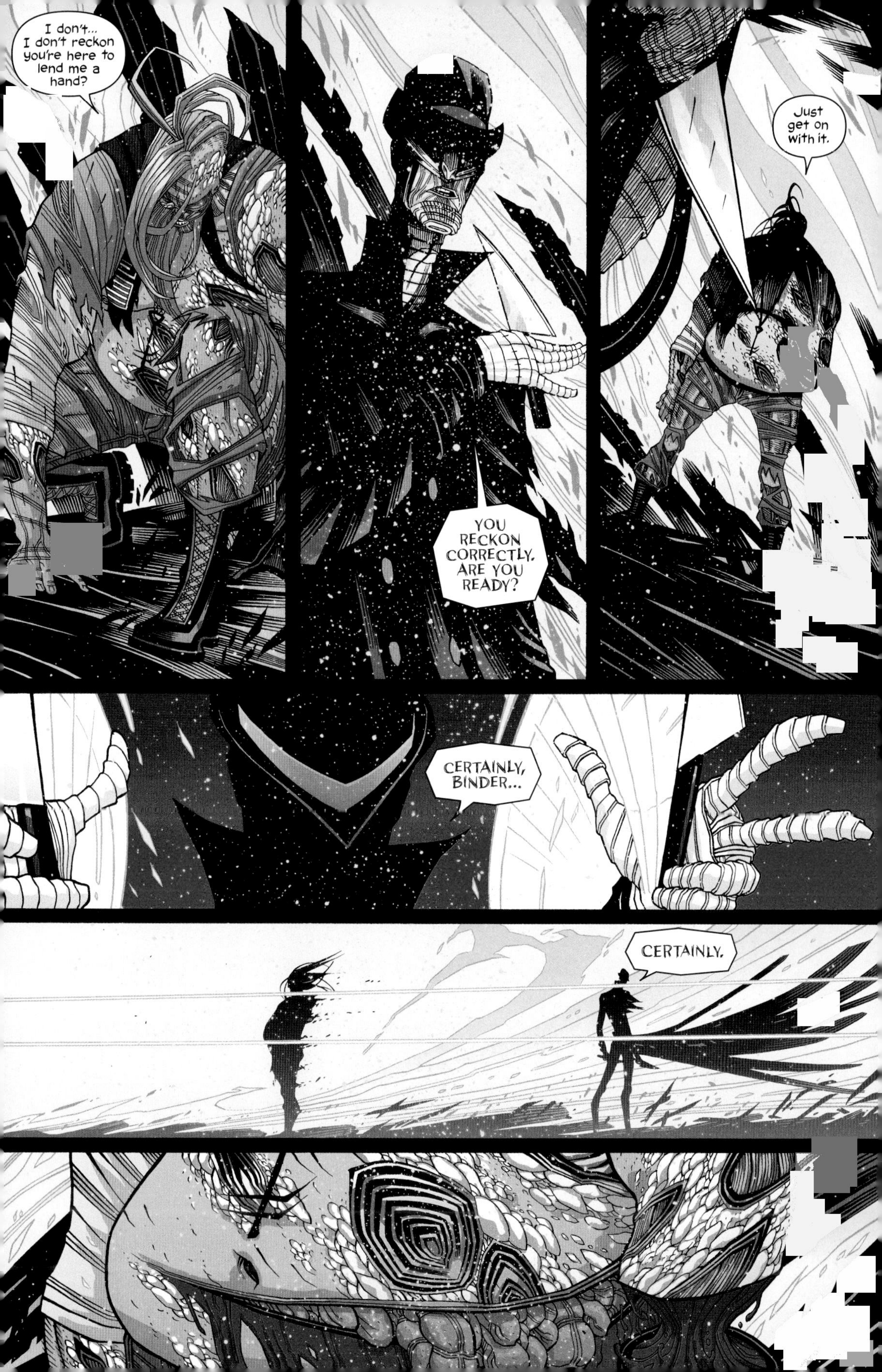
I don't... I don't reckon you're here to lend me a hand?
YOU RECKON CORRECTLY. ARE YOU READY?
Just get on with it.
CERTAINLY, BINDER...
CERTAINLY.

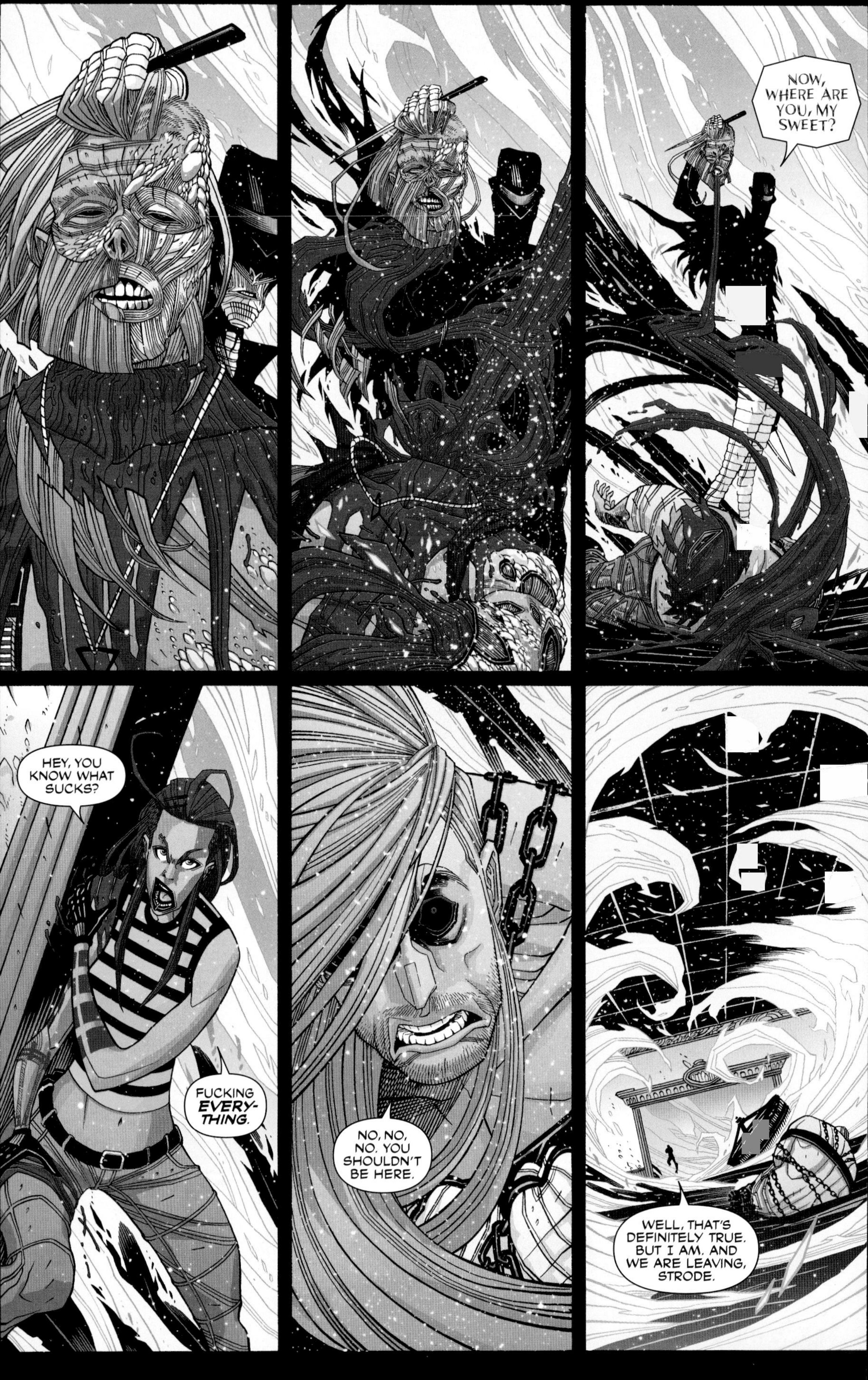
NOW, WHERE ARE YOU, MY SWEET?
HEY, YOU KNOW WHAT SUCKS?
FUCKING *EVERY-THING*.
NO, NO, NO. YOU SHOULDN'T BE HERE.
WELL, THAT'S DEFINITELY TRUE. BUT I AM. AND WE ARE LEAVING, STRODE.

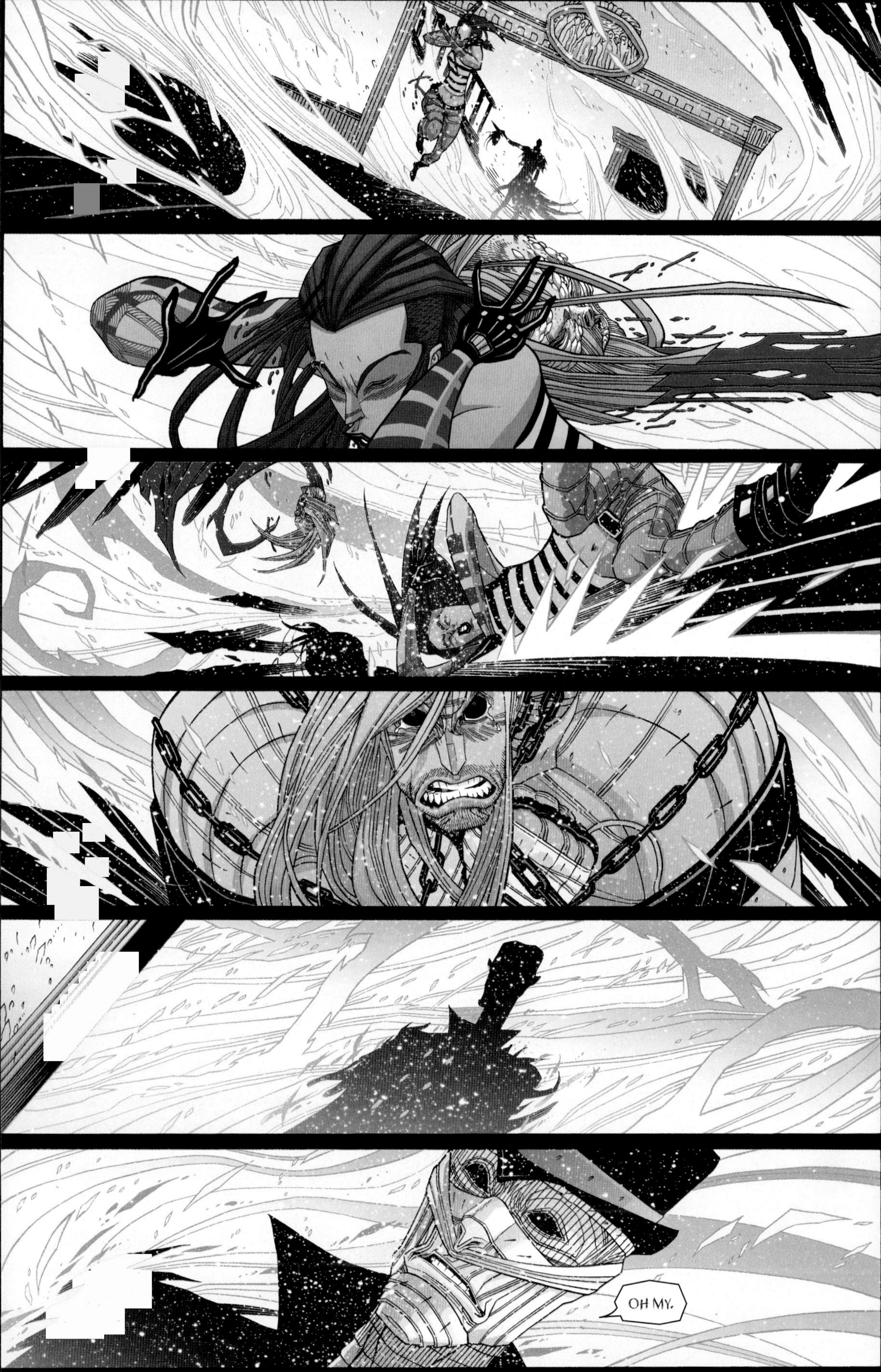
OH MY.

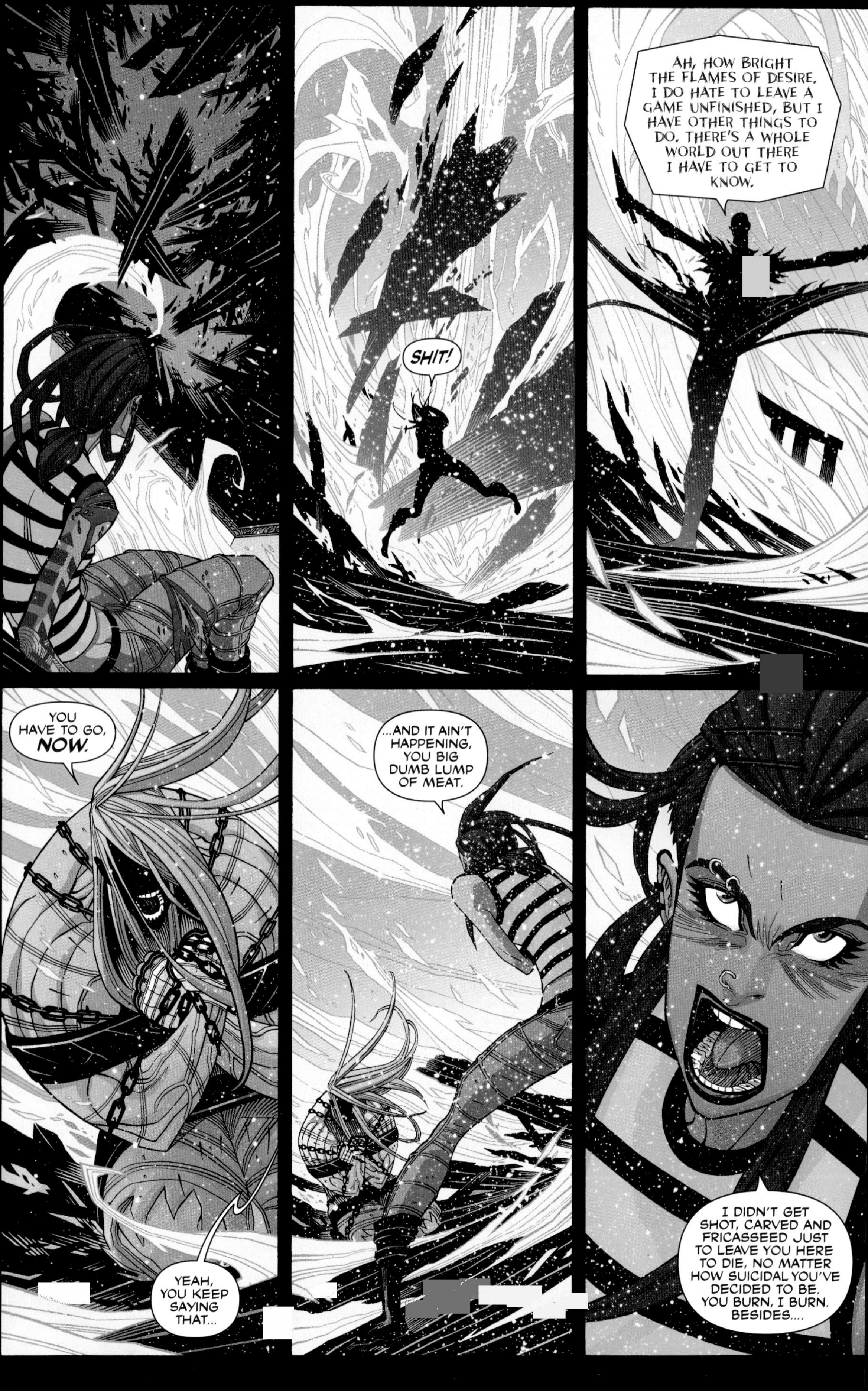
SHIT!
AH, HOW BRIGHT THE FLAMES OF DESIRE. I DO HATE TO LEAVE A GAME UNFINISHED, BUT I HAVE OTHER THINGS TO DO. THERE'S A WHOLE WORLD OUT THERE I HAVE TO GET TO KNOW.
YOU HAVE TO GO, NOW.
YEAH, YOU KEEP SAYING THAT...
...AND IT AIN'T HAPPENING, YOU BIG DUMB LUMP OF MEAT.
I DIDN'T GET SHOT, CARVED AND FRICASSEED JUST TO LEAVE YOU HERE TO DIE, NO MATTER HOW SUICIDAL YOU'VE DECIDED TO BE. YOU BURN, I BURN. BESIDES....

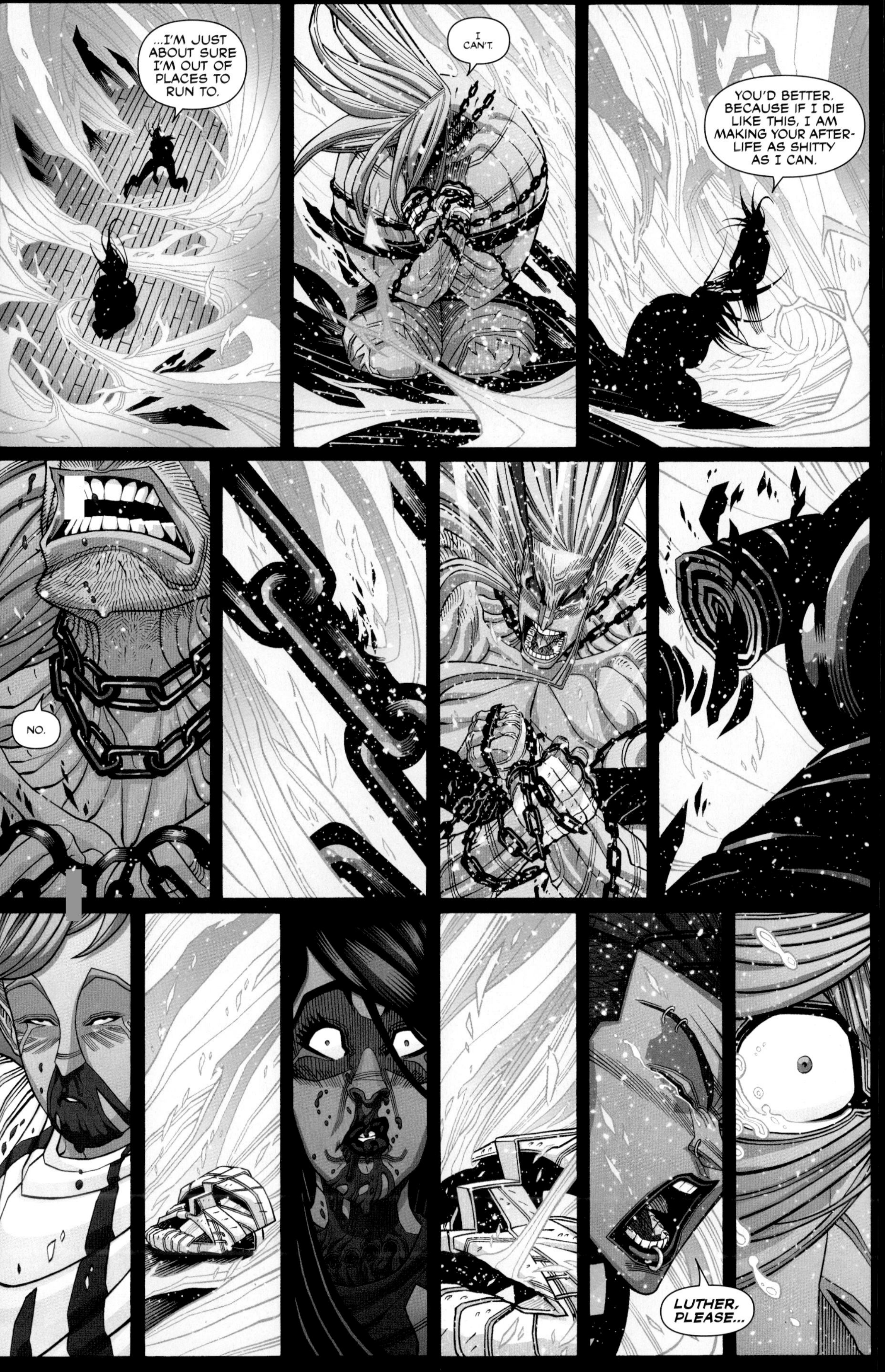
...I'M JUST ABOUT SURE I'M OUT OF PLACES TO RUN TO.
I CAN'T.
YOU'D BETTER. BECAUSE IF I DIE LIKE THIS, I AM MAKING YOUR AFTER-LIFE AS SHITTY AS I CAN.
NO.
LUTHER, PLEASE...

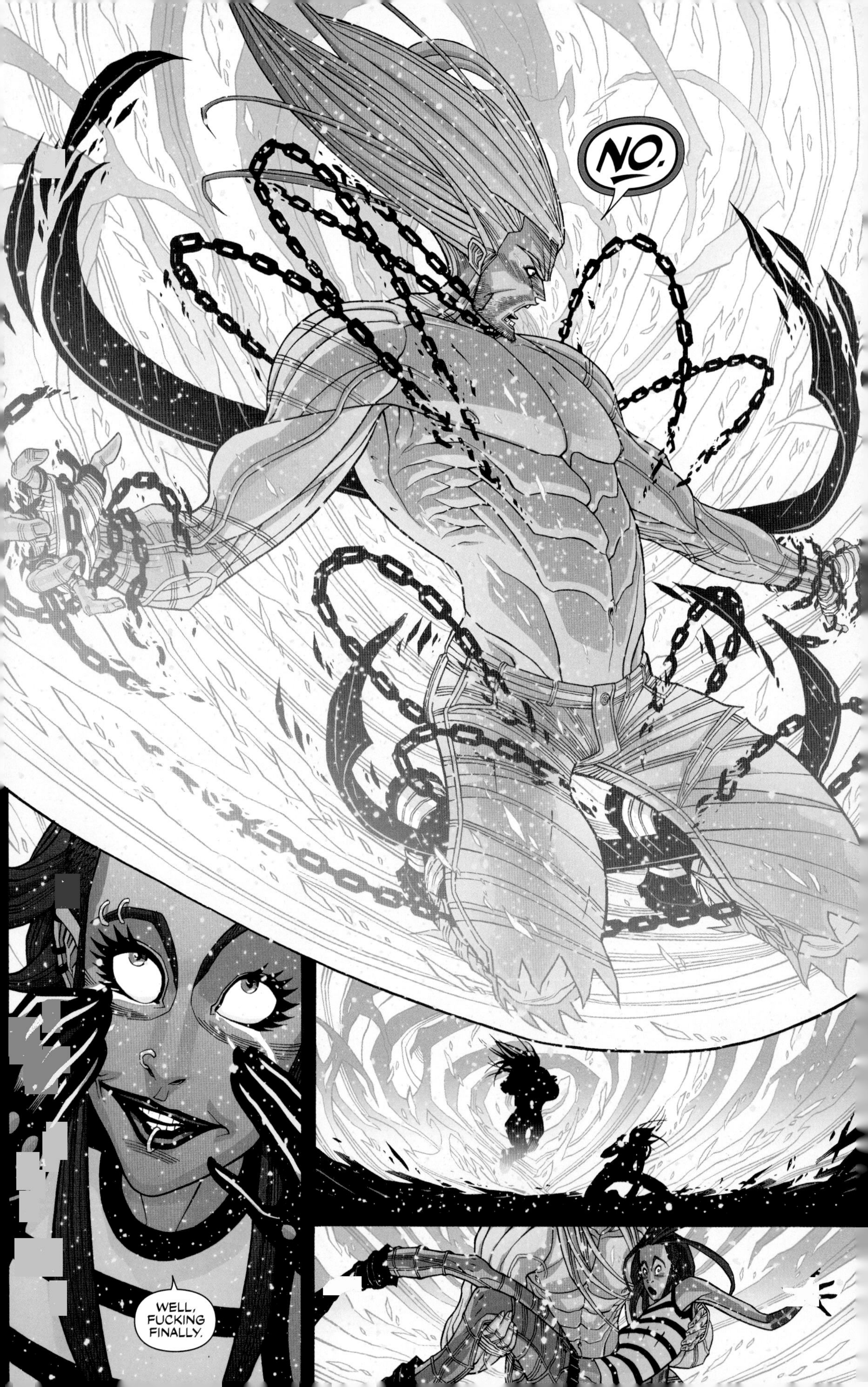
NO.
WELL, FUCKING FINALLY.

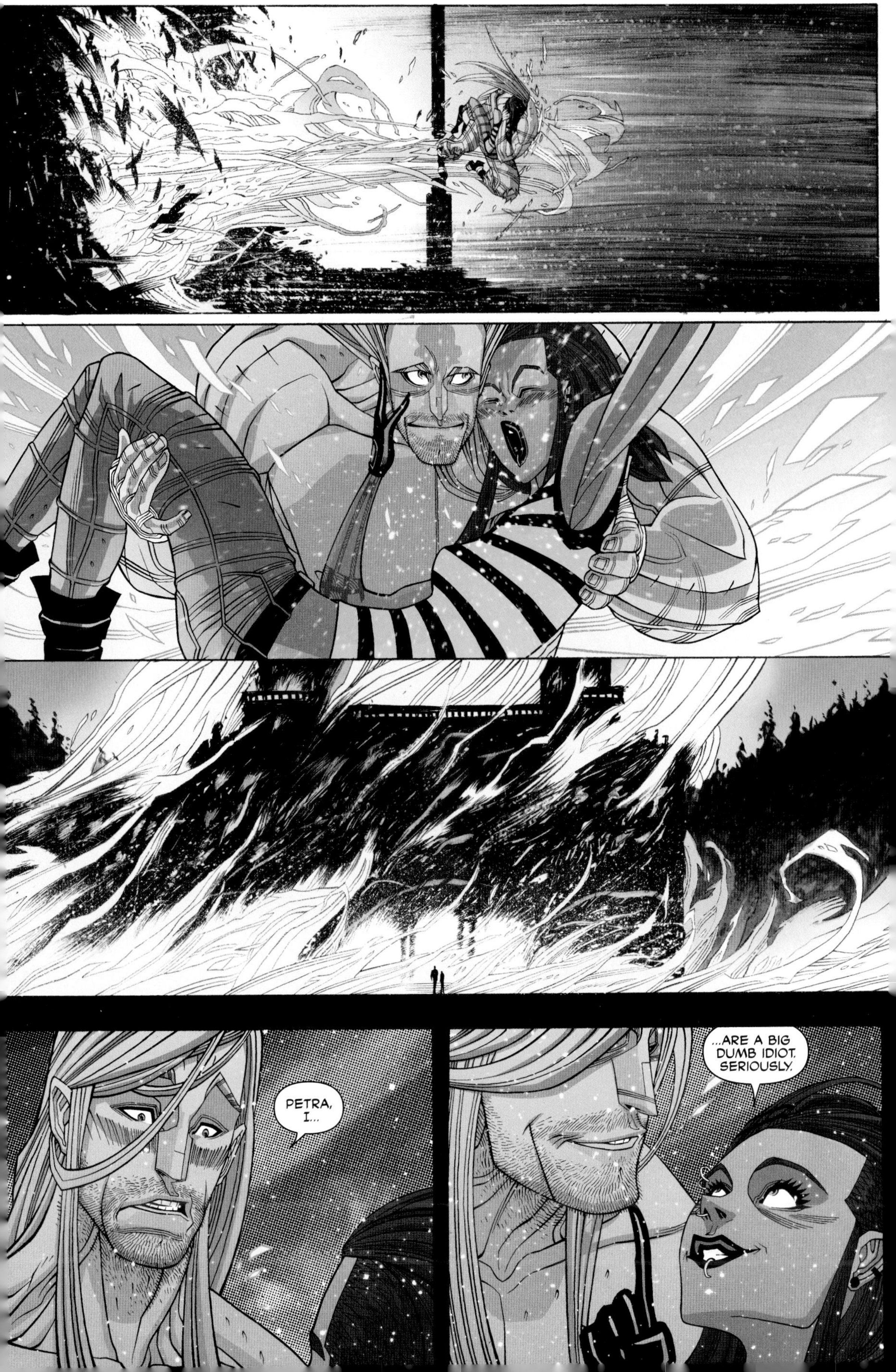
PETRA, I...
...ARE A BIG DUMB IDIOT. SERIOUSLY.

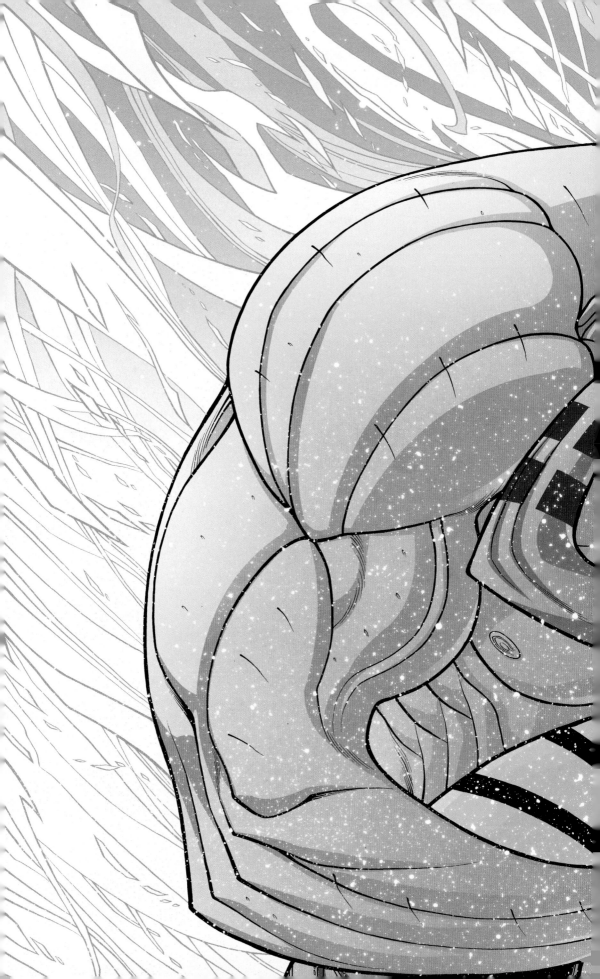

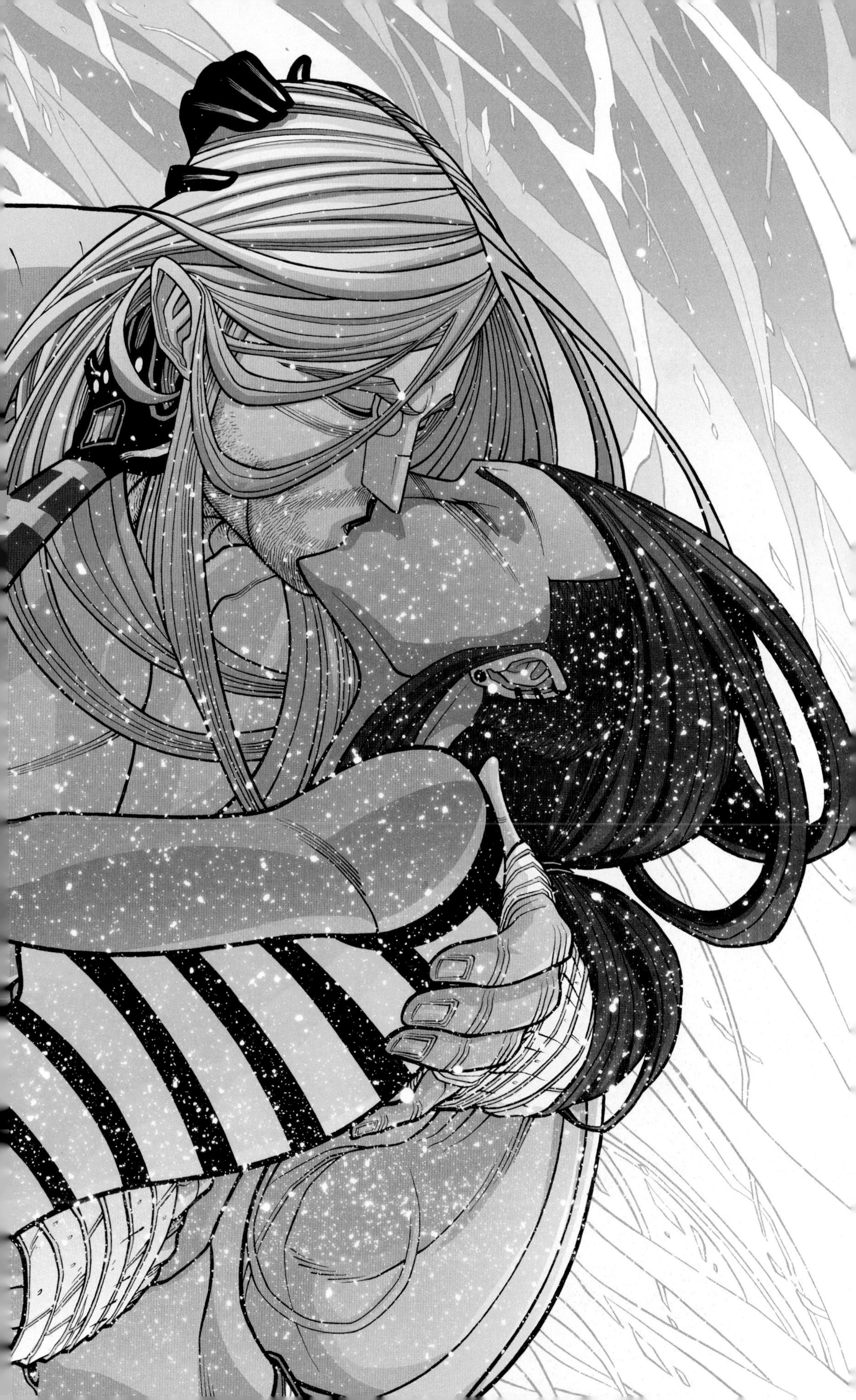

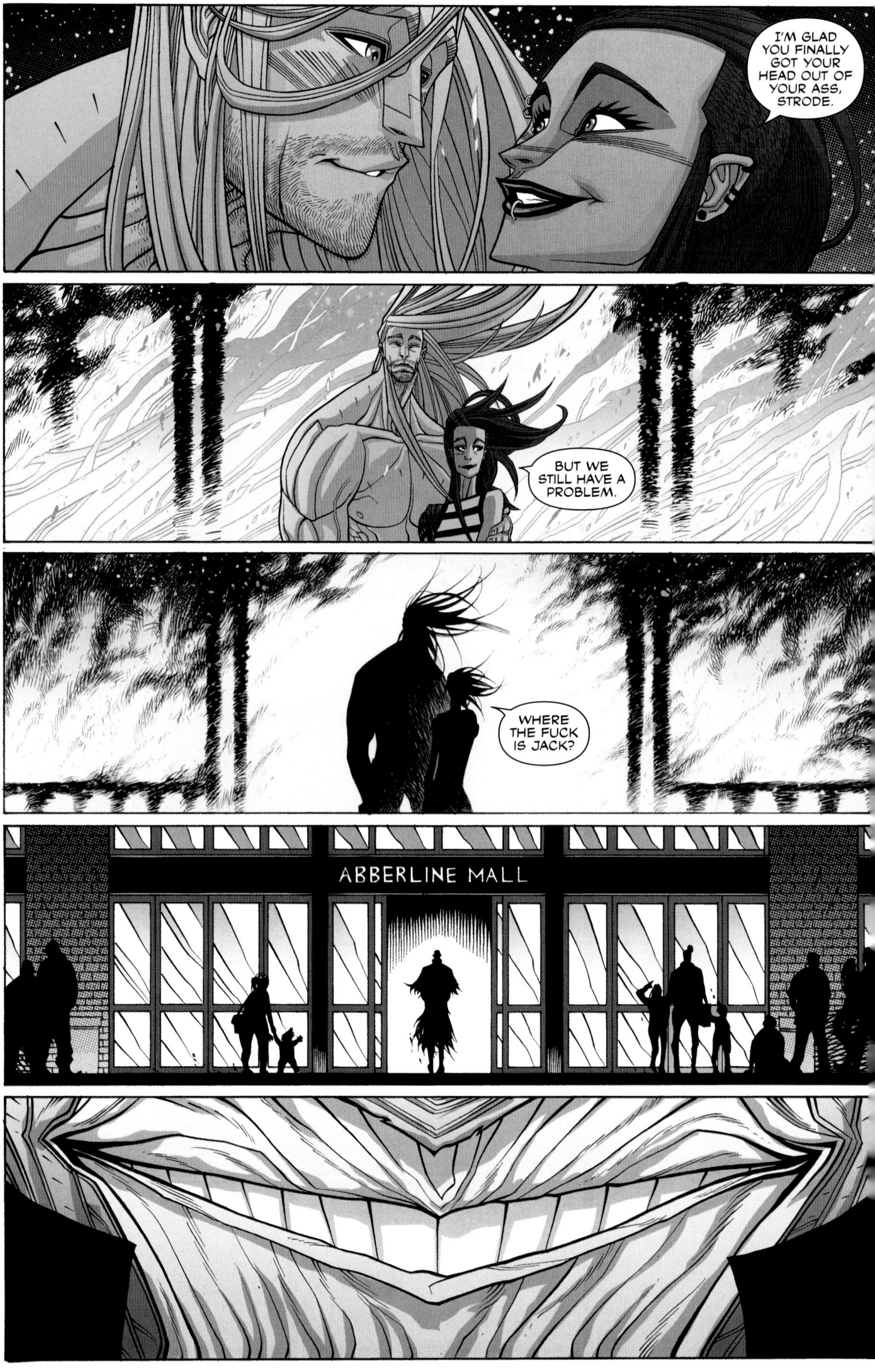
I'M GLAD YOU FINALLY GOT YOUR HEAD OUT OF YOUR ASS, STRODE.
BUT WE STILL HAVE A PROBLEM.
WHERE THE FUCK IS JACK?
ABBERLINE MALL

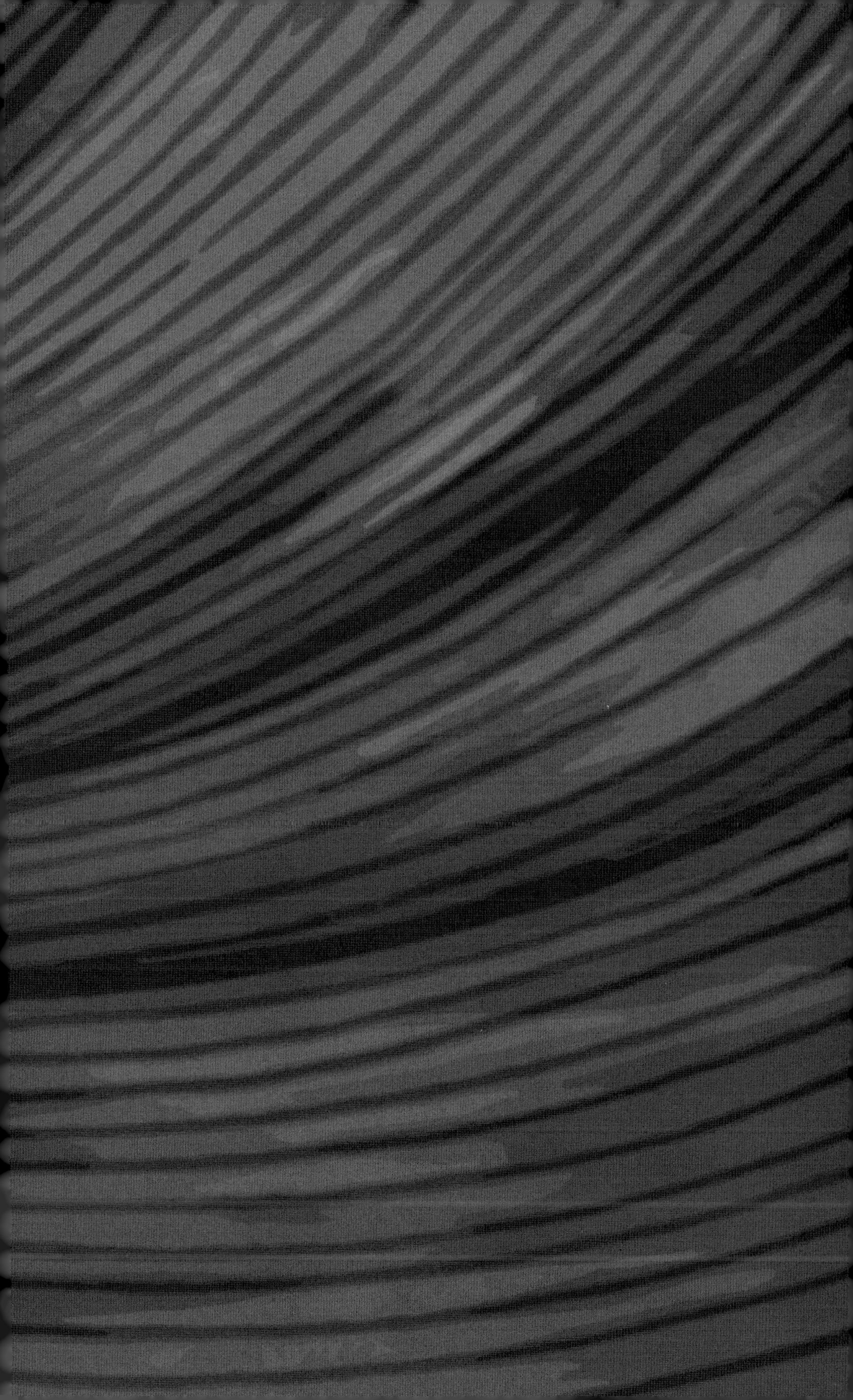

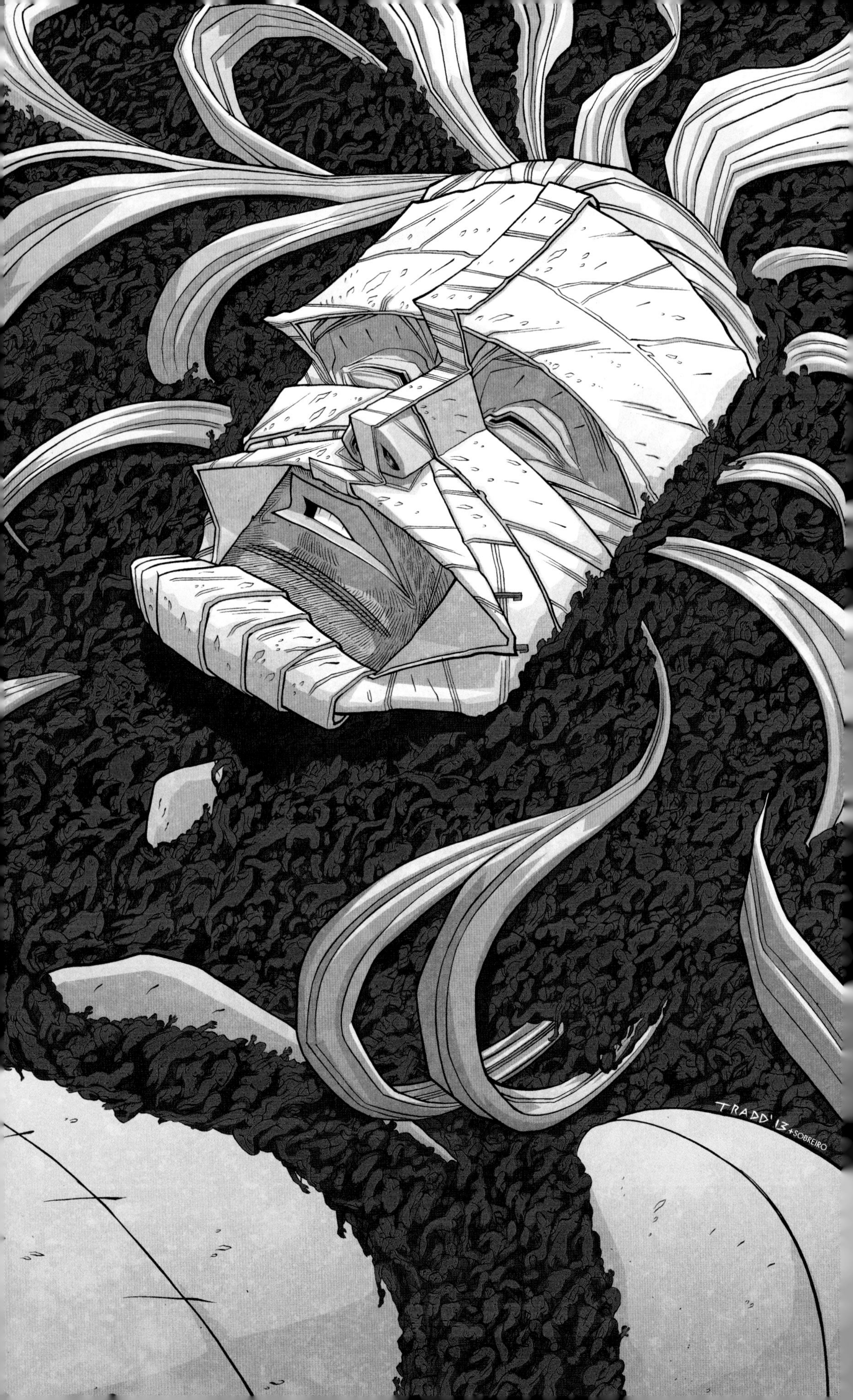
TRADD '13 +SOBREIRO

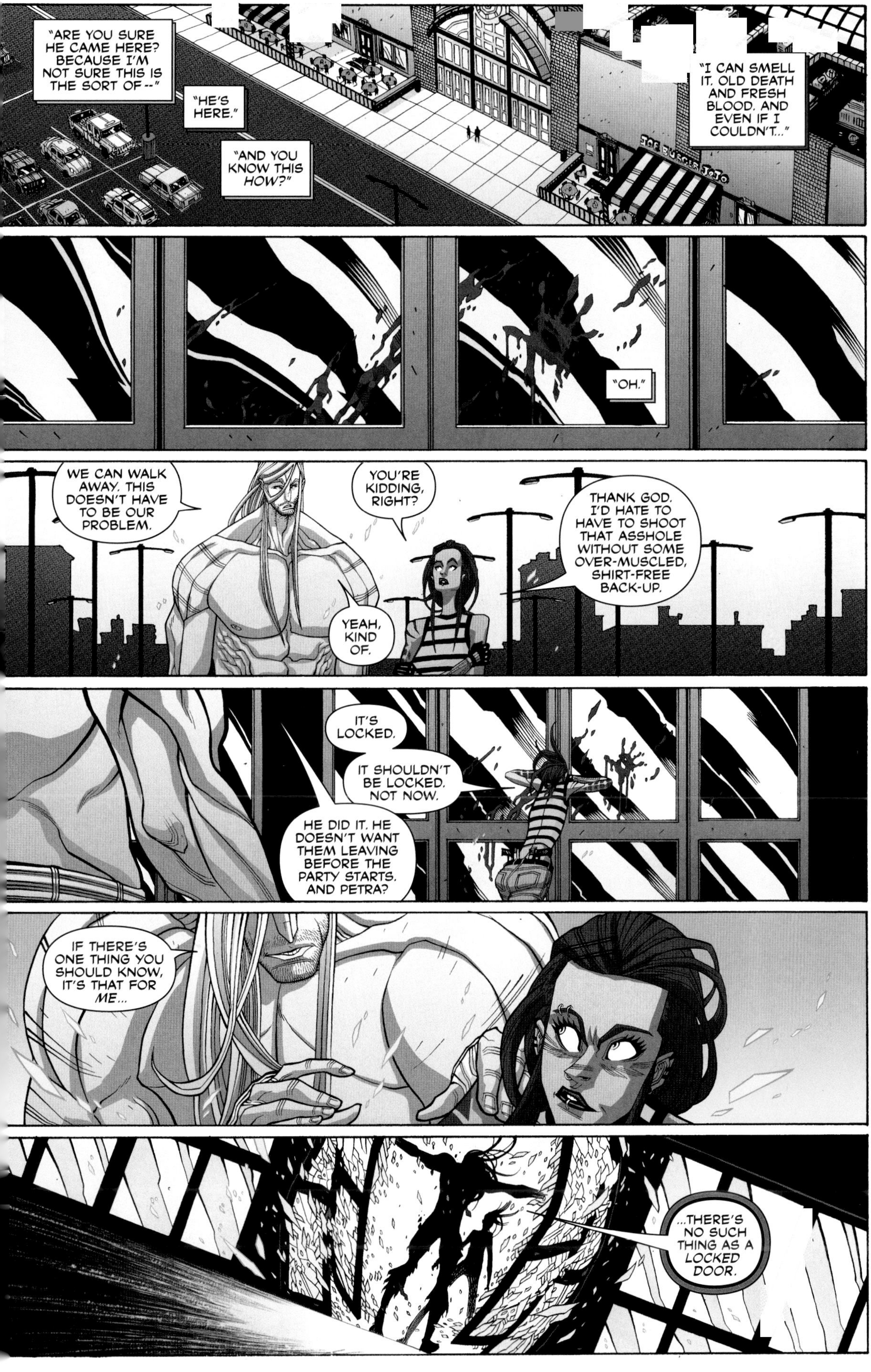

"ARE YOU SURE HE CAME HERE? BECAUSE I'M NOT SURE THIS IS THE SORT OF --"
"HE'S HERE."
"AND YOU KNOW THIS *HOW?*"
"I CAN SMELL IT. OLD DEATH AND FRESH BLOOD. AND EVEN IF I COULDN'T..."
"OH."
WE CAN WALK AWAY. THIS DOESN'T HAVE TO BE OUR PROBLEM.
YOU'RE KIDDING, RIGHT?
YEAH, KIND OF.
THANK GOD. I'D HATE TO HAVE TO SHOOT THAT ASSHOLE WITHOUT SOME OVER-MUSCLED, SHIRT-FREE BACK-UP.
IT'S LOCKED.
IT SHOULDN'T BE LOCKED. NOT NOW.
HE DID IT. HE DOESN'T WANT THEM LEAVING BEFORE THE PARTY STARTS. AND PETRA?
IF THERE'S ONE THING YOU SHOULD KNOW, IT'S THAT FOR *ME*...
...THERE'S NO SUCH THING AS A *LOCKED DOOR.*

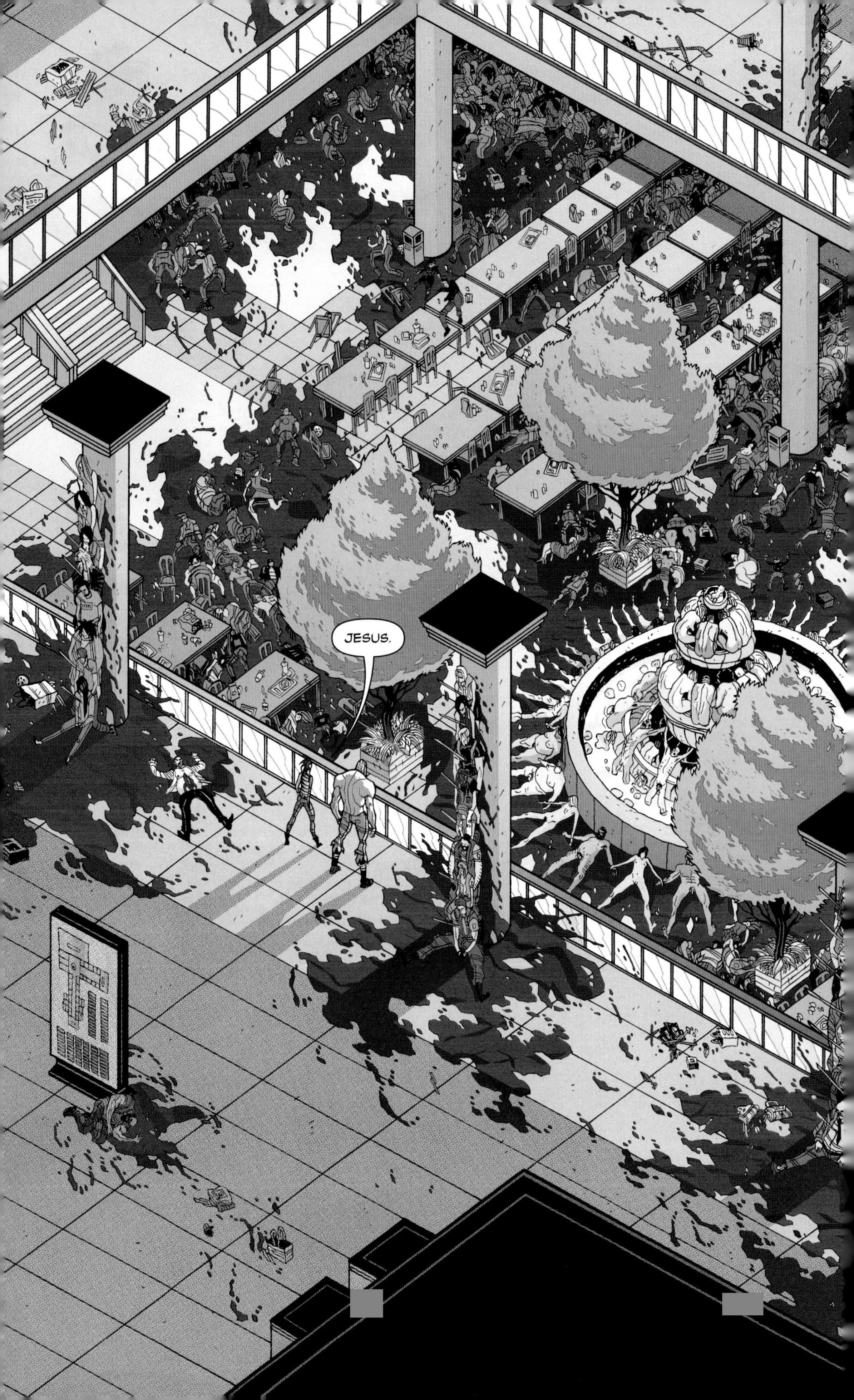
JESUS.

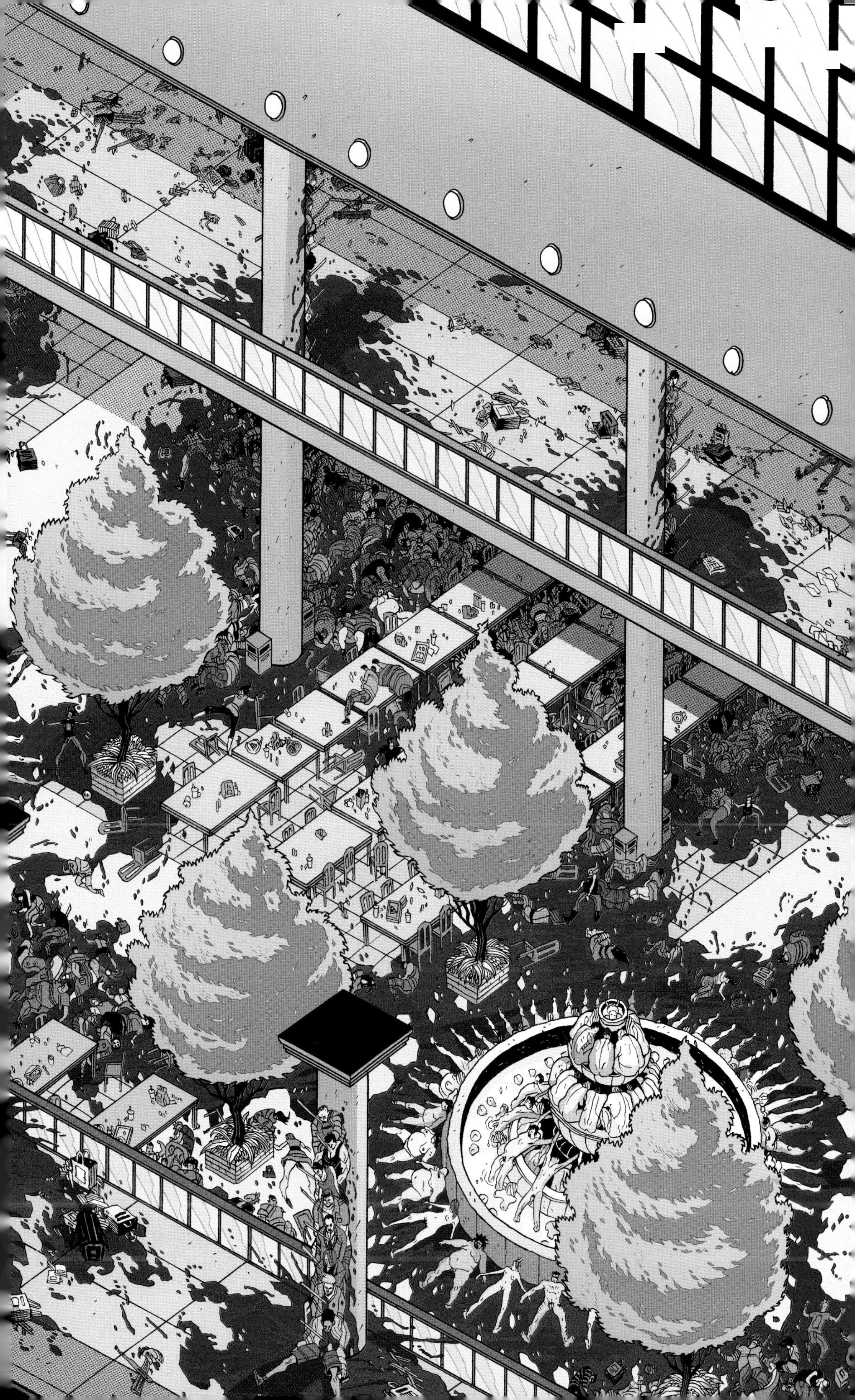

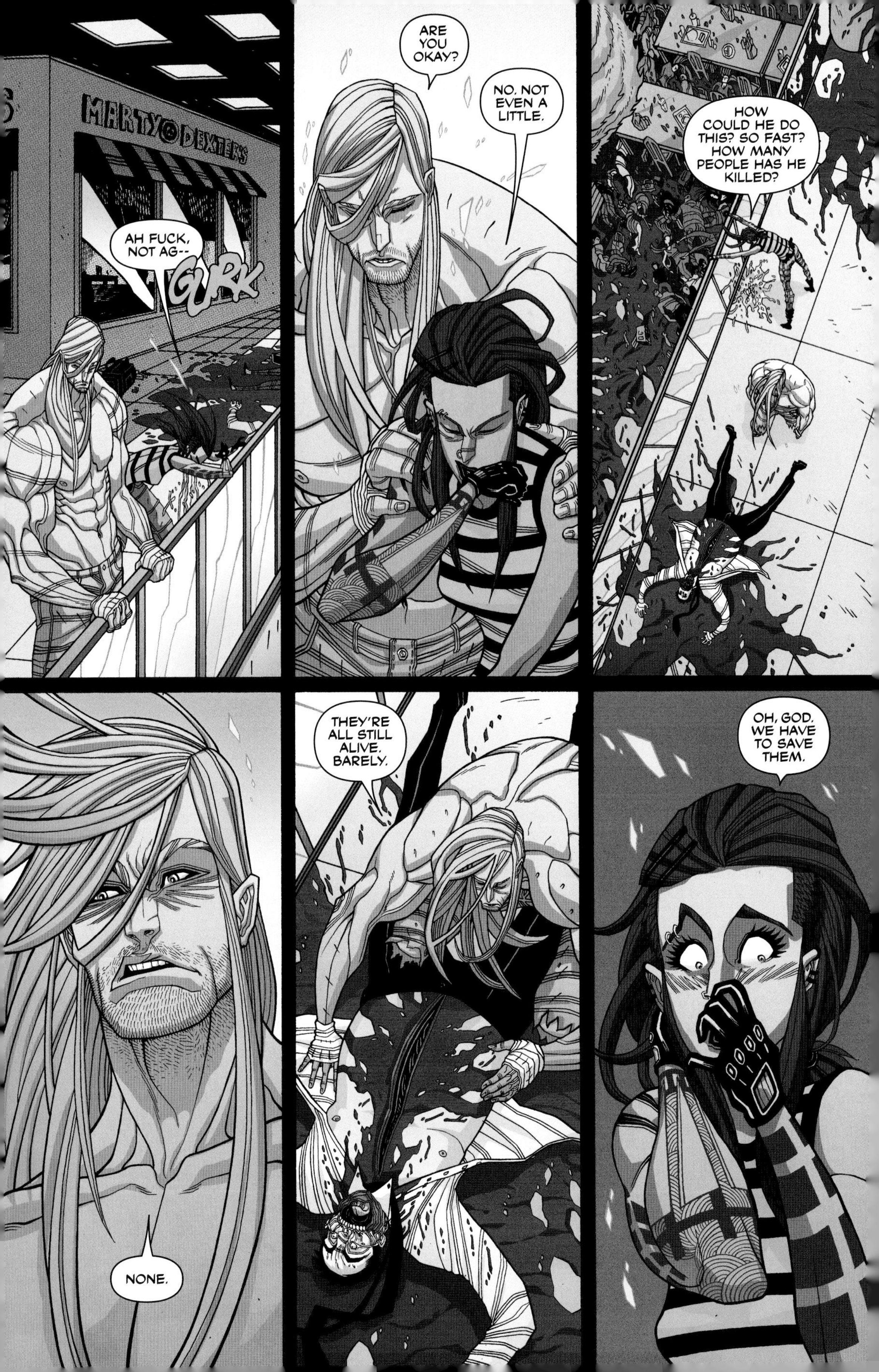
MARTY & DEXTER'S
AH FUCK, NOT AG--
GURK
ARE YOU OKAY?
NO. NOT EVEN A LITTLE.
HOW COULD HE DO THIS? SO FAST? HOW MANY PEOPLE HAS HE KILLED?
NONE.
THEY'RE ALL STILL ALIVE. BARELY.
OH, GOD. WE HAVE TO SAVE THEM.

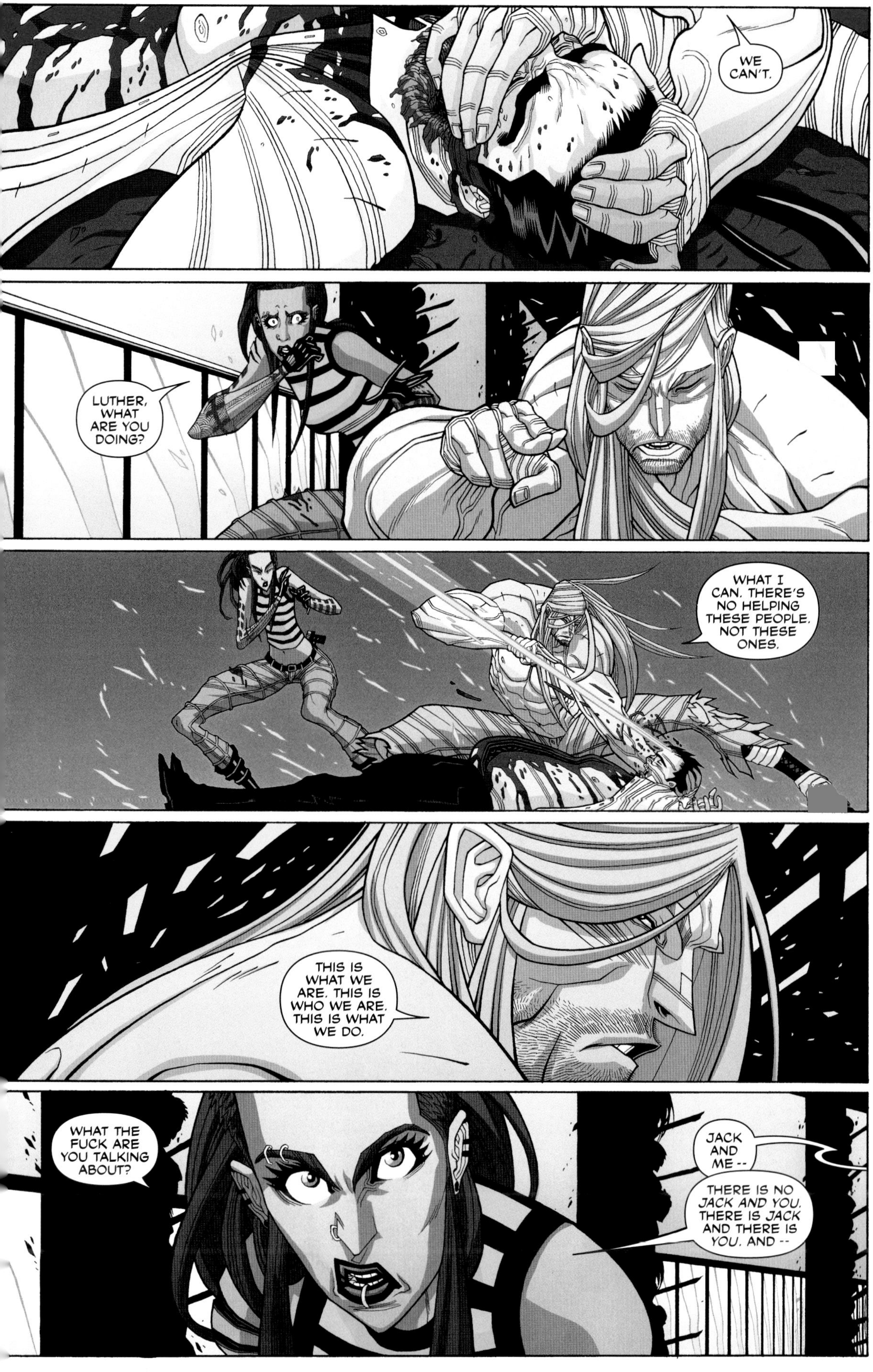
WE CAN'T.
LUTHER, WHAT ARE YOU DOING?
WHAT I CAN. THERE'S NO HELPING THESE PEOPLE. NOT THESE ONES.
THIS IS WHAT WE ARE. THIS IS WHO WE ARE. THIS IS WHAT WE DO.
WHAT THE FUCK ARE YOU TALKING ABOUT?
JACK AND ME --
THERE IS NO *JACK AND YOU.* THERE IS *JACK* AND THERE IS *YOU.* AND --

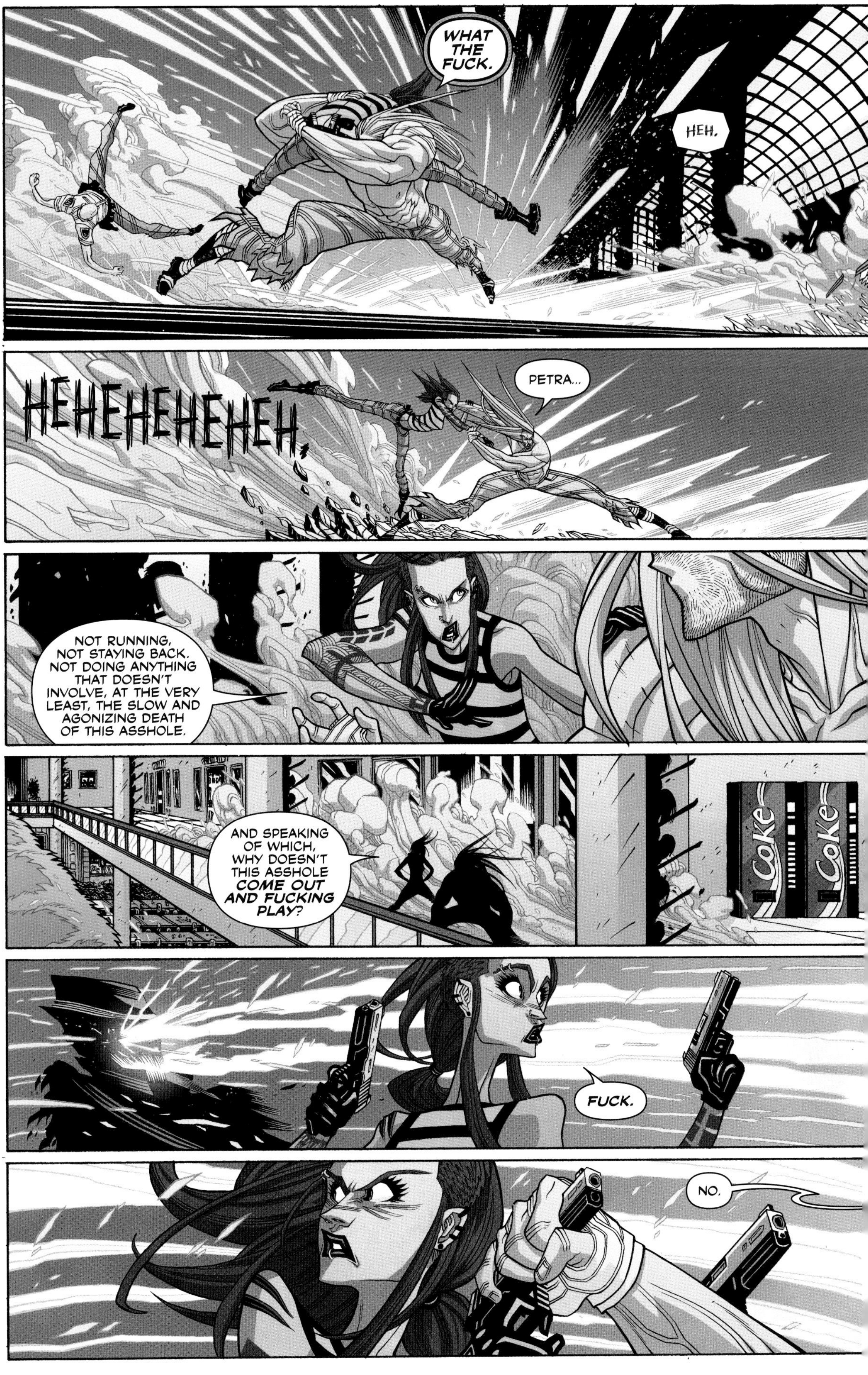
WHAT THE FUCK.
HEH.
HEHEHEHEHEHEH.
PETRA...
NOT RUNNING, NOT STAYING BACK. NOT DOING ANYTHING THAT DOESN'T INVOLVE, AT THE VERY LEAST, THE SLOW AND AGONIZING DEATH OF THIS ASSHOLE.
AND SPEAKING OF WHICH, WHY DOESN'T THIS ASSHOLE COME OUT AND FUCKING PLAY?
Coke
Coke
FUCK.
NO.

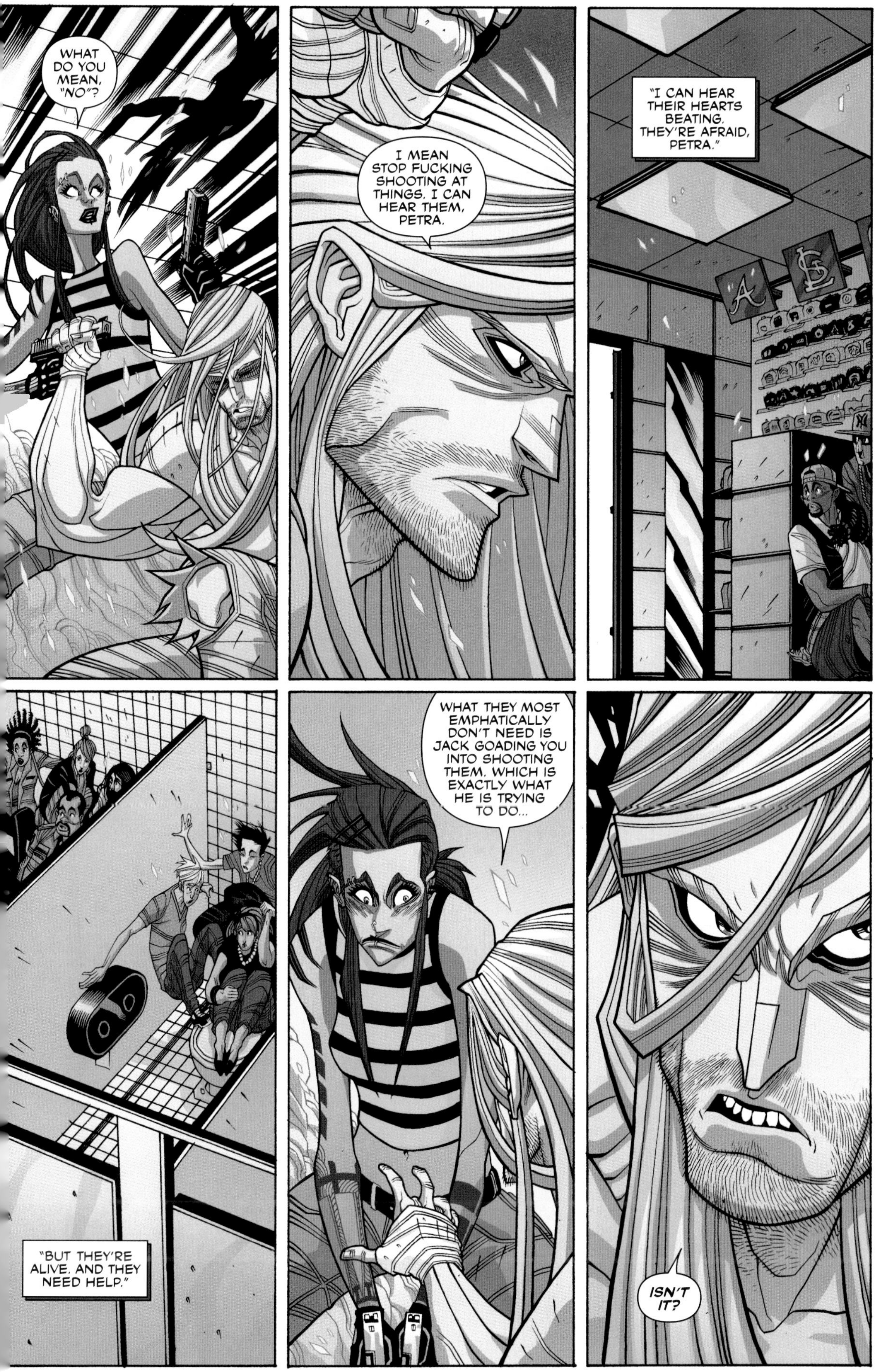
WHAT DO YOU MEAN, "NO"?
I MEAN STOP FUCKING SHOOTING AT THINGS. I CAN HEAR THEM, PETRA.
"I CAN HEAR THEIR HEARTS BEATING. THEY'RE AFRAID, PETRA."
"BUT THEY'RE ALIVE. AND THEY NEED HELP."
WHAT THEY MOST EMPHATICALLY DON'T NEED IS JACK GOADING YOU INTO SHOOTING THEM. WHICH IS EXACTLY WHAT HE IS TRYING TO DO...
ISN'T IT?

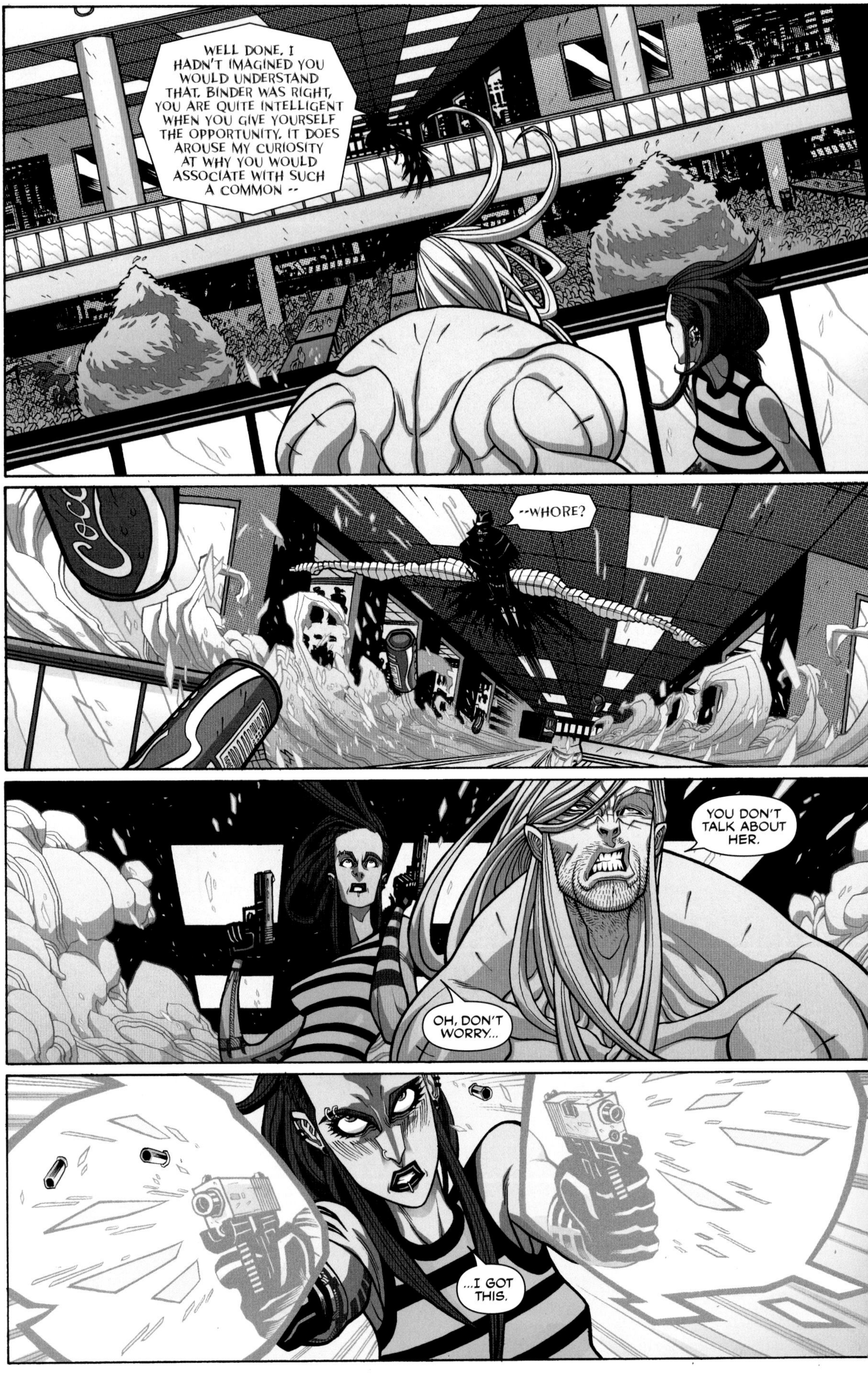
WELL DONE. I HADN'T IMAGINED YOU WOULD UNDERSTAND THAT. BINDER WAS RIGHT, YOU ARE QUITE INTELLIGENT WHEN YOU GIVE YOURSELF THE OPPORTUNITY. IT DOES AROUSE MY CURIOSITY AT WHY YOU WOULD ASSOCIATE WITH SUCH A COMMON --
--WHORE?
YOU DON'T TALK ABOUT HER.
OH, DON'T WORRY...
...I GOT THIS.

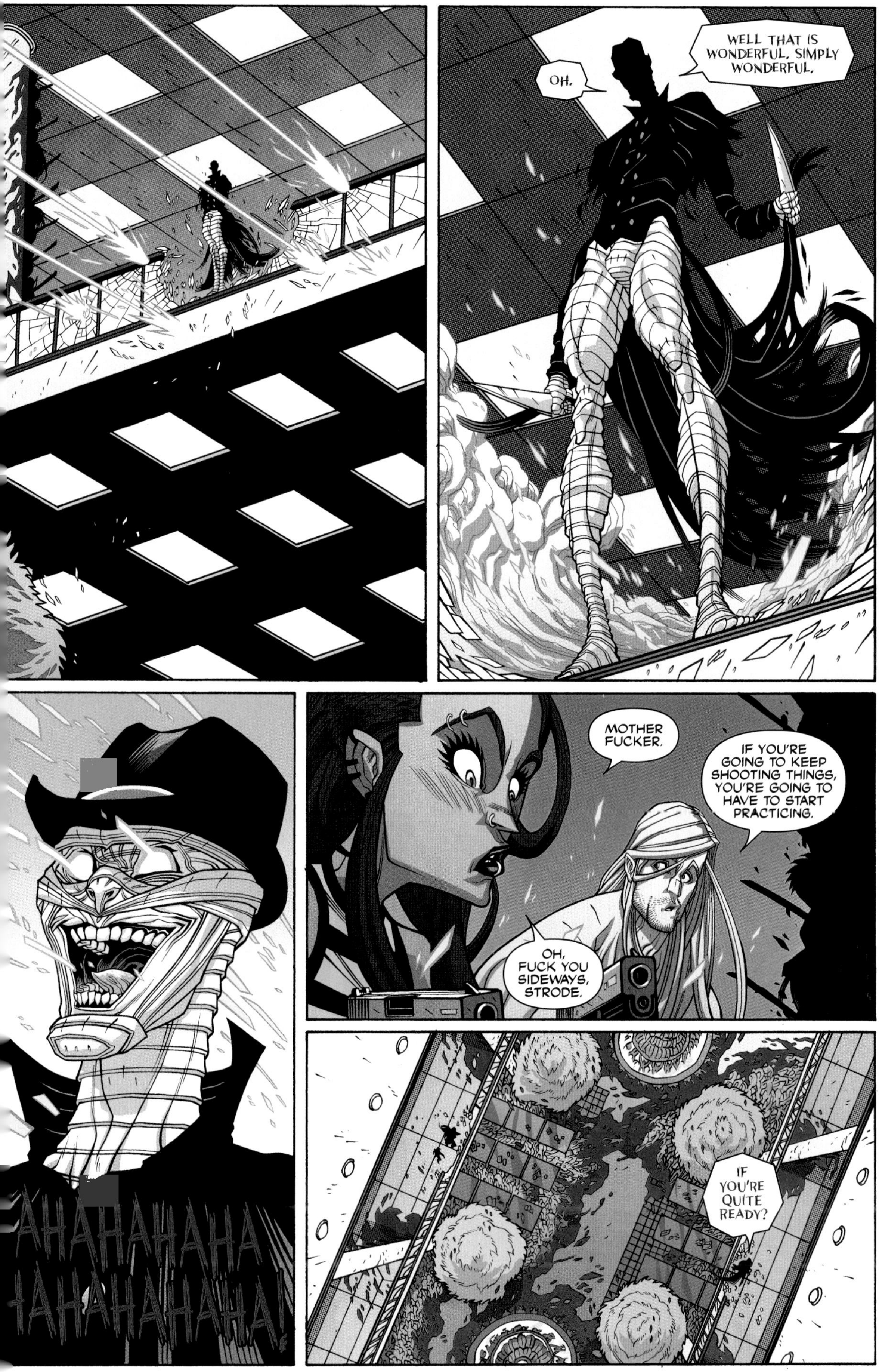
OH.
WELL THAT IS WONDERFUL, SIMPLY WONDERFUL.
AHAHAHAHA
AHAHAHAHA!
MOTHER FUCKER.
IF YOU'RE GOING TO KEEP SHOOTING THINGS, YOU'RE GOING TO HAVE TO START PRACTICING.
OH, FUCK YOU SIDEWAYS, STRODE.
IF YOU'RE QUITE READY?

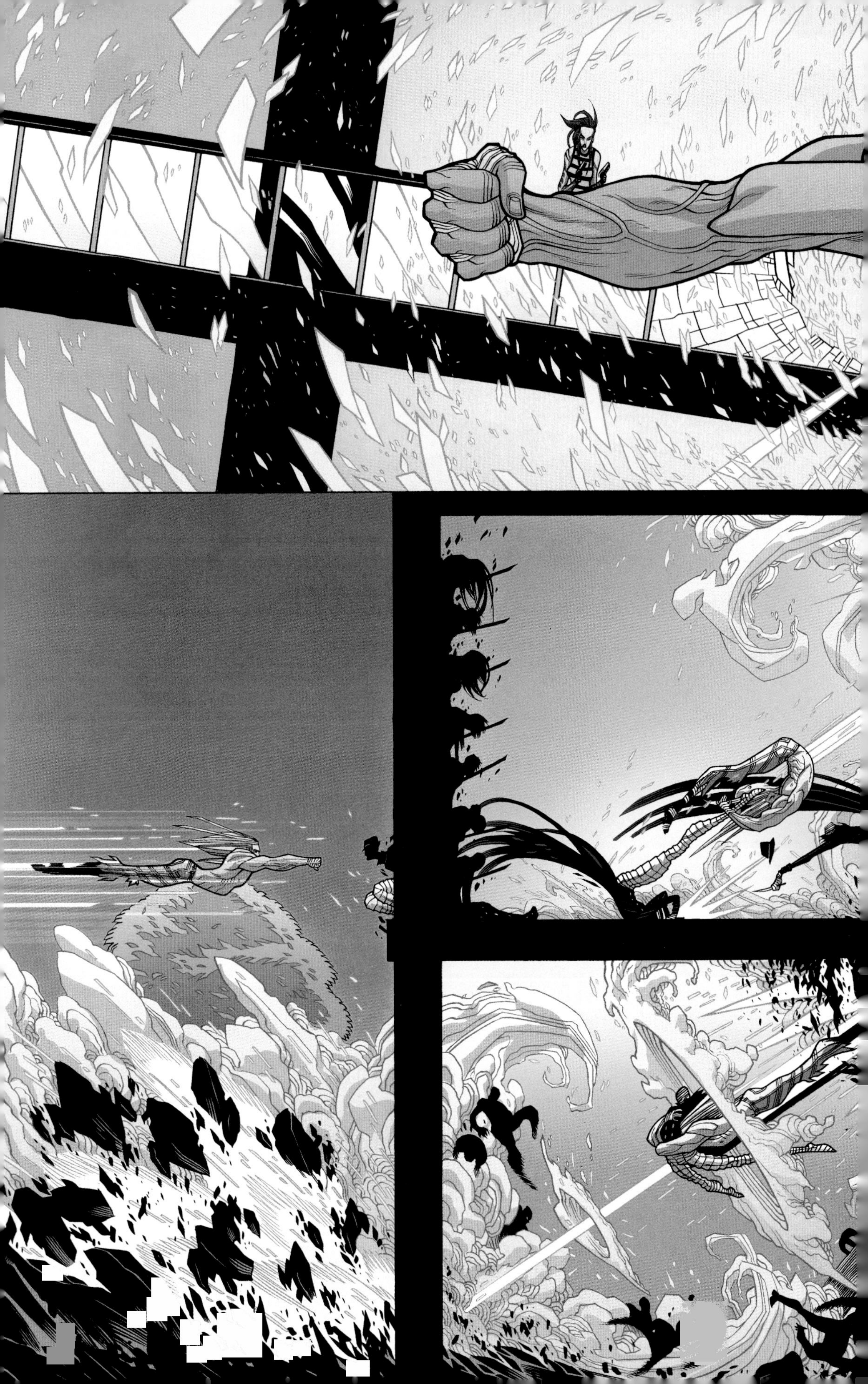

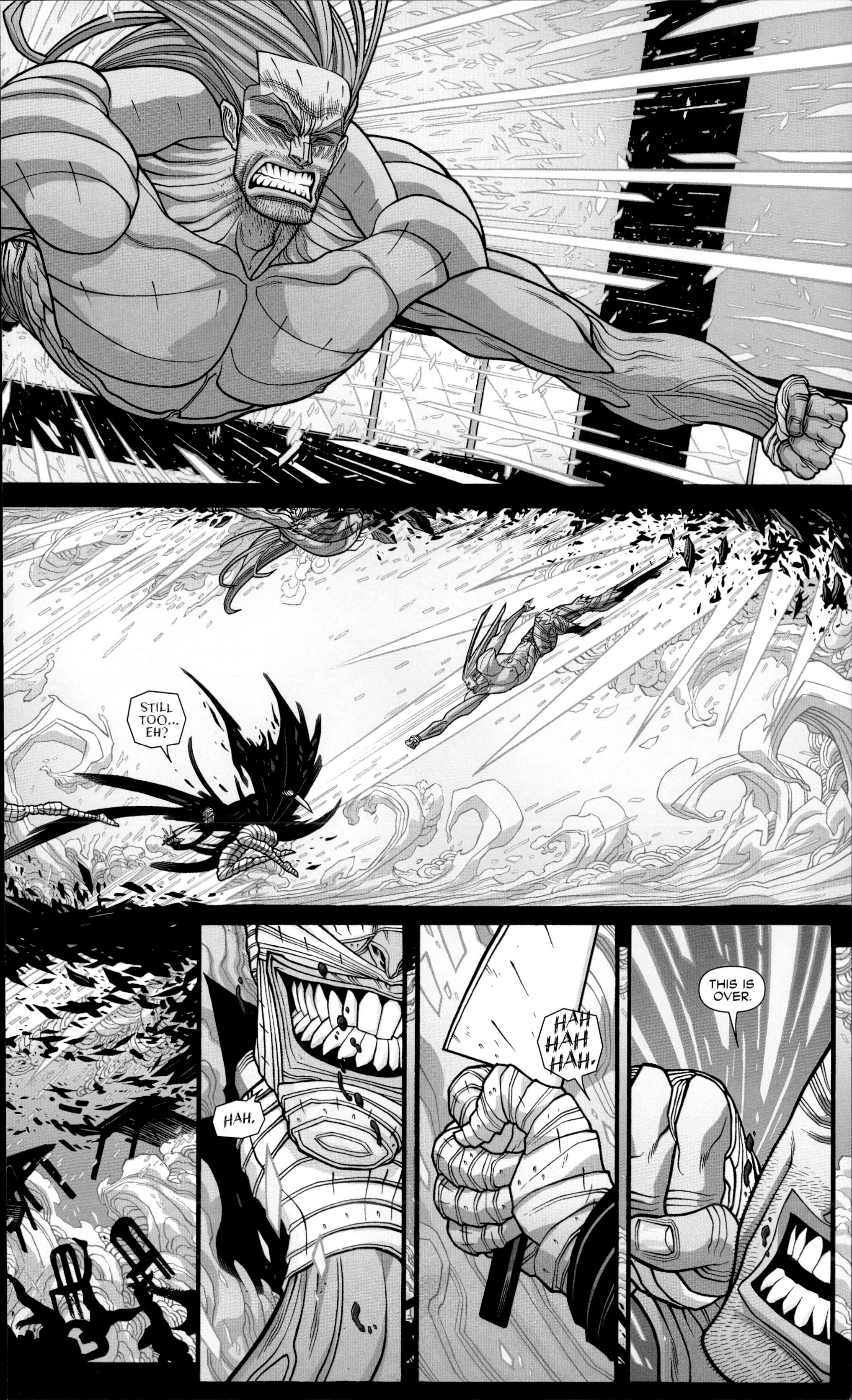
STILL TOO... EH?
HAH.
HAH HAH HAH.
THIS IS OVER.

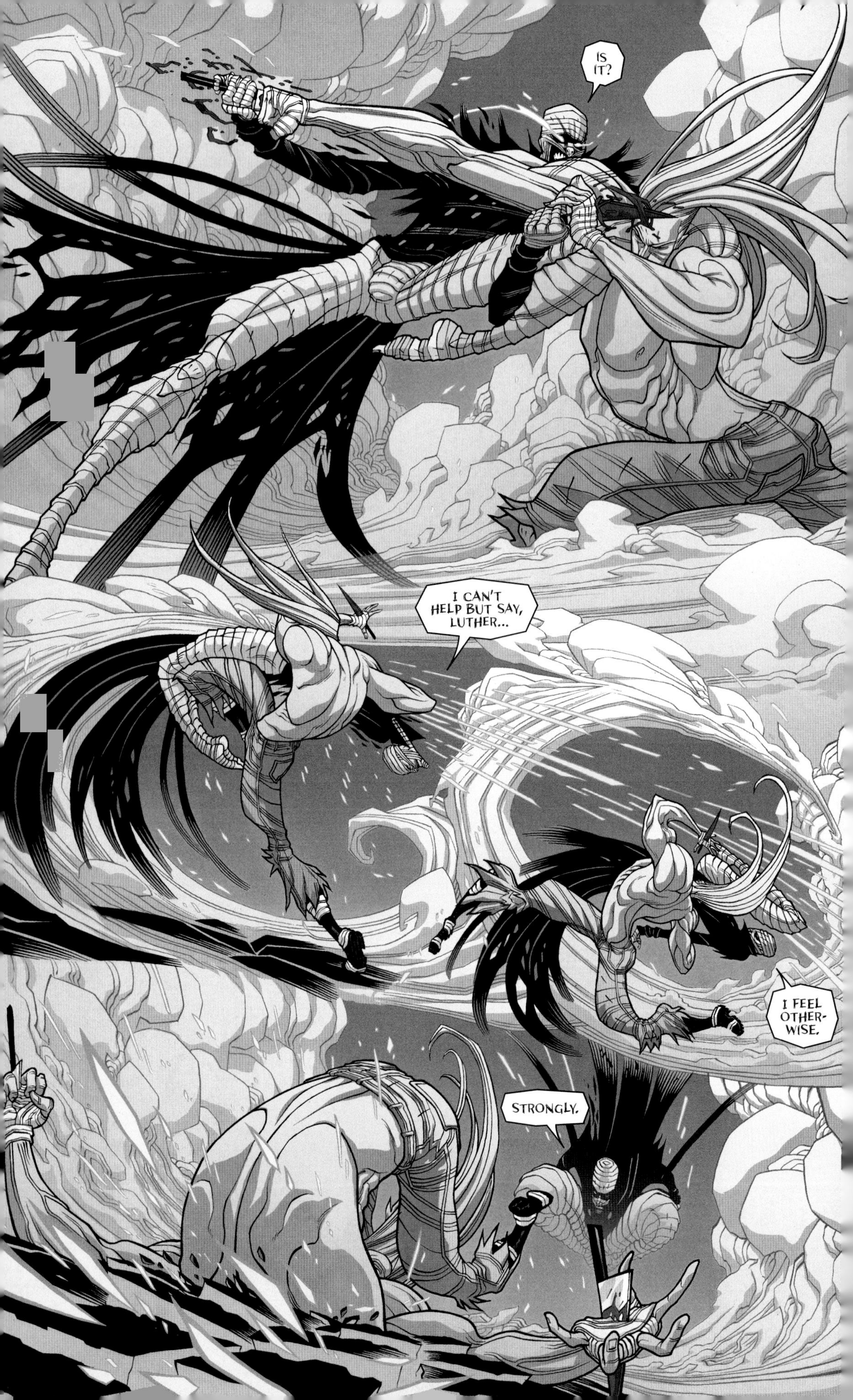
IS IT?
I CAN'T HELP BUT SAY, LUTHER...
I FEEL OTHER-WISE.
STRONGLY.

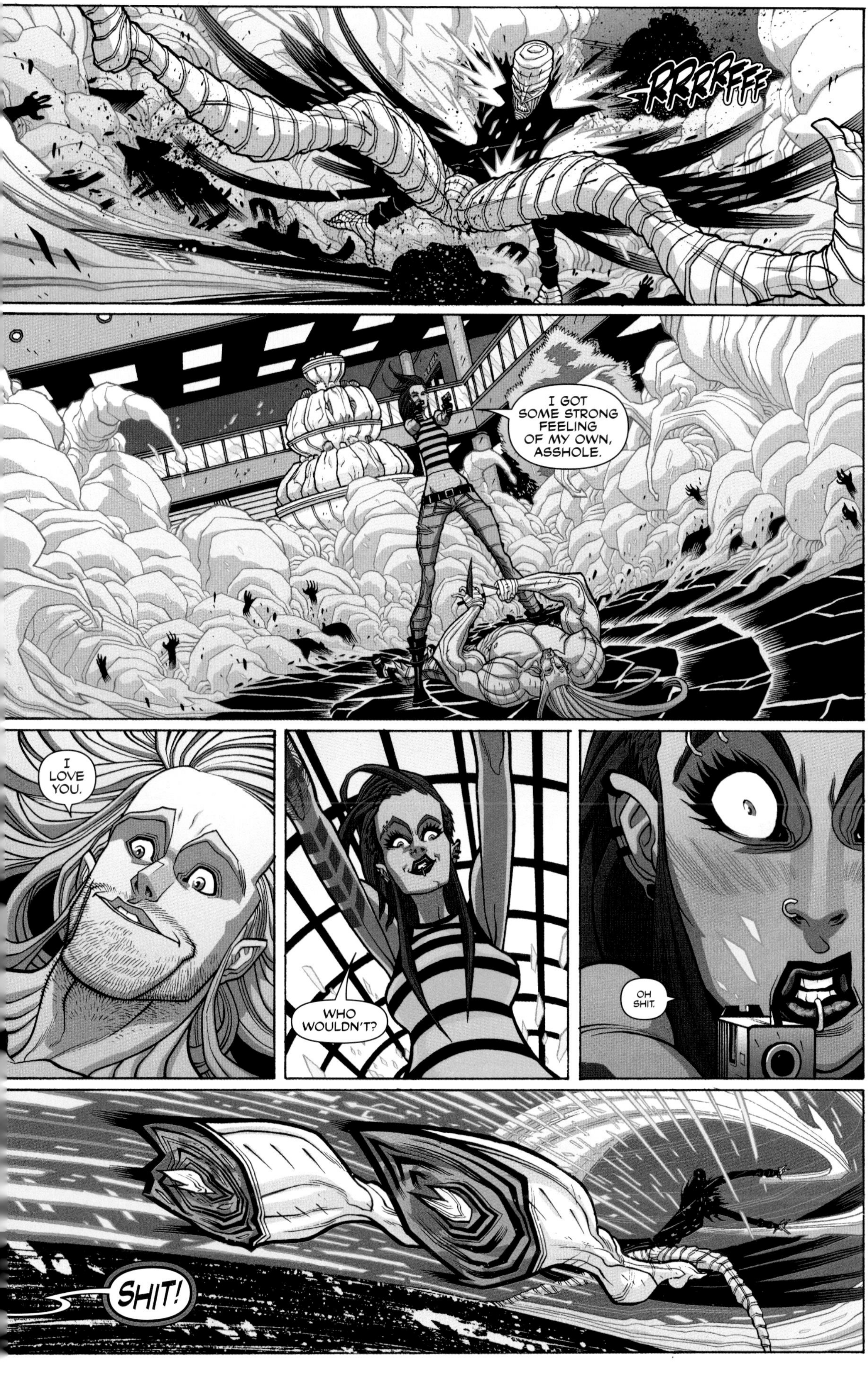
RRRRFFFF
I GOT SOME STRONG FEELING OF MY OWN, ASSHOLE.
I LOVE YOU.
WHO WOULDN'T?
OH SHIT.
SHIT!

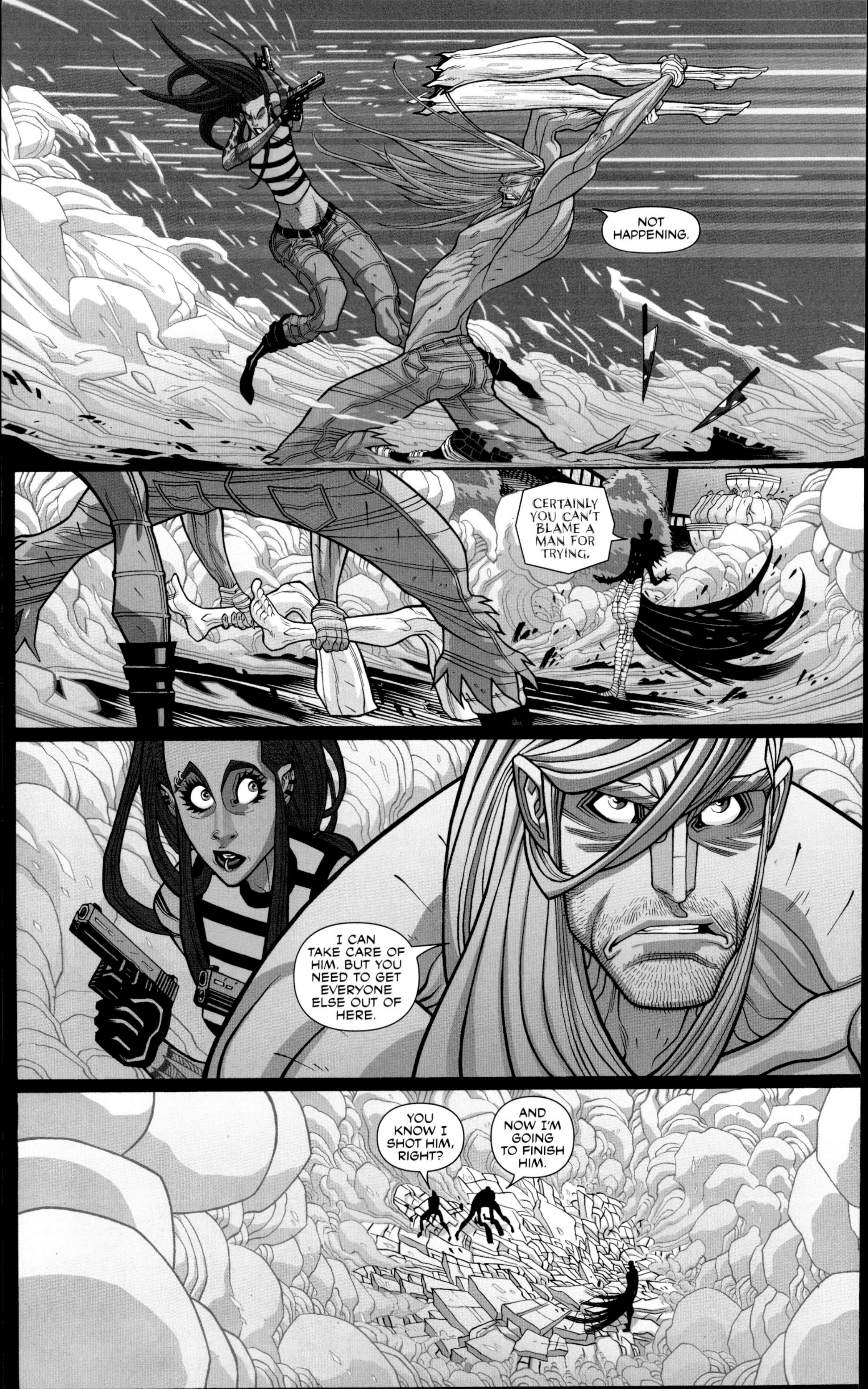
NOT HAPPENING.
CERTAINLY YOU CAN'T BLAME A MAN FOR TRYING.
I CAN TAKE CARE OF HIM. BUT YOU NEED TO GET EVERYONE ELSE OUT OF HERE.
YOU KNOW I SHOT HIM, RIGHT?
AND NOW I'M GOING TO FINISH HIM.

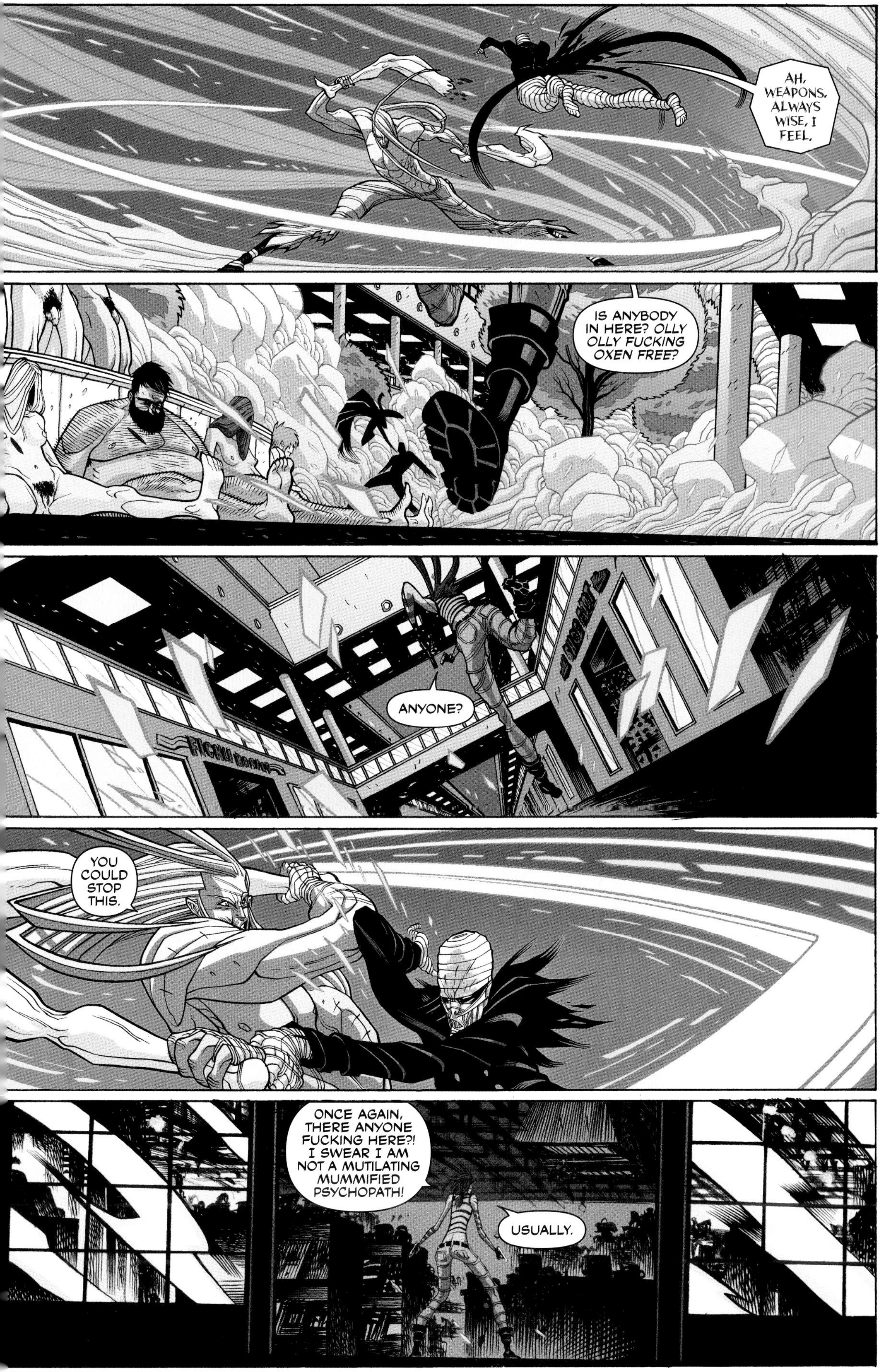
AH, WEAPONS. ALWAYS WISE, I FEEL.
IS ANYBODY IN HERE? OLLY OLLY FUCKING OXEN FREE?
ANYONE?
YOU COULD STOP THIS.
ONCE AGAIN, THERE ANYONE FUCKING HERE?! I SWEAR I AM NOT A MUTILATING MUMMIFIED PSYCHOPATH!
USUALLY.

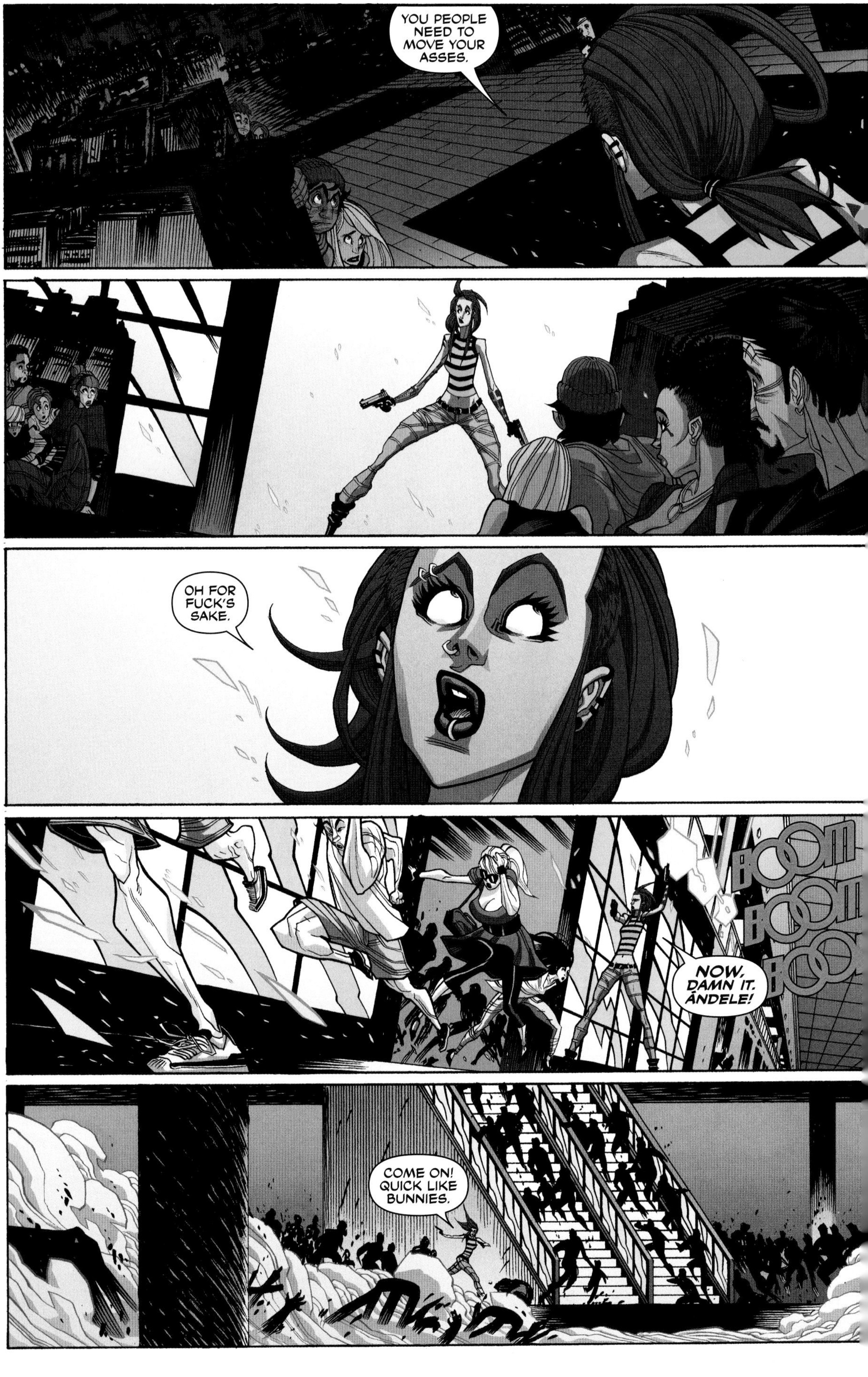
YOU PEOPLE NEED TO MOVE YOUR ASSES.
OH FOR FUCK'S SAKE.
BOOM BOOM BOOM
NOW, DAMN IT. ÁNDELE!
COME ON! QUICK LIKE BUNNIES.

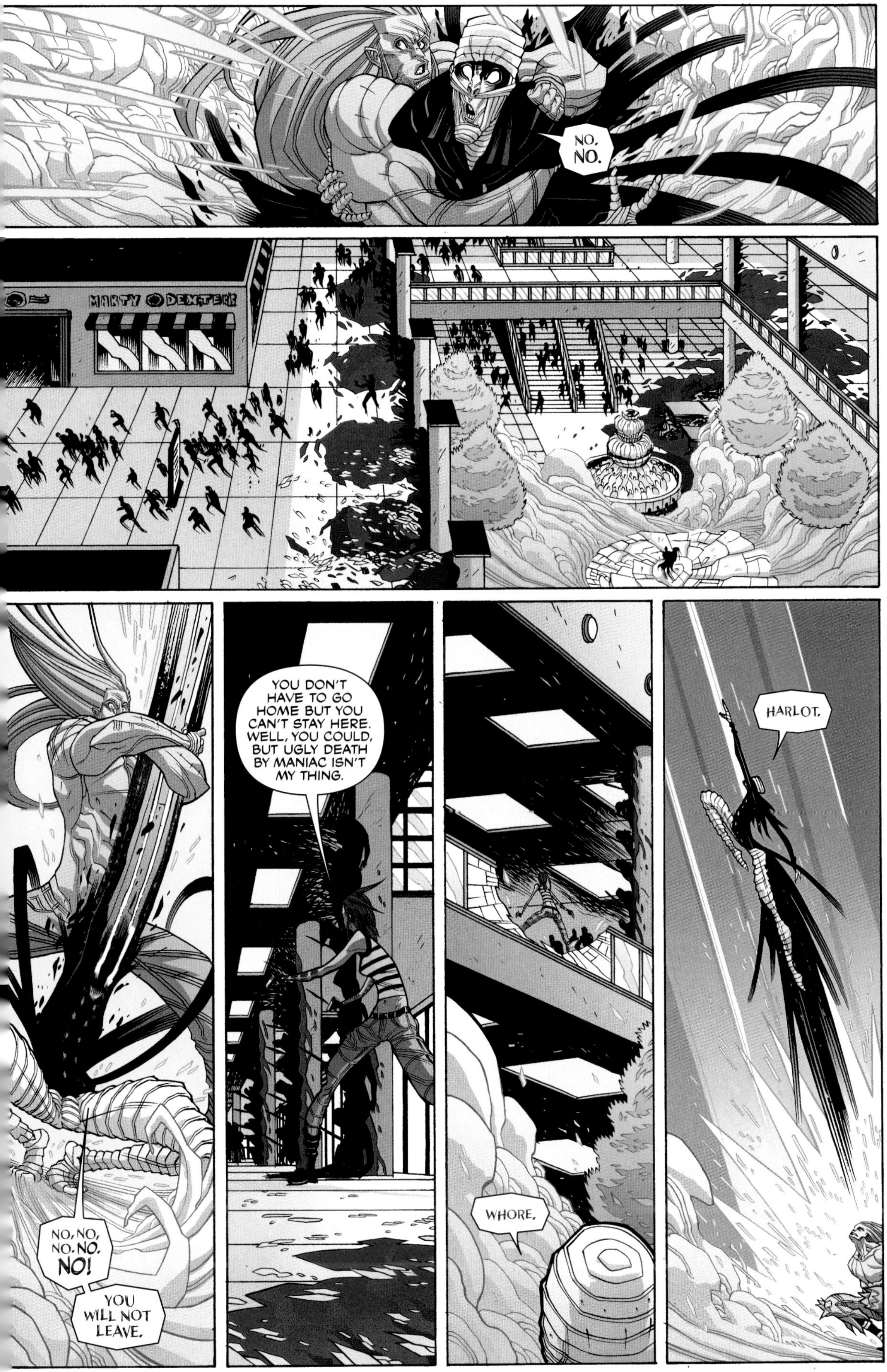
NO. NO.
YOU DON'T HAVE TO GO HOME BUT YOU CAN'T STAY HERE. WELL, YOU COULD, BUT UGLY DEATH BY MANIAC ISN'T MY THING.
NO, NO, NO. NO. NO!
YOU WILL NOT LEAVE.
WHORE.
HARLOT.
MARTY DEXTER

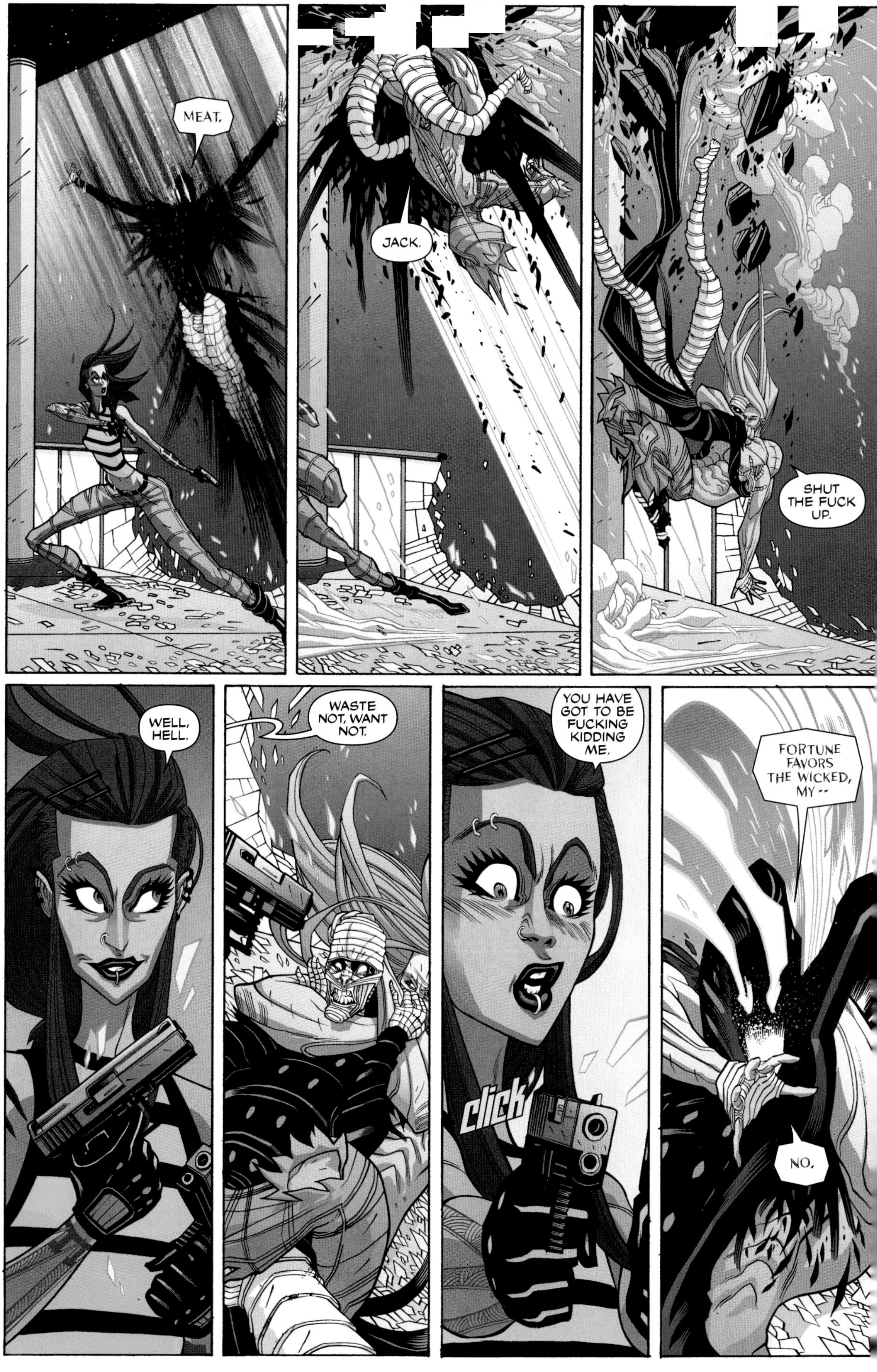
MEAT.
JACK.
SHUT THE FUCK UP.
WELL, HELL.
WASTE NOT, WANT NOT.
YOU HAVE GOT TO BE FUCKING KIDDING ME.
click
FORTUNE FAVORS THE WICKED, MY --
NO.

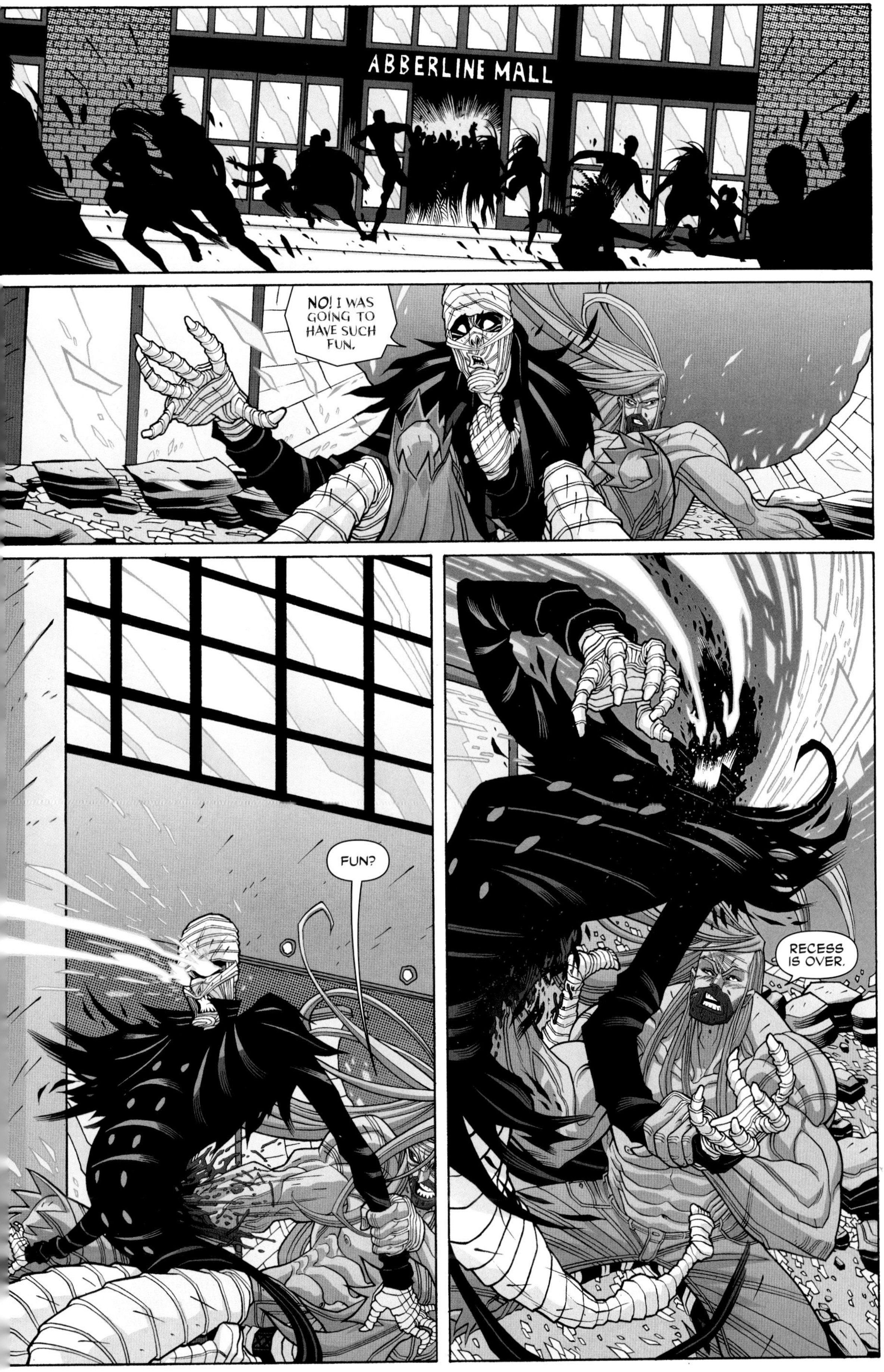
ABBERLINE MALL
NO! I WAS GOING TO HAVE SUCH FUN.
FUN?
RECESS IS OVER.

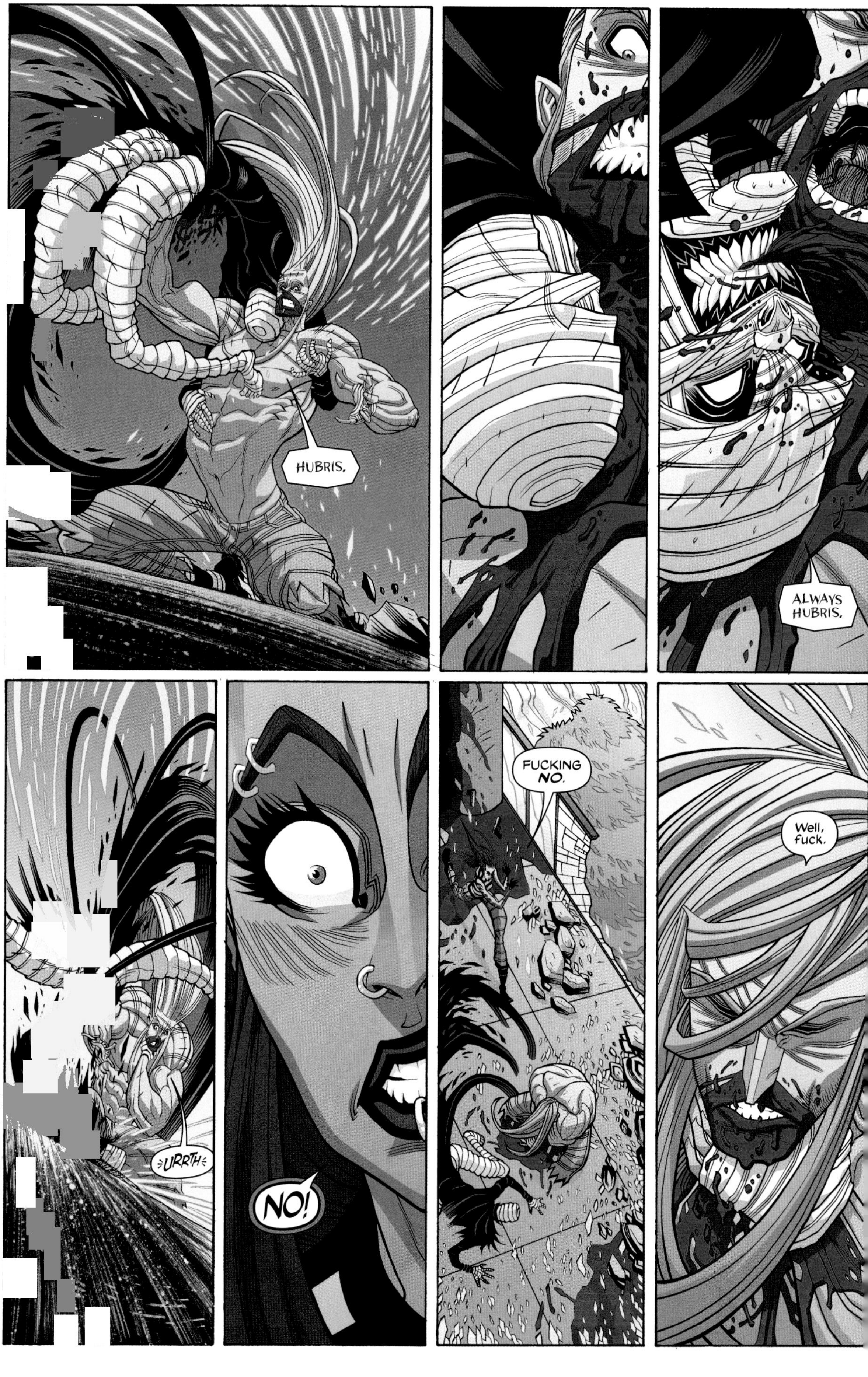
HUBRIS.
ALWAYS HUBRIS.
URRTH
NO!
FUCKING NO.
Well, fuck.

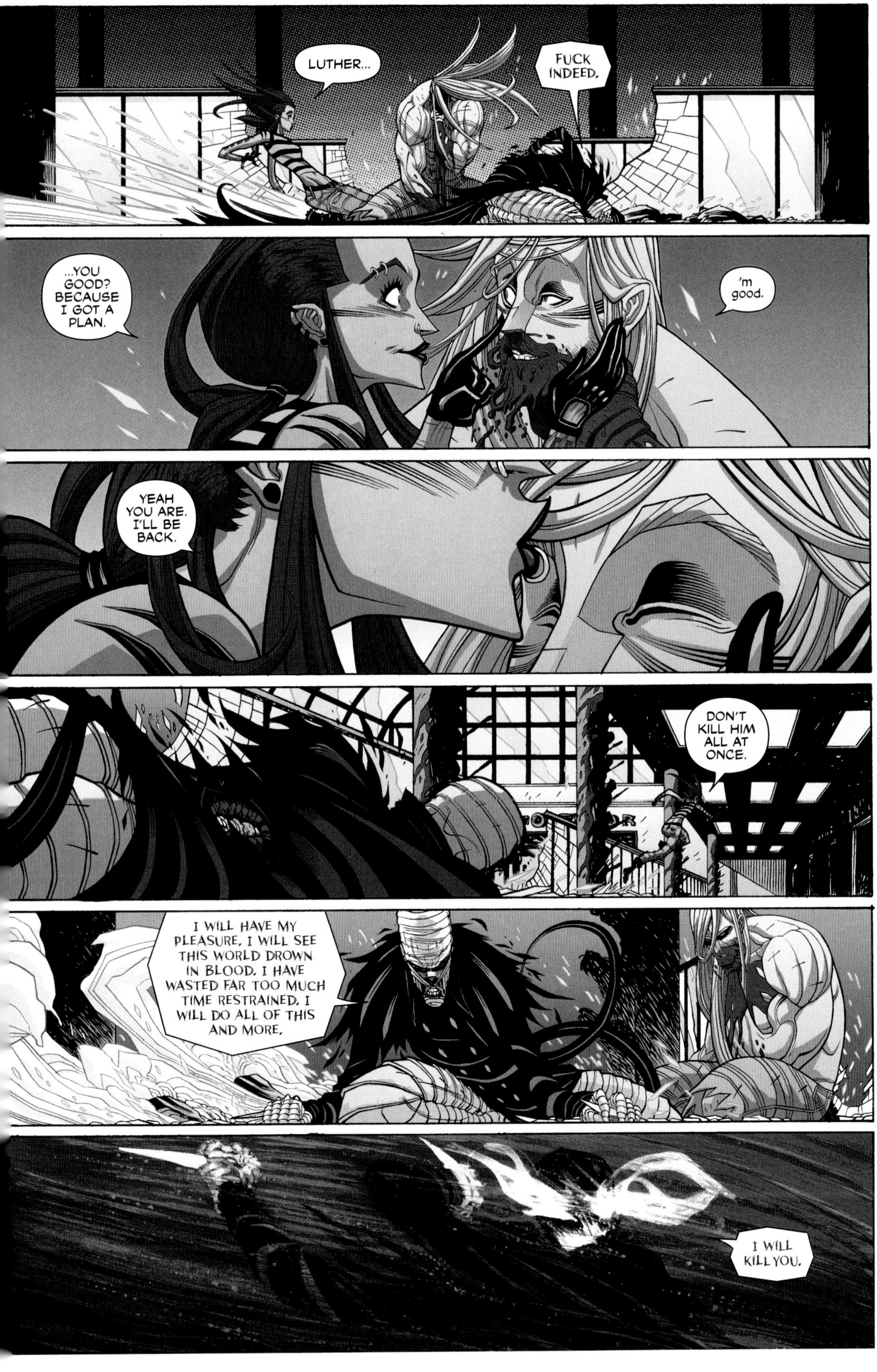
LUTHER...
FUCK INDEED.
...YOU GOOD? BECAUSE I GOT A PLAN.
'm good.
YEAH YOU ARE. I'LL BE BACK.
DON'T KILL HIM ALL AT ONCE.
I WILL HAVE MY PLEASURE. I WILL SEE THIS WORLD DROWN IN BLOOD. I HAVE WASTED FAR TOO MUCH TIME RESTRAINED. I WILL DO ALL OF THIS AND MORE.
I WILL KILL YOU.

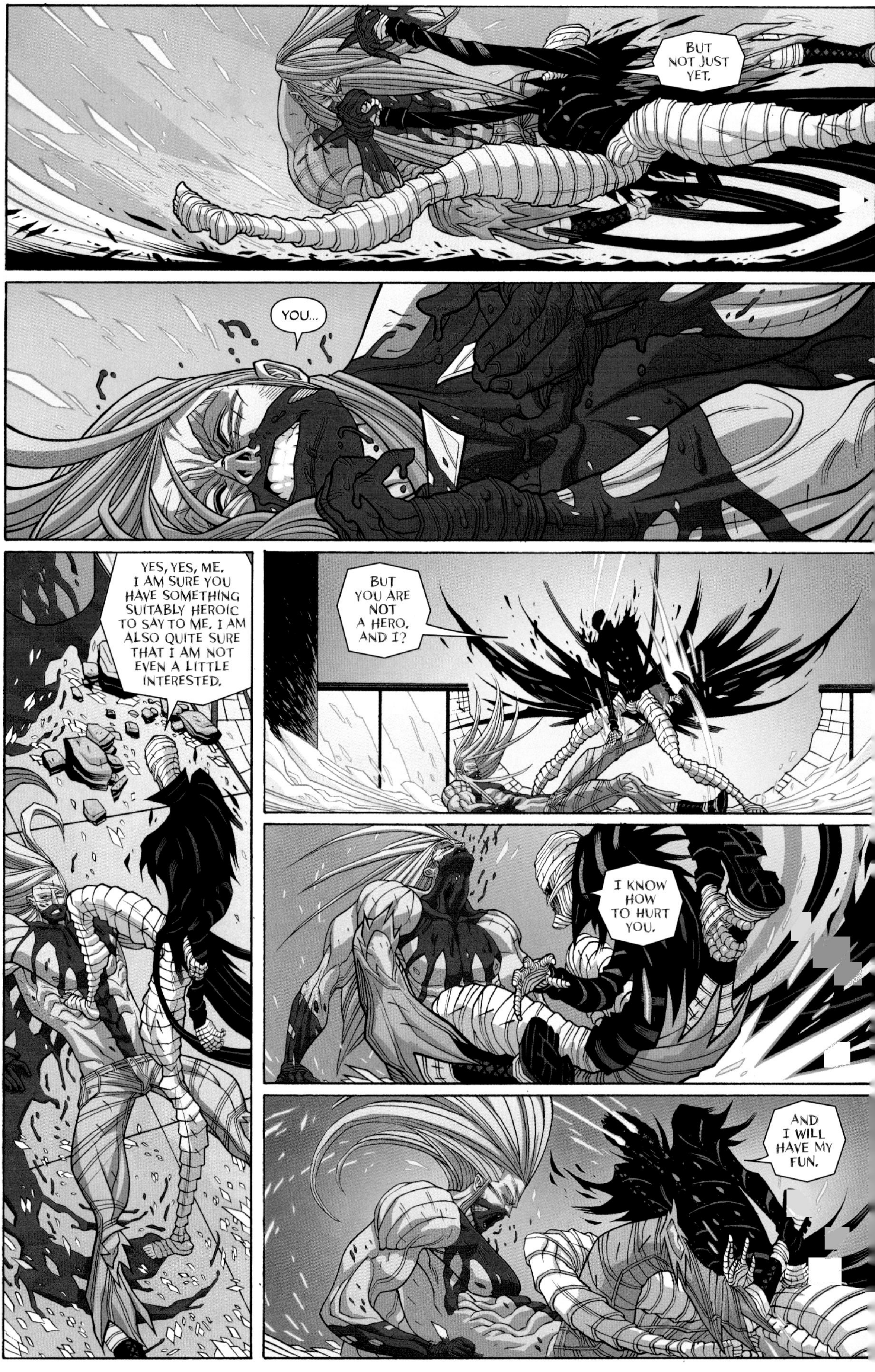
BUT NOT JUST YET.
YOU...
YES, YES, ME. I AM SURE YOU HAVE SOMETHING SUITABLY HEROIC TO SAY TO ME. I AM ALSO QUITE SURE THAT I AM NOT EVEN A LITTLE INTERESTED.
BUT YOU ARE NOT A HERO, AND I?
I KNOW HOW TO HURT YOU.
AND I WILL HAVE MY FUN.

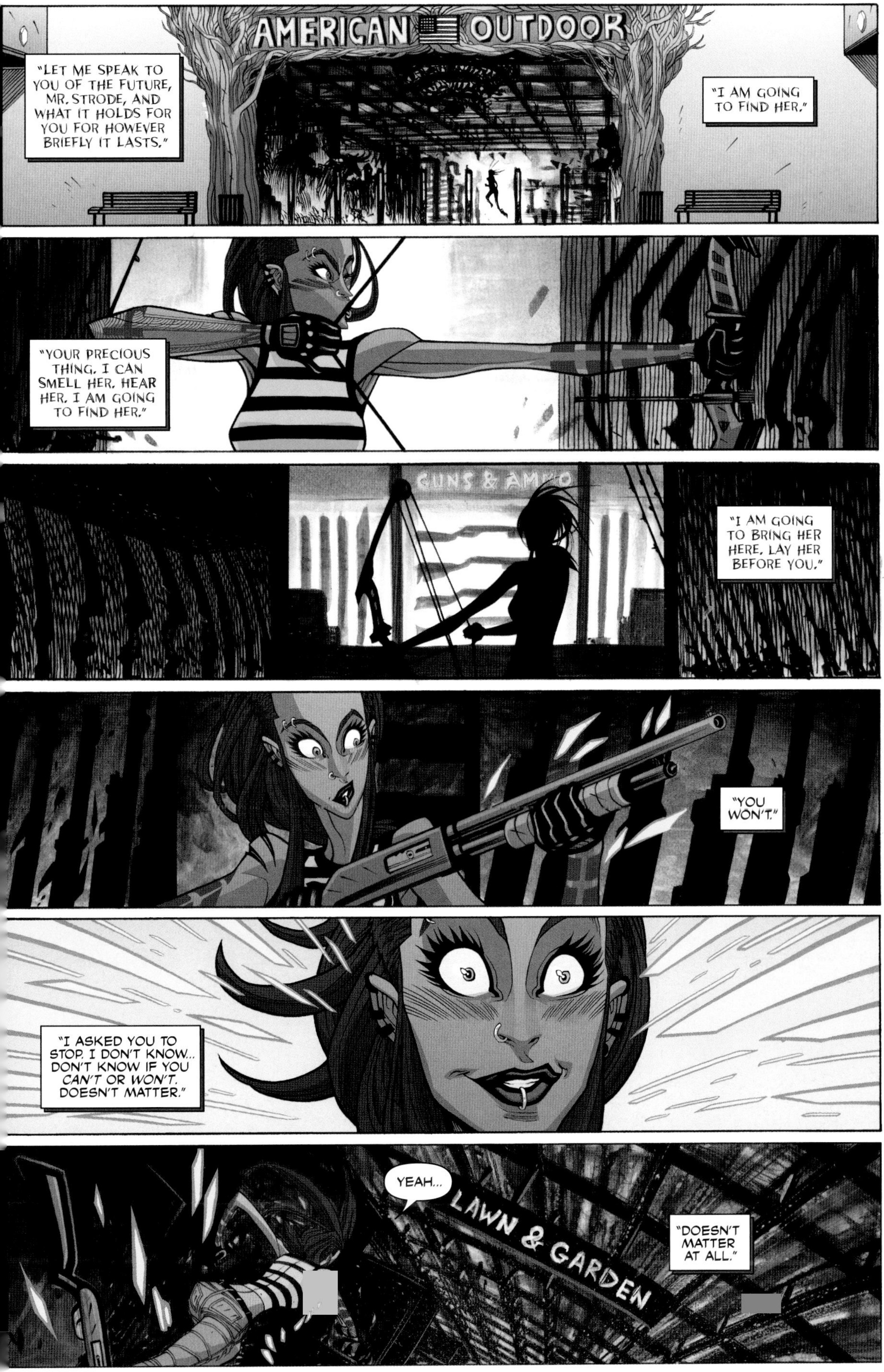
AMERICAN OUTDOOR
"LET ME SPEAK TO YOU OF THE FUTURE, MR. STRODE, AND WHAT IT HOLDS FOR YOU FOR HOWEVER BRIEFLY IT LASTS."
"I AM GOING TO FIND HER."
"YOUR PRECIOUS THING. I CAN SMELL HER. HEAR HER. I AM GOING TO FIND HER."
GUNS & AMMO
"I AM GOING TO BRING HER HERE, LAY HER BEFORE YOU."
"YOU WON'T."
"I ASKED YOU TO STOP. I DON'T KNOW... DON'T KNOW IF YOU *CAN'T* OR *WON'T*. DOESN'T MATTER."
YEAH...
LAWN & GARDEN
"DOESN'T MATTER AT ALL."

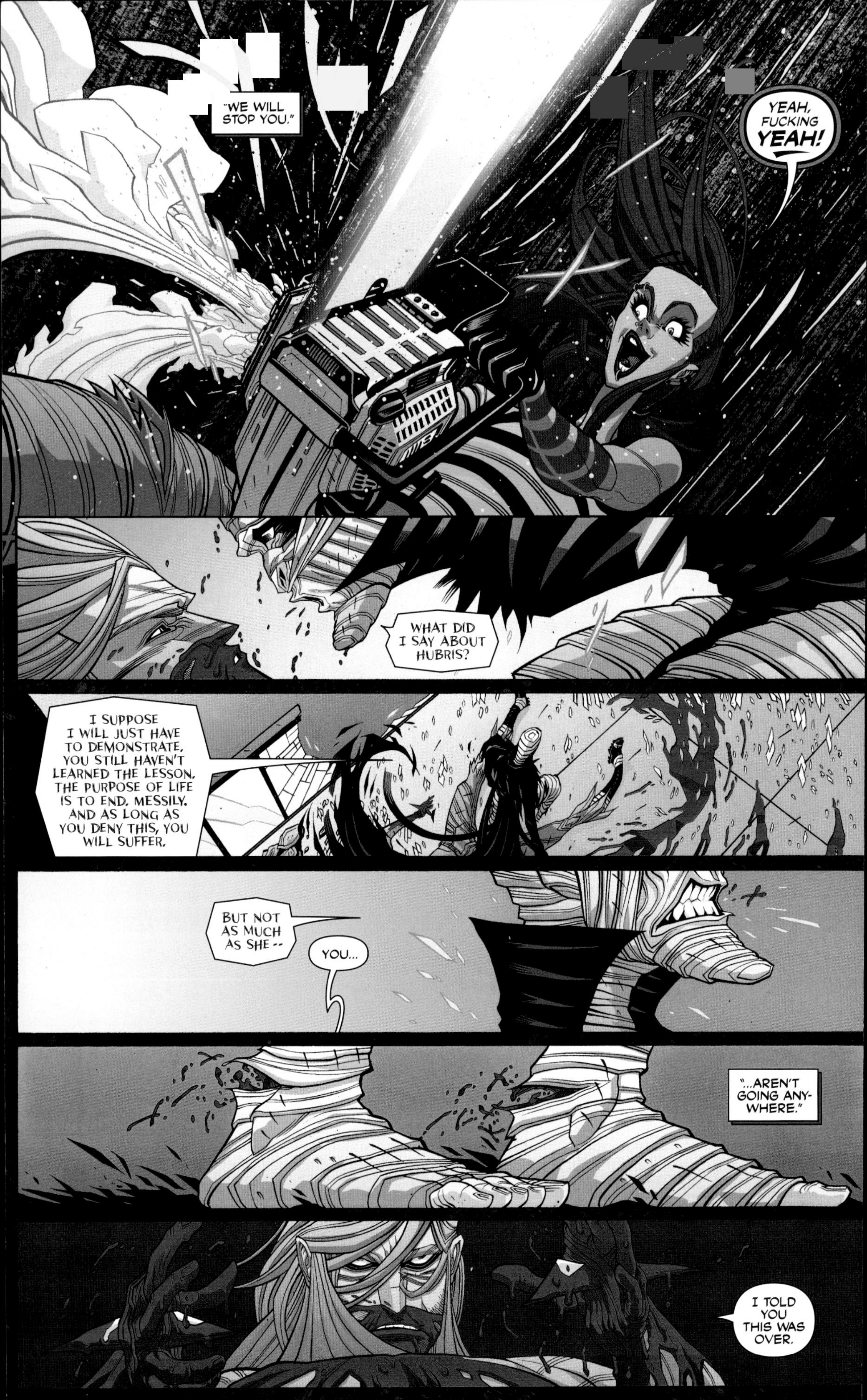
"WE WILL STOP YOU."
YEAH, FUCKING YEAH!
WHAT DID I SAY ABOUT HUBRIS?
I SUPPOSE I WILL JUST HAVE TO DEMONSTRATE. YOU STILL HAVEN'T LEARNED THE LESSON. THE PURPOSE OF LIFE IS TO END, MESSILY. AND AS LONG AS YOU DENY THIS, YOU WILL SUFFER.
BUT NOT AS MUCH AS SHE--
YOU...
"...AREN'T GOING ANY-WHERE."
I TOLD YOU THIS WAS OVER.

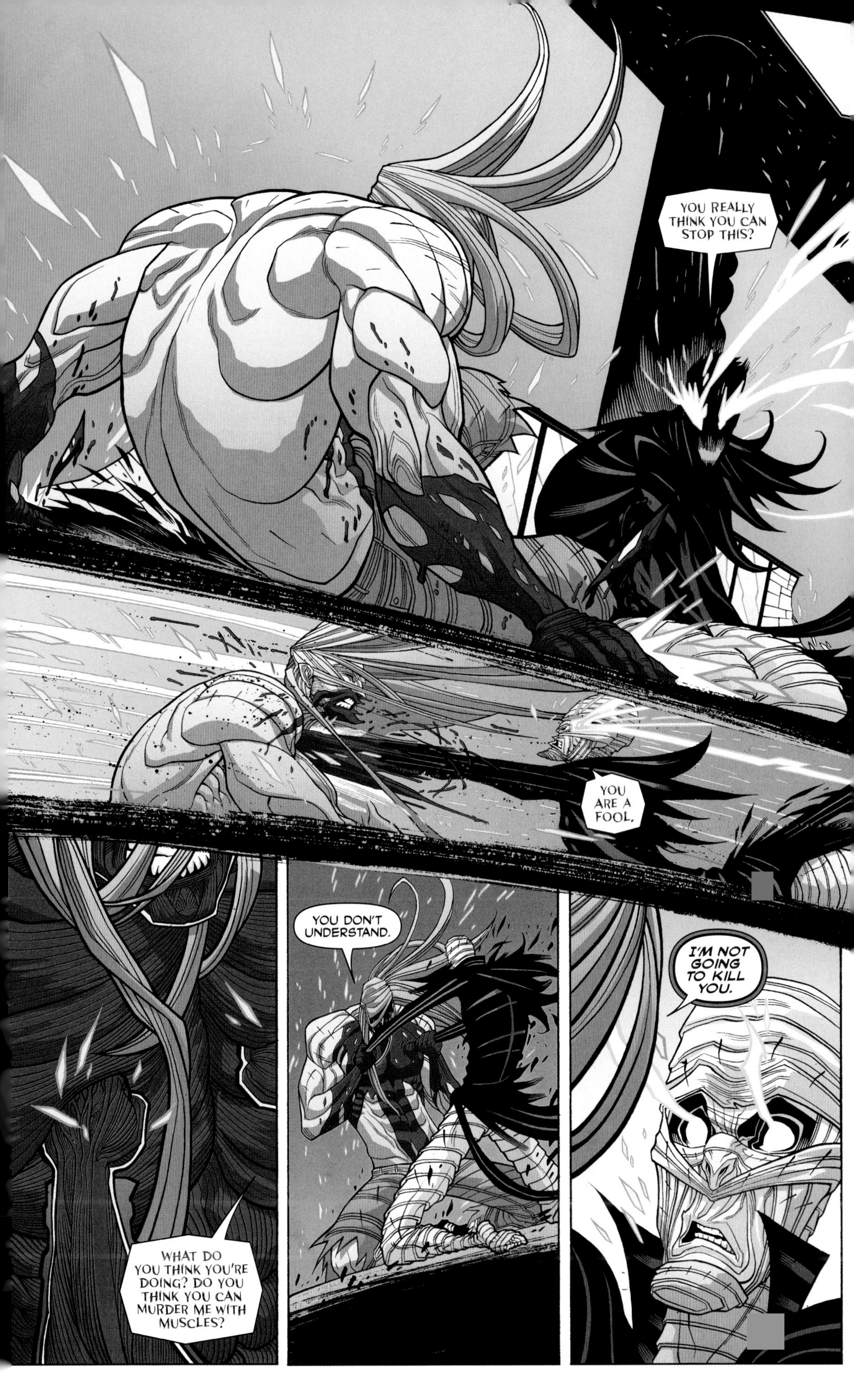
YOU REALLY THINK YOU CAN STOP THIS?
YOU ARE A FOOL.
WHAT DO YOU THINK YOU'RE DOING? DO YOU THINK YOU CAN MURDER ME WITH MUSCLES?
YOU DON'T UNDERSTAND.
I'M NOT GOING TO KILL YOU.

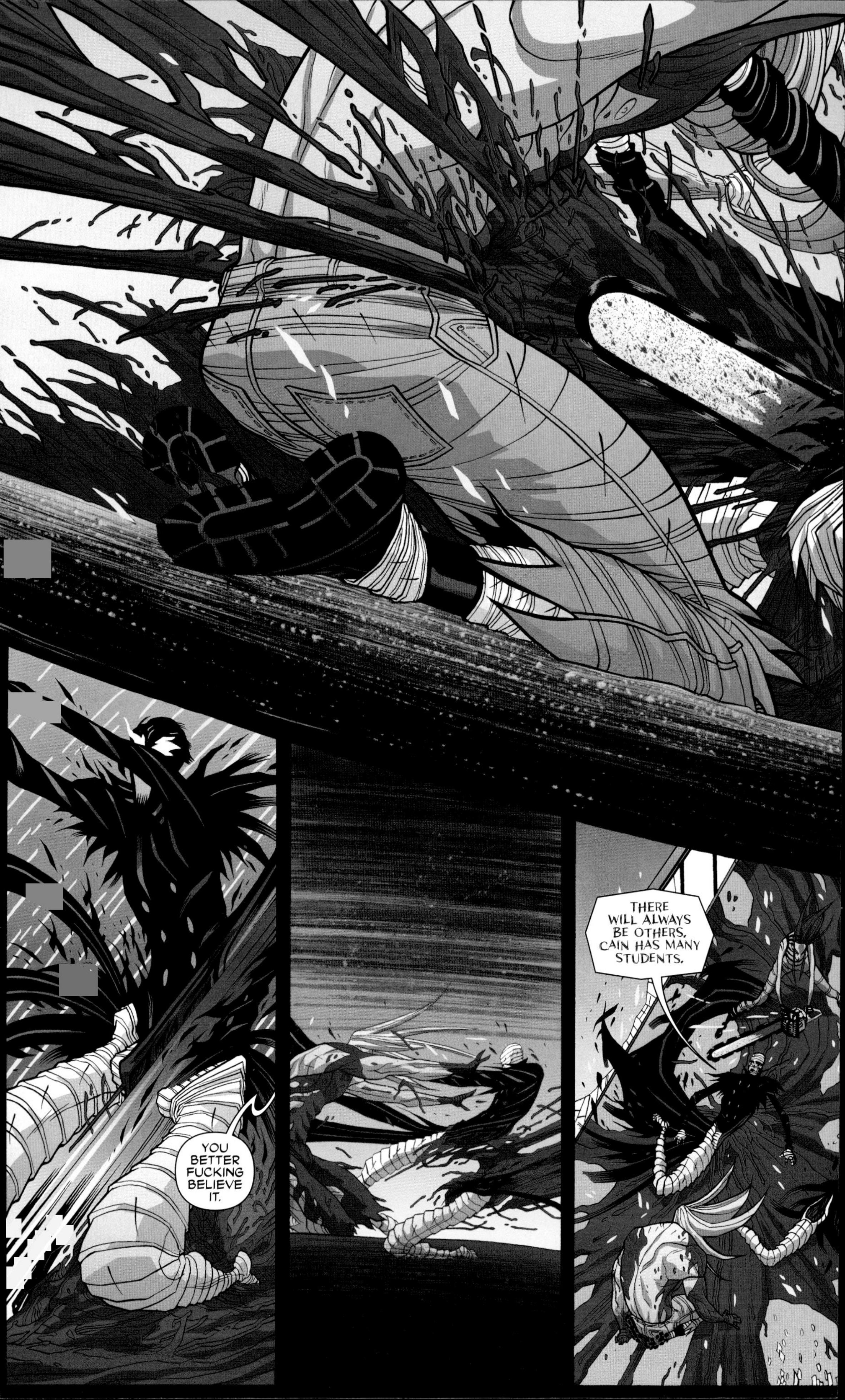
YOU BETTER FUCKING BELIEVE IT.
THERE WILL ALWAYS BE OTHERS. CAIN HAS MANY STUDENTS.

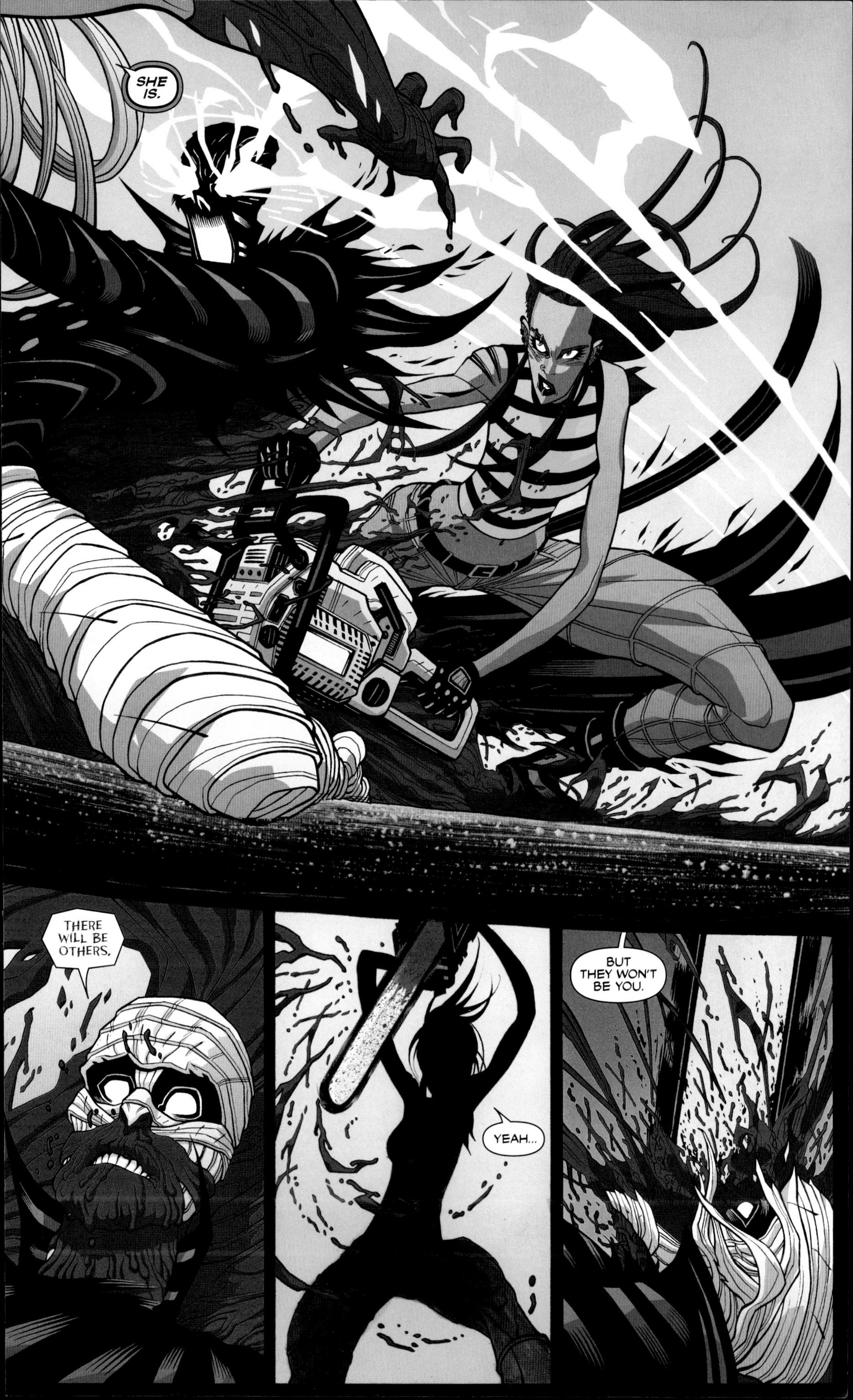
SHE IS.
THERE WILL BE OTHERS.
YEAH...
BUT THEY WON'T BE YOU.

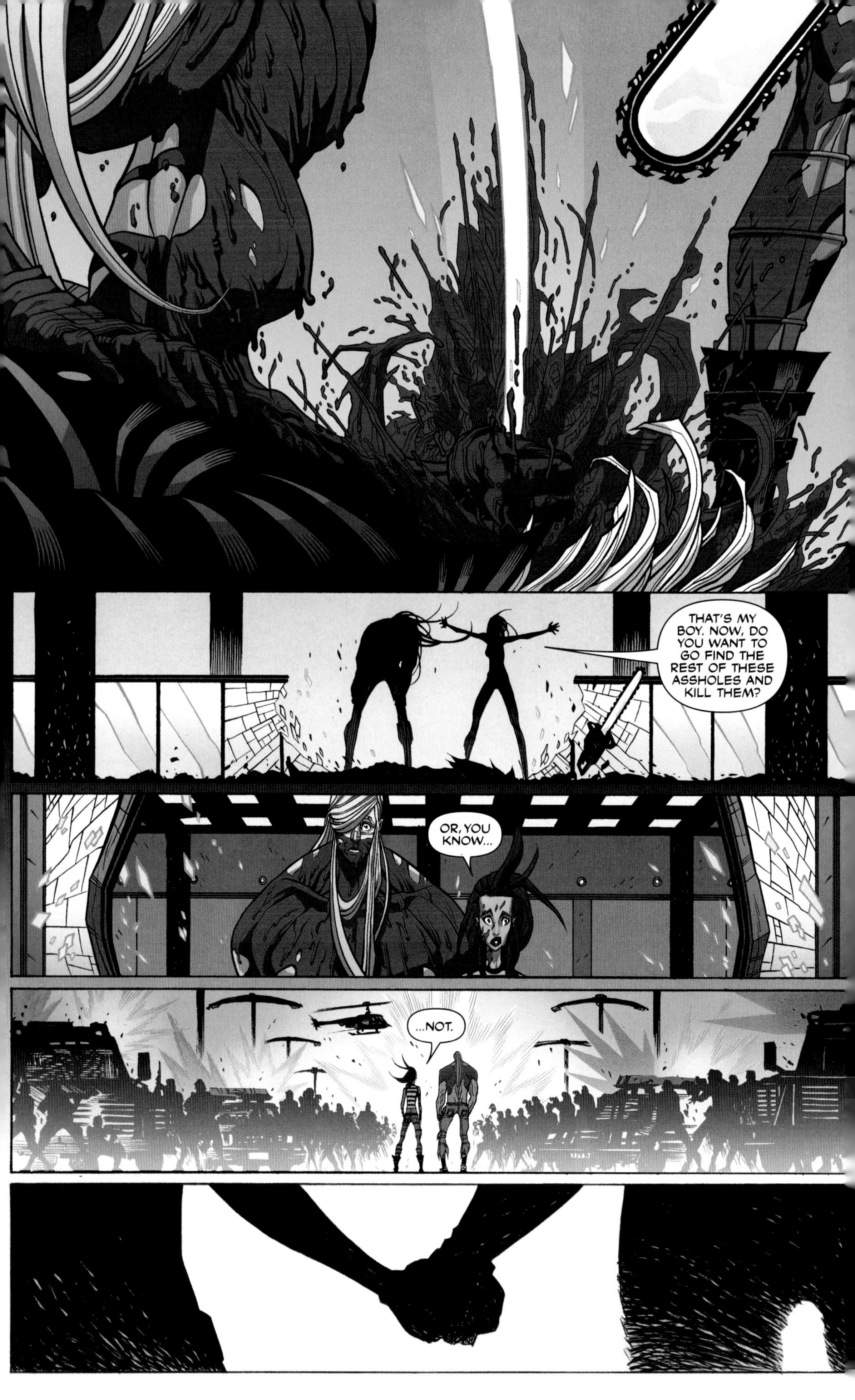
THAT'S MY BOY. NOW, DO YOU WANT TO GO FIND THE REST OF THESE ASSHOLES AND KILL THEM?
OR, YOU KNOW...
...NOT.

Justin Jordan lives in darkest Pennsylvania, and when not wrestling bears and growing an Old Testament level beard, he writes comics. He rebooted *Shadowman* for Valiant, and has written for DC, Marvel, and Avatar on various titles. You can reach him at *JustinJordan@gmail.com* or on Twitter at *@Justin_Jordan*, unless you're reading this 100 years in the future, in which case you can probably contact him with a Ouija board.

Tradd Moore lives in Atlanta, Georgia and draws all the time. Sometimes he takes a break to play Final Fantasy.

Felipe Sobreiro is the artist behind *The New Adventures of Sigmund Freud* and a handful of other short comics. He has been published as a colorist in *Heavy Metal* magazine, Image Comics' *Popgun* anthology, Alex De Campi's *Ashes* and a couple of BOOM! Studios titles, including the critically acclaimed *Polarity*. He currently lives in Brasília, Brazil's very odd capital city.

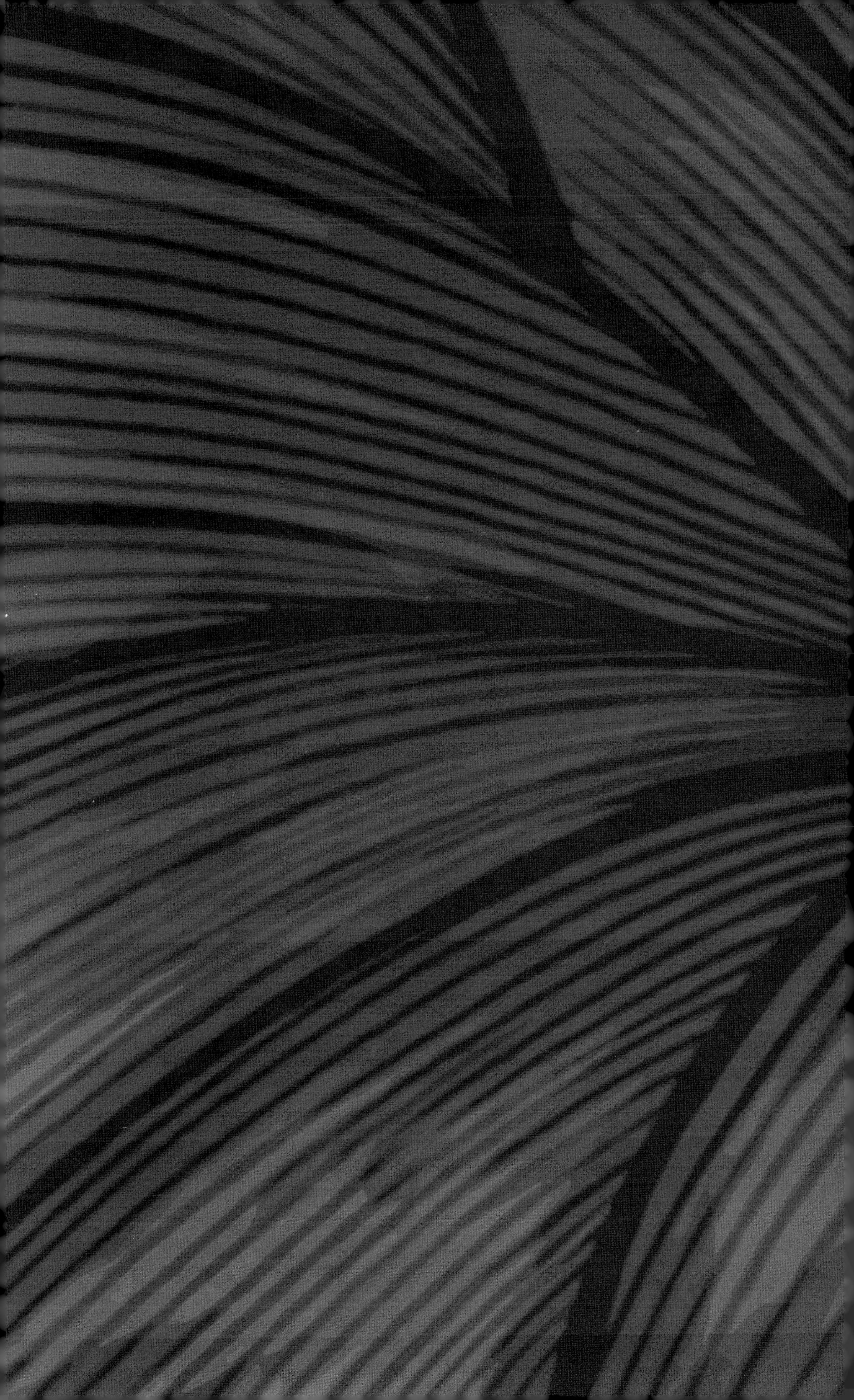

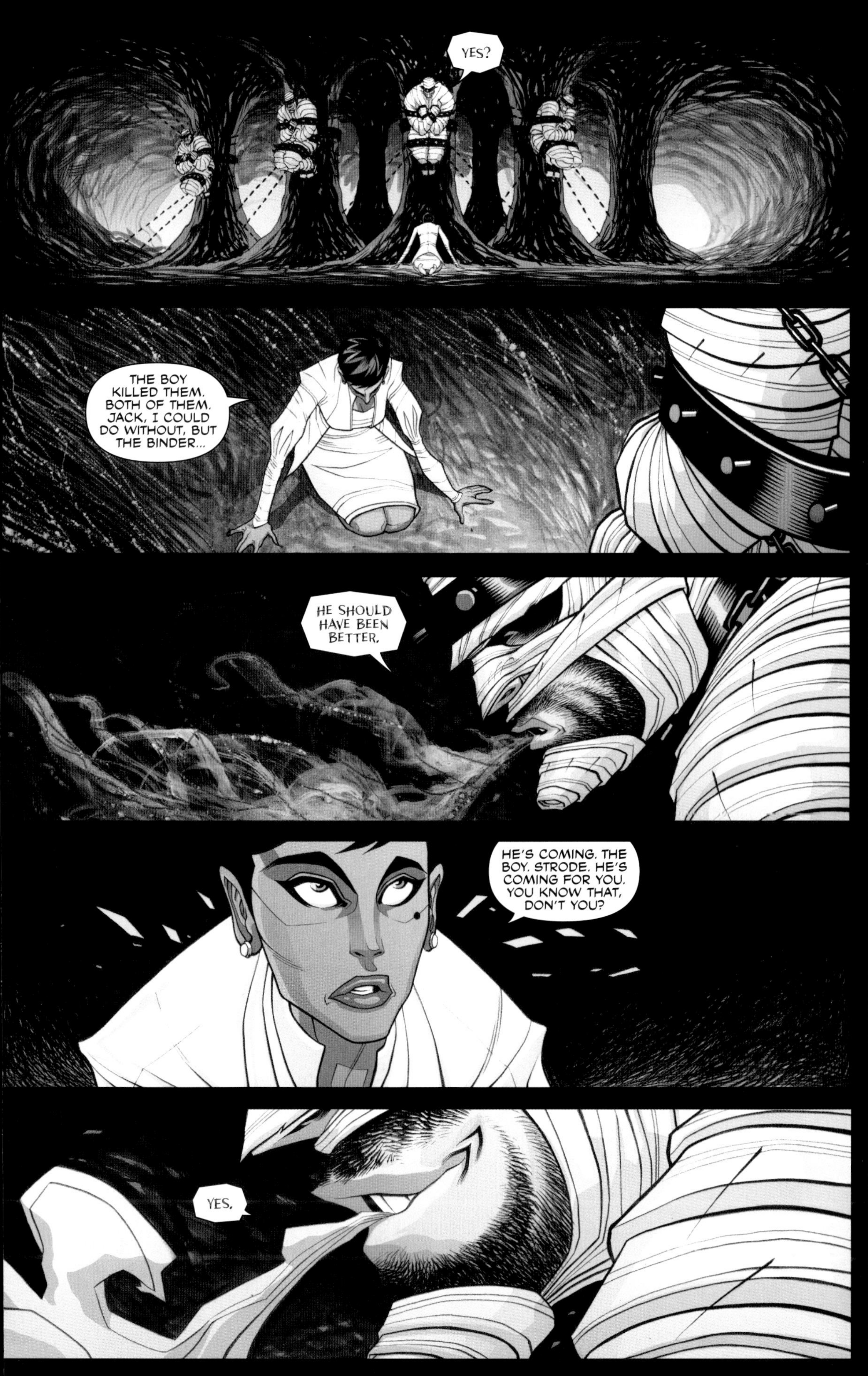
YES?
THE BOY KILLED THEM. BOTH OF THEM. JACK, I COULD DO WITHOUT, BUT THE BINDER...
HE SHOULD HAVE BEEN BETTER.
HE'S COMING. THE BOY. STRODE. HE'S COMING FOR YOU. YOU KNOW THAT, DON'T YOU?
YES.

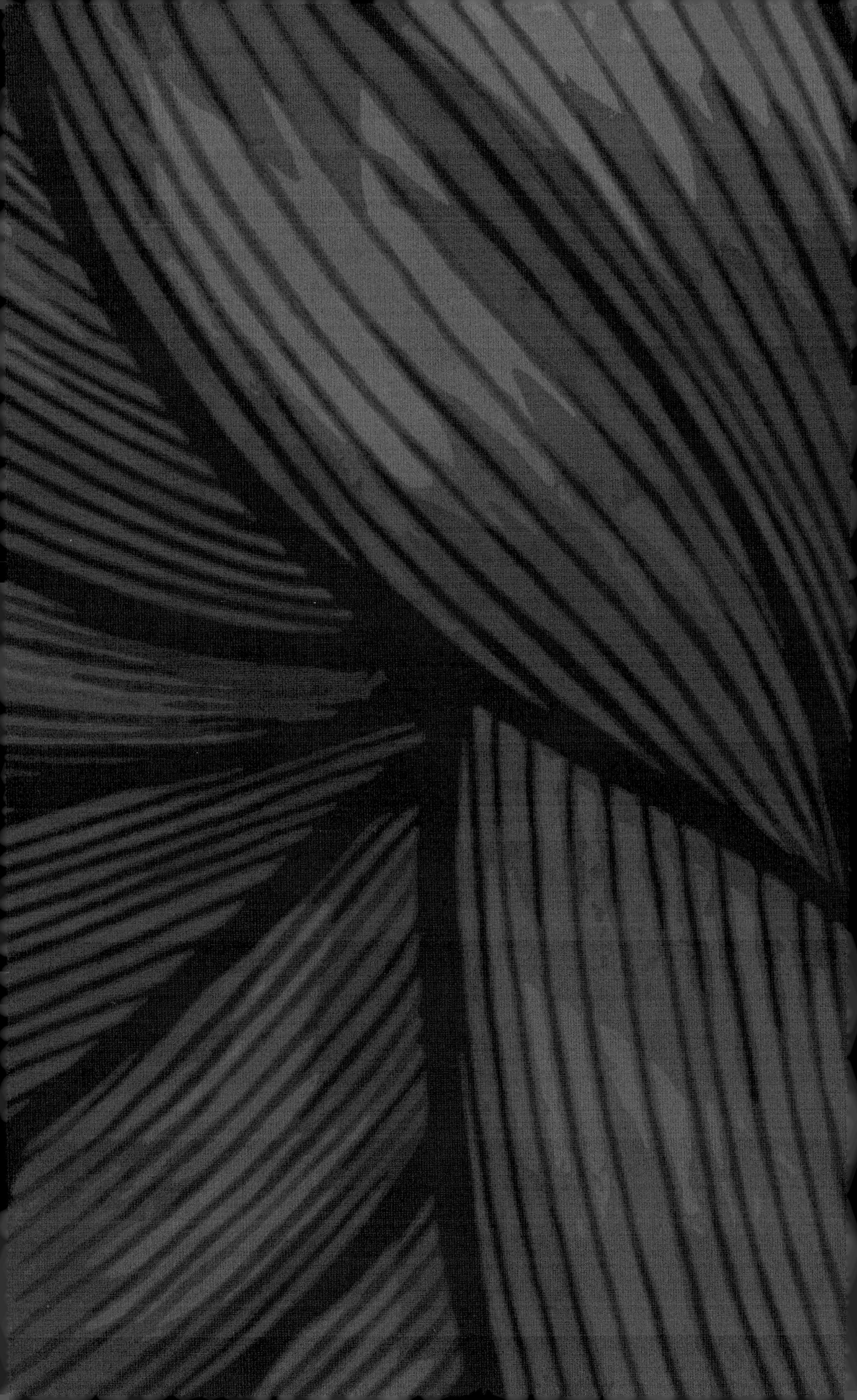

Hey! Here's a quick look at the cover process of

The Legend of Luther Strode #1.

♡Tradd♡

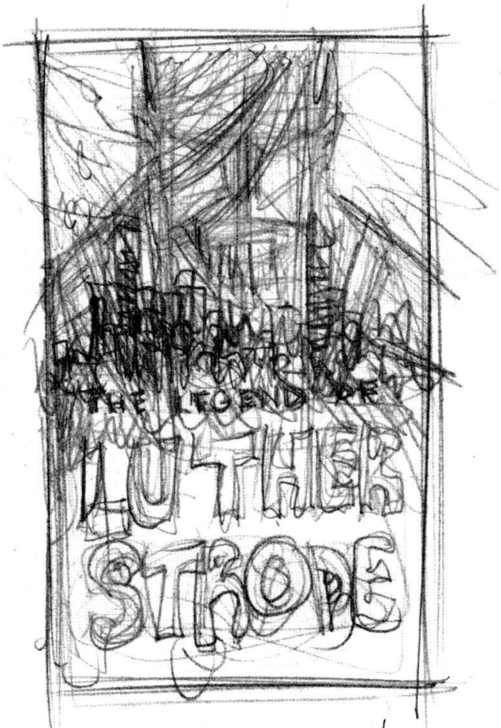
THE LEGEND OF
LUTHER
STRODE

1

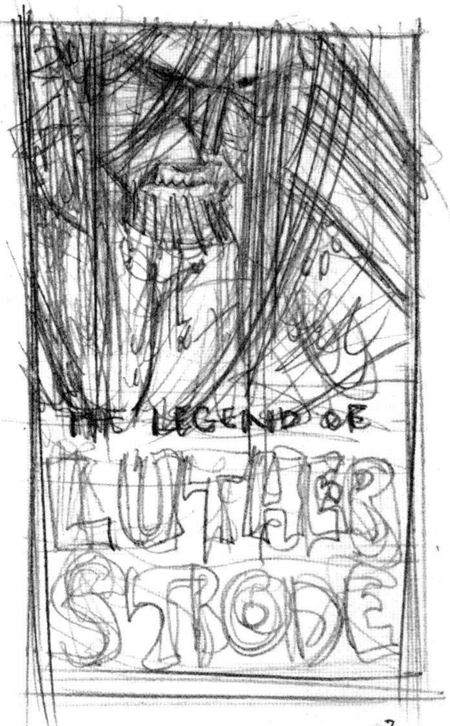
THE LEGEND OF
LUTHER
STRODE

2

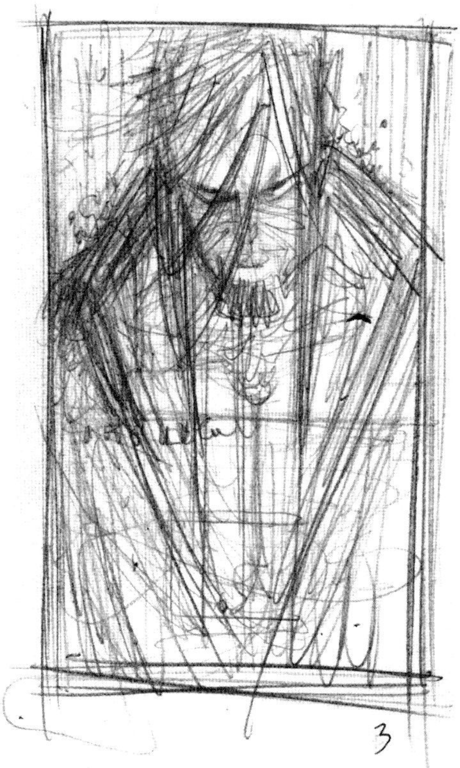

3

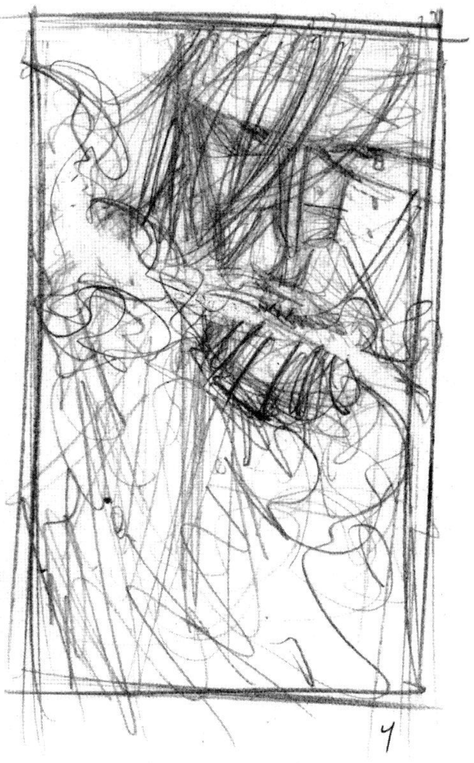

4

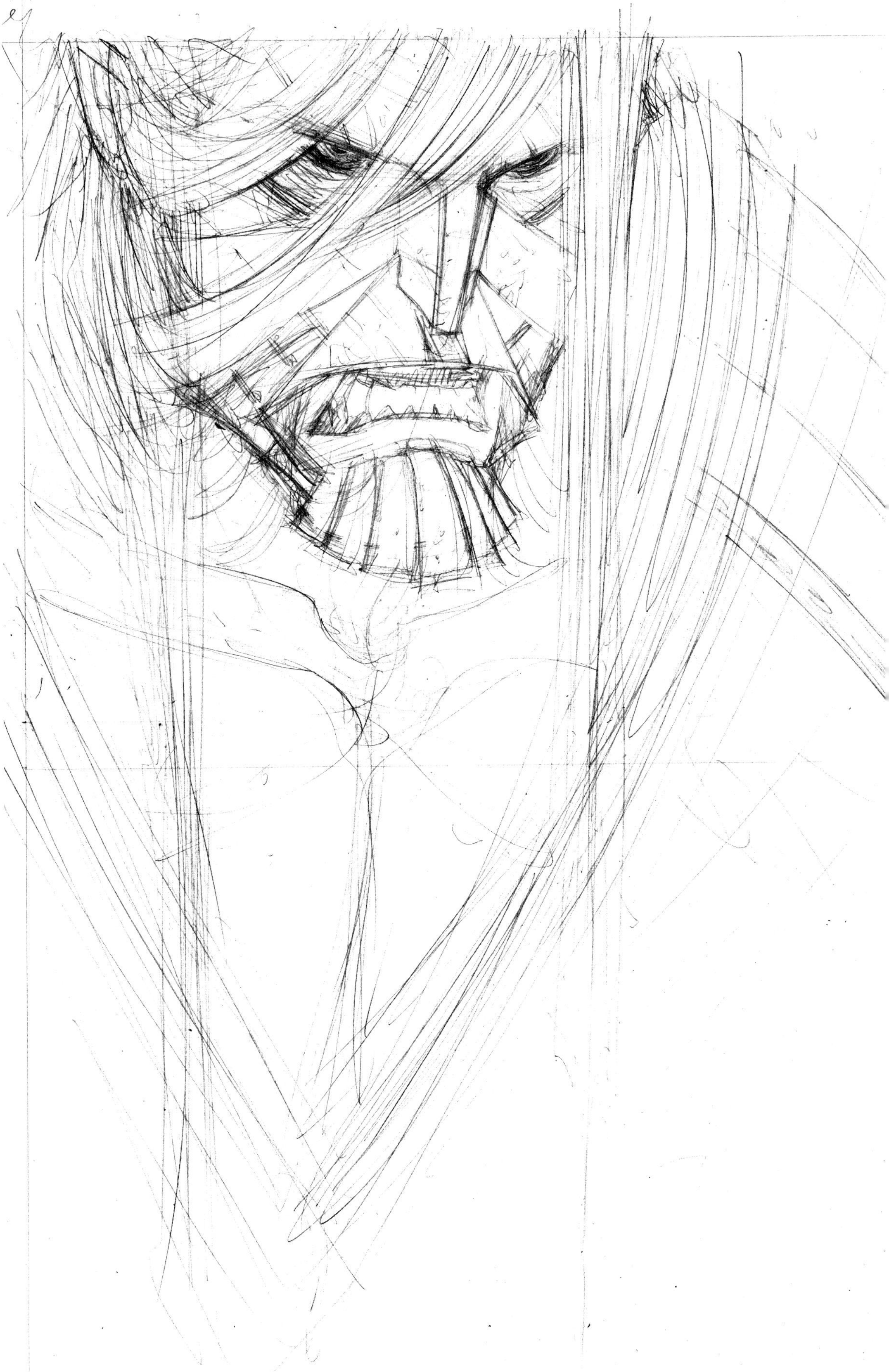

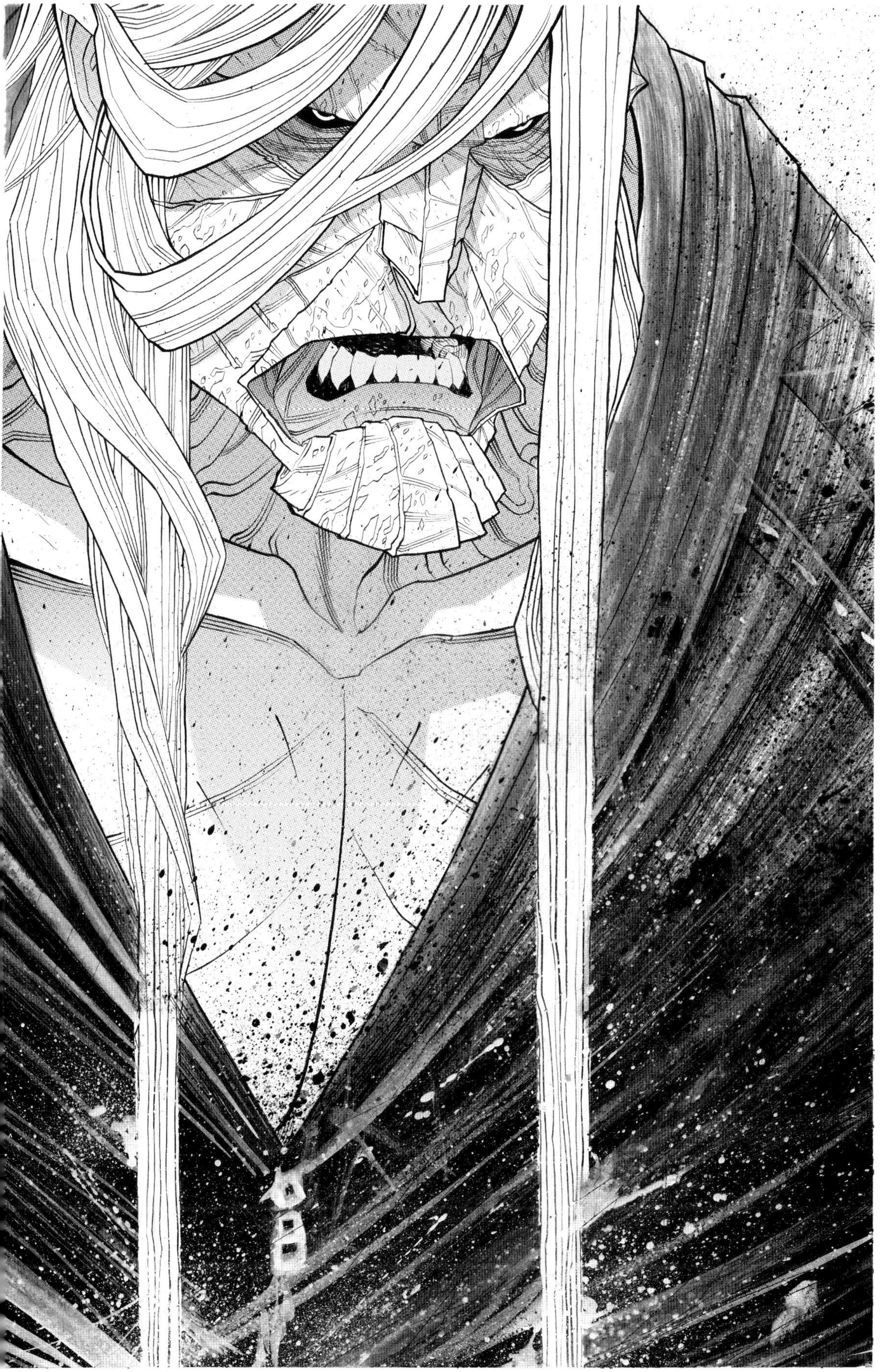

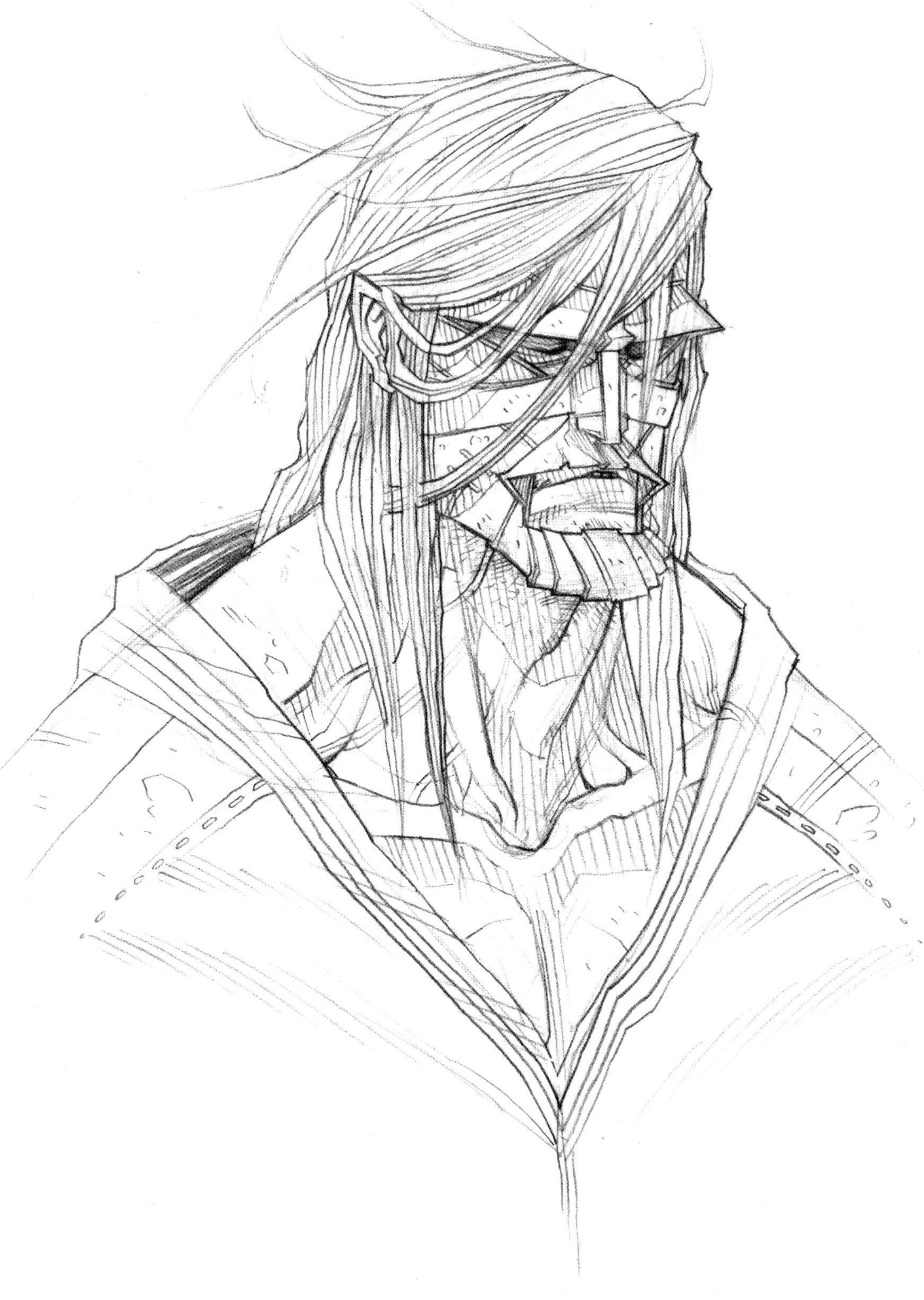

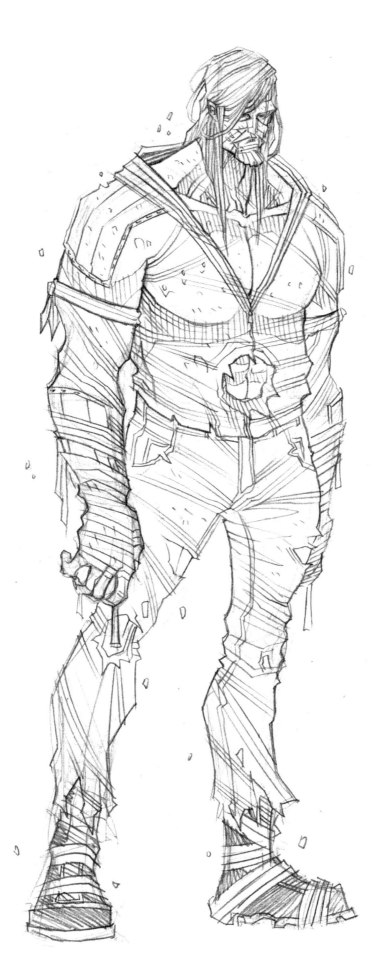

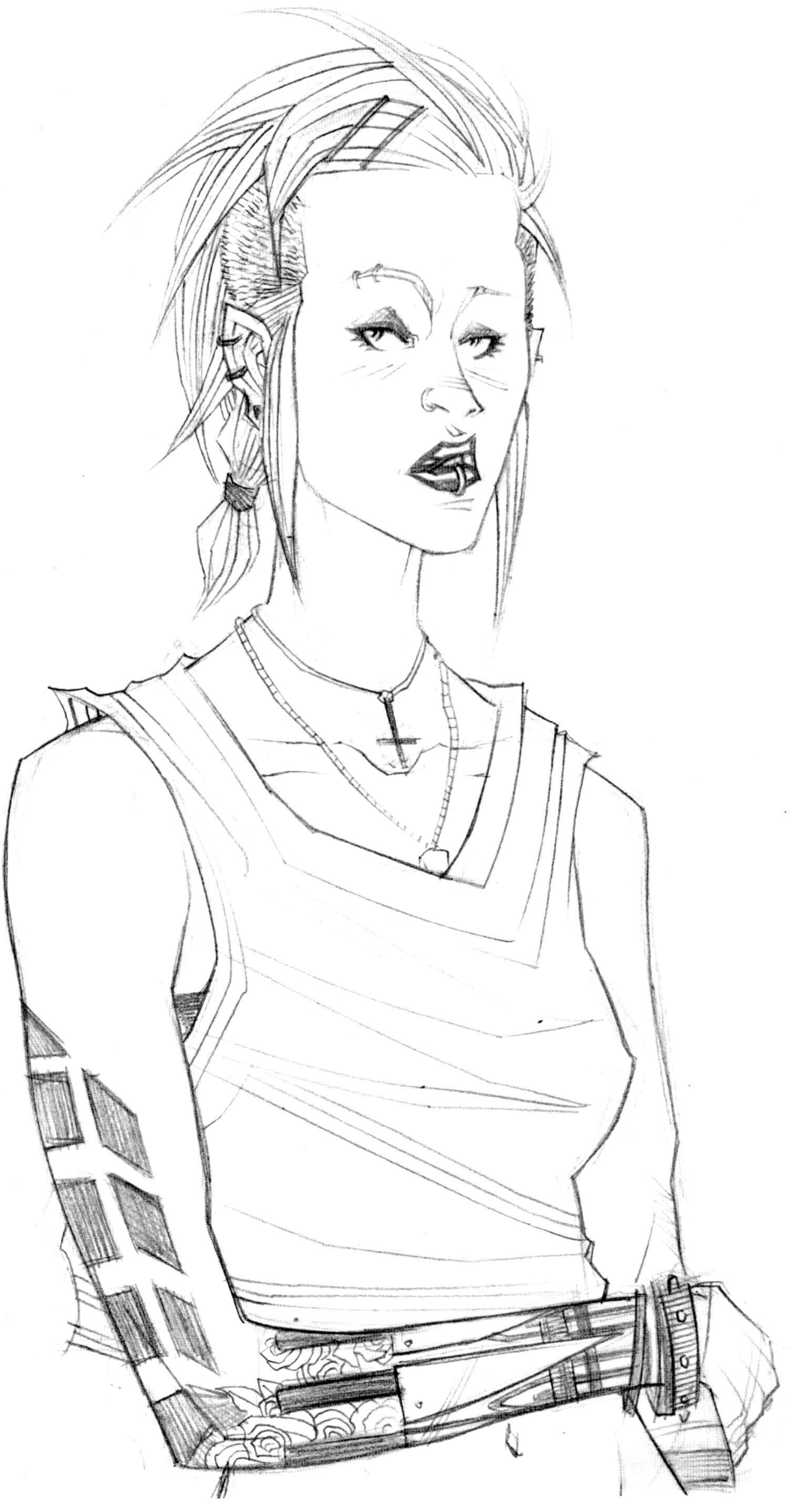

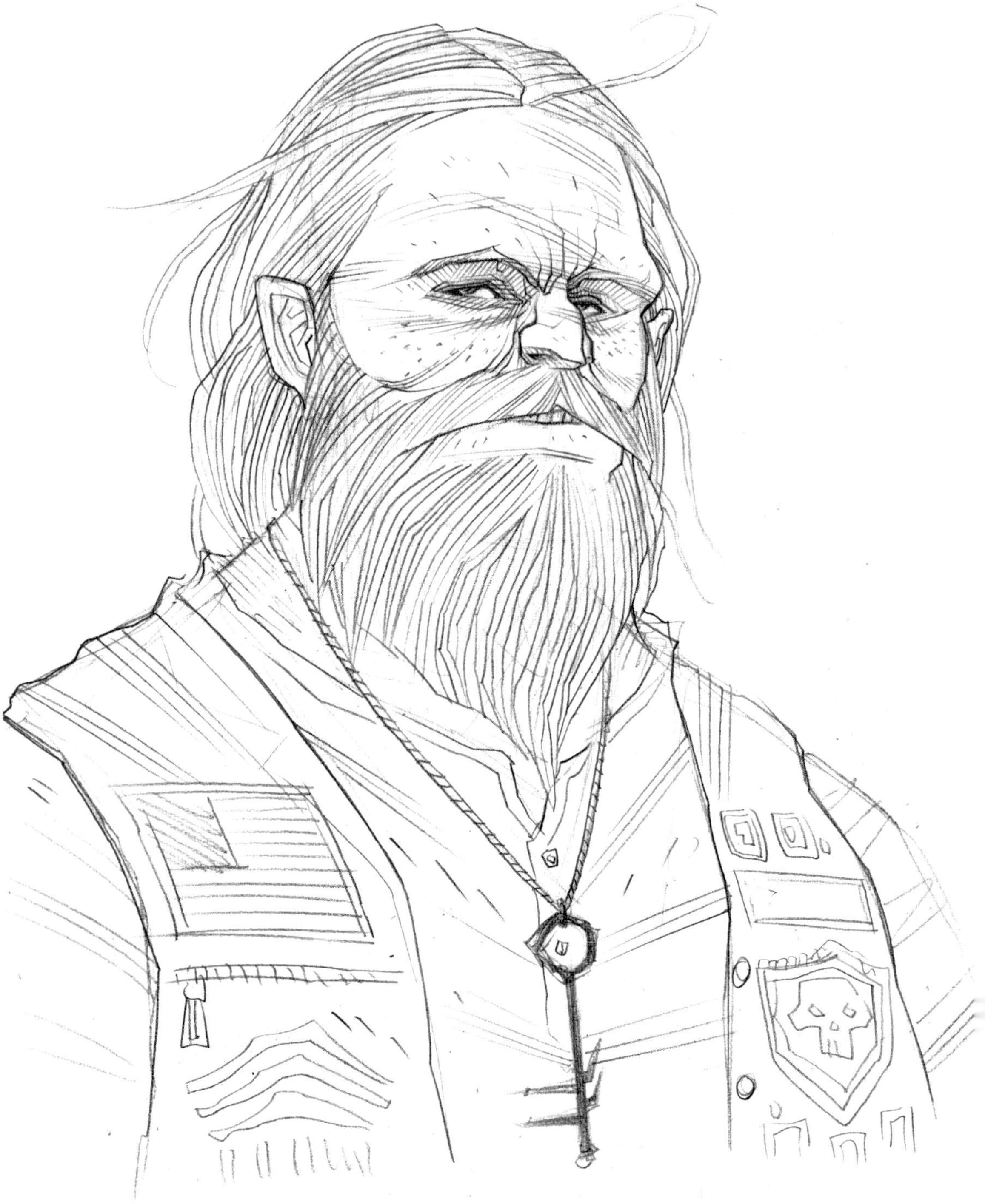

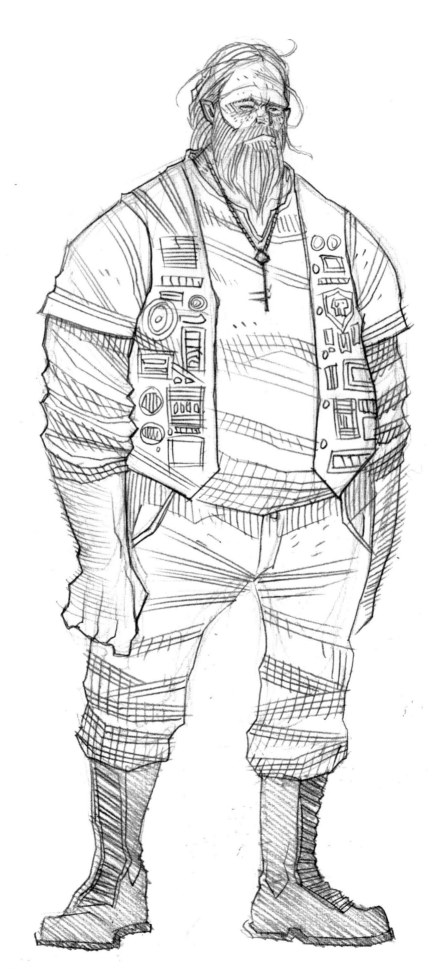

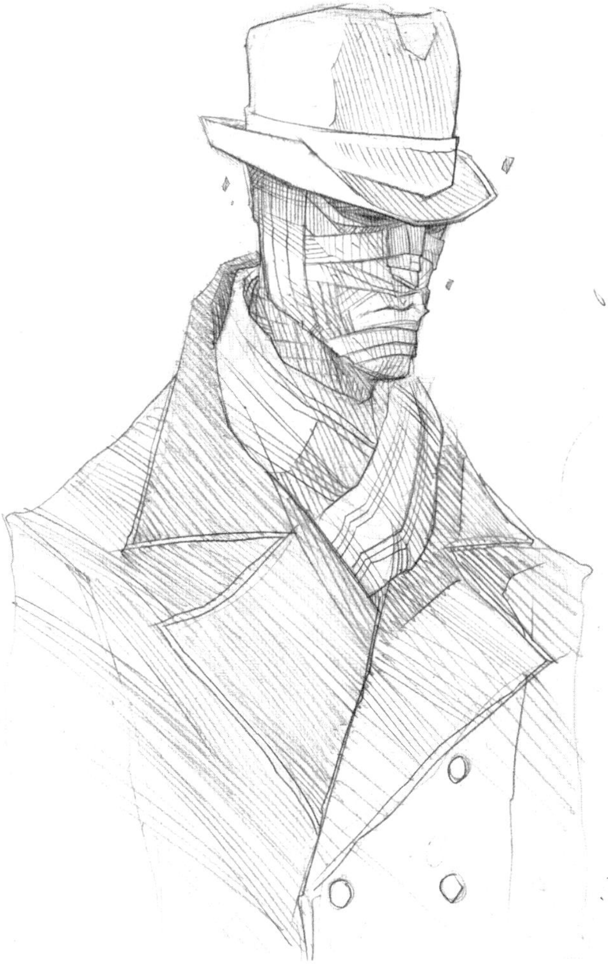

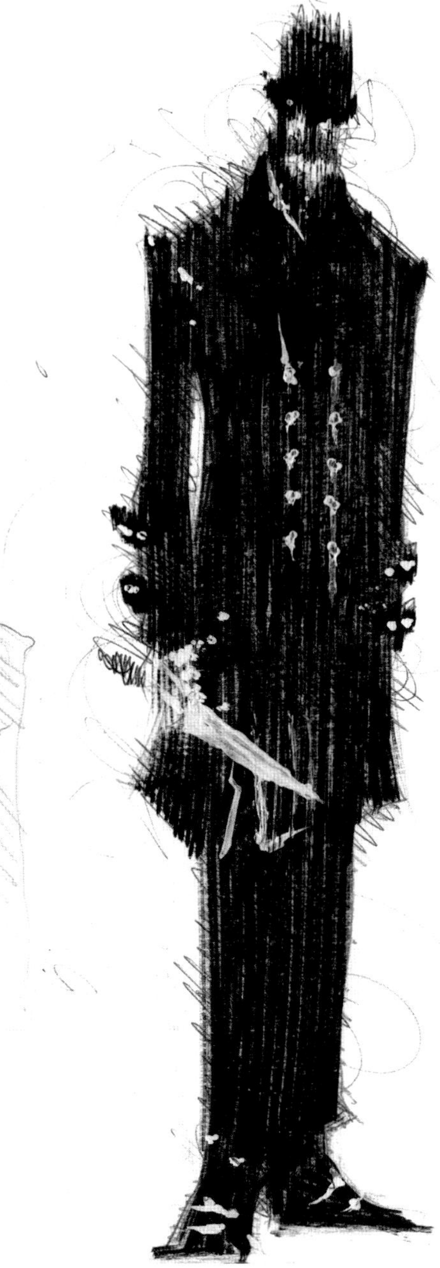

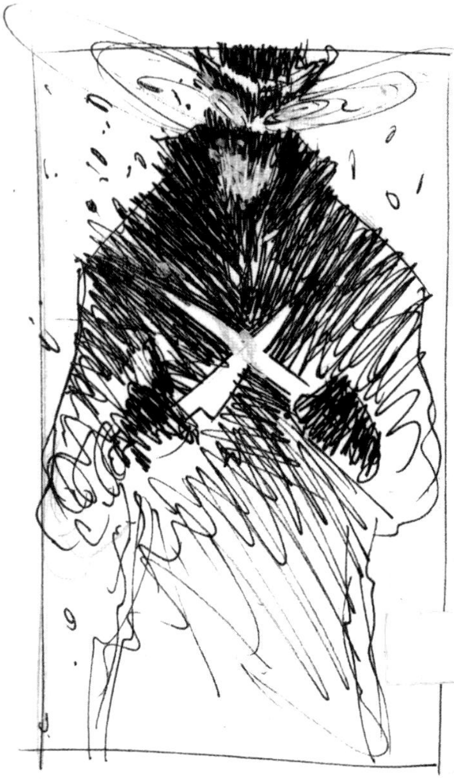

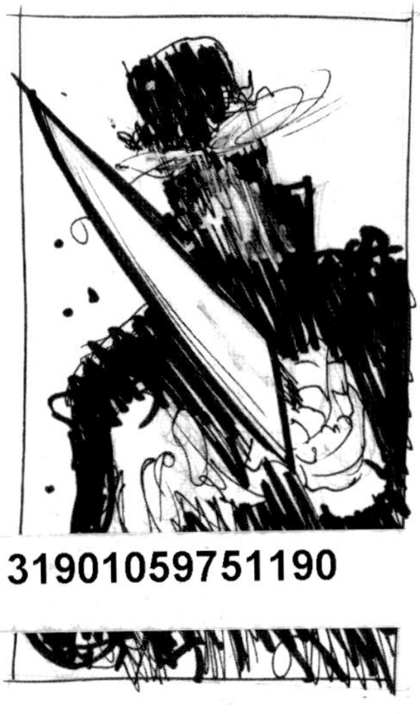

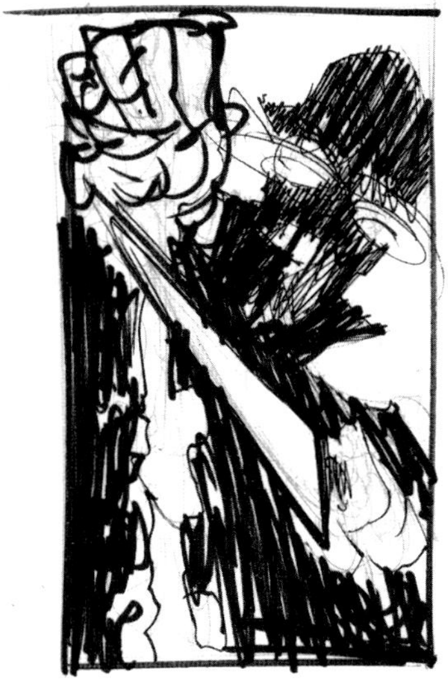